DATE DUE

JY 31 0?			

DEMCO 38-296

Living History

Living History

A   MEMOIR

Chaim Herzog

PANTHEON   BOOKS

NEW   YORK

Library of Congress Cataloging-in-Publication Data
Herzog, Chaim, 1918–
Living history : a memoir / Chaim Herzog.
p.   cm.
Includes index.
ISBN 0-679-43478-X
1. Herzog, Chaim, 1918–   . 2. Presidents—Israel—Biography.
3. Israel—History.   I. Title.
DS126.6.H47A3   1996
956.9405′092—dc20
[B]   96–14358
CIP

Random House Web Address: http://www.randomhouse.com/

Book design by Debbie Glasserman

Printed in the United States of America
First Edition
2 4 6 8 9 7 5 3 1

To Aura,
the partner at my side
in most of this saga

CONTENTS

Contents

ACKNOWLEDGMENTS

WRITING A MEMOIR is a labor of love. But love is not enough. Behind the writer there must be able and dedicated people. I was fortunate in this respect.

This book could not have appeared without the help of my very devoted and efficient personal assistant, Joan Gahtan, who coordinated all aspects of the preparation of the book from the outset. I am most indebted to her, as I am indeed to my entire office, headed by Sima Flit. In particular, my appreciation is due to Gali Harpaz-Matoki, my very able research assistant.

I am especially indebted to my editor, Peter Gethers of Random House, whose experience, personal ability, and advice proved of great value in writing this book.

A word of thanks to Esther Newberg, whose wisdom and publishing know-how were invaluable.

The wise comments and encouragement of my wife, Aura, were beyond measure.

Writing a book of such broad scope could not have been accomplished without the help of many others, too. To everyone involved in the production of this book, my sincere gratitude.

INTRODUCTION

I'VE ALWAYS BELIEVED that a voyage—with all its tumult, danger, exhilaration, discovery, and, ultimately, its inevitable closure—was a perfect metaphor for life. It certainly has been for my life, whose journey has gone down dirt roads as well as superhighways, crossed turbulent seas, and soared high on the mightiest of jet planes.

My journey began in Ireland, leading directly from the strife-torn aftermath of the 1916 Irish Revolution and the subsequent civil war of the early 1920s. I was educated in a Protestant school, though I grew up in a strict Orthodox home, always conscious that I was a Jew. To me, that fact, imparted so often by my father, meant that I was singled out as a member of a chosen people with a mission for doing good.

As a boy I left for Palestine and the Middle East, where I held my first rifle. The fierce pride in my origins, along with an overpowering belief in the justice of the Jewish cause, led me to swear an oath on that rifle that I would forever defend my people. Had I been apprehended at that ceremony, a meeting of the Israeli underground, the Haganah, held in a dark cellar in Jerusalem, I could have been sent to the gallows by the British Mandatory authorities. Yet, like all those who were with me, I asked no questions and had no hesitation. Nor was I afraid. My belief in the cause was so fervent, it did not even occur to me to be afraid.

My journey continued in the halls of higher education and back to Britain on the eve of World War II. This was the first of too many wars that I would see firsthand and the first time I saw the heights to which man can ascend when struggling for what he believes is a just cause. In London I saw the greatness of the British people during the indiscriminate bombing of their capital. In Jerusalem, years later, I saw much the same tenacity, bravery, and courage as the besieged and beleaguered Jewish people struggled to achieve their destiny.

In the British army, I served in northwest Europe and entered the concentration camps at the close of the war to find myself at the center of one of the monstrous happenings of all history. Here I saw the tragedy not only of the Jewish people but of the world. Peering at the core of man's evil only strengthened my conviction that the values inherent in Judaism could indeed lead to goodness, peace, and wisdom.

My journey led me past the destruction of Nazi Germany to the internecine war that ravaged Palestine, as Jews and Arabs battled for supremacy. I witnessed the heroic War of Independence, in which a small Jewish community, against overwhelming odds, achieved statehood after two thousand years. The dream on which I had been brought up became reality.

As my new country struggled through its youth, my journey continued to America, where I helped to form the first military relationship between Israel and the United States; back to Jerusalem, where I commanded Israeli troops in our state's first decade. Twice I was to head Israel's Military Intelligence; indeed, I was privileged to lay the foundation for it.

My path eventually turned to industry and commerce, the practice of law, broadcasting, and then to the Israeli political scene. On that crucial yet absurd stage known as the United Nations, I had the honor of defending Israel and the Jewish people before the world, giving full expression to what motivated me as a Jew and a Zionist.

The road led to the Knesset and, ultimately, to the presidency of Israel, where I completed two tours of duty in ten years. When I was elected, I remembered my boyhood, when my father rode me on his knee through the Holy Land, while he acted out the great events of Jewish history. How could I have imagined then that I would become a part of it, associated with David Ben-Gurion, Levi Eshkol, Golda Meir, Menachem Begin, Yitzhak Rabin, Shimon Peres, Jimmy Carter, Ronald Reagan, George Bush, Richard Von Weizsaecker, François Mitterrand, Margaret Thatcher, and Vaclav Havel. They were living players in what is to me the greatest game of all: maintaining and sustaining Israel as an essential force in today's world, at the center of world Jewry and, I hope, world peace.

My voyage has not yet come to its final port. When I disembark, I hope that everything my generation and I dreamed of and fought for will have come true. I pray that my children and grandchildren will see a strong and vigorous Israel at peace with its neighbors and continuing to represent the traditions that have sustained our people throughout the ages. I pray that the world will have taken even greater steps toward democracy and the guarantee of human rights, and that dignity will have become the universally accepted value of mankind. I wish for a world in which Israel vindicates its promise to be "a light unto the nations."

If it is people who shape history, it is also history that shapes people. My journey through this most extraordinary century has allowed me to write about both.

C.H.
July 1996

Living History

—◈◈◈—

Ireland

THE EARLIEST AUTHENTIC record of the Jews' arrival in Ireland is in the *Annals of Innisfallen*, which records that in "Year 1062: Five Jews came to Ireland from over the sea bringing gifts to Tordelbach who were again expelled over the sea." Tordelbach was a grandson of the great Irish king Brian Boru. Since Jews did not appear in England until after the Norman Conquest in 1066, these five must have come from France.

Since then, there has always been some form of Jewish presence in Ireland. Indeed, the Jewish community of Dublin is one of the British Isles' oldest. (Cromwell apparently wanted to encourage the settlement of Ireland by an industrious and substantial community that would form a barrier for him against the Catholic population.) The first synagogue in Ireland was established by Portuguese Jews in Dublin in 1660, and property for the first Jewish cemetery in that city was acquired in 1718.

Ireland's small Jewish community reflected the movement of the Jews from Spain, Portugal, Holland, Germany, and Eastern Europe. Thus, *Faulkners Dublin Journal*, the leading newspaper of the time, reported in October 1747 that "Last week some Jew Merchants of great Wealth arrived here from Holland in order to settle in Ireland."

In 1689, William III of England dispatched an expeditionary force to Ireland under the duke of Schomberg. The commissary-general was Isaac Pereira; another leading member of the force was Abraham Yadner.

In the early eighteenth century, there were four synagogues in Dublin. In 1876, the president of the Jewish congregation, a leading financial merchant named Lewis Harris, was the first Jew to win election to public office in Dublin, but he died a few days before he was due to be appointed lord mayor. In 1956 another Jew, Robert Briscoe, a prominent leader in the Irish struggle for independence, would assume the office of lord mayor of Dublin.

In the late nineteenth century, amid the repression of Jews in Europe, there was an enormous influx of Jews into the British Isles. Dublin's quota settled in the southern part of the city. An 1880 appeal for funds to build a central synagogue pointed out that Dublin's Jews comprised representatives of the community's founders "who may be said to be English or Irish Jews" and "a large body of foreign Jews who for the past eight years have made Dublin their residence and who generally outnumber the English-speaking Jews." The Cathedral Synagogue was consecrated in 1892 by the chief rabbi of the British Empire, Dr. Herman Adler, "in the presence of a congregation representative of the community, and including several of Her Majesty's judges and several other prominent personages of the Christian faith." It was here that I was called to the Torah as a bar mitzvah.

Jews also prospered in Belfast, where Sir Otto Jaffe was elected lord mayor in 1904, and in Londonderry, Limerick, and Cork. By the time I was born, there were approximately 5,000 Jews in Ireland.

If I'm to believe my birth certificate, I first saw the light of day on 17 September 1918, in the home of the local rabbi at 2 Norman Villas in Belfast. Nine months later my father, who was that rabbi, was invited to become chief rabbi of Ireland. That seat was in Dublin.

Belfast had been my father's first position in the ministry. He was born in 1889 in Lomza, Poland, a pleasant small town on a river, to Rabbi Joel Leib Herzog and Miriam Liba Cirowitz. My paternal grandfather was the son of the pious Rabbi Nafthali Hirsch Herzog, who served in Lomza. The Jewish community there, numbering approximately 10,000 at the beginning of World War II, was obliterated by the Nazis. The great synagogue, which dominated the center of the town, was destroyed, and all traces of the community were obliterated. At the entrance to what had been the ghetto, there is now a plaque.

In the course of a state visit to Poland in 1992, I was moved and honored to lay a wreath at that very spot. As I traveled around the countryside on that trip, the name of each town aroused memories of people who used to visit my family in my youth. As we neared Bialystok, I realized my wife's grandparents had come from there. Part of Aura's family had been driven out of Spain in 1492 and moved to Italy, where they became master builders. The prince of Zamosc, a Pole who had studied in Italy, took them back with him to Poland in the eighteenth century to build the town of Zamosc. Around 1875, Aura's grandfather made his way to the Holy Land, where he was one of the *Biluim*—the *"Mayflower"* generation.

My paternal grandfather was a great character, squat, bearded, heavily built, and with a deep, hoarse, resonant voice that I can hear to this day. He was a marvelous preacher, a tough and single-minded man, and his children were completely subservient to him. I adored him. When we were living in Dublin, I would go to the post office with my father every day to mail a card to my grandfather in Paris.

My grandparents lived very sparingly, as did all those in rabbis' homes in Eastern Europe. They had four children: a son who died in his youth; Esther, Helen, and the baby of the family, my father. Aunt Esther was a strange character who married a man named Reuben Goldberg in Paris. His family were very successful traders in ostrich feathers, with offices in New York and Shanghai. Esther graduated from the University of Leeds with a degree in music and wrote several books but, in general, lived a tragic life. She looked after her invalid sister, Helen, until she died. Her husband escaped the Nazis by fleeing to Shanghai but died soon after. One of Esther's two daughters, Annette, died in Auschwitz at the age of twenty-one.

Aunt Helen married a modestly prosperous Manchester wine dealer named Zadok Levinson. A portly, Dickensian figure, he seemed never without his gold watch chain or thimbleful of cherry brandy. Helen lost a baby in childbirth and, stricken by melancholia, never spoke again. Esther took her into her apartment in Paris—miraculously, even through the Nazi occupation. Near the end of Helen's life, they moved to Jerusalem.

My father grew up in straitened circumstances, and the memorial book of the community of Lomza* describes his home as an attic apartment. It became evident when my father was very young that he was a genius, so my grandfather devoted himself to teaching him rather than exposing him to the evils of the world or the rather inadequate yeshiva educational system. By the time my father was nine, he had acquired a reputation as an *ilui*, an outstanding thinker.

My paternal grandfather joined the early Zionist movement Hovevei Zion, and remained a member despite the unpopularity of its newfangled philosophy. He constantly espoused unpopular causes, had no idea of expediency, and always remained true to what he believed, no matter how

---

*Memorial books for most of the Jewish communities destroyed in World War II have been produced by the survivors of those communities.

great the cost. As one of the prominent spokesmen of the Hovevei Zion Movement, he was elected a delegate to the First World Zionist Congress in Basel in 1897. Unfortunately, his older son became fatally ill, and he was unable to attend.

THE VAST EMIGRATION from Eastern Europe to the United States in the late 1800s made many American communities attractive posts for European clergy. Motivated by the lure of the Promised Land, my grandfather accepted an appointment as the first rabbi of Worcester, Massachusetts. He lasted only six months, however, having apparently become involved in a conflict—another matter of principle—over his demand for the dismissal of the *shochet* (ritual slaughterer). Soon afterward, he was appointed rabbi for a congregation in Leeds, England, and the family moved there from Lomza.

Before the outbreak of World War I, the family moved to Paris, where my grandfather was appointed rabbi of the Orthodox community. Headquarters were at the synagogue on the rue Pavée, in the Jewish quarter known as the Marais.

My father, like many Jews who began life in Eastern Europe or the ghettos of the West, grew up with a background of Talmudic scholarship and a close adherence to the principles and precepts of Judaism. But unlike many from his background, he branched out into general studies, as other great Jewish contributors to philosophy, science, medicine, and politics did. As their field of studies expanded, they frequently cut themselves off from their religious origins; and many a full-fledged revolt took place as talented youths from the narrow, rigid background of Orthodox upbringing either opted for recognition in the field of Talmudic and Jewish studies or turned their backs completely on them. My father did both. He imbibed the Jewish culture and background, the Jewish beliefs and hopes, the Jewish dreams that culminated in the Zionist ideal. At the same time, his thirst for knowledge led him to become a scholar in fields as far apart as law, classics, mathematics, Oriental languages, and marine biology. He was driven by his own father, who never entrusted him to a center of Talmudic studies but remained his private teacher as long as it was feasible.

My father studied in England and France. He lived with, and traveled throughout Great Britain with, Rabbi Jacob David Werner, known as the Ridvaz, one of the greatest Talmudic scholars of his time. After testing my father for weeks, Rabbi Werner proclaimed him, when he was still very young, to be one of the world's outstanding Talmudists (by the age of sixteen my father knew the entire Talmud by heart). At the same time, he studied Oriental languages at the Sorbonne in Paris, and classics and mathematics at the University of London, where he received his doctorate. In his dissertation on marine biology he identified "The Royal Purple and the Biblical Blue," the shellfish that provided the purple dye for the holy garments in ancient Israel. (Later scientific research has vindicated all his findings.)

In 1916, my father received his first appointment, as rabbi of Belfast, in Northern Ireland. He was very much the absentminded-professor type, and his contemporaries related with amusement stories of his unworldliness. When my mother married him and came to Belfast, she found the floor under his bed covered with shoes, for every time a shoelace tore he simply bought a new pair.

In the rabbinical world, word was spreading not only about his Talmudic brain but also that he was a desirable catch for the right woman. Word was also getting around about the beautiful daughter of Rabbi Hillman.

My MATERNAL GRANDFATHER, Rabbi Samuel Isaac Hillman, had an unusual personality, intensely outgoing, dignified, full of humor, and very authoritative. Born in Kovno, Lithuania, he was married to Shaina, the daughter of Nafthali Hirsch Pakempner. They hailed from the Kurland district of Latvia, where German was spoken, so my grandmother was fluent in both German and Latvian. Her father was a prosperous trader, and the family lived comfortably. They were wiped out by the Nazis in World War II.

When my mother's father was rabbi in the small Russian town of Berezino (now located in Belarus), there was a riot in the fish market one Sabbath eve. A Gentile fishmonger came to my grandfather, complaining that all his money and his fish had been stolen. At the conclusion of the service, my grandfather mounted the pulpit and told the congregation about the complaint. He decreed that all fish thus acquired for the Sabbath were nonkosher (forbidden for Jews), unless those who were guilty left payment in his study after the Sabbath. The fishmonger was more than compensated; he emerged with a handsome sum far beyond what he expected.

My grandfather had two children, Uncle David, the elder, and my mother, Sarah, born in 1899 in Riga in Latvia. While a student in the *heder* (religious school) in Russia, Uncle David revealed unusual artistic ability. Though his caricatures and drawings of his teachers were superb, they brought on the wrath not only of those depicted but also of my grandfather, who did not think much of an artist's life. David Hillman graduated from the Glasgow School of Art and from the Royal Academy in London. A superb portraitist, he was nominated master of glass by the Royal Academy, a tribute to his impressive stained-glass windows, which adorn most of the important synagogues in Great Britain, as well as many public buildings in Israel. David's devotion to art was a lifelong source of tension with his parents. But as my grandfather lay on his deathbed, he called for Uncle David and asked his forgiveness.

My mother's father was a descendant of Rabbi Samuel Isaac Hillman, who, six generations earlier, was rabbi of Metz in Germany. In the introduction to his books, the rabbi of Metz maintained that he was a direct descendant of Rabbi Katzenelenbogen of Hamburg, who officiated in the seventeenth century. Rabbi Katzenelenbogen, for his part, maintains in the introduction to his Talmudic responsa, "Knesset Yehezkel," that he is descended from Rashi (Rabbi Shlomo ben Yitzchak), who lived in Troyes, France, in the eleventh century. Considered the greatest interpreter of the Bible and the Talmud, Rashi claimed descent from King David. (Once, when we lunched with Queen Elizabeth II at Windsor Castle, my wife, Aura, told her about this alleged descent from royalty. The queen smiled and said that she was also supposed to be descended from King David. "Welcome to the family," Aura responded without hesitation.)

DURING WORLD WAR I, there was a serious food shortage in Great Britain. The question arose in Jewish communities whether to authorize, for use during Passover, the use of such foods as rice, normally forbidden by the Ashkenazim but permitted by the Sephardim. A convention of rabbis was convened by my maternal grandfather, who presided over the religious law courts of Great Britain, the Beit Din, in East London. My father attended that conference, which was held at the Hillmans' beautiful old house next to the courts. During a break in the meeting, my mother brought in the tea. She and my father knew of each other—they even knew they were supposed to be meant for each other. She was truly beautiful, with large brown eyes and a lovely complexion. So while they were gazing at each other, she spilled the tray of tea all over him. Despite this inauspicious beginning, they were married in August 1917—and managed to live happily ever after.

THE CONFLICTS OF growing up as a Jew in Western societies have been chronicled by many great writers. On the one hand is the adherence to Jewish traditions and discipline imposed by parents who would tolerate no deviation from the straight and narrow path of Judaism; on the other hand is the continuing effort to assimilate, to be as good as non-Jews—if possible, to be even better. There is the inevitable fear of discrimination, whether direct or implied, and the inevitable desire to prove oneself. In this regard, my family was typical of those pulled between two distinct societies. My father was well known in Dublin for supporting the Irish in their struggle for independence; as we walked through the streets he was acknowledged with great deference, much as the leading Catholic clergy were. Yet, on many occasions stones were thrown at us by young urchins, who believed that this was the best way to settle the account with the Jewish people for allegedly crucifying Christ.

Ireland had no history of anti-Semitism, and while I did not feel outcast, I did feel different. I was always aware that somewhere in the background I was being judged by different standards. When a Jew was arrested for a crime, the entire Jewish community shuddered, because it was expected that all Jews would be thought guilty of that crime. There was an absence of psychological equality. Physically and psychologically, the Jewish community was closed in on itself. It had its own social organizations, Zionist organizations, and religious community. Very few Jews mingled socially with non-Jews. A visit from a non-Jew was a major event, and the best finery and airs were exhibited. There was always the feeling of inadequacy, and in many ways it was "them" and "us," but we strove to succeed among "them." As stories were brought back by tourists from the Jewish settlements in Palestine, Zionism—the concept of a Jewish state—emerged in our collective consciousness and added considerably to our sense of pride. As that consciousness expanded, it strengthened our entire community.

My parents set up house in Belfast, where they stayed for two years and developed lifelong friendships. When my father received his "call" to become chief rabbi of Ireland, they moved to Dublin, where they remained for eighteen years. He became a world figure, renowned as an outspoken scholar and master of many languages. He was offered the rabbinate in

Vienna, the chief rabbinates of France and Greece, and even the presidency of Yeshiva University in New York, but turned them all down because they would have taken him too far away from his father in Paris. He feared the effects of such moves on my brother and me, and I believe he also had a premonition of developments in Europe.

Many things happened in my father's life that indicated special divine protection—what a religious Jew would call *hashgacha.* In World War I, while engaged to my mother, he was asked to deliver a sermon at the magnificent Great Synagogue on Duke's Place in East London, where they were later married. When he was boarding the ship that would take him to England, he was called off—a member of the community was dying. So he missed his trip to London. The next day, at precisely the hour he was to deliver his sermon, there was a zeppelin air raid on London, and a bomb destroyed the pulpit on which he would have been standing.

Another time, he woke up screaming in panic on Rosh Hashanah night. The Ridvaz, who had ordained him as a rabbi, had come to him in a dream, dressed in white and wearing a *tallit* (prayer shawl). The Ridvaz said, "Tsarot al Yisrael" [tribulations on Israel], then disappeared. The next day it was learned that the Ridvaz had died at exactly the moment when my father had screamed. The next week, World War I broke out, with all the "tribulations" it would entail for the Jewish people.

During World War II, while my parents were traveling to America, they missed their ship, the *Robin Moore,* and were forced to sail on another. While crossing the Atlantic, the *Robin Moore* was sunk by a German U-boat.

FROM OUR CHILDHOOD my younger brother, Yaacov, and I had a very special relationship with my father. When it came to religious observance, my father was a strong disciplinarian, but in an extremely positive way. He invariably tried to explain the logic and advantage of our religion; he wished us to observe willingly rather than to simply impose his will. I may not always have wished to do as he wanted, but the gentle and civilized manner in which he expounded his views usually left little option. We never reached the stage of parent-child confrontation—which characterized so many Jewish homes at that time—that came from being caught between the Jewish community and the requirements of Irish, non-Jewish society. As a family, we tried to experience and enjoy both worlds. That was not always easy.

My father's greatest contribution to helping me to define what I am today came when I was a boy. He would spend hours with Yaacov and me, walking in the botanical and zoological gardens and relating all the plants and animals to some place or event in the Bible. As a result, I grew up with a strong sense of pride in my heritage. Under different tutelage I could just as easily have rebelled and broken away; the pressures to do so were certainly there.

I have vivid childhood memories of our annual family trips across the Irish Sea to England. I can still see my mother fussing over the luggage—my father was much too unworldly to deal with such mundane matters. After the long train ride from Holyhead in Wales, we were welcomed in London by my maternal grandparents and my uncle. Then we'd all ride in a horse and cab to their home in East London.

BEING JEWISH IN IRELAND was not our only cultural conflict. Being Irish in England was another.

Since the seventeenth century, when Cromwell ruled England, bitter strife and struggle characterized the relationship between the Irish people, the bulk of whom are Catholics, and the English Protestant aristocracy and settlers, who established themselves in Ireland's rich agricultural country. With their own language, Gaelic, and their very proud cultural heritage, the Irish endeavored to rid themselves of what they considered the British occupiers. The House of Commons struggled mightily with what seemed to be an insoluble problem. In 1916, in the midst of World War I, a comparatively small group of Irish patriots led the Easter Monday Uprising against the British forces and government. The revolution tore the country apart. Ireland had been an integral part of the United Kingdom since 1801, but as a result of the struggle, the Anglo-Irish Agreement of 6 December 1920 was signed. Twenty-six of Ireland's thirty-two counties were allotted to the Irish Free State; the remaining six counties of Ulster, which constituted Northern Ireland, were left an integral part of the United Kingdom. This arrangement in Northern Ireland, where the population is two-thirds Protestant and one-third Catholic, has been the source of the strife that has torn that province ever since.

My first vivid memory in Dublin was of the Irish civil war. The forces were set up on both sides of South Circular Road—we lived at No. 102—and fought each other from the rooftops. To this day I can recall the shooting. I was only around three years old but already quite inquisitive and probably too mischievous. As I wandered out into the front garden to watch the battle, a man driving a horse and cart went past and was shot dead in front of me. The windows of Williams's food shop, across from our house, were blown in. I recall the horse wandering aimlessly, a dead man lying on the cart in a grotesque manner, and mounds of fruit from Williams's windows cascading onto the street. The opposing sides beat on the doors with their rifle butts in order to search the houses. My mother, in hysterics, dragged me and my baby brother down to the cellar and locked us in a lavatory, while my father, who never knew fear, opened the door.

My father was an open partisan of the Irish cause. When Irish prisoners went on a hunger strike, he pleaded with them to cease endangering their lives. In many circles in Ireland, our family name is still associated with those who fought for liberty. The outstanding Jewish leader in the revolution was Robert Briscoe, later a member of the Irish Parliament (the Dail) and lord mayor of Dublin (his son, Ben Briscoe, also became lord mayor). The Jewish community as a whole gave a lot of help to the Irish. After the establishment of the Irish Free State, when Eamon De Valera was in the Opposition, he would come to visit, usually with Robert Briscoe, and unburden his heart to my father. He obviously never forgot these sessions, because in 1950, after the State of Israel was established, De Valera was one of the first foreign statesmen to visit. He dined with Ben-Gurion and Bobby Briscoe at my parents' home in Jerusalem.

THE JEWISH COMMUNITY in Dublin was a small, closely knit Orthodox community whose elders, and the bulk of its members, had emigrated from Lithuania. Noted for their learning and Talmudic scholarship, Lithuanian Jews were extremely honest and tolerant. These traits were certainly dominant in Dublin, where the religious and social life revolved around the synagogues. Rivalry between synagogues and the political foolishness that exists in every community were here, too. And colorful characters abounded. Small wonder that James Joyce chose Leopold Bloom in *Ulysses* from the area of Clanbrassil and Lombard streets, the center of the Jewish ghetto.

The Reverend Gudanski was the *hazan* (cantor) at the Adelaide Road Synagogue, which catered largely to Anglicized Jews, in contrast to the Greenville Hall Synagogue, which served the more Orthodox Eastern European community. His voice had seen its best days long before I was old enough to appreciate his chanting, but he still evoked respect and dignity. The *shamash* [beadle] was Mr. Isaacson, who had a dentist's sign outside his house and specialized in rather painful extractions since he deemed painkilling devices a needless complication.

But the Greenville Hall Synagogue was my favorite, because most of my friends from the Hebrew school *(heder)* attended it. Its cantor, the Reverend Rosenfeld, had an international reputation. He was aided by a choir led by Mr. Bryll, who later became a renowned cantor in London. The combination produced services of extraordinary beauty.

The central activity for children of Dublin's less Orthodox community was the scout troop. My parents would not hear of my joining it, despite my desire to. The life of the more Orthodox members was centered on the *heder.* There we had debating societies (in which the language was Hebrew), a vaguely scoutlike organization called Woodcrafters, and eventually the Habonim, a Zionist youth movement that later played a great part in the settlement of Israel.

The *heder* was, in many ways, the only contact with Jewish education for most of the students. Classes were held daily, and the headmaster in my early youth was Moshe Vilenski, a character out of some great Russian novel. He was small with sharp, foxlike eyes, a long red nose with spectacles perched at the end of it, a pointed red beard, and hair swept back and out. In his waistcoat he had a huge watch on a gold chain, and I have never ceased wondering at the durability and stability of that watch. Every so often he would take it out of his pocket, look at it, try to wind it, and then knock it with great strength on one of the desks. After looking at it again, he would give a grunt of satisfaction and put it back in his pocket. To emphasize his point, he would stab his long fingernail into a desk, leaving his mark not just on our education but all over the classroom.

When Vilenski left Dublin, his deputy, Hyman Schreider, took over. He tutored me for my bar mitzvah and was the most pedantic pedagogue I have ever come across. But he was an outstanding teacher of Hebrew grammar, and if I know anything about that subject today, it is thanks to him.

For my secular education I was sent first to Alexandra College, a girls' school with a kindergarten for both girls and boys. It was quite fashionable and not Catholic, which was probably why my parents sent me there. My first day of class marked my introduction to the non-Jewish world. One of my teachers, Miss Cherry, obviously remembered the devilish little boy I was then, because she wrote to me fifty years later when I was elected president of Israel.

From Alexandra I moved to Wesley College, an English-style Protestant school, whose most famous alumnus was George Bernard Shaw. For the school's 100th anniversary, they asked for a message from Shaw as part of their celebration. They wrote twice, but he did not reply. The third time, he answered, via postcard: "If you don't stop pestering me, I will write what I *really* thought about the place."

Wesley was coeducational, the morning prayers were nondenominational, the men and women teachers wore gowns, and many of the male teachers hit us on the head with books when they considered it appropriate, which seemed to be most of the time. Punishment was, as at all good English schools of the time, six strokes of the cane. Throughout my scholastic career I had my share of "sixes," both on my posterior and on my hand. We gradually learned how to put padding under our trousers and to hide horsehair in our fists, which tended to minimize the effect of the blows. The cane was administered by the headmaster, the Reverend Dr. J. J. Irwin, a pompous man who was not highly regarded. There was much speculation about his doctorate, rumored to have come from some unknown American college—a near disgrace for one in his position.

I don't believe I was an overly bright student, but I worked quite hard and came in first in the competition for the annual scholarship prize, which guaranteed me free tuition. I excelled in French, history, and geography, but schoolwork was not nearly as important to me as sports. *The* game in school was rugby, and from time to time I was included on the team. But most games were on Friday afternoons, and to play in the winter meant a desecration of the Sabbath, about which I was regularly admonished at home.

My desire to participate in sports created the inevitable conflict between my Orthodox upbringing and my need to be acknowledged as an equal in the complicated student hierarchy. All through these formative years, I grew up with a father who was a genius but extremely unworldly. My mother was the personification of practicality, a powerful figure and strict disciplinarian who dominated the home and, indeed, any organization with which she was associated. That my father's brilliance, scholarship, and character could be translated into the highest ecclesiastical position among the Jewish people was due in no small measure to the home that my mother created. Indeed, my parents were the parents of Dublin's Jewish community. Anyone in trouble came to my father. No Jew went to court against another; instead they agreed to a *din torah*, an arbitration based on Jewish law, presided over by my father. His word was final and he exercised his authority with tolerance and an understanding of the failings of human nature that could well be emulated by many spiritual leaders today.

Although the Jewish community was tiny, my father maintained excellent relations with the heads of other religions and was on particularly good terms with Cardinal McRory, primate of all Ireland. Once, at a state dinner in Dublin Castle, where my father ate nothing but fruit, the cardinal reproached him for not trying the excellent ham being offered. My father reportedly smiled whimsically and said, "Let us discuss this at your wedding."

My mother was very active in women's organizations and clearly the dominant individual at home. She was very pretty and gracious and, although petite, almost regal in her demeanor. Wherever her home was, it was a center of grace and culture and, later, in Israel, a magnet for much of world Jewry. She was to build the leading psychiatric hospital in the Middle East and would head the women's division of a political party. She was awarded two honorary doctorates and was an accomplished speaker.

As the family's taskmaster she disapproved of any tendency toward the lighter side of life; but for her, my father would never have written some of his great works. His impracticality placed a great burden on her; she had to run everything. We were always being besieged by *meshulachim*, emissaries from *yeshivot* throughout Eastern Europe and Palestine, as well as scholars from all over the world who simply wanted to talk to and learn from my father. Since he had no idea of administration, he blithely wrote checks to all who turned to him. I still recall the sense of doom when the bank manager called to advise my mother that our account was overdrawn and we were heavily in debt. From then on, my father would never write a check without my mother's signature on it.

My brother, Yaacov, was also quite brilliant. Eventually he studied law, took his doctorate in Canada, became minister in Israel's embassy in Washington and ambassador to Canada. He was the advisor and confidant of four prime ministers. Ben-Gurion admired him; Eshkol treated him as a son. For many years, he was responsible for Israel's diplomatic relations with the Vatican.

Summers we played cricket at the Jewish club—I was not very good, Yaacov was better—and in the winter we played rugby. In summer I went swimming almost every day with him, often cycling out to Blackrock or Kingstown (Dunlaoghaire as it is today). My first bicycle became a crucial symbol of freedom, and its acquisition was a major event. Hardly a day went by without a dramatic scene in which my mother would vividly describe the horrible fate that would befall me if I rode a bike on the streets of Dublin—histrionics accompanied by lurid examples. With the help of leaders of the community and especially of my father, I finally got a bicycle, but Yaacov had no such problem. On his bar mitzvah, while my mother smiled proudly, he was duly presented with his very own bike.

At one stage we both took up boxing. In Ireland, being a boxer placed you in a class by yourself. The idea of Jewish boys knocking the daylights out of the *goyim* filled these immigrants with satisfaction. While my father was secretly proud that we were following in the footsteps of the great Jewish warriors of the past—I was champion of my weight class —my mother thought the whole thing was a lot of nonsense. Once, when I arrived home with a bloody nose, black eye, and swollen ear, I got a long lecture and an "I told you so." My father fared no better for encouraging me.

WE STILL TRAVELED frequently to London to stay at Court Lodge in the East End, the official residence of the head of the Beit Din, who was my maternal grandfather. He was a very learned rabbi, the symbol of orderliness, and with two fingers typed out twenty-two volumes of an encyclopedic work on the Bible and the Talmud. The teeming East End had a daily Jewish newspaper, a Yiddish theater, and a strong and attractive mixture of Eastern European Orthodoxy with the dignity of Anglo-Jewry. I can still recall walking with my grandfather to the Great Synagogue on Duke's Place in Aldgate (later destroyed by German bombs in World War II). On Saturdays he'd be dressed in his Sabbath best, top hat and all, as we strolled through the streets crowded with Jews hurrying to or from prayer. Everywhere the Jews raised their hats and bowed to my mother's father. It was like walking with some form of prelate.

The aristocratic Jewish families—the Rothschilds, Sir Robert Waley-Cohen, the Sassoons—were leaders of the community alongside the rabbis and yeshivot. The chief rabbi in England was Dr. J. H. Hertz, who, though looked upon somewhat askance by the Eastern European rabbis because of his alleged lack of Talmudic scholarship, left an indelible mark on the community by virtue of his strong personality. My grandfather's working arrangement with him was basically "live and let live." A new generation of leaders—Chaim Weizmann, the first president of Israel, and his "court," the Marks, the Sieffs, the Sachers, as well as such great Zionist leaders as Sokolov and Shmaryahu Levin—were flourishing and centered in London. The sons of the ghettos were moving into mainstream commerce and the universities. They would become great bankers, merchants, writers, and academicians.

My paternal grandfather was rabbi of the Orthodox community, and on the rue Pavée we were in an Orthodox ghetto. The garden of my aunt's rented summer house in Ile Adam, just outside Paris, housed a veritable zoo, with wild animals in cages. I still remember the ferocity of Pierre, the landlady's pet gorilla.

The great event of this period for me was my bar mitzvah, and all my grandparents came to Dublin for it. I was called to the reading of the Law in the Adelaide Road Synagogue. My *haftarah* was from Isaiah. It held forth the promise of a great tomorrow, of an expansion of one's human borders, of a bright and hopeful future for the people of Israel provided they conducted themselves according to the precepts of the prophets of the Lord. My father's sermon was on that *haftarah* reading. Drawing the analogy between past and present, he said, "When these eyes are closed, and this voice is silent forever, you will remember what I have said to you today." And, indeed, I do.

The reception was in the Rathmines town hall, and the entire community came. Grandpa Hillman opened with a story about a cantor and a beadle in a synagogue, who used to play cards together. (Though my grandfather was unaware of it, this was exactly what our cantor and beadle used to do.) One day, while playing cards, the beadle asked to withdraw a card, maintaining he had made a mistake. The cantor refused to acquiesce, saying with a smile, "As it lies, so may it continue to lie." The next day was the Yom Kippur service, when the cantor traditionally falls on his knees in obeisance to the Lord and is helped to his feet by the beadle. The cantor dropped to his knees and prostrated himself before the Ark of the Law. When nothing happened, he whispered to the beadle, "Lift me up." The beadle replied, "As it lies, so may it continue to lie."

According to Jewish tradition, by being bar mitzvahed I entered manhood. My father uttered a prayer thanking the Almighty for having released him from the responsibility for my sins. I was now expected to become an active member of the community and to live according to the 613 precepts that are supposed to bind a Jew. When I went to synagogue with my father on a cold Dublin morning, I proudly laid phylacteries on my arm and forehead. Ambitious mothers of attractive Jewish daughters began to appraise me in a more serious—and threatening—manner. I was happy to be a boy no longer.

This joyous occasion was the last time our entire family was to be together.

During the feast of Succoth, in October 1934, I heard my father run to answer the telephone in his study. It was my aunt, in Paris, calling to say that he should come immediately. His father had died.

In Paris, my father made arrangements for the transfer of my grandfather's remains to Palestine. Little did we realize that this decision was to be the turning point in the history of our family.

After my bar mitzvah, my parents began discussing my future. Like many Jewish boys in the community, I would undoubtedly have studied medicine had I remained in Dublin. But my parents were somewhat concerned about what could happen to me in Dublin society. Part of the younger generation was turning away from the Orthodox fold. Their intermingling with Irish youth was beginning to lead to intermarriage, which shocked both communities. Dublin was not my parents' ideal for me. To give me the necessary Jewish educational background, it was decided I was to enroll at a yeshiva. I was given a choice: Poland, Switzerland, or Palestine. I chose Palestine. It turned out to be a critical choice as history moved on toward the Holocaust in Europe and Jewish independence in Palestine.

My decision meant traveling abroad and seeing the world. Several of my older contemporaries had returned to Dublin from the great *yeshivot* of Poland, better equipped to understand and confront the destiny of *being* a Jew. I was already an eager Zionist and longed to be part of the struggle in Palestine. In addition, life there seemed romantic and certainly less mundane than the normal route from medical school to middle-class existence as a general practitioner.

In 1934, the year my paternal grandfather died, my maternal grandfather, Rabbi Hillman, had retired to Jerusalem. Since arrangements had been made to bury my Paris grandfather in Jerusalem, it seemed the perfect time to make my break. And leaving the Irish-Jewish community behind was a huge break. I had many close friends, both boys and girls. I was involved in every aspect of daily and communal life. I had absorbed much of the Irish culture, which to this day I deeply love and admire. However, despite my love for the Irish people, I was ecstatic about making such an adventurous change in my life.

By Hebrew law, I was a man. Now it was time to really become one.

CHAPTER 2

Palestine

IN MAY 1935 my family sailed on the *Mariette Pasha*, with my paternal grandfather's remains, from Marseilles to Palestine. It was on board ship that I truly began to realize the oneness of the Jewish people. We sat praying as we crossed the sea, Jews from the United States, Ireland, Europe, North Africa (attired in Berber headdress), even Jews from the island of Djerba, off Tunisia, dressed in their flowing white robes. We spoke different languages, yet we were uttering the same prayers in Hebrew and feeling the same sense of awe and wonder.

Our short stopover in Alexandria was my first taste of the East and the Arab world. Half the population seemed to descend on the dock. Magicians performed their tricks, vendors proffered their goods, scantily clad boys carried brass pitchers and offered exotic drinks. It was Babel and pandemonium entwined, as fez-wearing Egyptian officials did their best to impose order. Even amid this chaos, I felt as if I were approaching home.

In Alexandria, we were met by the leaders of the Jewish community, and the chief rabbi took us to the Jewish school. My father asked one of the children to quote something from the Bible, and the child replied, prophetically, "Although you are small in your own eyes, you will be a leader in Israel."

From Alexandria we sailed to Jaffa, where we arrived, wearing our heavy European clothes, on May 15. The ship lay off the port, so lighters manned by Arabs—in traditional dress, with tarbooshes on their heads—unloaded us as well as my grandfather's coffin. Here we were, at last, in the land of our dreams, in the Promised Land. Arabs bustled around, shouting, screaming, and bargaining; Jews pushed each other, yelling, hugging, and laughing as they greeted relatives. It was brutally hot, with flies almost as thick as the dust. My maternal grandfather had come from Jerusalem to greet us, and quite a large crowd was there for the funeral cortege. I stood by my grandfather's coffin, which was placed on an open truck, all the way to Jerusalem, staring wide-eyed at everything.

The procession moved to the Great Synagogue of Tel Aviv on Allenby Street, where my father recited the kaddish and tributes were paid to my grandfather by the leaders of the city. From here our convoy proceeded up the Jaffa–Jerusalem road. Even today, I can recall the enormous emotion that overcame me at my first sight of Jerusalem, when I entered the city at the side of my grandfather's coffin. It was so glorious and yet so sad, so overpowering and yet so natural. Our first stop was at the Etz Haim Yeshiva, at the entrance to the city. Here rabbis and students emerged, and again the appropriate prayers were recited. We kept driving, and as the Jaffa Road unfolded before us, it is hard to say whether I was more astonished, exhausted, or dehydrated. By now, standing on the truck in the open sunshine in my flannel suit, with a tie and a trilby hat, I was in a very sorry state.

We made it to the Mercaz Harav Yeshiva, where Rabbi Abraham Isaac Kook, the chief rabbi of Palestine and a saintly figure, great scholar, and philosopher, came out and stood behind the truck. The prayers were recited, my father again said kaddish, and Rabbi Kook delivered a eulogy. When he finished, my father spoke. Though we did not attach any significance to this event, Rabbi Kook was in the last months of his life—indeed, this was his final public appearance. While my father was not a candidate to replace him, this meeting was later much remarked upon. My father was running for rabbinical office in Tel Aviv, not for the chief rabbinate. That he was the last man to follow Rabbi Kook on the podium, as it were, was later seen as a sort of passing of the rabbinical baton.

The cortege continued to the Mount of Olives, but because the custom in Jerusalem is for the son of the deceased not to go to the cemetery, we parted from the coffin and were taken to Patt's Bakery, a very famous institution in the city. In their small garden we recovered from the efforts of the day, and I first tasted cold fruit soup. I could not drink enough.

While in Palestine, we visited friends' orange groves and went to kibbutzim, but the bulk of our time was spent in Tel Aviv, where my father campaigned for the city's chief rabbinate. His main supporter was a Rabbi Yitzchak Pinchas, who was pushing his candidacy against the

Mizrachi (a religious party). My father met all the leading luminaries, religious and not so religious, demonstrating his Talmudic prowess, delivering sermons in the Great Synagogue, and giving Talmudic discourses both in the great yeshivot of Jerusalem and in centers of learning in Tel Aviv. In the yeshivot, scholars tried to upset his theses, interrupting his remarks and arguing vociferously, but he floored them with his phenomenal memory and profound understanding of the Talmud. By the time his trip was over, he had made an indelible impression. However, the struggle in Tel Aviv was a political one, and Rabbi Amiel of Antwerp, the Mizrachi candidate, won the war of backroom politics, receiving twenty-one votes to ten for my father and three for the renowned Rabbi Soloveitchik of the United States.

In due course, it was time for my parents to return home. I *was* home now. Arrangements had been made for me to board with Dr. and Mrs. Isaiah Wolfsberg, who lived on Rechov Hanevi'im (Prophets' Street), near the Abyssinian church, in an ancient Arab building replete with courtyard and pool. Dr. Wolfsberg, a pediatrician, and his wife, Sonia, were in straitened circumstances—the market was flooded with German doctors escaping from Hitler's regime—so, even though they were already short of space, with their own three children, they rented rooms to three student lodgers.

Dr. Wolfsberg's mother also lived with them. She refused to adapt to a new way of life, so I learned German willy-nilly from her and absorbed a great deal of European culture, to which I had not previously been exposed. In Ireland we grew up under the influence of the stage, the Abbey and Gate theaters, but I had not been exposed to much of the world of music. My Uncle David had a record collection of great operas in his art studio, and I would hear the majestic voices of Caruso and Galli-Curci emerge from the huge gramophone loudspeaker. But my introduction to great symphonic works, and my appreciation of them, came from the Wolfsberg family.

Because I was in Palestine to acquire a Talmudic education, I was placed in the preparatory class at the Mercaz Harav Yeshiva, otherwise known as the Mechina. And suddenly I found myself in the Middle Ages.

Yeshivot in Israel, by and large, were replicas of the great seminaries in Eastern Europe—but strictly Orthodox and, in most ways, totally out of touch with modern Zionist life. For me, coming from a Western-type Orthodox background, it was a shock, and I was not at all prepared for the new surroundings. I had come from another world, one with a coeducational school, teenage parties, and rugby. Now I was in the decrepit district known as Even Yehoshua, near Sabbath Square (an appropriate name, since any transgressor of the Sabbath who drove through the square was bound to be stoned). The small synagogue in which the Mechina was housed would have been quite at home in a Chagall painting. It was surrounded by a sea of mud in winter and enormous piles of dust in summer. Inside, around the traditional tile-covered stove, the devout sat all day engrossed in prayer or study.

The school comprised four classrooms—actually four tables—with a teacher at the head of each. The language of instruction was Hebrew rather than Yiddish, and the Mechina's restrictive nature reflected the approach to life of a small, Eastern European shtetl at the turn of the century. One day, I rode a borrowed bicycle there. I do not think I could have caused greater consternation or had a more horrified reaction had I brought in a ham sandwich.

The Mechina, so totally out of tune with the times, did not represent what I had been brought up to believe in: the pursuit, rather than the restriction, of knowledge and culture. Though in many ways I was psychologically part of the Mechina, I realized that it was not the background against which our national aims would or could be developed.

IN ONLY ONE RESPECT was there a synthesis between the antiquated orthodoxy of the yeshiva and the striving of the younger Zionist generation: most of the yeshivot students were members of the underground. (Curiously enough, this is not true today. At many yeshivot, service in the armed forces is frowned upon by the strictly Orthodox.) As a natural and necessary outgrowth of the Zionist struggle, the underground was created with the idea that all members should have full military training and preparation, since its entire purpose was to defend Jewish settlements and districts against Arab attacks.

The Jewish community in Palestine numbered about 400,000 in 1936. The country was administered by the British Mandate, an attempt to implement the Balfour Declaration of 1917, which encouraged the establishment of a Jewish national home in Palestine. In 1922, the League of Nations reaffirmed the Balfour Declaration and gave Britain a mandate to enforce it. Part of the Arab world acquiesced and accepted this decision, but the bulk opposed it. This is the basis for the Arab–Israeli conflict during the whole of this century.

The internal political situation was confusing, complicated, and chaotic. During this period, a sizable number of Jewish refugees were admitted from Germany, and this immigration brought many of the world's leading scientists, musicians, and doctors. It gave Palestine a core of forward-thinking intellectuals and a strong foundation of leaders committed to the idea of running their own country and capable of doing so. The Jewish community, known as the Yishuv, was a compact, well-organized unit living side by side with the British Mandatory Government (in which Jews and Arabs also officiated). Under the aegis of the General Federation of Trade Unions, there was the Histadrut, a form of state government within the official—meaning British—government. The Histadrut was run by the Jewish community and administered such aspects of public life as the educational and health systems, labor, and social security.

Simultaneously, as the Nazi regime was beginning its march of domination in Europe, many people in Palestine felt a sense of urgency to strengthen the Jewish community's hold and to create an infrastructure that would enable the absorption of persecuted immigrants. The Zionist movement had many important political supporters, including Winston Churchill. But the real struggle was on the ground. The Mandatory authorities were generally unhelpful and unsympathetic to the Zionist cause, and British fascination and alignment with the Arab world reinforced the growing Arab opposition to a Jewish state. The Arabs' feelings were all too clearly expressed in periodic and horrendous mass riots in 1920, 1929, and 1936. (In the 1929 riots in Hebron, my mother's grandmother was seriously wounded by Arabs. In a room in which seventeen people were massacred, she, an old lady of eighty, survived by successfully feigning death.) It was against this background that the Jewish community worked to expand and prosper—and develop an alternative government. We knew we had to be prepared for the inevitable day the Arabs decided to leave.

As with all governments, a military was needed, hence the birth of the Jewish underground. Like almost everything in Israel, particularly where politics is concerned, its structure was overly complicated.

The original underground, called the Haganah, was controlled by the ruling Labor Party, led by David Ben-Gurion, and had approximately

40,000 members. It is this segment of the underground that was eventually transformed into the basis for the Israel Defense Forces.

The British army was in Palestine ostensibly to keep the peace and protect the Jews from Arab attacks. However, there was much hostility between the British soldiers—and government—and the Jewish population. Many Mandatory authorities were pro-Arab and there were frequent clashes between the British and the Jews. That political rift brought into existence a new force in the underground, the Irgun Zvai Leumi, known as the Irgun (also referred to as IZL or Etzel), which adopted a more militant policy in combating the British.

The Irgun, with approximately 5,000 members, did not accept Ben-Gurion as their leader; the organization was linked to the right-wing movement Betar and later to the Herut Party, and was ultimately led by Menachem Begin. At times it acted more anti-British than anti-Arab, frequently attacking British troops. On one occasion, in retaliation for the hanging of several underground fighters, two British soldiers were hanged.

A third, very extreme underground movement, the so-called Stern Group (or Lehi), was led by Yair Stern. It was primarily devoted to the anti-British struggle. It has even been alleged that the group endeavored to develop a dialogue with Nazi Germany, at the outset of World War II, in an attempt to ensure German support for the Jewish struggle against the British in Palestine. Indeed, in 1940 it broke away from the Irgun, refusing to back Britain in its struggle against the Nazis. One of Stern's leaders was Yitzhak Shamir, later a prime minister of Israel. There was as much tension between the various underground organizations as there was between the Jewish community and the British Mandatory Government—and probably even between the Jews and Arabs.

I joined the Haganah as soon as I was able, at the age of sixteen. I knew from hints dropped by my roommate at the Wolfsbergs', a young man named Justman, that he was a member. It seemed to me that everyone was in the underground—even the Boy Scouts and the Labor Union Youth were fronts for the underground. Of course, nobody announced his membership, but from the odd glance, the occasional wink, the random remark, it was clear who was involved. In that regard, it was not unlike a fraternity: to be a member meant you were "in." But it also meant much more. A driving force inside me had been nurtured since the days of the long walks and talks with my father, and had turned me into a Jewish patriot. Linked with my religious upbringing was the overwhelming sense that the possibility of impending statehood meant that one could and *should* finally fight for this ultimate dream. One could no longer be outside the pale and expect to be a part of the new state.

The ceremony of joining the Haganah was moving and rather terrifying. I had received a message ordering me to be outside the Alliance Israelite School in Jerusalem, an ancient Ottoman-style building, at a specific time, and I was then taken down into a darkened cellar. Security precautions were heavy, and we knew full well that to be caught by the British meant a long prison term or even a death sentence. (Moshe Dayan spent several years in a British-run prison in Acre when his Haganah unit was caught in the act of military training.)

We were each given a rifle. It was the first time I'd ever held one, and it was a strangely thrilling and empowering sensation. The commanders of the district sat grim-faced at the table while we stood at attention. A Bible was placed on the table and we were sworn in. To this day, when Israeli youth join the military, they take the same oath, either on Masada or at the Wailing Wall.

Even though my father was a scholar and not a soldier, I knew I had his tacit approval; he would have done the same at my age. But my mother was terrified, especially since she discovered my underground affiliation accidentally during a visit. A salesman in a store was serving us— and he happened to be in my Haganah unit. Only in our society would a salesman tell your mother that you were in the underground. But despite her anxieties and fears, she did not interfere in any way.

And so began my military career. Although somewhat ragtag, the Haganah was a full military operation, all based on Ben-Gurion's vision that we must have a modern and efficient army to survive as a country. Accordingly, we were schooled in the use of weapons and went into the mountains for more advanced training. We were broken up into companies and divided according to districts; each company was responsible for the protection of a particular area against Arab attacks. Like any rebel or underground group, we were poor. When we went on patrol we were lucky to have even close to a sufficient number of weapons.

I was placed in a religious company, since boys professing religious faith were segregated at their request. (This foolish policy was abandoned after the War of Independence, when some religious communities lost great numbers, out of all proportion to their size.)

The Arab revolt, led by the Mufti of Jerusalem, Haj Amin al-Husseini, broke out in April 1936, and the British forces and police were now engaged in the bitter struggle against the Arabs. The fighting was fierce, with no quarter given and no holds barred. The British had no option but to turn a blind eye to the Haganah's activities; unofficially, they were forced to acknowledge that they needed us to defend Jewish villages and settlements against the Arab irregulars. As part of this policy, members of the Haganah, myself included, were officially inducted into the supernumerary police as *ghaffirs* (guards).

THE CITY OF JERUSALEM WAS, as it had been for centuries and is today, an extraordinary mixture of cultures. At the Zion Cinema on Saturday evenings, the Arabs, all men, sat bunched together, splitting seeds with their teeth and throwing them on the floor. The Jews also sat together, cooling themselves with ice cream. On both sides of the screen were translations, operated by hand, in Hebrew and Arabic. Many of the British were attired in formal gowns or black tie, having come from their everlasting dinner parties. This unique cross-cultural experience has given me a tolerance and appreciation for the foibles, customs, and beliefs of many different peoples.

As a member of the underground, I was assigned briefly to the Old City. I would travel through the Jaffa Gate in a specially built bus, the No. 2, which was just wide enough to negotiate the narrow streets of the Armenian and Jewish quarters. I was on duty in the Misgav Ladach Hospital, alone or with one other Haganah member, usually for a period of twelve to twenty-four hours at a stretch. This sublime example of the chutzpah of the Jewish forces was dictated by the almost total lack of equipment and personnel. Two men and one rifle were entrusted with the security of the entire Jewish quarter.

Once we were sworn in by the British as *ghaffirs*, our unit served in the Arnona district, between Talpiot and Ramat Rachel, covering the Arab village of Sur Bahr. Dressed in long raincoats and high Caucasian *kalpaks* (sheepskin caps), and armed with British Lee Enfield rifles, we patrolled the roads at night and searched anyone moving to and from the village. It was a comparatively quiet sector, although one of our members, the son of the rabbi of Lomza (where my father had been born), Shneor Gordon, was shot and killed in an Arab raid.

AROUND THAT TIME, I left the Mechina of Mercaz Harav and joined a more traditional yeshiva, the Hebron. Originally the Slabodky Yeshiva, named after a suburb of Kovno in Lithuania, it was headed by Rabbi

Moshe Mordechai Epstein. In the 1920s the yeshiva moved from Lithuania; during the Arab massacre of August 1929, in which part of Hebron's Jewish population was destroyed, many of its students were killed. It was then moved to the Geula quarter of Jerusalem, where I joined it.

Rabbi Epstein's son-in-law, Rabbi Yehezkel Sarna—a great character in his own right—was now in charge. This yeshiva was in the tradition of the great schools of Eastern Europe, teaching not only Talmud but also Jewish morals and ethics. Although many students, especially the Sephardis, studied in Hebrew, we were taught in Yiddish and lived on a pittance. Our food tickets were good at the local grocer's—who usually had great difficulty getting the yeshiva to reimburse him. Yet somehow, despite the lack of modern facilities, the haphazard administration, and the near-poverty of many students, I cannot escape the impression that this yeshiva was far more effective and not only produced far better leaders than those today and some of the nation's scholars, but also sent a high percentage to perform their national duty in the various underground movements. I doubt that that yeshiva now sends a single member to the Israel Defense Forces to protect the society that has given it the wherewithal to study and advance.

Four months after my arrival in Palestine, Chief Rabbi Kook passed away. The process of selecting his successor was long drawn out—and, of course, quite political. Many names were bandied about. First and foremost, what was needed was the excellence and erudition to sit in judgment as head of the Rabbinical Supreme Court. Since the British Mandate maintained the traditions of the Ottoman rule, the court had exclusive jurisdiction in such personal matters as marriage, divorce, inheritance, and alimony. This autonomous authority also applied to the Moslem and Christian communities; they, too, maintained their own independent legal status on such matters.

The chief rabbi, much more so in those days, was a central figure in community leadership. He represented the Palestinian Jewish community not only to Jews everywhere but also to Moslems, Christians, and the British Mandatory authorities. My father's scholarship was well known and established. Since he also met all the other qualifications, he emerged as one of two main candidates. The other was Moshe Charlap, the rabbi of a district in Jerusalem and the supervisor at Rabbi Kook's yeshiva. Though a great holy man, he had little experience of the world and was unlikely to display the kind of leadership needed at a time of great turmoil and change. So the lines were drawn—between the old and the new—and the battle began.

Strangely enough, many in the Mizrachi religious Zionist movement again opposed my father, although Rabbi Meir Bar-Ilan, its head, as well as a number of other leaders, supported him. But the party hacks preferred someone they could control, regardless of the effect on the rabbinate. My grandfather and Shaul Lieberman, Rabbi Bar-Ilan's son-in-law and one of the world's greatest authorities on the Jerusalem Talmud and Hellenism in ancient Israel, organized a small campaign staff. It was my own initiation to the world of campaigning. In the time-old tradition of Jerusalem and politics in general, there was quite a bit of mudslinging. The main objection to my father—that he held a doctorate—meant he had departed from the straight and narrow path of religious piety and was "tainted" by exposure to foreign intellectuals. This was one of the hypocritical aspects of Jewish religious life. Maimonides was worshiped, yet what he represented—a fusion and unity of the great civilizations of the world—was dismissed.

However, the heavy artillery of Orthodox Jewry was soon activated. Rabbi Chaim Grodzinski of Vilna and Rabbi Joseph Rozin of Dvinsk supported my father's candidacy, and as they were the greatest Jewish religious leaders of the age, their endorsements were vital. Gradually, the main centers of learning, the yeshivot, also endorsed my father; the secular community realized that the country needed a spiritual leader who would deal with and answer the problems of the time.

After a long and intense battle, the elections took place in an orphanage on Jaffa Road in Jerusalem, on 1 December 1936. I waited tensely at my grandparents' small apartment for the results. Suddenly we heard footsteps running up the stairs. Supporters burst in and announced the results. My father had won, thirty-seven votes to thirty-three, and we rushed to cable the news to my parents in Ireland.

The election marked a major advance on the part of the Orthodox community in Palestine. It was a statement that they were adapting to changing circumstances. In many ways, my father's appointment was a breakthrough, although sadly the progressiveness he brought with him has not been maintained over the years. Religious fundamentalism has recently become extraordinarily dominant among not only Moslems and Christians but among Jews as well. The Jewish fundamentalists are quite powerful in Israel because of their political clout and their voting blocs— and they basically blackmail the government to get what they want. Fundamentalists are anti-intellectuals interested not in the truth but only in furthering their own way of thinking and behaving. My father was a truth-seeker, and it was important to have such a man as a leader in the religious community. It is still important.

MY PARENTS SAILED from Marseilles for Haifa. I went to meet them in Alexandria, taking the trans-Sinai train, which was loaded with bedouin chieftains and their harems. The official welcome of the Alexandria Jewish community took place in the home of one of its leaders, a Mr. Nadler, who had created a candy industry in Egypt. His young daughter Leah was years later to become Mrs. Boutros-Ghali, wife of the secretary-general of the United Nations.

At Alexandria, I joined my parents' ship. As dawn broke I stood on deck with my father, who was normally very unemotional. But as we approached Palestine, as he saw the majestic Mount Carmel emerging from the morning mist and the city of Haifa growing up its slopes, tears welled in his eyes.

My parents had a royal reception in Palestine. The Jewish community knew that they were greeting not only a religious head but also a forceful representative in their political struggle. Cheering crowds lined the main street parallel to the port in Haifa; the procession was led by a ceremonial figure known as the *kawass*, who was wearing traditional Turkish Ottoman clothes, including a fez and an ornate sword, and carrying a silver-topped mace, with which he struck the ground as he advanced. This was a sign of honor, retained from the period of the Ottoman Empire. Behind him was my father, with his gold-topped walking stick and top hat. Next came the Arab mayor of Haifa, wearing his fez; the head of the Jewish community of Haifa, in morning suit and top hat; and the British district commissioner and various other luminaries.

This reception was gloriously typical of that time; every occasion was chosen to emphasize and celebrate our national aims, heritage, and spiritual leaders. It was of great psychological importance, an opportunity to express a feeling of pride despite the atmosphere of conflict with the governing authority. But today, that kind of pomp and ceremony would be reserved for a head of state—on a special occasion—or for visiting heads of state.

Leaving Haifa, my parents and I rode the train along the coast—stopping at various towns and settlements, where huge throngs turned out to greet us.

In Jerusalem, a large motorcade awaited my father, with all the heads of the Jerusalem community, secular and religious. Thousands gathered on Ben-Yehuda Street outside Amdursky's Hotel, where my parents were to live, to cheer their new chief rabbi. Father went out onto the balcony to greet them all.

Early 1937 marked the beginning of a new era in the religious, political, and social development of the country. My father would build not only a chief rabbinate much more attuned to modern times but also a Supreme Religious Court of Appeals, which, while adhering to *halacha* and incorporating the Jewish legal code, was responsive to the requirements of a new world. Having achieved the highest religious position in world Jewry, he would also lead a community in a modern secular society, free of many taboos that affected the Jewish, Moslem, and Christian religious communities in Palestine. He had grown up in a Western atmosphere, had proved himself academically in universities in Great Britain and France, and had observed the institutions set up in the new state of Ireland. All of this had left its mark on him. It was also to leave its mark on the chief rabbinate.

An office for my father was established in the new apartment, which was quite modest, and the secretary's room attached to it doubled as a small personal chapel for prayer. My own room was divided from the secretary's room by a folding door. Every morning a little after dawn, the stalwarts of my father's *minyan*, the ten male Jews, the minimum for congregational prayer, would enter the office and unceremoniously thump on the folding door. Heaven help me if I was slow about opening it or—God forbid!—tried to ignore the thumping; it would get louder and more insistent. It was almost like leading a double life—I was, after all, a young man, and growing up in an Orthodox background had never hindered my adapting to normal teenage development. To complicate things, I frequently returned from duty in the Haganah early in the morning. In all honesty, I cannot say that I became a devotee of early morning prayer. It was, frankly, somewhat of a nightmare.

The pressures on my parents left them little or no time for their children in these critical years. The conflicts created by the dictates of this new situation produced a certain antagonism on my part that would later be reflected in my approach to religious observance. It was clear, at least to me, that I was not going to follow in my father's rabbinical footsteps. My brother, Yaacov, had remained in Dublin to complete his studies and sit for his London matriculation. When he arrived in Palestine, in 1939, he became an indispensable aide and advisor to our father.

But though I may have been rebelling inwardly, I was deeply involved with the intricacies of my father's new job. The chief rabbinate was then just being constructed as a modern organization, and the main burden of its administrative aspect fell in no small measure on my untried and unworthy shoulders. My main contribution was the creation of an appointment calendar. Previously, there had been no organization of the chief rabbi's hectic schedule. Anyone who wished to approach simply came in, sat in the waiting room—which, after prayers had been concluded, was my bedroom—and waited.

It was a pivotal period, for my coming of age and for Palestine; we were, in a sense, growing toward adulthood together.

Opposition to the Zionist program had, to put it mildly, grown in the Arab population, which in Palestine was mobilized and led by its religious leader, the Mufti of Jerusalem, Haj Amin al-Husseini. Under the British Mandate, periodic riots and attacks on the Jewish community had occurred, and many Jews were massacred during the 1920s. In 1936, after the Arabs declared a major revolt, heavy losses were suffered in Jewish villages and towns throughout the country. The Jewish community, out of necessity, was developing and perfecting its defense system. The mufti's forces were waging guerrilla war against the Mandate—but not always very successfully—and many British soldiers were killed, which was why the British agreed to cooperate with the Haganah. In the Valley of Jezreel, Arab bands continually blew up the Iraq–Haifa oil pipeline. A young British officer, Captain Orde Wingate, organized special night squads from the Haganah—which included two youngsters named Moshe Dayan and Yigal Allon—and developed a very effective form of counterguerrilla warfare.

Against that background, ships with "illegal immigrants"—Jews from Eastern Europe who wanted to come "home" to Palestine—were being apprehended by the Royal Navy and the British forces. Many members of the Haganah and the Irgun were being arrested for their nonsanctioned counterattacks on the Arabs as well as for "smuggling" illegal immigrants into the country. In some cases the death penalty was the sentence. During all of this, enormous pressure was brought to bear on my father, by officials within the Jewish community and by those directly involved in the tragedies and traumas. When "illegal immigrants" were detained in Europe or members of the Haganah or Irgun were apprehended and imprisoned, our home was invaded by groups of hysterical relatives and friends, who assumed that my father was all-powerful and could obtain clemency or solve any problem. He would almost always use his best efforts, and I remember his taking the long walk to Government House, in search of the high commissioner, on many Sabbaths.

The Jews in Palestine were frequently at loggerheads with one another, and their wide range of political affiliations reflected different approaches to the implementation of the Zionist ideal. Unlike the two-party system in America and Great Britain, the electoral system adopted by the World Zionist Organization allowed for fragmentation into many parties. A minority party, often with a tiny membership, could join forces with other minority parties and frequently block—or, more often, blackmail—the majority parties. This system was adopted by the State of Israel and created a major problem in its political life. But in the 1920s and 1930s, despite the many differences, the entire community came together in defense of the life and freedom of those who were fighting for the cause. Shlomo Ben-Yossef—a young Irgun member who shot and killed several Arabs on a bus—was the first Jew sent to the gallows by the British. His execution aroused fury and bitterness that united the Jewish community politically and emotionally. It did not matter that much of the Jewish population was not supportive of people like Ben-Yossef or Aryeh Altman, who was also sentenced to death for smuggling arms into the country. Once they faced the gallows, the Jewish community rallied behind them as one man.

One night during Passover our house was invaded by a mob; I believe it was in connection with Altman's death sentence. They would not leave or allow us to celebrate the seder unless my father immediately obtained clemency for the condemned man. His sentence was commuted to imprisonment, but Ben-Yossef died bravely for the cause. My father was involved with many such cases and always used whatever personal influence he had. But he never succeeded in enlisting the help of the Vatican and of Pope Pius XII—neither during nor after the Holocaust.

In 1936, when my father became head of the Supreme Religious Court of Appeals, he was completing the second of five volumes of his great work, *The Main Institutions of Jewish Law*, a classic that revealed the enormous scope of his scholarship in Jewish, Roman, and English common law. He would later adapt the laws of the halacha, set out almost two thousand years ago, to the requirements of a modern society. He introduced amendments of great importance, including the right of a divorced woman to compensation for her work in the household over the years. In matters of inheritance, he adapted regulations existing since the second century to meet more modern requirements.

While these developments were taking place, I was still in the yeshiva, but my studies were preempted by my involvement with setting up meetings for my father at home. I enrolled at the Government of Palestine Law School in Jerusalem, having decided to pursue a legal career—I had grown up in an atmosphere dominated by the Talmud, after all. The school held classes in English at the Evelina de Rothschild School, one of the few institutions where Arabs and Jews mixed freely and taught each other. For a student, there was a particularly great advantage in belonging to a student and teacher body that comprised Moslems, Jews, and Christians: there were no classes on Fridays, Saturdays, or Sundays.

The burdens at home grew as I struggled to help my parents, stay involved with the Haganah, and keep up a social life. My natural tendency, which has never left me, is to engage in far too many activities at the same time, and it soon became clear that I was not going to achieve anything as far as my education was concerned if I stayed in Jerusalem. My parents agreed that I should go abroad to pursue my studies, and I enrolled at the University of London and applied to Lincoln's Inn to read for the bar. The decision was difficult for my parents—both my brother and I would be away from home—but they realized that there was little option if I was to make anything of myself. It was hard for me as well. My country—and it was now my country—was in a bitter struggle not only between the Jews and the Arabs but also between the Arabs and the British. Faced with the possibility of war in Europe and Hitler's threats, the British had decided once and for all to suppress the Arab revolt.

While I was preparing to leave, the Peel Commission, named for its chairman, Sir Robert Peel, was set up by the British government. Its purpose was to seek a solution to the Arab revolt. My father appeared before the commission, together with other Jewish dignitaries. Finally the commission recommended the partition of Palestine into three areas. The Jewish state was allowed approximately 20 percent of the area of Mandatory Palestine, including all of eastern Galilee, the Upper Jordan Valley as far as Beit Shean, the Valley of Jezreel, most of the Carmel range, and the coastal plain up to two miles south of the present port of Ashdod. Jerusalem and its environs, including Bethlehem, along with a corridor to the coast comprising Jaffa, Ramle, and Lydda, would remain under British Mandate. The rest of the country would become an Arab state.

The Zionist movement was torn by debate. David Ben-Gurion favored the plan. Great prophet that he was, he foresaw the Holocaust and maintained that a Jewish state, no matter how small, could save a great part of European Jewry before the mass slaughter. The Revisionist Movement, led by Zeev Jabotinsky, violently opposed the plan, and Ben-Gurion had many opponents in his own party, too, including Golda Meir.

My father had an ambivalent relationship with Ben-Gurion, who was unquestionably Israel's greatest figure. But even great men have flaws. My father, being an extraordinary scholar, especially in the secular field, did not fit into Ben-Gurion's conception of the traditional rabbi, and they never became close. However, my father supported Ben-Gurion's approach—he, too, was constantly warning the leaders of European Jewry about the imminence of the Holocaust, as Hitler's oppression of the German Jews became more and more severe. My father wrote impassioned letters to such leaders as the chief rabbi of Kovno in Lithuania, urging them to leave as soon as possible. Their soothing replies, however, reflected none of his urgency.

The Zionist Organization, under Ben-Gurion's leadership, did eventually accept the principle of partition as proposed in the Peel Report. In 1938 the British appointed the Woodhead Commission to study the possibility of implementing that report—and concluded that partition was impracticable. The British government decided to drop it.

When the time came for me to leave for London, we all hoped against hope that the 1936 occupation of the Rhineland and the 1938 rape of Austria would satisfy Hitler's insatiable appetite. But much of the world lived in a serene atmosphere of wishful thinking, with only one relatively solitary voice, Winston Churchill's, ringing out to warn humanity. But, as is so often the case, humanity chose to ignore it.

CHAPTER 3

The Outbreak of World War II

I RETURNED TO England in the summer of 1938, passing through Paris, where I saw my Aunt Esther, her husband, Reuben, and their children, Rosette and Annette (the last time I was ever to see Reuben and Annette). The Third Republic was eroding: premiers were changing rapidly, and the will of the French people to resist German aggression was being eaten away by governmental instability. There was also widespread corruption; the Nazis were even allowed to buy part of the French press. A left-wing coalition under Léon Blum was outspoken against Hitler, as were the Communists, but the political fragmentation prepared the way for the nation's inevitable collapse when it was overrun by the German army in the spring of 1940. The atmosphere in Paris was a mixture of apprehension, fear, and wishful thinking. Despite confidence that the French army could hold back and perhaps defeat the German army, the growing threat of the Nazi war machine was uppermost in everyone's mind. Many Jews in Paris had escaped from Germany and Austria, and many of them were endeavoring to cross the Atlantic or get permits to enter Palestine. But the policy of the British Mandate made it hard for a Jew to return to his or her homeland—even as an escape from Hitler.

In London, antiaircraft guns were being set up in Hyde Park and other public spaces. Shelters and trenches were being dug citywide, and gas masks were distributed, since it was assumed the Germans would, as they had done in World War I, use poison gas. But the calm and efficient British organization was lagging. Churchill's was still a lone voice ringing out against German aggression. Hitler was directing his attention to the Sudetenland in Czechoslovakia. He met with Mussolini, Edouard Daladier, the French premier, and Neville Chamberlain, England's prime minister, at Bad Godesberg. In September, a naive and duped Chamberlain arrived back in London with a piece of paper, promising "peace in our time." There was a tremendous wave of relief, but newsreels of the German entry into Czechoslovakia gave a true indication of the dreadful events ahead. As German tanks barreled forward, the Czech population stood by the roadside weeping openly.

And so, with war looming, I began my university education.

At first, I lived with my Uncle David, the artist, and his delightful Scottish wife, Annie Hillman, a doctor whose pleasant bedside manner was perfect for a general practitioner. I then moved to rooms rented to students in the same district, West Hampstead. I immediately became heavily involved in student activities—in the Jewish Society, the Zionist Society, the Inter-University Jewish Federation, and the University Liberal Society. Most of my activities were in support of the Zionist cause and its position in various Palestine endeavors. Palestine was, naturally enough, the subject of much debate in Britain, both in Parliament and in the media. My fellow activists and I faced considerable and unpleasant opposition not only from the Communists, who naturally reflected the policy of Moscow, but also the Fascists, who supported Hitler and Nazi Germany. My tendency had always been toward the liberal politics of the Labour Party, but the student Labour movement had by now been penetrated by the Communists and was gradually becoming subservient to the Communist ideology. It was incredible to hear so many intelligent and aware students parroting the simpleminded Marxist idiom. Many able and high-minded British citizens were becoming Communist agents— Kim Philby, Guy Burgess, and Donald Maclean, among others. But the Jewish students, who saw our cause as literally a life-and-death struggle, had no illusions about communism, and it became only natural to rally around those struggling against this insidious movement. By the outbreak of the war, the National Union of Students of Great Britain was completely penetrated by and, in effect, controlled by the Communists. We, the pro-Palestine Jewish activists, were pariahs in their eyes; they tried to portray us as exploiters, aggressors, colonialists, and Fascists. As always, no matter the battlefield, we seemed to be fighting against overwhelming odds and irrational forces.

In January 1939 my parents came to London to attend the St. James's Palace conference, convened by the British government to advance negotiations between the Jews and Arabs in Palestine. The Arabs refused to sit with the Jews, as usual, so the British held alternate meetings, first with the Jewish and then with the Arab delegation. The secretary of state for the colonies was Malcolm Macdonald, and it was this government under Chamberlain that produced the White Paper that limited Jewish immigration to Palestine and banned the sale of land to Jews.

The conference reflected the British government's anti-Zionist bias as well as the extreme differences within the Zionist camp and the internal strife among the Palestinians and Arab elements. Spurning any thought of compromise, the Arabs insisted on total and absolute adherence to their demands. Cooperation among Jews was not much better than between Jews and Arabs. There was disunity within the Zionist movement, which was represented by the official Zionist Organization and by a newer faction, called the Revisionist Movement. My father, foreseeing the possibility of a world war, approached both Dr. Chaim Weizmann, president of the Zionist Organization, and Zeev Jabotinsky, leader of the Revisionist Movement, with an offer to mediate, but to no avail.

I HAD BEEN instructed by the Haganah to join the university's officers training corps, and I took to my training eagerly; my one great advantage was that I'd held and used weapons in Palestine. We thoroughly enjoyed the camps and our training, and although the clouds of war were gathering, nobody knew how soon we would all be wearing uniforms, and how many of the men I trained with would make the supreme sacrifice in defense of their country's liberty.

This was an extraordinary formative period of my life. I had been quite shy and reserved, but my political activities helped me overcome my insecurities—I was suddenly quite a public speaker. My immersion in the British army developed and cemented my personality. I have been many things—statesman, diplomat, businessman, commentator, lawyer, family man—but perhaps more than anything, I consider myself a soldier. If one has a great cause, I believe nothing is so noble as the willingness to fight and sacrifice for it. That desire for commitment and strength came from my parents, I am certain. But the British army proved to me that I was strong and committed enough to actually become a soldier.

In the summer of 1939, as the political crisis escalated (Hitler's troops had entered Prague on March 11), efforts were afoot in Britain to step up production of military weapons and aircraft.

During that period, Yaacov concluded his studies in Dublin, and we met as he passed through London on his way to Palestine. Our brief moments together were filled with love, intimacy, and hope. My brother was never really young; he was always grown-up and serious. In his early teens, he was in regular correspondence with Clement Attlee, who became British prime minister after World War II. In many ways Yaacov was more like my father than I was: a true scholar and intellectual, yet with an instinct for the subtleties of politics. After our visit, he stopped off in France; he was the last of our family to see my aunt and cousins before the war.

ON 1 SEPTEMBER 1939 the Germans invaded Poland. The Polish army, living in the past with its splendorous but ineffectual cavalry, was no match for panzer formations and Stuka bombers. Britain and France had, months earlier, announced a military guarantee of Poland's territorial integrity. Left with no alternative, they issued an ultimatum: unless German troops withdrew from Poland, the guarantee would be invoked. The Germans rejected the ultimatum. Hitler, having sized up Chamberlain and Daladier, assumed they would not honor their obligations. But, like most dictators, he had misjudged and underestimated democracies. At eleven o'clock on Sunday morning, 3 September, the clear, measured voice of Prime Minister Neville Chamberlain came over the BBC. Britain was at war.

I went to keep an appointment, and while driving up Hampstead High Street I was signaled by police and air raid wardens, already on duty and in uniform, to seek shelter. The rising and falling wail of the sirens— a sound that was to accompany me not only in England but also in Israel—echoed everywhere. We were facing the unknown, but there was no panic. (The British *never* panic. Their stiff upper lips seem only to get stiffer.) As everyone was directed to the basement of the Hampstead Town Hall, I suddenly realized that I had not brought my gas mask with me. We were expecting the type of merciless air raid being described from Warsaw, accompanied by a poison-gas attack. In near panic, I reproached myself for having been so foolish and negligent. Luckily the "all clear" soon sounded—the alarm was false. Never before, and possibly never since, was I so frightened and lonely. I was completely on my own, cut off from my home and parents. I could not know what the future held in store—only that I was not yet in the army fighting the enemy, but still in civilian clothes.

As Warsaw fell to the Germans, the world was shocked by the announcement of the Molotov-Ribbentrop Agreement, one of the great betrayals of history. Stalin, who had the military power to thwart the

German plans, negotiated behind the backs of the Western Allies. As a result of his negotiations, Molotov, the foreign minister of the Soviet Union, and Ribbentrop, the foreign minister of Germany, signed an agreement dividing Poland into areas to be occupied once the German invasion was complete. Whole areas of Poland were to be occupied by the Soviet Union. Communists everywhere, including Britain, slavishly accepted the thesis broadcast by the Soviet Union, that the war against Germany was not a just one. For them, it became just only in June 1941, when Hitler turned on his newest ally and invaded the Soviet Union.

The ordeal of Polish Jewry began: the greatest Holocaust in history. Nearly all of Poland's three million Jews would be exterminated; some six million Jews, or one-third of the entire Jewish people, would be annihilated in the gas chambers and furnaces of the Nazi concentration camps. Ignorant of the historic tragedy about to unfold in Eastern Europe, I was more concerned about the situation in Palestine. There the large Italian army was poised in Libya, threatening Egypt and the Suez Canal.

Closer to my temporary home, the British began evacuating hundreds of thousands of children from cities likely to be bombed to the safer countryside. My uncle's children, coming from an Orthodox Jewish home, were sent to live with non-Jewish foster parents in Rickmansworth outside London. Separated from their parents, many children wound up sailing for America, and this difficult, rootless period created quite a few problems about their identity and religious orientation. Everything was now rationed—fuel as well as food—and it was not easy to drive long distances.

London University was also evacuated. My college, University College, merged with the University College of Wales at Aberystwyth, a small seaside town on the Irish Sea. We were accommodated in boardinghouses run by landladies who did not hide their disdain for youthful pranks and behavior. They adhered to the strictest rules of the Sabbath on Sundays; even playing cards was forbidden. On Sundays they all went to church, where they listened to the famous Messianic Welsh preachers. I learned to admire the Welsh people and their rich culture of poetry, music, and singing. Even in wartime their annual Eisteddfod festival of music and singing was a moving and beautiful experience.

I WAS ACTIVE again in the University Liberal Party. In Wales, too, the Communists had infiltrated the University Labour Party and were campaigning against an "unjust war." We struggled manfully against them, but they were powerful—and committed. It's interesting that for many generations the politics of the far left faded with the waning anger and passion of youth. But for my generation, ideology seems to have survived youth.

Then as now, I marveled at the gullibility of the Communists and the extreme left, while sympathizing with many of their causes. The Liberal Party was extremely sympathetic to our cause in Palestine, had a centrist approach in economics, and was capable of standing up to the Communist-controlled political groups of the time. My own leanings still reflect a liberal approach to social problems, a middle-of-the-road, free-market economic approach, and a rejection of colonialism. I have never understood the obsession to defend every thought and belief that emanates from a political group, whether right or wrong, rational or irrational.

I pursued my service in the officers cadet training unit, and was very active in the Inter-University Jewish Federation; I was also elected chairman of the Students Union of University College. We established a small synagogue in Aberystwyth, with local Jewish life centering on the few families already there and the Jewish students evacuated from London. The annual conference of the Inter-University Jewish Federation and of the National Union of Students was held at Leeds. It was there that I began to emerge as a leader of the Jewish students in Britain.

When the British forces were forced to evacuate from the French port of Dunkirk, in the spring of 1940, the political uproar in Britain rose to new heights. In Parliament, Leopold Amery shouted at Neville Chamberlain, "In the name of God, go!" Chamberlain resigned and Churchill took over, inspiring the nation with his "blood, sweat, and tears" speech and with his exhortation to fight on the beaches, to fight in the fields, to fight in the cities, never to surrender.

As the victorious German armies swept into Paris, Britain began to brace itself for an onslaught. Obsessed by a spy mania, the British were not prepared to distinguish between German and Nazi; all were regarded as potential enemies. German refugees were arrested and put in detention camps, and one of my roommates in Aberystwyth, Manny Goldschmidt, was deported to an internment camp in Canada. Most of the refugees were later released to join the British army's Pioneer Corps or special commando units, where their knowledge of German could be put to use.

For the summer vacation of 1940 I stayed with my aunt and uncle in London. We built a shelter in the garden against bomb attacks, and I volunteered for the local Home Guard, an auxiliary organization that protected vital points throughout Britain against German parachute operations. I took my dinners at Lincoln's Inn, where it was quite amazing to see bowler-hatted lawyers under the command of another bowler-hatted lawyer, drilling with the only weapon available to them: their rolled-up umbrellas. I shall never forget the commingled horror and thrill of Sunday, 15 September 1940. I was drilling with the Home Guard in Hampstead, which overlooks a good part of London, when air raid sirens suddenly sounded. Almost immediately, we saw the Luftwaffe coming from across the Channel, heading for the London power stations at Battersea on the Thames River. The armada came in waves. Facing it was a handful of Royal Air Force Spitfires and Hurricanes, many of them piloted by teenagers who only a few months before had been my classmates. The German bombers droned on toward their target, as the RAF attacked and dogfights ensued. In the fog of battle, amid the stutter of machine-gun fire, it was almost impossible to discern the enemy from the friend. From time to time, a plane peeled off from the battle, smoke pouring from it. When the results were announced, we knew that this battle would live on in history and would turn the tide of war, for the British had made it clear to the Germans that they could not seize command of the air in England, as they had in Poland and France.

Was I engulfed in fear? No, in awe and exhilaration at the sight of the RAF defending a great metropolis in full view of its citizens. These valiant men were not just *on* our side; they were our side. They were us.

IN THE AUTUMN of 1940 the wanton carpet bombing of English cities began, day and night.

One morning I awoke because of a sudden blast of cold air to find myself covered with broken glass. A bomb had exploded just down the road in West Hampstead, demolishing two houses and killing the inhabitants. Completely exhausted, I'd slept through the entire raid, never hearing the noise of the antiaircraft or bombs. Only the cold disturbed my slumber. Wrapped in blankets, I had avoided any injury from the shattered glass.

It is impossible to forget the screech of the air raid sirens and the feeling of impending disaster. You ran for shelter and waited in terrible silence for the distant humming of the planes' engines. Suddenly all hell was let loose as the antiaircraft batteries, positioned throughout London, opened up. To the orchestra of artillery fire and aircraft engines was added the dreaded whistle of falling bombs and the terrible crashes that followed. It was said that if you heard the whistle you were all right, because that bomb would not hit you. But that comforting thought never entered your mind as you hugged the ground, uttering a prayer. What was so amazing was how life continued in London under these onslaughts.

One evening I went to Leicester Square to see Charlie Chaplin's movie *The Great Dictator*. An air raid began but we never knew which guns were firing, those in the film or those defending us against the shower of incendiary bombs over the City of London. The blackout curfew in London was stringently enforced, but when we emerged from the cinema, the fire that had enveloped the city made it seem like daylight. We stood under the awning to avoid falling shrapnel. One could read the newspaper by the light that illuminated the skies.

The next day the people of London went bravely about their daily tasks, traveling to their jobs, clearing up the destroyed areas, helping each other. I saw a very great people in a very great time of crisis.

WHEN CLASSES RESUMED that fall, my college was transferred to Cambridge. I was somewhat intimidated by the atmosphere of the great old university, where the world's finest talent would be teaching me law. I was very active in Jewish and Zionist groups, none of which was particularly popular with the Cambridge Communists, as well as the Law Society, which had a particularly obnoxious member named Ashkenazi. Partly because of his very Semitic appearance, he was ridiculed and tormented. As a result, he went out of his way at every public meeting to attack Jews and the Zionist effort. It was insane, and I found it deeply disturbing to watch his self-loathing and self-destructiveness. At one meeting he proposed a resolution condemning the growing Jewish influence in the Law Society, a resolution so anti-Semitic it sounded as if it were being submitted by a Nazi sympathizer. I could not restrain myself. While he was speaking, I knocked him down with a well-placed uppercut to his chin. This caused quite a furor, but Ashkenazi never repeated his attacks.

On my arrival in Cambridge I volunteered for the officers cadet training unit and joined the cavalry squadron. Our major was from the 13/19 Lancers. An old-time cavalryman inside and out, he regretted that we had degenerated to a war in which the cavalry would have to fight in "smelly tanks and armored cars" rather than on horseback, as befit a true gentleman. We trained on Guy armored cars with 15mm and 7.5mm Besa guns (originally from Czechoslovakia) and Mark II tanks equipped with a Besa machine gun and a 2-pounder gun, but Major Watts saw to it that we learned to ride. We spent many hours wheeling and charging on horseback and learning to jump. During one particularly satisfying session, we all performed extremely well, whereas a cadet called Malik, an expert horseman from what is today Pakistan, who rather looked down on us all, was thrown quite fiercely from his mount.

More Jews were being evacuated from the bombed areas in London, increasing the size of our Cambridge community. The synagogue on Thompson Lane was the center of our life in the city, and we were invariably invited on the Sabbath to the homes of these Jewish evacuees. Many Jews had already settled in Cambridge. As members of the traditional Jewish community of dons and researchers, they set themselves apart from the newcomers and even looked down upon them.

But there were also brilliant scholars and genuine intellects. I have always tried to live in this kind of stimulating atmosphere, even while fighting for what I believed. This duality of thought and action has been the driving force of my entire life.

A third element must be added to thought and action: humor. Jews have historically had a sense of humor—believe me, we've needed it. During my student days laughter was crucial in helping us carry on as normally as possible. I was coauthor with my friend Helmut Lowenberg, later president of the Tel Aviv district court, of a musical skit about the Anglo-Jewish community that was actually staged. For months, Lowenberg and I went to the tiny Cosmopolitan Cinema, which specialized in Marx Brothers movies. We wrote down all of Groucho's and Chico's cracks—and then plagiarized them shamelessly for our production.

In June 1941, the German army invaded the Soviet Union. Its units swept along the Black Sea and the Caucasus, while other forces reached the gates of Moscow. We followed these developments with aching hearts. The Russian fight aroused everyone's imagination, for we realized what the momentous battle meant. The Nazi juggernaut would not spare the millions of Russian Jews, and once again our people were facing tragic days. Even so, few people dreamed of the terrifying events that were still to occur. Russia became popular, with the inspiring Cossack cavalry song on everyone's lips.

I am a fervent believer in the freedom of the press. At the same time, it should not under any conditions be allowed to endanger national security or basic personal and human rights. I have often maintained that had TV been able to bring the horrors of World War II into every living room,

Western public morale would have deteriorated to a serious degree and the West might well have been defeated. Democrats throughout the world should ponder this point. I have often thought that TV could also have led to our defeat in Israel's War of Independence.

The German armies now swept down through Yugoslavia and saved the Italian army from a debacle in Albania and Greece. The Balkans were subjugated, and the German army moved through Romania into the southern U.S.S.R. For us as students, the war was still remote. The movie news in the cinemas showed some of the action but it was all still vague and indistinct.

On 7 December 1941, Japan attacked the U.S. fleet at Pearl Harbor, and the entire course of the war changed. We followed with great trepidation the Japanese invasion of Southeast Asia, the fall of the Philippines, the sinking of the *Prince of Wales* off Singapore, the invasion of Burma and the threat to India, the struggle in China and in the islands of the South Pacific. But slowly the American economy was creating its own war machine, which of course would be the decisive factor in the Allies' victory.

I GRADUATED AS a bachelor of laws from London University in the summer of 1941 and immediately volunteered for service in the British army. As a resident of Palestine, I was not draftable for service, but I felt it was my duty to be part of the forces fighting Hitler in his war against the Jewish people. Pending my call-up I took my bar exams, and finally passed them in the summer of 1942. I was called to the bar on 17 November 1942.

Meanwhile, I began "deviling"—apprenticing as a barrister, as compared to a solicitor—at the chambers of David Weitzman, later queen's counsel and member of Parliament. I followed Weitzman around on cases and acquired respect for the British legal system, which shaped my own vision of how a government should mete out justice—except for their peculiar dress code. I purchased a secondhand wig and gown, and— on the surface, at least—I looked like an experienced barrister. My first brief was over a rental dispute and netted me all of two pounds, four shillings, and sixpence. Arriving at the Marylebone County Court, I was completely befuddled and enormously nervous, with no idea of what was going on. But I tried to look totally at ease. The opposing counsel mumbled something, and the judge mumbled back, but I could not grasp what they were saying. When the judge looked at me, I began to plead.

"Mr. Herzog," said the judge, "your opponent has given in, and your pleading is unnecessary." I hastily gathered my papers and fled, victorious on my first legal effort through no fault of my own.

The summer of 1942 ended with the first signs of life from our family in Paris since its occupation by the Germans. My Aunt Esther had stayed in Paris with her invalid sister, Helen. Esther's daughter Annette had been urged by the family to flee, but she was very attached to her mother. When she returned to Paris to see her, she was apprehended at the Vichy crossing line at Poitiers, having apparently been betrayed—denounced as a Jew—by the couriers who were shepherding people across. She was sent to Drancy, a French concentration camp, and handed over to the Germans, who shipped her to another concentration camp. The names of such camps were still unknown to the world. This one would come to be too well known, to the shame of all humanity: Auschwitz.

CHAPTER 4

On His Majesty's Service

On 17 December 1942 I joined the British army.

My father wrote me a wonderful letter. Although he was a man whose life was devoted to God and to the pursuit of abstract intellectual excellence, he showed a remarkable understanding of the realities of the world I was living in, and his letter supported my decision to become a soldier. My mother was, of course, upset at the path I'd chosen—what mother wouldn't be?—but she wisely kept her fears hidden and sent word of her love and desire for my well-being.

I was posted to the Royal West Kent Regiment in Maidstone, where I was introduced to the harsh realities of wartime army life—rising at dawn, washing in cold water in winter, sleeping on a straw mattress in a hut built for twenty-seven men but now housing over fifty. The man who had the mattress just a few inches from me was named Wells. I had never met anyone remotely like him. He spoke almost incomprehensible Cockney, lived strictly by his wits, and told me that he had even been involved in a case of attempted murder—he'd attacked a Canadian soldier in a brawl over a woman. He regaled me with his criminal and amorous exploits, which were usually enough to make my eyes pop. I had seen slums and poverty and read about crime, but here I was sleeping next to a would-be murderer and thief. But somehow, sharing army hardships erased any differences between us. If there was an enemy, it was your own sergeant-major, the man who made your life a living hell, not the Jews or Catholics or Protestants in your battalion. Wells was wary of me at first— he thought my chosen profession of law was too close to being a police- man—but we gradually became close friends. I even used to write letters to his girlfriends for him (writing was not one of his strong points). When the time came for us to go our separate ways, he cried.

WHILE TRAINING IN the Kent countryside, we learned how to kill with a bayonet. Despite my religious upbringing, I had no internal conflict whatsoever about preparing for bloody infantry fighting. I was there to fight the German Nazis; as a Jew I perhaps understood more than anyone else in my unit the significance of the struggle for which we were preparing ourselves. I was a soldier now—and happy to be one.

During this training period I received the nickname that has stuck with me. The platoon was at attention, drawn up for inspection, and a corporal was taking names. He came to me, stared me in the eye, and said "Name!" My reply brought the immediate response, "What in fucking hell is Chaim?!"

"It's Hebrew," I explained.

"Well, we don't speak fucking Hebrew here! This is the fucking British army!" he screamed.

One of the other Jewish boys in the company spoke up. "It means life," he said. "The English equivalent is Vivian."

The corporal turned back to me and said, "Right! From now on you're fucking Vivian!"

And so I have remained ever since.

In February 1943 I was transferred to the Intelligence Corps Training Depot at Wentworth Woodhouse, in Yorkshire. It was reputedly the largest house in Britain, with 365 rooms—one for every day, although I never bothered to count. Here we were subjected to the strictest discipline. We learned the basics of staff work; we studied security; we trained to live as small units on our own; and we not only mastered the motorcycle (standard equipment in those days for intelligence personnel), but went through a course of acrobatics on the slag heaps of the Yorkshire coal mines. On weekends it was occasionally possible for me to be with the Jewish community in nearby Sheffield, and special arrangements were made for Jewish soldiers in the camp to attend Passover seder. Across the common was an antiaircraft battery, manned (or womaned) entirely by the ATS female soldiers, whose presence diminished the omnipresent harshness of the military garrison atmosphere.

In June 1943, I was posted to the prestigious officers training school, the Royal Military College, Infantry Wing, at Mons Barracks in Aldershot. The training was brutally tough, and recruits were subjected to unbelievably strict discipline. I often heard the tale of the Scots Guards sergeant-major at Purbright, their basic training center, who, while with his family, saw an officer approach. He immediately slammed to attention, saluted, and called out, "Wife and children, attention!" The disciplinary training that lay behind the Guards' ceremonial excellence was the core of their superb fighting spirit and valiant behavior in action. On church parade every Sunday morning, on the order "Other denominations, dismiss!" we three Jews in the company would smartly step one pace to the rear, mount bicycles, and cycle to the military synagogue in Aldershot, where a rabbi officiated at services.

Meanwhile the war was being fought on the Continent, and my unit was being trained to participate in it. On the highest mountain in Wales, Mount Snowdon, in wild and beautiful countryside, we were tested to the limits of our endurance. There were wretched marathon marches day and night—and half an hour after we had fallen asleep we were awakened to go on yet another one. The training was designed not only to prepare us for battle conditions but also to separate the sheep from the goats and to reveal any problems that might confront cadets during the physical and mental strains of combat. Many men just could not stand up to the strain and were removed from the unit. It returned from the battle course with each of us a finely honed fighting machine and sharing the highest esprit de corps.

In September 1943, I received the King's Commission and was promoted to second lieutenant. In typical English fashion, there was great pomp and ceremony involved. We all had to order a dress uniform, Sam Browne belt, and the inevitable officer's swagger stick, and the parade itself was a splendid affair. But underneath the surface spit and polish, there was a great seriousness of purpose. I would now, I hoped, be playing a part, however small, in the life-and-death struggle of the free world against the Nazis. However, although I had purpose and a prestigious title, I still was not fully prepared to be an officer. The first time a soldier threw a smart salute at me I was completely flabbergasted and flustered, until I realized the change in my status that had occurred.

My first posting was to Oxford, to the Officers' Basic Course in the Intelligence Corps. Here I learned not only how to be an officer and a gentleman—partly thanks to the orderly who polished my shoes and equipment, acted as a valet, and catered to my every need—but also the basic elements of intelligence collection, collation, production, and distribution. I was introduced to all the possible sources of information that an intelligence officer in war can benefit from. I was trained to put the pieces of a puzzle into a logical form and developed an instinct for how, where, and to whom the collated material should be passed. We studied the German army, learning the order of battle, the breakdown of the army units on the various fronts, the organizational structure of the units, German weapons and their capabilities, the basics of prisoner-of-war interrogation, and similar aspects of the intelligence war. We studied the political issues facing us in the struggle against the Nazi war machine, and even the political, social, and organizational characteristics of our enemy. Good basic training in staff procedures and staff work enabled us to fit into any given staff structure. After six weeks, I graduated and was an intelligence officer.

During brief postings to Matlock, Derbyshire, and then back to Wentworth Woodhouse, I was able to spend my leaves in London, at the British Empire Officers Club and the Theatre Club, which was located in a cellar and was a center of the avant-garde. I joined the National Liberal Club because they offered free membership to nonresident officers, and discovered the dignity, decorum, and elegance of an old, traditional English club. The National Liberal was considered quite modern—women were allowed in the restaurant, although excluded everywhere else. One can caricature these establishments, but the more I think back to the quiet lounge—members dropping off to sleep after lunch, their heads hidden behind *The Times*, nobody at their side to bother them or tell them what to do—the more I revel in the British definition of what a civilized people should be.

In February 1944, I was shipped off for one month's attachment at Whitby, on the Yorkshire coast, to the 4th Battalion of the Black Watch, one of the famous Scots regiments. I was a young, "green" officer given command of a platoon and thrown in among highly experienced officers, but I very much enjoyed the regimental life. I loved to watch the bagpipers trooping the colors at sundown on the beachfront while the local population watched. I did find it very difficult to understand the Highlanders' deep brogue but gradually became accustomed to it. I can recall attending the trial of a Cockney soldier for returning late to barracks. He maintained that he was just incapable of understanding the orders that the sergeant-major had given. He received a nominal punishment from the company commander, an upper-class Scot, who turned to the sergeant-major and said, "The truth is, I don't understand you either." Once again, I got to know the ordinary British family—in the pubs, at local concerts, at "hops" in the church halls. I became very much a part of the day-to-day life in this small fishing town in Yorkshire and grew to love even its imperfections.

My next posting was back to Cambridge, where I attended a prisoner-of-war interrogation course and was further educated in the ways of the German army. By the time I was through I knew its entire organization by heart—infantry, armor, and SS groupings. Part of the time we lived as German soldiers, drilling in accordance with their style (left instead of right about-turn), training on German weapons, receiving German army pay books and German ration books, and studying German military slang. We wore German uniforms and were commanded by former officers from Polish Silesia who had served in the Wehrmacht. We went on sick parade as German soldiers and negotiated the bureaucratic procedures that a German soldier and officer would encounter. When we left this course, no German prisoner could mislead us with stories—we were almost as familiar with their daily life as they were. Our study of the Nazi regime and its history illuminated its hateful philosophy. We were subjected to interrogation under conditions that simulated capture by the enemy and were trained in the art of extracting information without letting the subject feel that it was important. We saw how to break a prisoner without touching him but simply by talking. While under interrogation, we were forced to stand at attention for hours, in blinding light, without food or drink for an entire day. One of the things I observed was that painful treatment frequently strengthened a prisoner's resolve *not* to divulge accurate information.

It was an extremely interesting study in psychology and later proved useful when I interrogated Hitler Youth and SS officers. Having grown up with a deep hatred of their enemy, they expected to be martyred, to be treated as *they* had been trained to deal with prisoners. But when they were questioned with humanity, the shock of it often led to a grateful flow of information.

After concluding the course in Cambridge, I was posted to Northern Ireland as intelligence officer on the staff of Lieutenant General Sir Alan Cunningham, commander in chief of Northern Ireland and later the last British High Commissioner in Palestine. I was stationed in the headquarters at Thiepval Barracks in Lisburn, not too far away from Belfast. This was my first conscious encounter with my birthplace, and I visited the house where I was born.

Our work included training the first American divisions to arrive in Great Britain in preparation for the invasion of Europe and also handling security in light of the hostile attitude of various elements of the IRA. I had special permission to go to Belfast in civilian dress—which was quite unusual. A good part of my time was spent politely dissuading match-makers in the local Jewish community from trying to hitch me up with attractive girls in the community.

In May 1944, I was posted as intelligence officer to the 45th (East Anglia) Division, headquartered in Haywards Heath, Sussex. Our division was responsible for the defense of southern England from Dover or Eastbourne to an area east of Southampton, a major concentration for forces gathering for the invasion of Europe.

The buildup gradually became evident everywhere, and our area was restricted; people could enter or leave only by permit. While traveling by motorcycle to visit various battalions, I could see the vast accumulation of materiel assembling for the invasion. All troops were restricted to barracks and were not allowed to communicate with their families in any manner; everything was strictly censored. This was the real thing.

Knowing that this was a concentration area, the Germans tried to penetrate it. One day we heard a buzzing noise, much like the engine of a small motorbike, in the sky. Then we saw a slow-flying object with flame emerging from the rear, coming right through the balloon barrage that covered southeast England and was meant to prevent low-flying aircraft from attacking us. Soon the noise stopped, followed by a tremendous explosion.

The divisional commander asked me for a report on this mysterious explosive. I immediately got in touch with Southeast Command headquarters and the War Office, which advised me that we'd seen the V-1 (later christened the doodlebug). This newly developed buzz bomb was being thrown into the works in desperation, and our area was soon subject to constant attack. But because their distinct noise preceded their attack, the RAF and the antiaircraft crews had little problem shooting them down, and they proved ineffective. The V-2, however, was not a pilotless plane but a conventional rocket, and it caused considerable damage and fatalities, particularly in London. There was no warning of its arrival—only after you heard the explosion did you know you were safe. (Almost fifty years later, during the war in the Persian Gulf, I was at the receiving end of attacks against Israel by Iraqi Scud missiles, the "great-grandchildren" of the V-1.)

By now I was a full lieutenant, my salary all of eighteen pounds per month.

In the first week of June 1944, restrictions throughout the area were tightened even more. All telephone calls were forbidden, all mail was stopped, and nonresidents could no longer enter, even to visit a loved one. Long convoys dotted the roads; the tension and excitement were palpable. One of the most momentous events in history was about to take place.

On the morning of 6 June I heard the voice of Dwight Eisenhower on the radio, announcing the invasion. The Germans had been fooled by the Allied use of a "dummy" army in East Anglia, and the concentration of troops in southeast England convinced them that the invasion would be in the area of Calais, when it was actually taking place in Normandy. Within the army, the mood was a strange combination of exhilaration and frustration. We envied those who had gone across, hoping that our turn would come soon. Despite the invasion, we were still being bombarded by the V-1 buzz bombs and the V-2 missiles.

As the battle raged across the Channel, I was transferred to a POW interrogation unit, pending my posting as a brigade or divisional intelligence officer in northwest Europe. Britain was fortunate to have many racetracks because they were invariably used for prisoner-of-war camps. For a short while, at a place called Kempton Park, I processed German prisoners of war brought over from France. I was then moved to Lingfield Park in Surrey, where in-depth interrogation was carried out with those prisoners considered important. I spent quite a long time with one captured German officer who had commanded a U-boat. At first, I saw him as a monster, but after several days of interrogation we developed a personal relationship. Suddenly he was an ordinary individual sitting in front of me and talking about his wife and his children. No training can prepare you for the reality that all evil and monstrous people are human, with many of the same foibles that you and I have. It is much easier to hate and kill a disembodied enemy than a person who appears to be human and normal.

WHILE IN MANCHESTER, I had visited my Uncle Zadok, my Aunt Helen's husband. She had remained behind in Paris with her sister, Esther, but he received an occasional letter from her via the Red Cross and sent her money to live on. The latest letter was the first indication that all was not well: my youngest cousin, Annette, aged twenty-one, had been deported. The last letter she wrote—in pencil without an envelope—was thrown out of the train taking her to Auschwitz and was delivered to her mother by French farmers. They would find hundreds of such letters after each train left for Auschwitz and, in most cases, made it a point of honor to deliver them. Writing about the three-day train journey, she expressed the usual hopes for a happy reunion. But it is clear that she had no illusions about her destination or destiny:

> I don't think I will be able to write to you, but don't despair . . . don't abandon yourself to distress. My morale is very strong. I have plenty of courage and hope. . . . There are thousands in my situation. I will return soon. Wait for me patiently, dear Maman.
>
> 1,000 kisses
> Nana

CHAPTER 5

The Fall of Germany

FINALLY, THE LONG-AWAITED day arrived, and I found myself en route to France about a month after D-Day. Two other officers and I formed an intelligence team, and we boarded an LCI (landing craft, infantry) at Southampton. Crammed together with 120 men, we spent a night in Southampton Sound, sleeping in our seats, and sailed early the next morning. The sea was rough and everyone on board—including me— was seasick. We approached the Normandy coast at Arromanches, only to find life on land no more pleasant. We lived in tents in an endless sea of mud, under incessant rain.

The transit camp was not far from Bayeux, which had miraculously been spared during the invasion and where I was able to buy a pair of boots to help preserve me from the mud. But since we had our army rations and food was scarce for the French civilians, all we were permitted to buy was Camembert cheese. The only commodity that seemed plentiful was Chanel perfume, of which I had no pressing need.

A week passed. Not only did the rain never let up, but we were entering one of the coldest winters in European history. My first hot bath in a tub was such a great event that it warranted a letter home. To stave off the cold, we were allowed a daily issue of rum, one bottle of whiskey per month, and three bottles of beer per week.

The Allied breakout from Normandy was under way. Our small team was attached to the Guards Armored Division advancing northward on the right of the British forces. In Normandy we passed through the ruins of Caen, which fell to the Allies after bitter fighting. (Many years later, as president of Israel, I would plant a tree there.) We also left behind the vast graveyard in the "Falaise pocket," where approximately 100,000 German troops were surrounded and destroyed in a fierce battle, a defeat reputedly second only to that at Stalingrad. Our division crossed the River Seine at Vernon and advanced rapidly, liberating one town after another as the entire population rushed into the streets to cheer us on. We reached Brussels in early September.

The roads were so jammed that our tanks could advance only with great difficulty. They often disappeared under throngs of women who climbed up to embrace the troops. Wine flowed freely, flowers were thrown, fresh fruit was handed out. Troops disappeared into private homes, and control became almost impossible. Furthermore, supplies to the British forces had become inadequate. As a result, opportunities to exploit our military success were missed, and the Germans were given time to recover.

Eventually our team established itself in Bourg Leopold. I received permission to go to Paris for the weekend, and on a Friday night, just before the Sabbath, I walked into my Aunt Esther's apartment. Our reunion was made even more moving by my aunt's mistaken insistence that Annette had survived Auschwitz. She would believe that to her dying day.

My aunt had taken in my Uncle Reuben's nephew, his wife, and an orphan girl she had adopted before the war. She had also taken in a man and woman whose apartments had been appropriated by the Germans. Reuben had long before fled via Vichy to Shanghai, where he died during the war. Several non-Jews were very helpful to my aunt; they hid her in their apartments when a hunt for Jews was on. The story of their nightmare emerged. Money had seeped through to her via the Red Cross from my Uncle Zadok in Manchester, as well as from Uncle Reuben in Shanghai. I tried to press money on her, but she would not take it unless I agreed that she could give it to more deserving people. She had kept some wine in anticipation of liberation, and I made kiddush, the sacramental blessing, on it.

My grandfather's synagogue on the rue Pavée had been damaged by the Germans, so I went to the Sabbath service in the Cathedral Synagogue, on the rue de la Victoire. Paris was as beautiful as ever; nothing about the people seemed to have changed.

Thanks to the unusual appearance of my British uniform, strangers invited me for drinks or into their homes for meals. The Americans who had liberated the city were now part of the scenery but no longer very popular. Already gone were the special emotions aroused by the liberation. Now the Parisians were back to their daily struggles and facing an extreme shortage of food and medicine. Members of the surviving Jewish community literally fell on me, embracing me. Listening to their stories, I realized the importance of the national home and independent state that we dreamed of and prayed for. I felt privileged to have served in the war, and I resolved to make every sacrifice to achieve that independence.

While on another leave from the front line to see my family in Paris, I watched the ceremony in the Champs-Elysées on 11 November 1944, when the French Resistance forces and French army troops paraded down the wide boulevard, led by Churchill and De Gaulle in an open car. If ever one can be aware of a moment that will live forever, it was this.

As an intelligence officer temporarily detached from the Guards Armored Division to the Third British Division, I was part of the first Allied formation to cross into Germany. We crossed at Sittard in Holland and moved on to the town of Geilenkirchen. The moral as well as the historical significance of the action was not lost on this young Jewish officer from Palestine, among the very first Jews in the world to cross as a free man into the hated Nazi Germany, the scourge of our people and of mankind. I shall never forget the moment we crossed the border in the mud, slush, and snow. The small customs building was abandoned; the border barrier, with its Nazi insignia, lay broken in a ditch. The German troops were still fighting what was later known as the Battle of the Rohr. We crossed the frozen Rohr River on ice. By the time the supply echelons arrived, there had been a slight thaw, and many of them were killed by mines—which we avoided only because they had been buried under the thick ice.

As division intelligence officer, I was responsible for directing all intelligence sources, assigning patrols and observation posts, evaluating reconnaissance photographs, monitoring radio traffic, updating the brigade or divisional commander, projecting the enemy's future moves, and keeping all appropriate levels rapidly and well informed. At this particular time, as we rolled through the little villages and farms, and as the overwhelmed German troops surrendered, my most important job was to interrogate them and gather information that would direct our forces and artillery in how and where to proceed. Our division entered Germany before the Russian forces invaded on the eastern front. Immediately to our right, the American Ninth Army broke in and took the town of Aachen. Sometime later, during Hanukkah, I was in what used to be the main street. It was now nothing but a path between two endless piles of rubble; the city was completely destroyed. Here and there a white flag hung from a ruin, indicating that Germans were living in the cellar. Occasionally I saw them moving around furtively, emaciated, covered up against the cold, scavenging for food that Allied soldiers might have thrown away. As an eyewitness to the "master race" burrowing in the ruins for crumbs, I was now able to comprehend the final and absolute destruction of Nazi Germany.

A Jewish sergeant was working with me, and we lit three Hanukkah candles on the fender of our weapons carrier. The third candle was significant because it was my father's birthday. American troops passed us and waved. I like to think that some Jewish soldiers among them took comfort from our candles.

THE WINTER OF 1944–45 was extraordinarily severe. Most of Europe was covered with snow, everything was frozen, and some of our trips across Belgium and Holland were nightmarish. On one occasion, I was certain I was going to freeze to death. Interrogating German prisoners of war, I could well understand the trauma that the Russian winter had left on them. I spent Christmas Eve, 1944, in Mechelen, in Belgium, and the local festivities were a brief respite to a very bleak Christmas. One record was played over and over again, Irving Berlin's "White Christmas."

As New Year 1945 was rung in, I was in the village of Stein, in Holland. Mid-December had seen the last major German counterattack, the Battle of the Bulge, launched in a desperate attempt to break through the Ardennes, reach the key port of Antwerp, and stifle Allied moves toward Germany. The Ardennes front was very lightly held, and the German attack caught the Allies with their pants down. Gathering information from prisoners became more important than ever, as the Germans were obviously developing a completely new strategic and tactical plan. English-speaking Germans managed to infiltrate the American side, engaging in sabotage, wreaking havoc behind the lines. Life became extremely perilous. Everyone was stopped and searched regularly, particularly by American sentries who were not satisfied with passes and passwords. To pass the regular grillings and interrogations, one had to have an intimate knowledge of day-to-day life in the U.S. I was constantly questioned about the last World Series results, about which I knew very little. I managed to pass because not only did I know that Sinatra's first name was Frank, but I could sing—or croak—four or five of his hit songs.

Many of the Belgian and Dutch towns I was in had sustained little physical damage, but the people in them had suffered great psychological and emotional traumas. Wherever I went, I met people who had fought bravely against the Nazis, but many others were accused of having been collaborators or just plain cowards. It caused a horrendous split in society, which cannot really be imagined by someone who has never been under attack. I was billeted in the home of a very wealthy and influential man in Mechelen. Each evening he would produce a superb bottle of choice French wine and invite me to join him for a drink. I sensed that he was doing his best to ingratiate himself with an Allied officer, although I could not imagine why. Since my billet was very attractive, it was soon given to an artillery general. A few days later, I learned in the local pub that my ex-host had been detained as a Nazi collaborator. There was no greater sin to a survivor of the war. Here and there small mounds of stones had been placed by the underground to mark the site of a local citizen's execution by the Germans or their collaborators.

I now rejoined the headquarters of the 32nd Guards Brigade in the Guards Armored Division in Holland. We were due to break back into Germany in the area of the Reichswald under the command of the First Canadian army. My work was concentrated on preparing a clear battle picture of the German forces in the area. Our mission was to break through the Reichswald, clear the Rhineland town of Gladbach, and close in on the Rhine in an attempt to destroy all German forces between the Rhine and the Meuse.

Only one road ran through the Reichswald, and the Germans had flooded the low-lying land to the north. The area was heavily mined, and Rhineland towns such as Cleve and Goch had been converted into fortresses ahead of the Siegfried Line. The houses of these German frontier towns had been specially constructed for battle, with concrete basements with slits in the walls through which weapons could be fired. To the east lay another very difficult nut to crack, the Hochwald forest.

The Allied forces hung on every piece of intelligence that my colleagues and I were extracting from prisoners taken along the front. All activity was concentrated in the dark, so the Germans would not get wind of what we were doing. Thirty-five thousand vehicles were used to bring up the men and their supplies, five bridges had to be constructed over the Maas, and one hundred miles of road had to be made or improved.

I found the work thrilling, if extremely stressful. We had to know the order of battle of the German forces facing us, exactly where the minefields were, and what the best areas were for bridging operations. It was vital to be aware of the morale of the other side. We learned that it was not very high, largely because, for the first time, the Germans were fighting on their own soil, and the probable outcome of the war had dawned on them. It was essential to know what routes we could safely take through the ruined towns of Rees and Wesel. Every additional item of intelligence—the location of German reserves, the routes of movement of those reserves, the kinds of armored equipment they had available—was of vital importance.

But the most important element of all, the weather, was out of our control. The ground was frozen, which was essential if tanks and vehicles were to proceed without difficulty. The Allied attack began on 8 February 1945, just as a sudden thaw set in. It was a major operation. Behind a curtain of fire, the advancing troops moved forward in an ocean of thick, nearly impenetrable mud, and the tanks became bogged down. The Germans breached the banks of the Rhine upstream, and the floods started to rise, spreading over the one road through the Reichswald. Thousands of tanks and trucks tried to make their way along, creating an enormous traffic jam, but the inexorable advance soon brought about the fall of Cleve. The battle developed into a slogging match, as Allied forces inched forward in the mud and rain. Their training, guts, and battlefield leadership were the decisive factors, with the brunt falling on the battalions. For five long weeks the bloody battle continued, until the U.S. Ninth Army was able to cross the swollen Rohr River, and the southern prong began to move northward. The Germans' fate was sealed. By 10 March the battle was over, and our forces advanced to the Rhine.

In this attack our forces defeated three panzer, four parachute, and four infantry divisions. We took 16,800 prisoners; enemy casualties were almost 75,000. Our casualties were almost 16,000 (slightly less than what the State of Israel has incurred in all its battles since its establishment).

As we prepared for the next assault across the Rhine, I was again at the center of the preparations. Once more the importance of intelligence could not be underestimated—a lesson I would take with me to Israel.

The army was to attack on a two-corps front between Wesel and Emmerich. To hide our preparations during the day, a continuous smoke screen was put down along the riverbank, but when the wind shifted, it blew the smoke toward us, and everybody got sick. So much for the best-laid plans.

On the evening of 23 March 1945, all hell broke loose. Two Allied airborne divisions were dropped behind the enemy's first line. I was standing on the banks of the Rhine with a group of German officers who had been taken prisoner. Seeing this overwhelming expression of military power, they were overtaken by despair. Several of them told me they finally realized that any further attempt by Germany to defend itself was now criminal because of the cost in life and property.

We crossed the Rhine at Rees, where not a single structure was still standing. We made our way through roads once lined with buildings and homes. Here and there the terrified inhabitants, in total shock, emerged from cellars or scuttled through the ruins. As we moved up along the Rhine, we saw the tragedy of war in completely human terms. The roads filled with sickly people, all their worldly possessions in a knapsack, the forced labor that had been taken from all over Europe. As Germany was collapsing, each of them was trying to find his way home.

Now the drive into the heart of Germany began. All the bridges were blown up and many roads cratered. I moved with a small unit along the eastern bank of the Rhine, and before we knew it, we were in a small Dutch town, Enschede. As the streets filled with the cheering populace, shots were fired, and German soldiers, hands behind their heads, were led out by the Dutch underground. Dutch women and the collaborators who had fraternized with the Germans were rooted out mercilessly, and as crowds jeered and cursed, they were forced to stand in the town square in front of the church. To the insults and applause of the crowds, the women's heads were shaved—the fate of all women in liberated territories suspected of fraternizing with the Germans. As we pushed slowly forward, a white sheet or towel or handkerchief was hanging from almost every window. Thousands of German refugees were now thronging the roads as well. When one talked to them, they cringed, denying all responsibility for Germany's crimes. As we moved past groups of slave laborers along the road to freedom—Russians, Poles, Dutch, Flemish—I looked in vain for a yellow Magen David.

Passover had been a depressing affair. I was too far forward to be able to attend a seder organized by the Jewish chaplains, and I spent the night in a slit trench covered by a tarpaulin as the concentrated artillery of the Allies pounded away. My friend Sergeant Ogus, from London, was with me, and I had received a small bottle of wine and a pack of matzot from the chaplain. I made kiddush in the trench—although I could hardly hear myself—then we ate the matzot and, in a very abbreviated ceremony, repeated the time-honored prayer, "LeShana HaBa'a BeYerushalayim" (Next Year in Jerusalem).

Victory was clearly in the air, and I was anticipating home leave to see my family after seven years. (Today I hear complaints about the lack of leave in the Israel Defense Forces. My sympathy is not aroused; in the wartime British and Allied forces, we were allowed compassionate leave only after five years away from home.) However, before I could go, my brigade still had to advance across Germany. After we crossed the Ems

River at Lingen, it became clear that we would have to fight to take the strategic port city of Bremen. While preparing for this attack, our brigade headquarters came under artillery attack, and one of the shells exploded quite near me, the force knocking me to the ground. I picked myself up and was happy to find that I was unhurt except for a loud ringing in my left ear. It continued for months on end; my eardrum had been damaged beyond repair. (I have gone through life with it, doing my best so that my impaired hearing should not be too noticeable. Years later, while being tested for a liaison pilot's wings in the Israel Defense Forces, I succeeded in bluffing my way through the hearing test. I was placed in a sealed compartment, and a woman in the next compartment pressed all sorts of instruments that emitted sounds. By watching her face, I could guess when she was activating a sound for my left ear, and I managed to scrape through the test.)

During the battle for Bremen, we were warned that a German underground resistance movement, the Werewolf, was being organized, but there was no sign of it. White sheets fluttered from almost every window as we passed. One moment the Germans were putting up the bravest resistance in a hopeless situation, and the next, they were passively surrendering by the thousands.

Even before Bremen fell, the world had finally been exposed to the horrors of the German concentration camps when Bergen-Belsen was liberated. The shocking revelations of Nazi bestiality were trumpeted by the international press. In battle, we had heard rumors of the camps liberated by the Soviets, but they did not move with a large press corps, as did the British and American forces. Even with unsophisticated communications technology, the world could see and feel the evil that had been perpetrated. The impact was almost too painful to bear.

My first personal encounter with this horror was at a small concentration camp just outside Bremen. It was a terrifying sight, one I will never forget. The floors of the filthy huts were strewn with emaciated figures clad in striped pajamas. Many of these poor souls could not even lift themselves up; a tortured smile was their only greeting. Nearly all of them suffered from dysentery, and the stench was indescribable; our corps commander, General Horrocks, was overcome and vomited. He immediately ordered the nearby towns and villages to clean up the camp and care for the prisoners, who nonetheless kept dying at an alarming rate. When the villagers arrived to confront their nation's atrocities, neither I nor anyone else I knew saw any expression of horror or remorse at the brutalities done in their name. For Germans to say, then or today, that they knew nothing of what had transpired—as nearly every German claimed—was a desperate lie. I was there. I saw the faces of the ordinary citizens. I saw the close proximity of the towns to the camps. I smelled the rotting corpses of the Jews and Gypsies and Poles. Believe me, the German people had to have known—the truth was omnipresent and inescapable.

The horrors of the large concentration camps were revealed to an unbelieving world when Bergen-Belsen fell to the British Eighth Corps, who were fighting and advancing on our right flank. When there was a lull in the fighting, I drove to Bergen-Belsen, having heard whispers of the atrocities that had occurred there. The sight of the living, emaciated skeletons was by now horribly familiar to me but that familiarity didn't make it any less terrifying. The entire scene was made more apocalyptic—if that's even possible—by the fact that, because typhus raged throughout the camp, the wooden barracks were being burned to the ground. I told some of the survivors that I was a Jewish officer from Palestine. They all burst into tears. It was all I could do to keep from doing the same. I became friendly with some of the survivors. It was most gratifying to see them recover, in essence to return to being human beings.

On 5 May I was summoned to corps headquarters and informed that the entire German army corps facing us was about to surrender and I was needed as a liaison officer. At 2:30 P.M. General Gunther von Blumentritt, his chief of staff, and several staff officers arrived, immaculate in their military greatcoats. They sat at a table in the center of the room. General Horrocks, in casual battle dress, entered and seated himself alone directly opposite the Germans. Using an interpreter, Major Freddy Hindmarsh, he issued orders for surrender, warning that they must be obeyed scrupulously. "We shall have no mercy if they are not," he said, his rage barely contained. "Having seen one of your horror camps, I am no longer concerned with my moral responsibility for your German soldiers." One of the German generals jumped up. "It was not us," he interjected. "The army had nothing to do with those camps." Horrocks replied that the S.S. guarded the concentration camps and could not escape responsibility. "The world will never forgive Germany for those camps," he whispered. It was all surreal. The murder and torture were nearly over, the madness was ending, and we were sitting in a civilized manner with those responsible, as they obsequiously surrendered.

I became part of a team of British and German staff officers created to supervise the surrender and concentration of German weapons. It was a logistical nightmare for an army such as ours to absorb the enormous German army facing us. Moving them to prisoner-of-war camps, commandeering the equipment and arms, and organizing the transport and feeding of hundreds of thousands of soldiers was an overwhelming task. Entire divisions—which had been fighting us only days before—were now standing at attention before us, waiting to be fed and cared for. Or, as the case might be, punished.

At 9:30 P.M. on 1 May 1945, on the orders of Admiral Doenitz, Hitler's nominee as Führer successor, Hamburg Radio had announced that Adolf Hitler had committed suicide. The announcement was followed by selections from Wagnerian operas, followed by the slow movement of Bruckner's Seventh Symphony. It was an extraordinarily emotional moment. This epitome of evil, who had brought so much misery, destruction, and cruelty on the world, the man who had brought mankind to the lowest level of barbarity that it had ever known, was no more. Many of us cheered, others wept. Some listened in stunned silence. Doenitz immediately set up a government in Flensburg, on the Danish border.

On 8 May 1945, when Germany's final surrender took place, I was in the main street of Bremerhaven, the port north of Bremen. I thought of how privileged I was to be there—a soldier, placed among my sworn enemies, able to savor total and complete victory. And yet I was overcome by a feeling of melancholy. I had fought them for so long. Here I was, walking amid German units that four days earlier would have shot me on sight. Though we were fighting no more, I could not erase my desire to do battle with them. They were no longer my enemies, but they were not my friends.

Our division moved up into Cuxhaven. The Royal Navy had not yet arrived, and a unit of German naval minesweepers was tied up at the dock. Nobody knew what to do with them. As was inevitable when anything unexpected turned up, the job was given to the intelligence officer. I was taken on board and received by Oberleutnant Von Bisterfeld, who commanded the ships. He saluted me and said, "I am proud to have been a Nazi." I was completely unprepared for this. He was the first German I had met who not only admitted that he was a Nazi but proudly proclaimed it—a complete change from the cringing Germans I had met all across the country. I asked if he was proud of the atrocities that had occurred in the concentration camps in his name and in the name of his party. He insisted that it was all propaganda and lies, that no such thing could happen under a German regime. Rather than argue with him I said, "If I could succeed in convincing you that what I am saying is correct, what would you do then?" He immediately answered, "I would go on the bridge of my ship, call together my crew, and do the most extreme act that a German officer can do. I would announce that I am ashamed to be a German officer."

I asked two officers to escort Von Bisterfeld to Sandbostel. It was on the road to Hamburg and had a concentration camp and a prisoner-of-war camp. Von Bisterfeld was shown around the concentration camp and then taken to the prisoner-of-war camp, where the German army commander was hospitalized. The commander told him about everything that had transpired in the camps, omitting no details. Von Bisterfeld returned to his ship, white as a sheet. From the bridge of his ship, as crews of the minesweepers were gathered on deck, Von Bisterfeld told them what he had seen and heard. To a deafening silence he announced, "I am ashamed to be a German officer."

WITH THE CONCLUSION of hostilities, I was promoted to the rank of general staff officer (III) intelligence and sent to a camp in Barfeld, a small village about an hour's drive from Luneberg, where the Second British Army headquarters had established a small team of interrogation officers. We were trying to uncover all the Nazi leaders, who were doing their damnedest to hide their identity if already captured, or their whereabouts if they were not. Accordingly, anyone connected with important Nazis was concentrated at Barfeld—assistants, office personnel, drivers, secretaries, and servants. We gradually amassed a comprehensive dossier on each Nazi leader, which we hoped would lead to his capture. As important Nazis were caught they were held at Barfeld for initial interrogation. The summer days were hot, and prisoners lay around in bathing costumes, sunning themselves, while we sat in stuffy little huts, plowing our way through the vast amount of material that was becoming available.

It was at Barfeld that Heinrich Himmler surrendered. He had been in Flensburg and had escaped with an adjutant and a bodyguard. But the Allies had published a book, which was in the possession of every Allied checkpost, listing those who must automatically be arrested. For each function of government or the military, a rank was specified above which all the holders had to be immediately apprehended. (For instance, in the fire brigade service only those ranked general and above were wanted.) Himmler made his way north on the Cuxhaven Peninsula with his two aides, who had false documents identifying them as privates in the GFP

(Geheime Feld Polizei), the equivalent of the British field security. Ever conscious of rank and status, Himmler had designated himself a sergeant in the GFP. He could not bring himself to be a lowly private, even when running for his life. Unknown to him, the automatic arrest category of GFP personnel was sergeant and above. As Himmler and his companions were crossing a bridge in the small town of Bremervorde, northeast of Bremen, they were stopped at a British military checkpoint. When they produced their papers and Himmler's rank—counterfeit though it was—was discovered, he was immediately arrested. Because he had shaved off his mustache and wore a black eyepatch, he was unrecognized.

He was moved to another facility near Bremen, Westertimke, which had been a concentration camp. Here he was processed, and when the money found on him was seen to have a Flensburg stamp on it, the processing officer realized that a field security sergeant from Flensburg— where many Nazi leaders had been headquartered—could certainly have pertinent information about the whereabouts of missing leaders. Accordingly, "Sergeant" Himmler was unceremoniously loaded onto a truck with his two faithful companions and transported to Barfeld.

On Himmler's arrival, the Barfeld camp commandant, Captain Smith, was having lunch with a group of officers. A sergeant-major burst in and announced that a prisoner was insisting that he see the commandant. Smith replied that the prisoner should wait outside. When lunch was concluded, the German "sergeant" came in, clicked his heels, and dramatically announced, "Ich bin der Reichsführer der S.S." ("I am the commander of the S.S.")

Captain Smith calmly asked who the sergeant's companions were. Himmler replied that they were his adjutant and his bodyguard. They'd been arrested because they had refused to leave his side. Himmler's eyepatch was removed, and he was told to sign his name. His signature was then checked against those of all the Nazi leaders—compiled in a book issued by Supreme Headquarters intelligence—and when they matched, the highest-ranking Nazi officer yet had been captured.

Himmler was immediately stripped and searched, and a cyanide capsule found in his clothes was confiscated. He was covered with a blanket while a call was put through to Colonel Michael Murphy, chief intelligence officer at Second Army headquarters: "Guess who we've got?" There was an explosion at the other end, and orders were given not to interrogate the prisoner—not even to touch him—until Murphy himself arrived.

Asked about the concentration camps, Himmler tried to portray them as prisoner-of-war facilities. A stack of magazines from all over the world was placed in front of him. In detailed descriptions and with graphic photographs, they told the terrifying story. Confronted with the evidence, Himmler denied any knowledge of the camps. This had been done by others, he said. It was all unofficial.

Himmler then asked to be taken to Field Marshal Montgomery or Winston Churchill. He had come forward of his own volition, he said, because he believed that Russian forces could and now would sweep across Europe, and he was prepared to place his S.S. forces at the Allies' disposal. This cold-blooded mass murderer was actually proposing that we join forces.

When Colonel Murphy arrived, he wasted no time on ceremony, sweeping Himmler out with "Come on, you bastard!" There was not even time to photograph him. At Luneberg, Himmler was examined at Second Army headquarters by a military medical officer. When he reached Himmler's mouth, Himmler jerked back his head and bit down on a capsule of cyanide concealed in a tooth cavity. Despite efforts to save him, he died fifteen minutes later.

Why he chose that moment to die—he could have done it any time after his capture—we'll never know. Perhaps he realized how hopeless his situation was. Perhaps he feared the kind of torture that he had sanctioned. Then, too, perhaps he realized that he would be forced to confront the truth that was more than even he could bear.

I saw Himmler only briefly and heard him say only a few words. Out of his gleaming Nazi uniform he looked like a drab and unimposing clerk, like the kind of man we pass every day in the street.

In this period, I was appointed to a committee headed by Brigadier General Bill Williams, the brilliant chief of intelligence under Field Marshal Montgomery. This committee was to decide on the organization of intelligence in the British Zone of occupation. Thus I had a minor hand in setting up an intelligence organization. In a few years' time, when I was entrusted with the job of organizing the Israeli military intelligence, this appointment would prove invaluable.

IN AUGUST, WE RECEIVED news that the atomic bomb had been dropped over Hiroshima and Nagasaki. I do not think anybody appreciated the significance of what had occurred; the details of the carnage were yet to emerge. In the army, all we knew was that the Japanese surrender was a godsend. Most of the army in Europe had expected to be transferred to the Pacific theater. It now appeared that we might soon return home.

Soon afterward, the phone rang in my office in Nienburg, where I was working in counterintelligence. At the other end was Major Beresford at BAOR (British Army of the Rhine) headquarters. He asked if I knew of any officer in the corps who spoke Yiddish. This was the last question I expected to be asked, and I wondered why he needed such a person. He explained that a conference of Jewish displaced persons was to be held in the British Zone at Bergen-Belsen. The policy of the occupying powers had been to ignore the existence of Jews as a separate entity; they were being recognized only as Poles or Russians or Hungarians. The Jews were fighting this policy, and units of the Jewish Brigade Group—raised from soldiers who had volunteered from Palestine to join in the war and had served in North Africa and Italy—were helping them. Central to this question of identity and recognition was the organization required to transfer Jews from Europe to Palestine.

Field Marshal Montgomery and General Templer, the military governor, were to receive the British Jewish delegation to the conference. They realized that to know exactly what was going on, they needed an officer who spoke Yiddish and could report back to them. I got the job myself— I would go to the conference.

The opening of the conference was a terribly emotional experience; never have I been so moved as when we sang our national anthem, "Hatikvah." The emphasis of the conference was on the major problems facing Jews and Palestine—recognition of homeless Jews as a separate entity, immigration to Palestine, and, above all, the conditions in the camps and the attitude toward the DPs of the British authorities and the respective commanders in those camps. There was remarkably little compassion for the Jewish survivors. It was as if the authorities were saying, The war's over and there were some bad times, but now let's pretend that none of it ever happened, so we can all go back to normal life. The problem for the Jewish DPs was that there was no normal life to go back to.

Members of the Jewish Brigade were present, as was a Jewish corporal from Palestine in the British army named Grabovsky (who would later serve as chairman of the Defense and Foreign Affairs Committee of the Knesset). Standing on the platform in his British uniform, he delivered a passionate call for revolt against the British. He minced no words. The British presence in Palestine and Germany, he said, was specifically intended to repress and suppress the Jews. He was not altogether wrong, but it was not wise to deliver such a speech while wearing a British uniform. Indeed, a major in the military government who spoke fluent German informed me that he was going to institute proceedings for a court-martial against Corporal Grabovsky. He gave me what he thought was the gist of the speech, which had been delivered in Yiddish, and I told him that I did not see anything seditious in it. Yiddish, though similar to German, had many important differences, I told him, and I would be obliged to testify that his allegations were incorrect. After a rather heated argument he backed down. I had saved Corporal Grabovsky from a court-martial.

ATTEMPTS TO RETURN to normalcy reflected the resilience and discipline of the German people. I spent a couple of days in Hamburg—the Hamburg Opera was operating again—and I went to a Yom Kippur service in Hanover, attended by some three hundred Jewish troops. The tasks needed to prepare the synagogue were carried out by uniformed German prisoners of war, who also served the meals before the fast. A year earlier we would have been doomed to death in the gas chambers. Now they were helping us prepare for our holiest day.

When my application for home leave was finally approved, I went to Celle airfield (near Bergen-Belsen), got a ride to Paris on a British army plane, and then hitched a plane ride to Naples. Before I knew it, I was on a Dakota flying to Cairo, from which I traveled by train to Jerusalem, arriving on a Friday morning. Because I might walk into my parents' home in the midst of my father's chaotic Friday morning gathering—the great rabbinic scholars of Jerusalem met to hear and argue with him on a weekly basis—I strolled up Jaffa Road. As I wandered past the post office and the Generali Building, I could feel the unique rhythm of this mystical town. The Arab merchants and effendis with their tarboosh and kaffiyah, the British policemen with their pith helmets, the Palestine police with their Circassian fur hats, the bearded Orthodox Jews, some of whom I recognized—here was this wonderful human symphony being played in front of me. As I feasted my eyes on the eternal city of Jerusalem, I realized that I was truly home.

One disturbing foreshadowing occurred; there was a scuffle in the streets, and an area was cordoned off by the police. Everybody within it was checked for identification, the result of the British trying to stop Jewish immigration into Palestine. The British soldiers were beginning to feel the effect of the Jewish resistance, and there was a strong undercurrent of hostility. Seeing my uniform, the British police officer saluted smartly and apologized for any inconvenience, and I was on my way. Little did he know!

Walking leisurely, in the early afternoon I arrived at the home in Ibn Ezra Street that I had never seen before. The magnificent house, built in my absence, befitted the chief rabbi, and my arrival was greeted with a kind of euphoric hysteria. When things calmed down, I began to adapt to again being the boy who had left home seven years earlier. My little brother, Yaacov, had become a political and social activist and leader. We had not seen each other for a long time, but we had a history to bind us, and I liked and respected the man he had become.

After a rejuvenating month of rediscovering Jerusalem and my family, I returned to Germany, where I was made responsible for all military field security and the counterespionage network in Brunswick, the nearest large city to the demarcation line with the Russians at Helmstedt, and for a good part of the area from Wolfenbuttel to Göttingen. Helmstedt was honeycombed with coal mine tunnels that crisscrossed under the demarcation line and became a major route for agents and spies. This area was a vital link in the renewed operation of Aliyah Bet, which organized the so-called illegal immigration of Jews from the Eastern Zone on their long odyssey to Palestine.

I did everything I could to aid this unofficial cause. I arranged for Danish border guards to be replaced by boys from the Jewish Brigade, making it easier for Jews to move through the border; a Russian Jewish colonel helped with rail transportation. American chaplains created fictitious units for which rations and transport were drawn, in order to move and feed Jewish refugees in the Aliyah Bet pipeline. Regardless of the uniform or the rank or the insignia, every Jewish heart beat as one. Never have I seen anything as expressive of the unity of the Jewish people and their willingness to sacrifice in order to save each other.

As chief of security, I was under instructions from the British Labour government to encourage the growth of democracy in the German political system. Many émigrés who had fled from Hitler now returned to Germany, joined by those who had languished in concentration camps. What I was witnessing was all of Europe pulling itself up by the bootstraps in an effort to restart civilization.

In June 1946, I was promoted to a lieutenant colonel's post in the rank of major and moved to Bremen and Stade as intelligence officer responsible for these provinces in the British Zone. The population in the area was approximately two million. My father and brother arrived in Frank-

furt, in the American Zone. My father was on a rescue mission to redeem
Jewish children from the Catholic churches and monasteries where they
had been hidden during the war—in those instances when the Church
had chosen to side against the Nazis. My father had gone to see Pope Pius
XII, who had not been very helpful, and was now traveling to Poland,
Czechoslovakia, Holland, and Italy to restore the children to their rightful homes.

This was the second time my father had called on Pope Pius XII. On
each occasion he found him most unhelpful and unsympathetic—and
even hostile. Tens of thousands of Jewish children had been hidden by
Jews and Christians in monasteries and churches throughout Europe. In
many places, they were not being allowed to reassume their Jewish identity or return to the Jewish community. Many children were not even
aware that they were Jews, having been too young to be aware of their
real identity when they were hidden. My father asked the pope to issue
instructions to churches, monasteries, and other institutions to allow
these children to return to their families or to the Jewish community. He
refused. It is almost unfathomable that he did refuse and totally unfathomable why. Perhaps he was unwilling to relinquish his hold on these
new Catholic converts. Perhaps it was for the same unknown reason that
the Church gave so much help to fleeing Nazi war criminals. I suppose
we will never understand the motives. But, nevertheless, my father,
backed by an important Jewish committee based in Switzerland, and
with considerable support from local Catholic authorities and people like
Queen Wilhelmina of the Netherlands, was to bring back to Israel thousands of Jewish children who would otherwise have been lost.

ONE MORNING IN STADE I came down to the officers' mess to a very tense
atmosphere. The hostile silence and tension that greeted me soon disappeared, but it was a rather unpleasant example of what it so often means
to be a part of a group, yet also separate. When I saw the newspaper
headlines, I realized why. There had been a bombing at the King David
Hotel in Jerusalem. The bomb was set by the Irgun, a Jewish underground organization, to protest British rule in Palestine. They had picked
Jerusalem's best hotel because it not only billeted many British soldiers
but also housed the offices of the Palestine government and the military
headquarters. Ninety-eight people had been killed. The Irgun had smuggled milk cans loaded with explosives into a wing of the hotel and deto-

nated them. The attack was condemned by the Jewish Agency and the Haganah, but the damage had been done. Of all the underground operations in the struggle against the British, none caused as much death and destruction.

As a result of the bombing, the British rounded up and arrested many Zionist leaders in Palestine whether or not they were involved with the Irgun or the bombing. The British wanted to apprehend all the leaders of all the Zionist groups, including David Ben-Gurion and Yitzhak Ben-Zvi, who both managed to escape to Paris. I was given leave and went to Paris, where my father was searching for Jewish displaced children. He asked to meet with Ben-Gurion in an attempt to come to grips with the escalating violence and potential revolt in Palestine. I attended that session—my first encounter with him—at the Royal Monceau Hotel, but, unfortunately, nothing particularly productive came of the conversations.

I WAS BACK in Germany for Rosh Hashanah, and I went to Hamburg for the New Year services. The heavily bombed city was still in ruins, with tens of thousands of people buried beneath the rubble. The once great Jewish community numbered scarcely one hundred, a depressingly high proportion of whom were soldiers. The Jewish chaplain had arranged meals for our troops in the Jewish restaurant, and we hosted the congregation at all our meals. It was moving but very depressing.

PREPARING TO RETURN to Palestine, I was torn by the thought of having to abandon the fascinating work I was doing—I was now advisor to the new military governor, General Brian Robertson—and return to student life.

Serving in the British army had brought about a great change in me. I had been thrown into the deep end of the pool and forced to swim. I had never led men before, especially in a wartime situation, but I liked it and was good at it. I had spent years on my own, confronting life-or-death situations. The army had strengthened my social beliefs; I was now a full-fledged backer of the Liberal Party and had great sympathy for the Labour Party. Wartime conditions had led me to understand people and appreciate their problems and to discover a facility that would prove an invaluable asset: the ability to sum people up accurately, to read their thoughts and nature as they talked to me. It had doubtless been developed in the course of interrogating German soldiers. I had succeeded on my merits and proved myself in the British army, and never did I have to compromise my opinions or beliefs.

But the time had come to join the struggle for freedom in Palestine. I had already learned much of what I needed to know, and someone of great importance was waiting for me. Back home was the girl I was going to marry.

CHAPTER 6

————— ∞∞∞ —————

The Return to Palestine

IN RETROSPECT, OUR marriage seemed dictated by fate. During my 1945 home leave from Germany, I had tried to cram a social life into those thirty days. I met my student friend Aubrey Eban, later to become Israel's ambassador to the United States and the United Nations as well as foreign minister and deputy prime minister under his Hebrew name, Abba. Aubrey was then deputy head of the British Army Middle East School of Arab Studies, in Jerusalem. He was married to Suzy Ambache, whose family lived in Cairo; originally from Palestine, they had been driven out by the Turks in World War I. During dinner with Aubrey and Suzy, I mentioned that I'd passed through Cairo in my complicated hitch-hike home. The next time I went there I had to visit the Ambache family, they said.

On my way back to Germany I called on them at their beautiful house in the prosperous Zamalek district. Mrs. Ambache was ill, so I was greeted instead by the youngest of the three Ambache daughters, Aura. I found myself falling in love the moment she opened the door.

Aura had just returned from South Africa, where she had studied science, mathematics, and astronomy at Witwatersrand University. She accepted my invitation to dine that night at the British Officers Club on the banks of the Nile—but only with her mother's permission. (In the French-oriented European society of Cairo, young women were not supposed to go out unchaperoned.) After much hesitation and discussion, a neighbor of ours in Jerusalem, the wife of a supreme court justice on a bedside visit to Mrs. Ambache, gave her stamp of approval.

By the end of the evening, it was clear to me that I had found the girl

I'd been looking for—Aura was vivacious, intelligent, charming, and most attractive. But there was one problem: I was due to leave the next morning for Italy. That was when Fate stepped in—my place on the plane had been taken. Someone had been given a higher priority, and the next plane wouldn't leave for several days. I immediately called Aura, and the romance flourished. Being bumped from that flight not only threw me into the arms of my future wife but saved my life. The plane crashed in Tobruk.

Aura and I were in love. We met, on another brief leave, in Switzerland, and got to know each other through our letters. In a strange way, we shared our thoughts and feelings more intimately than we might have been able to do in a mundane year of dating. After a year, the Ambaches came to Switzerland for their summer vacation. Aura and I met in Zermatt, and I popped the question on a small bridge overlooking a mountain stream. Luckily for me, the answer was yes. Even more fortunately, for me, when I finally returned to Jerusalem, Aura was waiting. She had been the only foreign student accepted in a training course established by the political department of the Jewish Agency to create a diplomatic corps for the state-to-be.

ASIDE FROM MY JOY at reuniting with Aura, there was not much joy in Palestine in early 1947.

Over 100,000 British troops were stationed there. The British forces were worn out by the war, and the Jewish community was angry with British restraints and generally resentful in the wake of the Holocaust that had wiped out six million of our people. As a result, the tension and hostility reached new heights. There were daily attacks on the British troops—and daily retaliations. Within a few months after the end of the war, Churchill's Conservative Party was defeated in the elections and the new Labour Government proved to be most hostile to the Jewish cause. Particularly unsympathetic was Ernest Bevin, the new foreign secretary, a laborer turned politician and diplomat. Ben-Gurion had the vision, very early on, to realize that Palestine could not depend on Britain's friendship and protection forever—nor should we. He had insisted that Jewish forces prepare to fight as an army, not merely as local security units. This decision would ultimately prove to be our country's salvation. We had a highly motivated and armed underground force chafing under and rebelling against the restraints of the British army. With our extraordinary underground army came a certain confidence. As the British clamped down harder and harder, we were confident enough to fight back—and with a vengeance. As Ben-Gurion said in the midst of the war, "We'll fight Nazi Germany as if there's no British Mandate, and we'll fight the British Mandate as if there's no Nazi Germany." In the midst of all this, Bevin announced that the British would withdraw from Palestine and hand the matter over to the newly formed United Nations.

I had a tremendous internal conflict. Being a member of the British army was a big part of my identity. One day I found myself sitting in an officers' mess in British army headquarters as a major, a big chief. The next day I was suspect by every British soldier I passed, simply because I was a Jew. During the war, 30,000 Jews had served as volunteers in the British army. Now we were all enemies.

The daily attacks on the British forces were undertaken primarily by the underground Irgun and Stern Group. The Haganah, of which I was still an active member, was too busy preparing to become the army of the new state. I now found myself at the bottom of the ladder, as it were, another demobilized soldier looking for employment. My standing in Germany was of no interest in Palestine.

A permanent conundrum of the State of Israel is that we are a community whose core is a peaceful and thoughtful religion, yet we live in a nearly constant state of war. I had come to grips with those seemingly diverse paths; I had no problem fighting for what I believed in, whether it was religious, social, or personal. But my father was in a slightly different position. He was the religious leader of the Jewish community, and part of his leadership involved being a realist. As a realist, he could not be merely a man of intellect; he had to be a man of action or at least acknowledge that many of those he served were men of action. So during this period, my father had much to do with the underground forces and their activities. Yaacov was his go-between. He accompanied our father on visits to leaders of the Irgun and the Stern Group after they were arrested for the King David Hotel bombing and exiled to Eritrea and Kenya. The internees included Yitzhak Shamir, later to be prime minister of Israel; Meir Shamgar, later chief justice of Israel; and Shmuel Tamir, a future minister of justice. His visit was approved by the British, and all facilities necessary for travel were placed at his disposal. My father did his best to inspire courage and confidence in them. He was a man of peace but he couldn't sanction the restrictions of the Mandate. To make matters even more complicated, both morally and practically, everyone—including the British—had to pretend that the underground armies didn't exist. (The British authorities occasionally used the Haganah for certain duties, even though they were sworn to destroy it.)

The surreptitious arrangements between my father and the underground's headquarters were in the hands of my brother, and Yaacov was perfect for this role. He had a trusting relationship with my father, was a natural-born diplomat, and was valued by officials who dealt with both the British and the underground organizations. While I'd been away, Yaacov had developed a strong working relationship with Ben-Gurion and particularly with Golda Meir, the two heads of the Labor Party. Golda, who became Israel's first foreign minister and later prime minister, was then head of the political department of the Jewish Agency (the equivalent of foreign minister). In political clout, she was second only to Ben-Gurion.

As the new kid on the block, I was not yet part of any behind-the-scenes wheeling and dealing. I had the utmost esteem for Ben-Gurion—our Washington, Lincoln, and Jefferson combined—and much respect for Golda. She had a tremendously strong personality and was revered, a feeling elicited by her Yiddishe Momma way of speaking. I later watched her become cut off from these same people, her constituency. She was a wonderful representative to the American Jewish people, who fawned over her and still think of her as synonymous with the State of Israel, but she was not very effective and indeed was very limited as a prime minister. Nonetheless, the dominant Labor Party gave great support to my father's and brother's efforts to unite Palestine's various factions, as the key to our success and even to our survival.

One story that made the rounds of the official Middle East created considerable mirth. It was of Yaacov's making arrangements for the trip to Kenya. The sergeant at the air reservations desk in Cairo, who was allocating seats in the RAF plane, asked my brother what unit my father was serving in. Taken aback but always with his wits at his command, my brother replied, "The army of the Lord." The sergeant dutifully noted this, then asked what my father's military rank was, to which my brother replied, "Field marshal." This was also duly noted. He then asked my brother what his military unit was, and Yaacov answered, "The same as my father, the army of the Lord." When asked for his rank, Yaacov allowed that in light of his father's rank, he was entitled to be a colonel. The plane reservations were duly filled out.

There was one very moving story about my father's trip to see the internees. En route, the plane landed at Jedda, in Saudi Arabia. A high dignitary met my father and took him into the refreshment tent, prepared for VIPs only. And VIPs did not include Jews. When my brother asked the dignitary why this warm and gracious welcome, he replied, speaking of my father, "I can see he is a man of God."

WITH HOSTILITY BETWEEN the Jews and the British troops growing worse each day, something was bound to cause it to explode into open hatred. That something was Dov Gruner.

Dov Gruner was a soldier in the British army but also a passionate Zionist and committed member of the underground. Dov participated in an attack on a British police station, was caught by the British, and was immediately sentenced to hang.

It is essential to understand the extent of British Mandate–ordered repression. Nazi Germany had created the ultimate threat to Jews and to the idea of a Jewish homeland, not only by spewing overpowering messages of hatred toward Jews but also by destroying an enormous percentage of the world's Jewish population. From an emotional and psychological, as well as practical, viewpoint, and from the simple need to ensure survival, it was critical for Jews to band together and create a home state in which they could thrive and feel safe. The European Jews who survived the Holocaust needed such a home *now*. But the British Mandate prevented any influx of Jews to their own homeland. The Arabs objected to more Jews entering what they considered to be their home. The British, still clinging to their Lawrence of Arabia fantasies, sided with the Arabs against the Jews. The British made sure that Palestinian Jews remained and could survive, but they were determined to keep more Jews from coming in and upsetting the Arabs any further. The attitude of the Jews, of course, was British rules and regulations be damned. Our people needed a home and it was our right and our responsibility to provide it.

European Jews were constantly trying to smuggle themselves into Palestine illegally. Boats carrying "illegal" Jews "home" would try to land. British naval vessels would lie in wait for them to get close to shore and then ram the boats. Many people drowned, and many lives were lost. The survivors, who had escaped from the horrors of the German concentration camps, were now placed in concentration camps, built by the British, in Cyprus. But even this human tragedy was less important to the British than their damned quotas.

The British did not really want to hang Dov Gruner. No one had been killed in the police station raid, and they expected him to plead for leniency. He did not. An extreme nationalist, he realized that his death could unite an entire people in their fight for independence. So Dov insisted—despite pleas from such high-ranking Jews as Begin and Ben-Gurion—that the sentence be carried out. He believed the cause was more important than his life.

Dov's sister, Helen Friedman, came from the United States, and my parents took her into our home. We spent those final, terrible hours of Dov's execution and funeral with her. Dov's martyrdom was agony to watch, partly because of our helplessness. But some of the agony was also due to our respect for what Dov was doing.

Forty years passed before I saw Helen again. I was president of Israel and the principal speaker at a ceremony in newly renamed Dov Gruner Square, in Ramat Gan. The ceremony marked the anniversary of the last execution of Jews by the British. Overall, twelve members of Etzel and Lehi had been executed.

Two other Jewish boys went to their deaths with extraordinary bravery and courage. Meir Feinstein, a member of Lehi, and Moshe Barazani, a member of the Irgun, were sentenced to be executed after a firefight between their underground organizations and British soldiers. The boys under sentence had plans for their hanging. A grenade hidden in an orange was smuggled in to them, and they were going to explode it in the gallows room, killing themselves and as many of their British captors as possible. Completely unaware of their plan, my father sent Rabbi Jacob Goldman, his devoted secretary, to the two boys on death row, with orders that they were not to be without a Jewish religious presence at the moment of their execution. Feinstein and Barazani begged him not to stay, but Rabbi Goldman insisted that he must obey my father's instructions. Knowing that they could not carry out their plan unless they were willing to kill Rabbi Goldman, Feinstein and Barazani exploded the grenade in their cell several hours before they were to be executed. No one else was present. They held the explosive between their bodies as they embraced.

In 1947, WITH THE once-glorious British Empire in the last stages of collapse, the vicious circle of violence continued in Palestine. The British kept hanging Jewish resisters, and Etzel and Lehi retaliated. Two British sergeants were kidnapped and hanged in Netanya, on the coast north of Tel Aviv. The message was clear: if you hang our boys, we'll hang yours.

The turning point, certainly the most dramatic, was the Haganah-orchestrated voyage of the *President Warfield*, nicknamed *Exodus* and immortalized in Leon Uris's novel. Four thousand European Jews were aboard the ship when it attempted to land in Palestine. They were intercepted by the British navy, taken off protesting and resisting, and forced onto a British merchant ship which took them to Port de Bouc in France. The French offered asylum, but the Jews refused to leave the ship—they were going to their homeland or they were going nowhere at all. In burning heat and amid horrendous conditions, these brave souls stayed aboard for one month. Three immigrants died, and hundreds became sick and injured.

Humiliated at the world media's exposure of their barbaric policies, the British did the ultimately stupid thing: they sailed the Jews back to Hamburg, the original port of embarkation. Then President Harry S Truman stepped in, insisting that 100,000 Jewish immigrants be allowed into their homeland immediately.

YET, EVEN IN SUCH turbulent times, ordinary life manages to continue and even thrive. And in the ordinary life of Chaim Herzog and Aura Ambache a wedding date was set, 8 May 1947. A large wedding in Jerusalem would have been inappropriate during such struggle and hardship, and an event such as this, held by my parents, could not help but be major. With her unfailing common sense, my mother decided that the ceremony would take place at the delightfully rustic Pension Meir, in the small village of Gedera in the south of Palestine.

My mother, who was extremely strong-willed, did not at first support my choice of Aura as my lifelong mate. She had already chosen a wife for me from a list of local Jewish girls, having forgotten that I was no longer a boy but an independent and headstrong man. Her father, Rabbi Hillman, ultimately overcame her resistance through a combination of humor, common sense, and oratorical skills.

On our way to Gedera, our car was stopped by a British patrol at Latrun, later the site of several bloody battles. The soldiers checked the wedding cake by prodding it with bayonets. Nothing more dangerous than vanilla icing was found.

The wedding was modest but very beautiful, done in my mother's usual dignified style, and my father and grandfather officiated. We were all seated together, men with women, without even a thought of separation. Today, it would be inconceivable for a member of the chief rabbi's family to have such a wedding. The atmosphere created by the extreme religious elements would forbid men and women to be seated together.

After our honeymoon in Nahariya, I returned to work at a law office, and Aura attended the school of diplomats. We settled in an attractive house in Talpiot at the southern edge of Jerusalem. Our immediate neighbor was Shai Agnon, one of Israel's greatest writers and the nation's first Nobel laureate in literature. Meanwhile, the struggle continued. The British set up security zones in Jerusalem, entire areas were sectioned off by barbed wire, and special passes were needed to move between security zones—all this in reaction to activities of the Jewish underground. I arranged to get an ID card with a photo in my British army uniform. Identifying me as a liaison between the Jewish Agency and British government officials, the card made it easier for me to move around in the Arab districts and let me bypass much British harassment. Usually when they saw my photograph on the identity card they saluted and I simply went through. One day an overly zealous Arab Legion guard from Jordan decided to scrutinize the card. If he discovered my Jewish credentials on the back of the card, I was in serious trouble. I suddenly shouted at him—a button was undone on his tunic—berating him for being slovenly and demanding his name in an imperious British military tone. He slammed to attention and apologized, and I excused him, pocketing my identity card. My bluster may have saved my life.

Daily life was so violent and irrational that in the door pocket of my little Morris Minor car I carried a German parachute jump knife from a German battalion sergeant-major taken prisoner on the Rhine. I kept it ready for anyone who tried to jump on the car's running board as we drove through the dangerous Arab areas.

I WAS APPRENTICED to David Goitein, originally from England, an outstanding trial lawyer who reputedly rescued many from the gallows. We had a sizable Arab clientele, primarily from large Arab villages in the Hebron Hills. I spent much time with our Arab clients and acquired an intimate knowledge of life in Arab villages. The office was in a dignified Turkish building on King George Street called Talitha Kumi; the portals still stand.

Despite internal divisions and struggles in Palestine, one could mingle freely with various elements of the population in government offices and the judicial system. British judges, robed and bewigged as if in London, maintained a reserved sense of decorum and dignity. The Arab officials, senior and minor, added a Levantine and colonial character, whereas the Jewish personnel contributed a European flavor. To say that friendships developed between members of these groups might be overstating the facts, but we were all, for the most part, courteous and professional.

By 1947, THE PRESENCE of nearly 100,000 troops had become an intolerable financial burden on a British government still reeling from a paralyzing war. That summer Ernest Bevin, the foreign secretary in the Labour government (and allegedly an inveterate anti-Semite) dramatically announced that Britain had decided to withdraw from Palestine and drop the Mandate in the lap of the United Nations, which immediately created the United Nations Special Commission on Palestine (UNSCOP).

Summoned to a special meeting of the Haganah, I met David Shaltiel, head of the intelligence service (Shai) and later commander of Jerusalem during the War of Independence, for the first time. The Haganah was setting up a department to monitor UNSCOP, which was considered our most realistic opportunity to establish a legal and official State of Israel. Confronted with worldwide opposition to the Zionist position, we knew that our political future was in the hands of the United Nations.

Shaltiel offered me the chance to head the Haganah's new operation, at the cost of giving up my work in the law office. There was only one answer I could give. I was at last to have a real function in my people's historic struggle, to become involved in developments that I believed would change our destiny. I agreed immediately.

My office was on the fourth floor of an apartment building on Hillel Street, next to the famous Eden Hotel, a meeting place for Jews, British, and Arabs. Since UNSCOP's members came from Sweden, Australia, Guatemala, Uruguay, Czechoslovakia, Holland, and India, to name but a few nations, we divided ourselves into teams. The Arab team would cover all UNSCOP's contacts with the Arab world. Another team would find cooperative members of the press to help us stay abreast of UNSCOP's dealings with the media. A special team looked after the commission's ensuing social contacts. Hotel employees were organized so that not one piece of paper on commission members' desks or in their wastebaskets would go unnoticed. Telephone lines were monitored, and every aspect of their lives was surveilled to give us a clear picture of their hearings, discussions, and inclinations. When the time came, we hoped that appropriate pressure could be exercised in the UN and in friendly governments. In addition to coordinating and presiding over this activity, my job was to draw conclusions and submit situation reports and evaluations to the Jewish Agency.

IT SOON BECAME CLEAR that the commission was tending toward partitioning Palestine into two states. That was confirmed in their report submitted on 31 August 1947 to the UN General Assembly. The majority recommendation was to separate Palestine into independent Jewish and Arab states linked in economic union (a minority report favored a united federal Palestine); Jerusalem was to become an international enclave under UN trusteeship.

"Chaos" best describes the intricacies of daily life during this period. Government offices, divided between British, Jews, and Arabs, were paralyzed. Most ordinary services were rarely available; municipalities were incapable of performing their normal functions. The British divided Jerusalem into "security zones" surrounded by barbed-wire fences; entrance was permitted only with an official pass. Food and water were limited, and entire areas were placed under curfew for days. Not a soul was allowed to walk the streets without a special license from the authorities, and flouting these regulations could mean death by shooting. Palestine was slipping toward anarchy. The Jewish community, which had created a state within a state, did its best to maintain an orderly form of daily life. It was easier in areas such as Tel Aviv, where there was no Arab minority, but Tel Aviv was a frontline area, bordering on Jaffa, which had a large Arab population. Things were spinning out of control.

At the United Nations General Assembly in New York, debate continued. The Arabs rejected UNSCOP's proposed partition, which would have given them a Palestinian state. As was to be the case time and again, the Arabs were never willing to accept less than 100 percent of what they wanted and refused to compromise. The British, too, opposed partition. Given their strongly pro-Arab recent history, their choice was not surprising. The United States supported the UN proposal, as did the Soviet Union, whose UN delegation was led by Andrei Gromyko. For them this resolution was a means of eliminating British colonialism in Palestine.

At one stage, the Americans, led by Secretary of State George C. Marshall, opted for a UN trusteeship proposal instead of independent partitioning. This setback led to the famous meeting between Chaim Weizmann, soon to become the first president of Israel, and President Truman. After that meeting, President Truman gave full support to partition.

On the never-to-be-forgotten night of 29 November 1947 the entire nation was glued to the radio as Moshe Medzini, correspondent of Palestine Radio, reported that the General Assembly was voting to decide whether we would achieve statehood. One by one the name of each member nation was called and each announcement was made—Yes, No, or Abstention. The United States, the Soviet Union, and France voted in favor; Britain abstained. Finally, the announcement was made; the recommendation had been adopted by a vote of thirty-three in favor and thirteen against, with ten abstentions.

Pandemonium broke out and the entire Jewish population was seized with joy. For that moment, all bitterness and remorse over past injustice disappeared. In Tel Aviv, in Jerusalem, in every town of Palestine, Jews poured into the streets cheering wildly. People of all ages spun around in euphoria, dancing the hora.

Aura and I drove to the headquarters of the Jewish Agency, established as the representative body of the Jewish community in Palestine and comprising Zionists and non-Zionists. Joining the crowd on the balcony, we stood by Golda Meir and watched the throngs dancing in the Agency quadrangle below. Jews clambered into the patrol cars of the British forces and drove around as the Zionist flag was hoisted everywhere.

WHILE THE JEWISH COMMUNITY danced in the streets, a sullen Arab population reacted violently against the UN decision. Arab rioters marched on the commercial center of Jerusalem, looted and burned Jewish stores, and attacked Jews in the streets before advancing into the center of the city. The British police seemed powerless. Attacks on urban transport, the Achilles heel of the Jewish community, were carried out, and the toll of lives mounted. Throughout the Arab world, rioting took place against Jewish communities. In Aden, eighty-two Jews were massacred and four synagogues were burned. Jewish homes were destroyed. The Arabs swore to fight the partition resolution to the end. Jerusalem, despite the British presence, became a divided city. Points of contact in government offices and institutions between Jews and Arabs were set even farther apart.

The British announced that they would withdraw from Palestine in May 1948, and the UN set up a special commission to effect the transfer of power to the new Jewish and Arab states. Meanwhile the battle continued. Convoys were regularly attacked along the roads by Arab terrorists and villagers. Gradually, these convoys were escorted by makeshift armored cars built in small workshops throughout the country. People traveled in iron-clad "coffins" between Tel Aviv and Jerusalem. These armored buses trundled along, escorted by armored trucks manned by Palmach boys and girls clad in balaclava knitwear, their hair flying in the wind, armed at best with homemade Sten guns. They were no match for the armed guerrillas operating against them, but they fought against tremendous odds and wrote one of the noblest chapters in the battle for Israel's independence. The wrecks of their trucks and armored cars lie strewn along the road to Jerusalem today in mute testimony to their bravery and self-sacrifice.

As the rioting spread and the Jewish community braced itself for the painful transition to statehood, I was invited by the head of the Jewish Agency's Security Department, Yehezkel Sahar, to become his deputy. A month after I began my activities, Sahar was chosen to be the first chief of the Jewish state's police force-to-be, based in Tel Aviv. I suddenly found myself responsible for direct liaison between the Jewish and British authorities, including their dreaded Criminal Investigation Department (CID) and the British armed forces. The tensions and mistakes—indeed, the chaos—that characterized our society were all concentrated in no small measure in my office.

With the British less and less willing to offer protection against Arab attacks, our only real means of retaliation was the Palmach, the mobilized striking force of the Haganah, led by Yigal Peikovicz (later Allon). The Haganah was trying to adapt to a constant state of guerrilla warfare, and some of its commanders were lackluster and mediocre; others achieved their position because of political affiliations rather than military ability. A lack of imagination, an absence of discipline, and a tendency to ignore details made the difference between success and failure in a military operation. It was a miracle that we had the courageous and effective Palmach organization.

Early in 1948 a major Haganah military operation was mounted. A force of thirty-five boys was dispatched to the Etzion Bloc, south of Jerusalem, which had been besieged and cut off by Arab guerrillas. Very little planning or thought went into this counterattack. A ridiculous attitude that "everything will be all right" pervaded our military planning at this stage. After setting off from the Hartuv area across the Hebron Hills, the troops were sighted by an Arab shepherd and attacked by thousands of Arab irregulars. The Haganah soldiers withdrew to a hill and held out until they were wiped out to the last man, fighting to the final bullet. We had to plead with the British to help us locate the bodies and make burial arrangements.

As sporadic fighting spread throughout Jerusalem, Aura and I moved from Talpiot, where we were somewhat isolated and where my job would have left her alone at night, to a newly reconstructed apartment next to my parents' home. Soon after we moved in, the *Palestine Post* building, over a mile away, was blown up by Arab terrorists, killing and wounding many innocent people; the blast ripped our newly hung curtains to pieces. I ran all the way and found the building in smoldering ruins, the printing press destroyed, as people wandered in shock, searching for friends and trying to retrieve documents and files.

The next day the *Palestine Post* appeared on a small sheet. Its most popular feature, Column One, was written by an Englishman named David Courtney, and it began "Words are louder than bombs." Publication of the paper the very next day was testimony to the spirit of the Jewish population in these harrowing circumstances.

IN FEBRUARY 1948, Aura was ordered to Tel Aviv. She was working in the Haganah and had to make arrangements to bring a generator from the Dead Sea Works (we were always scrounging for electricity and power—not to mention food and water). On our way to the bus station, we saw a British army truck with troops in it. As we headed off in the armored bus, there was an enormous explosion. When we were safely inside the "Jewish State" and could breathe freely, we learned that the truck had been loaded with explosives. The troops included British turncoats who had gone over to the Arabs and set off the bomb. Over fifty people were killed and many hundreds wounded. We had escaped by a mere few minutes.

Around this time, the UN advance group for the implementation of the UN partition resolution arrived. Five countries were represented and the group was headed by Pablo Azcarate, who had been the Spanish republican ambassador to London. The Jewish Agency, which had accepted the partition resolution, welcomed them and appointed Walter Eytan and me as liaison officers. The Arabs announced a boycott of the commission, totally rejecting the UN resolution. The British, in accordance with the hostile attitude of Bevin and of Sir Henry Gurney, the chief secretary of the Palestine Government and a rabid anti-Zionist, also boycotted the group, refusing to cooperate in any way.

Colonel Ragnvald Alfred Roscher-Lund, the commission member from Norway, was an honest and outspoken career officer with whom I became very close. (He was later posted as military attaché to the Soviet Union, and when he did not hide his views about the regime he was obliged to leave as persona non grata.) I set about proving to him that despite skepticism in UN circles encouraged by the British, who maintained that we would be wiped out after they left, we could and assuredly would overcome our problems. The British and Arab attitude toward the commission members made my job a lot easier. I got word to Ben-Gurion that it was crucial to get them on our side, and he gave me full support. I believe I was quite successful in showing that Israel could survive as an independent unit. Roscher-Lund's reports were certainly supportive.

On 1 March 1948, I took Roscher-Lund to lunch with Reuven Shiloach, an intimate advisor to Ben-Gurion. Aura had become assistant to one of our great scientists, Aaron Katchalski, in a Haganah department set up to mobilize scientific ability for our defense effort. Unbeknownst to me, she had a meeting at the Jewish Agency that morning with Leo Kohn, head of the Political Department. Leo had ensconced himself in Golda Meir's room, right above the entrance; my office was down the corridor.

Nearby was Ben-Gurion's. Like the other members of the Agency, he was then in Tel Aviv. While I was bantering with the secretaries, there was a tremendous explosion and the world went black. After getting my bearings, I opened the door and a thick cloud of dust rolled into the room. Gradually, ghostlike apparitions began to grope their way out of the rubble, and blood was everywhere. Shiloach's cheek was gashed (leaving a lifelong scar); Elias Sasson, later a minister in the State of Israel, had blood pouring from his forehead; Gershon Avner, in the office next to mine, was covered with blood and blinded from glass shards.

Rushing into the corridor, I saw Aura lying amid the ruins. Stunned, I asked her, "What are *you* doing here?" She had been so concerned about my fate that she fainted when she saw me. With the help of Aaron Katchalski, I carried her down to an ambulance. In the back lying on a stretcher was the headless corpse of the guard who moments before had become suspicious of a car parked in front of the Agency. When he attempted to move it, a powerful bomb blew it up. I covered the body with a blanket and we were rushed to Bikur Holim Hospital. Aura had a bad concussion, and her eyesight was in danger. Delayed shock laid her up for almost two months. To this day, she has many scars in her scalp.

Seventy people were wounded in that explosion and thirteen killed, including our very close friend, Zionist leader Leib Jaffe. Although the Jewish Agency was in the most heavily guarded area of Jerusalem, it was still vulnerable. The car with the bomb belonged to the American vice-consul.

It had driven up and was admitted into the courtyard, having been stolen that day by the vice-consul's Arab driver.

Assured that Aura was being well cared for, I arrived at Roscher-Lund's cellar office in the security zone. Only then did I realize that I was covered with dust and my shirt was soaked with blood. I took Roscher-Lund to the Agency and showed him the ruins. Workers were already laying bricks and repairing the internal damage to the building. As secretaries cleaned up and workers moved silently carrying bricks, his eyes filled with tears. "Such a nation will never be defeated," he said.

Every day brought its dead, its wounded, its maimed. Sheer logic dictated that we stood no chance of survival. However adverse our circumstances would later become, they never descended to the depths of 1948, when our daily existence hung on a fragile thread. But we were too preoccupied with survival to understand or appreciate what little hope we had. A special feeling united us as a people, and we had no alternative. If we wanted to live as we wished to live—as we knew we had to live—we had to face the shocks and adversity.

Jerusalem was eventually so besieged that food and supplies could be brought up from the coast only by convoy. Our security personnel, guarding the convoys with a minimum of weapons, had to face overwhelming numbers of Arabs as well as the blatant hostility of the remaining British troops. Although any Arab or Jew risked a death sentence for carrying weapons, the British rarely enforced the law. When they did, they invariably disarmed our personnel, leaving them at the mercy of the Arab mobs.

While showing Roscher-Lund our military capabilities around the country, we came upon the tail end of a convoy moving slowly toward Jerusalem. It was a motley collection of trucks, loaded with produce, negotiating the hills with great difficulty. Many trucks had armored cabins for the drivers, and the convoy was escorted by the armored "tin boxes" of the Palmach. Their youthful faces looked at us curiously as we passed by. As we entered Jerusalem, crowds awaited the convoy, for the food and medical supplies made the difference between continuing our struggle or giving in—and being massacred. This convoy was one of the last to reach Jerusalem before the siege became total. The Hadassah convoy, several days later, did not. Perhaps no adversity was as tragic as what happened to that convoy.

The Hadassah convoy, much like the one we had passed, was moving from Jerusalem to Mount Scopus, filled with doctors, nurses, and medical supplies bound for the Hadassah Hospital's exhausted staff. Arabs intercepted the convoy and surrounded it for hours, pouring murderous fire into the vehicles while British forces stood by, watching passively; the seven-hour attack left seventy-seven dead. Of twenty-eight people saved, only eight were unhurt. Doctors, nurses, and hospital workers were massacred in full view of a British military unit.

At this point, Ben-Gurion decided to move to the attack. A supply of weapons from Czechoslovakia, mainly rifles, landed secretly by air, bypassing the British embargo. Within four days, the largest Jewish force activated so far, comprising 1,500 men, launched Operation Nachshon, designed to capture the heights along the road to Jerusalem, including Latrun. This territory was crucial if additional convoys were to reach Jerusalem. My task was to activate our friends among the British so that their reaction would be minimal to nonexistent.

The bloody seesaw battle went on for almost a week not only at Latrun but also at Kastel, an ancient Roman encampment and Crusader castle that dominates the closest approaches to Jerusalem. The death of Abdel Kader el-Husseini, one of the most powerful and popular guerrilla leaders, had a devastating effect on the Arabs' morale. (His son, Faisal Husseini, was to conduct political negotiations with Israel on behalf of the Palestinians almost fifty years later.) The Haganah finally gained control, and three of the largest convoys ever assembled managed to reach the city. The final convoy saw heavy fire, with many killed and wounded, and six trucks were abandoned. My secretary Rachel's husband, Maccabi Moseri, was killed in this battle. When it was over, Jerusalem was saved. At least for the moment.

IN 1948, THE TRADITIONAL Passover seder was held in a city under constant shelling by the Arab Legion. The most familiar sound in the streets was from whizzing bullets, and every household had its collection of spent shrapnel. Because the cemeteries were now cut off, a makeshift graveyard was opened at Sheikh Bader near the western approaches to Jerusalem. As the battle became fiercer and the siege tightened, bodies were buried in back gardens. A wild weed that was edible and could be cooked became a staple. A city of 100,000 was quickly reaching the stage where each inhabitant would be living on three slices of bread a day, with one pail of water per family for drinking, cooking, and washing.

My father tried to help stop the destruction of the Holy City, cabling Christian religious leaders worldwide to rally support against the profaning of Jerusalem. But it was to no avail—the Christian world was not interested. On the eve of Passover he went to the central seder of the troops to impart his strong belief and faith that Providence would guide us through this seemingly impossible situation. I, too, believed in Providence, but not in leaving our future in its hands only. I believed in fighting for that future.

My wartime experience stood me in good stead. Walking with Aura in Jerusalem, I suddenly heard a familiar whistle, immediately threw her to the ground, and flattened myself against the pavement. A split-second later, a mortar shell crashed into the street and exploded not more than fifty feet away. Others were not so lucky. One of our friends walked out of his house with his wife. Within one step, she dropped dead by his side, struck in the head by a bullet.

By 26 April, when the central post office closed down, the stores of Jerusalem had long since been emptied, and tax collection had ceased. The Jerusalem Municipality no longer met, as the Jewish members turned themselves into a council. The British, aware of the gradual takeover by local authorities of their central authority, would neither condone it nor surrender any portion of their sovereignty to enable the country to be administered in any form.

At the end of April and the beginning of May the Palmach attacked the Arab-held area of Katamon in Jerusalem. I was asked to try to work out a cease-fire in Katamon by Brigadier C. P. Jones, who commanded the Second British Brigade. As an intelligence officer in Germany, I knew him when he was chief of staff of the 30th British Corps. Surveying the Katamon battlefront, he turned to me and said, "Just like old times." "Yes," I replied, without a smile, "but this is different. This time we're not on the same side."

I began my negotiation with the Arab representative, Anwar Nusseibeh. Later the Jordanian minister of defense and ambassador to the Court of St. James's, he would eventually become the unofficial ambassador of King Hussein in Jerusalem, but at that time he refused to meet with me face-to-face. An Arab would not dignify a Jew with a direct meeting. Jones had to go back and forth between our two adjacent rooms, carrying proposals and counterproposals. My purpose was, in fact, not to make a negotiated settlement but to drag out the talks; it was clear to us that we would soon complete the capture of Katamon. My stalling was quite successful and years later Anwar Nusseibeh told me that he still resented the manner in which he had been outmaneuvered.

We were now preparing for the final withdrawal of the British, and all the planning in Jerusalem centered on our takeover of the security zones as soon as the British evacuated them. Along with Eliezer Kaplan, the senior member of the Jewish Agency left in Jerusalem and later the first minister of finance in the State of Israel, I met with General Gordon Macmillan, who was commanding the British forces in Palestine. We tried to come to an understanding whereby we would be allowed to take over specified areas by agreement with the British, thus avoiding unnecessary bloodshed. Macmillan was sympathetic, but he clearly believed that we would not survive for very long after the British left. We accomplished little and said farewell. He was obviously not happy about the manner in which the British were leaving, but it was equally obvious that he could do nothing about it.

On 7 May 1948, seven days before our official declaration of independence, Lieutenant Colonel Oscar Norman, chief of military intelligence, invited me to meet him at General Macmillan's residence. Seven British soldiers had died in an attack near Tel Mond by the Stern Group, and the British were now prepared to take violent action against the Jews. As a first step, every armored vehicle—the only thing that ensured what little freedom of travel we had—would be confiscated and destroyed. I protested that the entire community could not be held responsible for the actions of a small group, but he was not sympathetic. Later that evening Roscher-Lund told me that the British were looking forward to additional operations by the Stern Group so they could settle accounts with the Jews once and for all. He was convinced that this time the British were extremely serious.

On the morning of Friday, 14 May, the British flag was lowered in Jerusalem, and Sir Alan Cunningham, the high commissioner for Palestine, drove out of Jerusalem in his bulletproof Daimler followed by the last British civilians and troops. Units of the Haganah moved rapidly to take over the evacuated offices and positions. The thirty-year British rule of Palestine had ended with a blot on their record, a period of shameful and disgraceful behavior in their long and proud history.

As soon as the British were gone, the firing intensified, and Jerusalem became an inferno. Artillery and mortar shells poured into the Jewish half of the city, machine guns stuttered, and rifle shots crackled as bullets flew everywhere. All hell had broken loose. Shaltiel, the commander of Jerusalem, asked me to make my way to the French consulate general, in the dangerous no-man's-land between the King David Hotel and the Jaffa Gate of the Old City. René Neuville, the consul general, was a member of the so-called Consular Truce Commission. He, along with the American consul general, Thomas C. Wesson, and the Belgian consul general, Jean Nieuwenhuys, had been trying to negotiate a cease-fire with the Arabs. Their attempts did absolutely no good; Wesson was, in fact, killed by an Arab sniper. Shaltiel wanted me to reach Neuville as a desperate means of reaching a cease-fire, and he gave me full authority to agree to it. A driver from the Jewish Agency took me at breakneck speed to the consul. We passed an area of large pipes, prepared for construction, lying in an open area, approximately where the Hebrew Union College now stands. Hiding in the pipes were Arab snipers, and a bullet grazed my driver's head. He would never again have to bother parting his hair.

The consulate lay between the two front lines between the Old City walls and the Jewish city. Shells and bullets were landing everywhere. Sixty French citizens had moved into the consulate for protection. In addition, Neuville had arrogated to himself a particular status, both as a Catholic dignitary and as the French representative in Jerusalem. Seeing himself responsible for the Holy City, he held decided opinions on France's special role as defender of the faith in the Holy Land. He was convinced that Jerusalem must be internationalized, and while generally friendly to the Zionist cause, he passionately rejected any claim we had on the city. Highly nervous, excitable, and quick to anger, he was not exactly the best interlocutor in negotiations for a cease-fire. Eight of Neuville's nine children were in the consulate at the time, and every time the building was hit by a bullet or a shell landed nearby, he would erupt in an explosion of uncontrollable hysteria. To say the least, it required a lot of patience to talk to him. Because of the constant spray of bullets, many of which flew through the windows, we spent most of our time crouched on the floor. Nieuwenhuys was also there, along with my friend Roscher-Lund.

I advised Neuville that I was authorized to negotiate a cease-fire, and he immediately telephoned his contact on the Arab side, who agreed to a temporary cease-fire. I phoned Shaltiel to tell him of the time of the cease-fire; orders were issued to the Jewish forces. But a few minutes after the announcement, heavy firing broke out from one of the Arab sectors. I was in the consulate from midday until 9 P.M., as the same pattern of events kept repeating itself. Each time we negotiated a new cease-fire, the Arabs—who had no control over the irregular groups operating—took advantage of it to open fire and bombard us. At one point, a mortar shell landed on the grounds of the consulate. Neuville broke down completely and hurled epithets at me, accusing the Jewish forces of trying to kill everyone in the consulate. Roscher-Lund, one of the few to remain calm,

went out into the garden to see the hole created by the explosion, and
told Neuville that the mortar that fired the shell was sited in the Arab Old
City. Roscher-Lund said that he had unjustly vilified me.

I knew that Ben-Gurion would announce the creation of a Jewish
State that afternoon, although I had no details and certainly not the name
of the state. At 4 P.M., with everybody sitting around morosely and ner-
vously, listening to the shooting and shelling and waiting for yet another
telephone call from the Old City telling us that the Arabs had agreed to
yet another cease-fire, I announced to Neuville and Nieuwenhuys, "I
wish to make it clear to you now that as from this moment I represent a
Jewish State which has just been proclaimed." This was all Neuville
needed in order to throw yet another tantrum. He launched into a diatribe against the Jewish State, the Jews and Arabs in particular, and as
near as I could tell, against everybody else he'd ever met or heard of.
Roscher-Lund came over demonstratively, shook hands, and congratu-
lated me on our independence.

Inside the French consulate, I didn't feel very independent. Bullets
came through the open windows, and by nightfall six of us were wounded.
Madame Neuville, in direct contrast to her husband, remained calm
throughout the proceedings and even brought a makeshift meal for those
in our negotiating room. Despite the extreme danger, she did not forget
to serve a good French wine. Avoiding the bullets, she crawled on the
floor to pour it.

After nightfall—and countless cease-fires—I proposed that we attempt
to get back to the Jewish city. I would take anybody who wished to go,
including the wounded. After notifying the Haganah headquarters, our
group, which included Nieuwenhuys, Roscher-Lund, several others who
opted to accompany us, and the six wounded, moved stealthily out of the
building along the narrow road. Roughly opposite the entrance to the
Apostolic Delegation we negotiated a break in the wall of the King David
Hotel, slowly making our way through the gardens, to the thump of
mortar shells and the staccato of machine-gun and rifle fire, under a sky
lit by the crisscross paths of tracer bullets. The doors leading into the
large hall were smashed, the curtains torn and flapping, doors swung in
the wind. Apart from the shooting, nothing could be heard but the bang-
ing of open doors and windows and the tinkle of glass as a bullet shattered yet another pane. We crossed the central reception hall and made
our way out into the street facing the YMCA. We had no idea where our
forces were as we groped our way to what we hoped would be safety. It
was pitch black—electricity had long since been cut off in the city—as

we moved slowly toward the corner of King George Avenue and what is now Jabotinsky Street. Suddenly, out of the darkness, some figures emerged. They were Jewish soldiers. When I saw Aura that night, I realized that when I left her to go to the French consulate that morning, she had not expected to see me alive again.

Between 15 May and 11 June our civilian casualties reached 1,738, including 316 killed. The capture of Jerusalem was the major objective of the Arab armies, even as life-and-death struggles were going on throughout the country. News filtered in of the fall of the Etzion Bloc on the Hebron Road after a frontal attack by the Arab Legion forces. After a heavy battle the survivors surrendered, only to be murdered in Kfar Etzion by the Arab irregulars and villagers. Those who fell into the hands of the Arab Legion were treated as prisoners of war and transferred to the prison camp at Mafrak in Transjordan. The tragedy unraveling before us could be measured by the increasing number of bereaved who attended the synagogue services on Saturdays.

Water no longer flowed through the city's pipes. To receive their daily ration from the water tanks, people lined up with their containers at fixed places and fixed times, despite the sniping. Very little fuel remained, and in the first week of May all bus and private-car traffic ceased. Fuel was rationed and allowed only for the military, for ambulances, and for essential hospitals, bakeries, and industrial plants. The gloomy stillness that pervaded the city was broken only by the explosions of shells and the rattle of gunfire. Business was paralyzed; there was no contact with relatives or friends outside the city. Everyone was treated equally, which contributed considerably to morale. There was no distinction between the ultra-Orthodox and the nonreligious, or between the rich and the poor. The spirit that sustained us came, I believe, from a collective feeling that we could not and would not be defeated, that ultimately we had to be victorious.

CHAPTER 7

The Struggle for Independence

THE WAR OF INDEPENDENCE was, in essence, Israel's only chance to prove that it could survive without the protection of the British Mandate. Now that we were left to defend ourselves, most of the world—especially the Arab world—expected us to wilt in the face of powerful anti-Israel forces or, in the event of hostilities, to be wiped out. But we had spent two thousand years searching for an established homeland. Now that we had one, it was inconceivable that we would give it up.

The odds were definitely against us. We were able to mobilize a force of only 45,000, which included some 30,000 men and women whose functions were basically limited to local defense, particularly in the villages; it took time before they could be included in the field forces. That left us at the outset with a full-fledged fighting core of 15,000. Our air force consisted of eleven single-engine light aircraft. Our navy had a few motorboats, several frogmen, and about 350 men whose main experience was smuggling immigrants into the country. Despite the popular conception, our army was not particularly unified or disciplined. The two right-wing underground organizations, the Irgun, under the command of Menachem Begin, and the Lehi, or Stern Group, which had never accepted the authority of the Haganah Command, were integrated into the Israeli army only after serious struggles and internecine bloodshed.

The war had erupted as a series of urban hit-and-run encounters that left scores of dead, maimed, and wounded civilians. Our transport systems were under constant attack, and many attempts were made to cut communications between Jewish centers. But the main worry, even greater than the attacks on isolated Jewish settlements, was that once the regular Arab armies entered the war, our positions in Jerusalem would be seriously threatened.

ON 21 MAY 1948 Yigael Yadin, the chief of operations of the Israel Defense Forces, ordered me to report to Tel Aviv. I said farewell to my parents and to Aura, knowing that this parting could well be our last. Being an Israeli in time of war—which in those years was basically all the time —created new norms, and people's lives faded into the background. We tried to behave unemotionally but nonetheless, whenever I parted from Aura, I felt as if I were leaving part of myself behind.

I made my way to the makeshift landing strip in the Valley of the Cross. A Piper plane landed to pick me up but the plane had aroused the interest of the enemy and shells began dropping around us. I clambered on board and the young pilot immediately took off for Tel Aviv. It was not exactly what I would call a good omen.

Yadin told me that Shlomo Shamir was establishing a new armored brigade and wanted me for his second in command. The brigade would try to take Latrun, the key to controlling the approach to Jerusalem.

Located on the road to Jerusalem, Latrun sits atop the Valley of Ayalon, the scene of battles of Joshua, the Maccabees, and Allenby's army, the perfect strategic location for a military stronghold. Control Latrun and you can block anyone attempting to get into or out of Jerusalem. And when the Seventh Brigade was formed, Latrun was controlled by the Arabs.

Shamir ordered the brigade into battle immediately. I told him that it made no military sense whatsoever to attack without adequate intelligence, proper training, and, in many cases, with soldiers who were new immigrants who had been imprisoned in camps by the British and barely knew how to handle a rifle. Furthermore, mortars had not yet arrived, there was no artillery, we had no air support, and the brigade was missing a key piece of equipment—water bottles. We were to attack in a heavy heat wave, through fields of ripened wheat covered by clouds of irritating flies, using soldiers who were completely unaccustomed to the brutal heat and the local conditions. In short, we'd be a primitive army charging up a hill to be slaughtered.

Shamir's request for postponement of the attack was not greeted enthusiastically. Ben-Gurion had decided that Jewish Jerusalem could be saved only by taking Latrun and opening up a supply road; any military activity at Latrun would tie down the Arab Legion and prevent their moving forces into Jerusalem. In response to our cable, we received one signed by Yadin, the chief of operations: we were to attack "at all costs."

In fact, Israeli forces had taken control of Latrun in April, in the so-called Nachshon Operation. However, because of the steady advance of Egyptian forces from the south toward Tel Aviv, and our fear that they would reach what is present-day Ashdod—another site we could not afford to lose—the Givati Brigade, whose forces were holding Latrun, was ordered to withdraw only weeks after capturing it. From 15 to 18 May, Latrun was empty. Then, on the 18th, the Arab Legion moved the bulk of its forces as Glubb Pasha, its English commander, realized its vital central importance. If our brigade had moved one week earlier, we would have met only the opposition of local villagers. Instead, we were about to attack an area held by two battalions of the highly trained Arab Legion, which was commanded and led by British officers and was the best-trained military force in the Arab world. Glubb Pasha was completely devoted to the Arab cause.

Our mission was to open the road to Jerusalem and move a convoy of desperately needed supplies that stood by at Ekron, ready to follow our brigade into the beleaguered city. The brigade was then to advance into the mountains toward Ramallah, north of Jerusalem, thereby removing Arab pressure in that area. It was to be coordinated with operations by the Palmach Harel Brigade in the Jerusalem Corridor, which would strike north from Kiryat Anavim and Bab-el-Wad toward Ramallah, as well as by the Etzioni Brigade in Jerusalem itself.

Meanwhile, we had moved forward to Kibbutz Hulda, where we established our headquarters. The attack was planned for shortly before midnight on Saturday, 22 May. The 32nd Battalion of the Alexandroni Brigade was ordered to capture the police station and the village of Latrun. A battalion of the Seventh Brigade was to cover Alexandroni's right flank in order to secure the Jerusalem road.

But the timing and discipline were woefully faulty. Instead of attacking toward midnight, under cover of darkness, the Alexandroni battalion was not ready to move until 4 A.M. the following morning, just as the first rays of dawn appeared. By the time the advance unit reached the Latrun–Jerusalem road, it was in full view of the defending Arab Legion. Completely exposed, the Israelis came under withering fire that obviated any possibility of attack. It suffered serious casualties and was forced to withdraw almost immediately.

Simultaneously, the battalion covering the right flank came under fire from Arab irregulars occupying the villages of Beit Jiz and Beit Sussin, which we had assumed were empty. As we tried to extricate ourselves, sniping from the flanks and rear intensified. The Arab Legion and artillery pounded the area mercilessly. Broken and in disarray, we struggled to retreat to the high ground, held as a firm base by the Alexandroni battalion. The first battle for Latrun was over, a major defeat.

After analyzing our mistakes, we decided to change strategy. We would attack and occupy the villages of Beit Jiz and Beit Sussin, which would give us a line along the high ground facing Latrun. Even if we failed to take the main road, this would help get supplies into Jerusalem. We decided to adopt a form of rank insignia so that troops would recognize their commanders, thus allaying much of the battlefield confusion. Equipment arrived and our troops were trained to use it, but we still had no supporting artillery. Intelligence was almost nonexistent, and all we could rely on was our own patrolling; we held no prisoners and received no indication from GHQ about the nature and strength of the forces facing us. Our untrained troops couldn't tell the difference between armored cars and tanks.

At this point, one of the special figures of the war, Mickey Marcus, arrived. Colonel Marcus was a retired American Jewish army officer whom Shlomo Shamir had convinced to help train the emerging Israeli army. Courageous, athletic, and extroverted, he had unusual leadership abilities and could adapt to the informal and ill-organized partisan type of army being created under fire out of an underground force. He participated in many operations himself, gaining the respect of Israeli commanders, who regarded outsiders with considerable suspicion. He would later be designated to command the entire Jerusalem front and create a divisional force that would take on the entire Arab Legion. But his immediate goal was to capture Latrun.

Marcus knew we could not repeat our disastrous tactics; and Yadin's cable, ignoring our plea for postponement and ordering us to move forward "at all costs," enraged him. It was grounds for a court-martial, he felt. This time, our brigade would again advance on the police fortress at Latrun, but the 52nd Battalion of the Givati Brigade, attached to us, would move to the right of the attacking forces and take the villages overlooking the village and fortress. This would cut off the Latrun enclave and trap the Arab forces therein unless they rapidly withdrew—which would be equally acceptable. We had received a number of ancient 65mm French guns (called Napoleonchiks, to reflect their age and ineffectiveness). The attack began in darkness, as three battalions led by an "armored" battalion under the command of Haim Laskov moved toward the fortress. The 52nd battalion under the command of Colonel Yaakov Prulov advanced as planned across the road to Jerusalem and made for two villages, Deir Ayub, halfway up the Latrun hill, and Yalu at its summit. We did not know that Arab forces had already begun to withdraw for fear of being cut off. They anticipated our strategy but had no plan to counterattack.

Laskov's forces entered the police fortress under devastating fire. The people of Israel were fighting for their very existence, and that meant *all* people, men *and* women. I can still recall with emotion the death of one radio operator, a young girl called Hadassah Lipshitz. She was in one of the halftracks, a light armored truck, left over from World War II and primitive even at the time. She was on the radio to us at headquarters when she was shot—and she talked to us, getting weaker and weaker, until the moment she died. As a staff officer, one who plans the battles, you don't see the deaths as they happen. You hear noises and you see flames. You only see the death afterward when the bodies are collected. I've never been sure which is worse for commanders, to see those around them go down in the midst of action or to see the cold bodies in the quiet of the aftermath, knowing their heroic sacrifices were made at the commander's direction. I suppose the answer is that both choices are equally terrible and wasteful.

The 52nd Battalion encountered slight opposition and endured a number of wounded. We were on the verge of victory until—for reasons that historians are still endeavoring to discover—it suddenly withdrew. The Arab Legion could breathe again and abandoned their own preparations to withdraw. Marcus rushed to cable Ben-Gurion that the armored battalion had been outstanding and the artillery had operated satisfactorily, but the infantry had been a disgrace. A court-martial was in order. The mysterious pullback cost us victory as well as lives and is the subject of much argument and controversy; none of the opinions and theories is particularly satisfying. We had to try again.

After the first attack, we had cleared the two Arab villages of Beit Jiz and Beit Sussin. After the second battle, we carried out a reconnaissance *parallel* to the Jerusalem–Tel Aviv road at Latrun, sheltered by a range of hills from the Arab Legion observation posts. The reconnaissance group included Mickey Marcus, Shlomo Shamir, our engineering officer, Markowich, and me. We came to an Arab orchard, in which figs and pomegranates grew in abundance. As we advanced along it, our path punctuated by the occasional shelling, we realized the possibility of an alternative road to Jerusalem. The orchard ended on a bluff some four hundred feet high, but if we could negotiate the bluff so that vehicles could move up and down it, we could use that route to move supplies to the city.

I was immediately sent to Tel Aviv and gave Ben-Gurion a list of heavy earthmoving equipment and the number and type of workers required to turn this path into a traversable road. I suggested that we put hundreds of porters at the bluff to take supplies from trucks, which could approach through the orchard. Porters would then carry the supplies to the valley below, where trucks from Jerusalem would be waiting to take the supplies back to the city. Ben-Gurion immediately gave orders to supply every-thing we needed.

This momentous development opened the supply route to Jerusalem even before the first truce was negotiated. Using bulldozers, tractors, and manual labor, the engineers began the nearly impossible task of creating a passable road to the bluff at the head of the orchard and a road to the val-ley below. At night, against the background of Jordanian shelling, the scene was almost unreal: hundreds of porters silently carrying food and supplies down the hill to waiting trucks and jeeps and even mules. Even herds of cows were led along this route because we desperately needed to ship beef into the city. Hollywood later made a movie of this extra-ordinary operation, *Cast a Giant Shadow*, with Kirk Douglas as Mickey Marcus.

After a few days, the road down the hill—hereafter known as the Burma Road—was completed. I cabled headquarters suggesting that for-eign correspondents be sent in, to prove to the outside world, as well as the Arab world, that we no longer depended on the UN to get food into Jerusalem. The journalists reported that we did indeed have our own road to the Holy City.

Soon thereafter, and partly due to the building of the Burma Road, the so-called First Truce was negotiated. The Arabs realized they could not take Jerusalem, could not invade us and push us back into the sea, so for the first time in more than half a year, the guns were silent in the new na-tion of Israel. In the final analysis, despite the failure of the attack, there is no doubt that the struggle for Latrun, which pinned down two Arab Legion battalions, preventing them from moving into Jerusalem, was a prime factor in saving Jewish Jerusalem.

Using the Burma Road, Mickey Marcus went up to Jerusalem in prep-aration for his appointment as commander of the Jerusalem Division. He did not get very far. He stayed with a Palmach battalion at Abu Ghosh, a small Arab village just outside Jerusalem, where he apparently decided to spend the night. In the middle of the night, to answer the call of nature, he climbed over a stone wall on the perimeter of the battalion area, covering himself in a white sheet. Because Abu Ghosh was so near the Arab Legion and guerrilla positions to the north of the Jerusalem–Tel Aviv road, Israeli sentries were on the alert. One sentry, aware that Arabs could attack at any moment, saw an individual dressed in white, which could be traditional Arab garb. The sentry called out for him to halt. The figure in white answered in English, which the sentry knew was spoken by the British commanders of the Arab forces. Without hesitation he fired one round, and his aim was extraordinary. The bullet pierced Marcus's heart, killing him instantly.

Deep sorrow descended as news of Marcus's death spread like wildfire. He was a genuine and beloved hero, devoted to our cause. He had come to Palestine in secret because by helping us he was breaking American law (hence his code name, Stone). His death hit me very hard, for we had talked so much about our dreams for the future. One night I was standing on the Burma Road near the serpentine track that mounted the bluff. People were moving supplies, and the area was covered in a heavy cloud of dust. Suddenly a hush fell as a jeep with a coffin strapped to it slowly made its way up the bluff, moving toward the coast. It was Mickey. His body was on its way to the airport, where it would be flown to West Point for burial. Watching the jeep disappear, we felt orphaned—and in a sense we were.

A few years later, as military attaché in Washington, I was privileged to accompany David Ben-Gurion, on his first visit as prime minister to the United States, to lay a wreath on Mickey's grave.

ALTHOUGH IT WAS still risky, I decided to take the Burma Road and visit my family in Jerusalem, accompanied by Reg Heap, a Canadian who manned a machine gun, and an intrepid driver from the brigade. We drove through the dark silence, expecting to be attacked at every turn and corner, and entered the deserted streets of Jerusalem without incident. If there is any pleasure in going off to war, it comes in returning home from battle. My parents and Aura were beside themselves with joy, but like everybody in Jerusalem they had lost weight and looked drawn and haggard, having been living—literally—hand to mouth. I saw a city existing under cover in shelters or in whatever structures were still standing. I saw people picking weeds for food and burying their dead in backyard gardens, sustained by their determination and inner strength. As in wartime

London, I saw the greatness of a people in extreme adversity, and it thrilled me to the core.

I HAD BEEN COMPLAINING vociferously that there was no professional intelligence organization in the Israel Defense Forces, and at one meeting with Ben-Gurion, I insisted that I was being wasted. The army was suffering casualties because of the absence of an effective intelligence organization. I knew I could change all that. I had not been appointed to military intelligence, despite many pleas, because I had been in the British army—ironically, the very experience that qualified me for it. A ridiculous and politically based rivalry had developed between the Haganah and Palmach forces on one side and those who had served in the British army in World War II and graduated from its ranks on the other. The ex–British army people had a different approach from that of the "partisans" in running an army.

Ben-Gurion favored the former, convinced that the Israelis had to adopt world standards of military strategy and organization. But Yigael Yadin, who was chief of operations (and later deputy prime minister in Menachem Begin's government), had grown up in the Haganah with no formal military experience and was clearly prejudiced against the British army people and approach. I refused to back away. The Haganah intelligence organization (Shai) had no inkling of modern military intelligence organization and procedures. They were incapable of helping us survive the immediate battle and of preparing for future battles. Like anyone in power, they guarded it jealously, and so it was up to Ben-Gurion to cut the Gordian knot and insist that Israeli intelligence be restructured and reorganized. In the final analysis, I was appointed deputy director of military intelligence, working under Isser Beeri, a product of the Haganah school of thinking. We would both have the same rank, however: lieutenant colonel.

As I approached my new job, I was wary of the political entanglements and conscious of the responsibility on my shoulders, but I was thrilled and satisfied. I was going to be one of the principal architects of the brand-new Israeli military intelligence organization.

CHAPTER 8

Intelligence—Phase I

ISRAELI MILITARY INTELLIGENCE is now considered one of the best organizations of its kind in the world. This was not always the case, nor was it a simple matter to build the organization into what it is today.

Before statehood, Israel's military intelligence was controlled by the Shai, which was developed by the underground Haganah. Historically, this makes perfect sense. Palestine had been besieged by sporadic outbreaks of violence ever since the early 1920s. Arab political resistance to the Balfour Declaration and, later, to the Palestine Mandate, led to rioting and attacks against Jews, which became more serious and violent as time passed. Massive riots, including vicious attacks on isolated Jewish settlements and populations, took place in August 1929, and prolonged guerrilla warfare developed over the next several years. To combat it, Jewish volunteers were mobilized to concentrate on defending settlements and lines of communication. But because of the exigencies of the situation, the Haganah, which organized these military volunteers, gradually began to become a quasi-military organization designed to face up to the new Arab threat.

During the Arab revolt (1936–39) the Haganah developed its intelligence organization, the Shai, an acronym for Sherut Yediot, or information service. A security service combined with a form of intelligence service, the Shai handled all aspects of defense for the Jewish community and mounted intelligence operations against Arab organizations and centers of activity. Many Jews who could pass freely as Arabs did so as spies in the service of the Shai. As a result, every Arab village was mapped out to the last detail, and there were files on every Arab community covering population, weapons, topography, and defenses.

At the head of the Shai in early 1948 was Isser Beeri. Tall and domineering, he had grown up as part of the Jewish establishment in Mandatory Palestine. He was quiet and taciturn, but his calm demeanor frequently belied his zealotry and extremism—traits that would ultimately end his career. Although charming and personable, he was extraordinarily ruthless, bore grudges, and harbored hatreds. It would not be much of an exaggeration to liken him to some of the heads of Soviet intelligence and security. He was single-minded and tough with a degree of intransigent fanaticism.

At the beginning of the War of Independence, there was no intelligence organization capable of providing the basic and current information required by our army. The Shai's informants were not always reliable, and their reports were somewhat suspect because of their lack of military background. It was impossible to evaluate any information that arrived from the Arab world; the unprofessionalism of our system made it impossible to collate or check it or separate the important from the unimportant. The intelligence organization, such as it was, repeatedly failed to correctly evaluate invasion plans of the Arab armies. Before the first Latrun attack, for example, the Seventh Brigade received "intelligence" that led us to believe that we would be attacking Arab irregulars rather than the Arab Legion. This crucial error caused unnecessary deaths and much suffering. Between the first round of irregular fighting (29 November 1947–15 May 1948) and regular battles leading to the First Truce (15 May 1948–10 June 1948), the absence of valid intelligence could be directly linked to the loss of life we suffered. The political, emotional, and ethical effects of these losses forced the issue of intelligence gathering to the forefront of political thinking.

It was Ben-Gurion who decided to reform the entire Israeli intelligence organization, on the urging of Reuven Shiloach, one of his principal advisors. Ben-Gurion was not a professional, by any means, but, as with many areas of military strategy and organization, his instincts were accurate and superb. After consultations with Chief of Staff Yaakov Dori and Shiloach, he ordered the dissolution of the Shai, and the transfer of its functions to other bodies proceeded immediately. On 12 July 1948, Ben-Gurion noted in his diary:

Together with Reuven [Shiloach], the functions of Isser [Beeri] and [Chaim] Herzog were decided upon. They will deal with combat military intelligence, the security of the armed forces and counterintelligence, radio monitoring, censorship, special operations. They will have a central service [corps] and services [representative sections] in the brigades.

Isser Beeri will run the service. His principal deputy will be Chaim Herzog, who will also represent the service on the General Staff. The monthly budget will be 13,000 Israeli pounds, in addition to the maintenance of the soldiers. I have issued orders on this subject.

I had a clear picture of what I wanted: an organization that would encompass every aspect of intelligence work. The Haganah's fieldwork had to be translated into modern military terms. First of all, the director of military intelligence had to be the intelligence officer of the chief of staff as well as of the general staff; thereby he would have a direct link to the crucial decision makers. He had to be backed up by departments headed by experts who specialized in each of the Arab armies facing us. We also needed a specialist to cover the local Palestinians and their activities. I had to create a situation in which Israel would never be taken by surprise. To ensure our very existence, we had to always be several steps ahead of our hostile neighbors.

We immediately began an enormous research operation based not only on information gathered clandestinely but also on the vast material readily available to every intelligence service in the world. It has never been popularly recognized that openly published material—technical magazines, scholarly publications, mainstream books and newspapers published in nations with a free press, and international media—can be the most important source of intelligence. It was essential to have a section that would set up a central library devoted to subjects of interest to students of the Middle East, a section that would receive and read the Arab press and monitor public radio stations of Arab countries, and a section that would subscribe to and cover professional publications from all over the world relating to every aspect of the Middle East. Furthermore, we required a section for collecting and producing detailed maps, which would place its knowledge and resources at the service of all the other departments.

According to my plan, the collection division would control all activities whose purpose was clandestine as well as overt gathering of information. The leading element was (and is) electromagnetic monitoring, primarily of radio traffic at all levels, including the technical level—among brigades and field units. We immediately began to organize air reconnaissance and air photography capability and to develop agent. who could operate behind enemy lines and in enemy countries and report on developments and deployment. For the interrogation of prisoners we required trained personnel—and we had to begin training that personnel.

Intelligence from the collection division would then be funneled into the research division, which would absorb and evaluate it and produce military estimates for the command and political leadership level. Our next objective was to develop a department for editing the assembled material and conclusions arising from it. We began to assemble a team that could distribute selected information to the command level as rapidly as possible.

The next major element was security and counterintelligence. It was quite clear that our enemies would be trying to do exactly what we were trying to do, and this effort obviously had to be blocked. For this purpose, a field security division was established, based on the British system, with responsibility for internal security and counterespionage within the armed forces. An adjunct to this responsibility was military censorship, to prevent the publication of classified material—indeed, of any material of possible use to the enemy. We had an advantage here: most of the people involved in this work under the British in World War II were readily available, and we moved quickly to bring them into the fold. With these departments in place, we could concentrate on filling in the gaps—for instance, other aspects of security and intelligence were covered by the department controlling military attachés sent abroad, whose job was to include being part of the effort to collect military intelligence. With extra work in this area, we were able to prevent unnecessary leaks.

When my plan was ready and documented—with a reasonably realistic budget—I met with Isser Beeri in one of the Shai's hideouts, which fronted as a book publishing company on Ben-Yehuda Street in Tel Aviv. Beeri confirmed his understanding of Ben-Gurion's instructions, acknowledging that I was exclusively responsible for both the military intelligence aspects of our new organization and for creating the departments that would form the basis of the new military intelligence corps. I understood that, as the nominal head, he would deal with matters outside the scope of military intelligence. I made it clear that I would represent the organization and be responsible for presenting any intelligence evaluations to the chief of staff and the general staff. On 20 August 1948 I presented the plan to Ben-Gurion.

One thing I was not privy to—it later came as a total surprise—was that Beeri had retained exclusive control of a special operations unit, a kind of private army that was a holdover from the Shai's internal security division. This unit operated in secret for six months and, on one occasion, was allegedly used to falsely incriminate someone who was, in Beeri's view, suspect. In December 1948, it was exposed in a huge and painful national scandal. The body of a murdered Arab informant, Ali Kassem, was discovered. It was rumored that, suspected of treason and of being a double agent, he had been killed on Beeri's instructions.

This was just the beginning of the discoveries of Beeri's alleged abuses of power.

Soon after I joined them, intelligence acquired a large house (called the Green House) in Jaffa. In my office there I found in a desk drawer a military beret, a pipe, and some personal papers and photos. After a bit of digging around, I discovered that they all belonged to Meir Tubiansky, a major in the British army in World War II. I knew a little about him. In June 1948, he had simply disappeared, and his wife came to my father, in his role as chief rabbi, for help in finding him. It was most perplexing and disturbing that Major Tubiansky's possessions had now surfaced in the Green House.

Investigators discovered that during the siege of Jerusalem the Shai had concluded that Jordanian artillery was firing on targets in Jerusalem that were stations for generating electricity. The supply of electricity was directed by the Haganah. Suspicion fell on Tubiansky, the go-between of the Haganah and the electricity authorities, who were British and were regarded as very pro-Arab. Tubiansky was summarily arrested by the Shai and at the outset of the First Truce was taken to an Arab village, Beit Jiz in the Latrun area. Beeri ran a so-called field court-martial that was nothing more than a kangaroo court. Although he denied any wrongdoing, Tubiansky was sentenced to death with no recourse to proper legal procedures. A firing squad of Palmach soldiers was sent to the village, told that he was a spy, and executed him within hours of his trial. When the story emerged, Ben-Gurion ordered an inquiry, and Isser Beeri and the members of his so-called court were arraigned in October 1949.

A dignified Beeri behaved like a soldier during his trial. He assumed full personal responsibility, refusing to implicate anyone, and showed no remorse. One of the most damning transgressions was that in an attempt to prove that Abba Khoushi, the mayor of Haifa and a prominent labor leader, was unpatriotic, Beeri had allegedly falsified documents that he submitted to Ben-Gurion.

Isser Beeri was convicted, sentenced to a day in jail, and dismissed from the army in disgrace. He died a few years later, sick, forlorn, and broken. Major Tubiansky was posthumously rehabilitated and buried in the central military cemetery with full honors.

THE MOST AMAZING aspect of the Israeli system at that time was the extent to which it was dominated by the personality of David Ben-Gurion. He ruled with an iron hand and could be ruthless, especially in going after his opponents on the left wing. He had a longtime bitter rivalry with Dr. Chaim Weizmann, the great scientist and Zionist leader who became Israel's first president, and was determined to limit the authority of the office. That's why the position was considered ceremonial for so many years—not for any parliamentary or legal reason but because our first prime minister so opposed our first president.

But Ben-Gurion overcame his flaws and built up powerful national support. The genius of his vision was nothing less than the creation of the State of Israel and an army to keep it alive. Any problem concerning that vision could be resolved only by Ben-Gurion. He dealt with an enormous number of political matters, one of which was my intelligence plan. He approved it almost immediately.

One rarely meets a figure like Ben-Gurion. He was frequently preoccupied with minor issues and even minor administrative chores (he personally wrote his notebooks with a carbon copy, noting the details of every meeting in his office). Yet in making major decisions he revealed a quick perception and understanding even of subjects and issues in which he had no expertise, and he exerted his authority so that the decision was implemented. Looking back, I sometimes find it difficult to realize that I was privileged to know and serve him.

Immediately after he approved my proposals, I began to search for anyone with military intelligence experience in the British army. The special Arab Reconnaissance Unit of the Palmach was transferred to us. Composed of fluent Arabic speakers who could pass as Arabs in Arab districts, it operated with extraordinary danger to its members; two of them were executed by the Egyptians as spies in Gaza, and a third went to his death on the gallows in Amman, Jordan, never revealing that he was Jewish. The unit set up bases of operations in Damascus and Beirut, using appropriate "covers" and transferring intelligence from behind Arab lines to the Israeli forces. It even created an interurban taxi service between Damascus and Beirut.

In the search for former British army personnel, we combed the staffs of universities, where we found willing recruits who had worked with the

British forces in interception of radio traffic, carrying communications intelligence, and related areas. We also found officers who had been involved in Royal Air Force intelligence work, and libraries and research institutes supplied personnel able to take advantage of the most important source of intelligence, published material. A Dutch officer who had served in Java and had been a Japanese prisoner of war became the intelligence officer of our central command.

During the war, I had attended a course organized by MI-9, of the Department of Military Intelligence in the British War Office, which planned the escape of prisoners held in German camps. The War of Independence had dragged on long enough so that we had a considerable number of Israeli prisoners of war in Jordan. It became clear that we had to organize direct contact with them and begin to plan for their escape. A recent immigrant, John Furman, had been a major in the British army and held the Military Cross for his actions in escaping from an Italian prisoner-of-war camp. Entrusted to set up a department in Israeli intelligence, he soon organized direct contact with Israeli prisoners in Mafrak, Jordan, sent direct instructions, and began facilitating their escape. Before any practical use could be made of this advance, an armistice was signed with Jordan, and the prisoners were returned to Israel. But now we had the know-how—and the means to use it.

In August 1948 we opened a course for intelligence personnel. Our new organization was being recognized as successful, and we soon expanded it, producing for the army a reserve of intelligence officers to serve at the battalion, brigade, and command levels. Intelligence was now being scientifically evaluated, edited, and distributed in daily, weekly, and monthly intelligence reports. We set up departments capable of handling enemy documents, interpreting aerial photographs, producing maps, and conducting prisoner-of-war interrogations. We were soon coordinating the efforts of air force intelligence and naval intelligence, and the heads of both sections became part of my immediate staff. All the time I had a major struggle with army authorities trying to obtain priority in the allocation of personnel with a suitable standard of educational, technological, and linguistic abilities.

I laid great emphasis on effective staff work and complained bitterly to Yadin, the chief of operations, about how army staff negligence—due to lack of education and proper training—endangered our operations. But gradually, I found experienced staff from the British army, the Shai, and the Palmach. The military-censorship staff was entirely British-trained and had worked during the war in that area. By censoring our soldiers' mail we registered their opinions and issued reports about their morale. In Israel's evolving society, in which public opinion polls did not yet exist, this was a very useful way to learn how we could serve those who were fighting for our survival.

FROM THE OUTBREAK of the War of Independence, hundreds of Jews with military experience, the so-called *machal*, poured in to offer their service in the armed forces. They were a devoted group but included some rather strange characters. First and foremost was Mickey Marcus. Ben Dunkelman, winner of the Distinguished Service Order in the Canadian army's battles in the Rhineland, singled himself out in command of the Seventh Brigade's campaigns in Galilee. Bernard Grigg, a former member of the British Brigade of Guards, fought bravely beside the defenders of Negba in 1948 in their struggle against the Egyptian invaders. Though his English behavior and appearance evoked suspicion at times, there was no doubt in the kibbutz about his bravery and willingness to face danger.

One extremely odd character claimed to have been awarded the Distinguished Service Order as a colonel in the South African army and to have been a senior member of the South African embassy commercial staff in London. His stupendous résumé led to great rivalry among the organizations seeking to acquire him: he was asked to form an army staff college, he was offered a prominent position in the Foreign Office, several groups were bidding for his services. During the fighting in the Galilee, in November 1948, I invited him to accompany me on a visit to my former brigade at Sassa, near the Lebanese border. Fighting broke out and we came under fire, and after observing this superman under battle conditions, I told General Yadin that if this South African had been a colonel and received a DSO, I would eat my hat. I had seen his reaction when the battle plans and area maps were presented—he had never even been on a battlefield. I asked Eli Kirschner, head of the South African Zionist Organization in Tel Aviv, to confirm the man's claims. He was, of course, an imposter: a lieutenant in a native unit court-martialed and reduced to private. Confronted by Yadin, he admitted that he had just been trying to get ahead in Israeli society. He was never heard of again—at least in the society he was trying to enter.

Despite such eccentric lapses, our military system was beginning to turn into an efficient machine. What characterized us, and indeed the spirit of the times, was the comparative youth of the military leadership.

Yadin was chief of staff in his early thirties; Rabin commanded a brigade in battle in his twenties; Yigal Allon was an outstanding army general when he was barely thirty; and indeed I turned thirty during my service as director of military intelligence. We faced crushing responsibilities and tremendous pressures in an atmosphere of constant struggle and hardship. We were working all night, sleeping barely five hours a day. But somehow we did not think of ourselves as young or inexperienced. We simply accepted an abnormal situation as very natural. So, despite my youth, when there was talk of replacing Beeri with another one of Yadin's cronies, I put my foot down: if I was not given full responsibility, I would not stay on. In January 1949 I took over as director of military intelligence.

In every area of Israeli's development, everything was new—opportunity and idealism were limitless. Ben-Gurion was our Jefferson and Washington. Reuven Shiloach was the *eminence grise* of intelligence, setting the tone and starting the Mossad (the equivalent of the CIA). Yehezkel Sahar, formerly of the British army, was inspector general of police. He and his deputy, Yosef Nachmias, created procedures and regulations that have served the force well. Isser Harel, the first head of the general security services, became head of the Mossad after Shiloach left in 1954. Six years later, in an operation organized by Harel, the Nazi criminal Adolf Eichmann was kidnapped in Argentina and brought to Israel for trial. Such was the group I grew up with professionally.

THE YOUNG STATE'S ABSORPTION of hundreds of thousands of Jewish immigrants was one of the great operations in history, and being part of it was moving and thrilling. Iraq's entire Jewish population, 160,000 members of a community that flourished there for over 2,000 years but were now oppressed by fanatic Islamic groups, arrived by air via Iran. The entire Jewish community of Yemen, cut off from the world for some 2,000 years, crossed the deserts to Aden and in the dramatic "Operation Magic Carpet" was flown to Israel. There was rapture when they emerged from their closed society to find themselves in a nation that spoke the same language, said the same prayers, and celebrated the same religious holidays. Yet these Yemenites still cling to their folklore, special dress, and unique appearance. That's one of the joys of Israeli immigration. We don't demand conformity; we embrace all new cultures as we integrate them into our society.

A large influx soon began to arrive from the North African countries, particularly Morocco, and huge transit camps were set up on the Mediterranean in France and Italy. From these points refugees from Nazi concentration camps and anyone who managed to escape through the Iron Curtain from Eastern Europe were shipped to Israel.

Absorbing these immigrants would have been beyond the ability of a well-established, prosperous country, let alone one newly born and struggling to feed and defend itself. Hundreds of thousands of men, women, and children were concentrated in tents in transit camps known as *ma'abarot.* There was no privacy and conditions were appalling. An embryonic educational system for children was established, but they suffered from the intense heat and dust in the summer, and wallowed in the mud of winter rains. At one stage there was no grain whatsoever left and no money to pay for a shipment due to arrive from America. Again, it was David Ben-Gurion who not only held the struggling nation together but also found solutions to these overwhelming dilemmas.

At our prime minister's urging, Yadin moved the army toward performing functions over and above purely military duties. It became involved in instructing farmers. Agricultural programs were instituted in which the army engaged in the actual production of fruits and vegetables to help relieve the food shortage. Staff officers were allocated to deal with the absorption of the immigrants, and the army even developed its own radio service. Yadin's plan to introduce an army television service was vetoed by Ben-Gurion, who resisted any attempt to introduce television for as long as he was prime minister. It's hard to say he was wrong. I'd like to see what Israeli culture—or any culture, for that matter—would be like today without the all-intrusive proliferation of witless TV shows.

With this tremendous effort, Israel's security was bound to be affected. In September 1949 I warned Yadin that we were taking too great a risk by drastically cutting down forces everywhere to deal with our internal problems; meanwhile, the Arabs were growing in military strength and beginning to penetrate our borders. The Israel Defense Forces had only three full-time brigades at their disposal, while the Arab armies numbered twenty-four brigades, including 800 armored vehicles, at least 200 tanks, 350 field guns, and 520 warplanes. Amid a vast effort to create and establish a state—having just lost 1 percent of our population in the War of Independence, faced with a tripling of our population, and trying to create bases on which to feed, educate, and house a vast number of immigrants—we were now surrounded by a growing Arab power motivated by the Israeli War of Independence to drive the new state into the sea. I even warned of the danger of chemical warfare; my sources revealed that Arab armies were beginning to interest themselves in such weaponry. Indeed, in 1966, the Egyptian army would use poison gas in its invasion of Yemen.

In May 1949, as Ben-Gurion was inspecting a monitoring unit of our military intelligence organization, he said, "What do you need to ensure that every bit of information available reaches you?" After a moment, I answered, "Give me $250,000 and I will do it." That was no small sum in those days and circumstances, but I decided to seize the moment. I made a few other demands, too. In his diary, Ben-Gurion noted, "An important and widely encompassing project has been created. Herzog wants a quarter of a million dollars for additional equipment and an establishment of 1,200 people. His first request is to be granted without delay. His second request has to be examined . . ." Like everything else, the financial administration of Israel was in its infancy, haphazard and disorganized. David Horowitz, director-general of the treasury and later the first governor of the Bank of Israel, nearly had a seizure—the country did not have enough money to buy food, he said. We ultimately compromised on $150,000.

In light of the shortage of resources, I found myself jockeying for any advantage I could muster. I proposed that intelligence be given top priority for university graduates who had taken relevant classes and were about to enter national service. I even convinced certain universities to broaden their syllabus to cover key subjects required by intelligence, such as Arabic and Islamic culture.

My main purpose was to establish one military intelligence service that would answer the requirements of the newly born state. Not an easy task. There was no clear delineation of responsibilities among the various civilian, military, and political intelligence and security agencies that had developed out of the Shai and the Jewish Agency. There was a tremendous amount of infighting. Ben-Gurion examined the possibilities of reorganizing the intelligence community and on 8 February 1949 he noted in his diary:

> I examined the intelligence services with Yaakov Dori (the Chief of Staff) and Herzog. . . . We delineated four major services—a service to combat crime in the police, a military intelligence service (against foreign enemies) in the army, a general security service for internal matters. This service will be represented in the Foreign Ministry, which will be coordinated with the military intelligence. In this service there will be representatives of the internal security service controlled by the security center but posted to the foreign service.

The fourth service to which he referred was the Mossad, which was responsible for foreign intelligence. I proposed relieving military intelligence of any responsibility for internal security, with the exception of field security within the army; this should be entrusted to a special security organization directly responsible either to the minister of defense or the minister of the interior. They would encompass all security responsibilities, including counterintelligence, internal security, control of borders, entry and exit from the country, distribution of passports and granting of visas, and a central security data base.

I also advised Reuven Shiloach as we proceeded to construct the Mossad. As early as September 1948 I noted that it was vital to set up a central intelligence committee that would deal in broad principles, divide areas of responsibility among intelligence agencies, and supervise their work. This committee was set up in April 1949 and began coordinating, setting priorities, and eliminating overlapping between the services. On 1 July 1949, I was named acting head of the committee in my capacity as chief of military intelligence.

The human spirit is amazing. Even amid extraordinary pressure and exhaustion, it strives for normalcy. Which I suppose is why our first son, Joel, was born on 3 October 1949. While it may seem a bit strange to bring a new life into a world where the struggle to survive is overwhelming, it made perfect sense and gave me an even greater reason to continue. I had seen my dream come true—the Jewish State existed. Now my dream for my children and for their children was to live in it free of the strife and hatred and suffering and fear that my generation had known. I felt an even greater urgency for my work and what I considered my mission.

ISRAEL'S WAR OF INDEPENDENCE can be likened to the Battle of Valley Forge. A ragtag army, imbued with the spirit of nationhood and guided by a great leader, rose to defeat the regular military forces facing it. It withstood invasions and hardships and internal bickering and military errors. Finally, an armistice agreement with Egypt was drawn up in Rhodes by Dr. Ralph Bunche, the acting UN mediator. It was signed on 14 February 1949, to "facilitate the transition . . . to permanent peace." An armistice agreement with Lebanon was signed on 23 March, and with Transjordan on 3 April in Rhodes. After difficult and protracted negotiations, Syria fell in line on 20 July. Israel's borders, recognized by these agreements, included more than had originally been envisaged in the Partition Agreement. Western Galilee, the whole of the Negev, and the corridor to Jerusalem, including the western part of the city, were now included in the Jewish State. We had won—decisively.

Peace came as a tremendous shock to the Arab world. It had been convinced there would be no problem annihilating the embryonic Jewish State, and the defeat of the Arab armies greatly affected the regimes in Arab countries. They lost face not just in their own eyes but in the eyes of the world. The inherently corrupt nature of the regimes, which had much to do with their defeat, was revealed to the Arab masses, and a series of upheavals followed in every nation involved. In Egypt, Prime Minister Nuqrashi Pasha was assassinated, and on 23 July 1952, the so-called Free Officers Junta, headed by General Muhammad Naguib and Colonel Gamal Abdel Nasser, carried out a coup d'état deposing King Farouk and exiling him. All political parties were dissolved; members of Parliament, who had "betrayed the trust of the people," were sentenced to long prison terms. A personal struggle for power developed between Naguib and Nasser. Naguib demanded the restoration of the constitutional regime and the return of the army to the barracks. Naguib resigned in February 1954 as president, prime minister, and chairman of the Revolutionary Council and then, in a rapid military coup, was returned to his post as president. But Nasser stirred up opposition within the military forces, and Naguib was compelled to appoint him prime minister. Nasser soon removed Naguib and consolidated his own position as leader of Egypt. He was to be a major unsettling element in the Middle East and, in June 1967 in the Six-Day War, would lead his country to defeat and disgrace. In Lebanon, Prime Minister Riyadh a-Sulh was assassinated in 1952. King Abdullah of Jordan was assassinated during that same period as a result of his desire to normalize relations with Israel. His grandson, later King Hussein of Jordan, was at his side when he was murdered. Through all this, the armistice agreements remained an uneasy and unreliable form of contact with the various Arab countries. The mandates of the armistice were ignored and discarded by the various sides whenever it was necessary.

Although the War of Independence was now officially over, the battle for Israel's independence was really just beginning.

CHAPTER 9

Washington

IN THE EARLY days of Israel's existence we had a surprisingly arm's-length relationship with the United States, which stemmed from the Truman cabinet's ambivalence toward us. George Marshall, the secretary of state, and Clark Clifford, administrative assistant to President Truman, were the spearheads of the opposing official points of view: Clifford wanted the United States to recognize and throw full support behind our emerging nation; Marshall did not.

This was the beginning of the repressive and destructive era of McCarthyism, and Americans seemed to see Commie spies under every leaf of every Israeli tree. While we could have gone Communist in our formative years, we most definitely did not—yet another important decision made by David Ben-Gurion and one fully supported by the people.

The Labor Party, which dominated Israeli politics and political thought from the beginning, had its roots in both Jewish and socialist values and traditions. Israel's purpose was not to be just another state but to be a light unto the people. Unlike the heads of our neighboring Arab states, Israeli leaders lived quite simply, even parsimoniously. To this day, they live comparatively simply, with few of the material trappings generally associated with political power. From the start, we mixed ideology with practicality, and both elements pointed us westward.

One of the very first decisions that had to be made was whether we should have an American or a Russian orientation, and there was pressure from both sides, as there was in those days on any emerging nation. Leftist elements obviously wanted Russian-style communism. But a Communist society was never a realistic choice for Israel.

Herut, the other dominant party and generally further to the right than Labor, was solidly pro-West, as was the Liberal Party. As was Ben-Gurion. Deciding that a Western link was Israel's main hope for long-term survival, Ben-Gurion believed from the outset—and history has certainly borne him out—that the Arabs had to feel that Israel had a firm and total commitment from America. Then and only then would they work toward peace.

But our early relationship with America was rocky. First and foremost, we needed military aid; our army was anachronistic and our budget totally incapable of altering that situation. But the U.S. refused our pleas. Truman, a genuine friend to the Jews, maintained a complete embargo on sending weapons to Israel. Ironically, Richard Nixon—who, records reveal, didn't much care for Jews—turned out to be one of Israel's greatest friends from a military viewpoint. But in the late 1940s, starry-eyed American politicians, like their British counterparts, cherished their romantic image of the Arabs and were wary of committing to a relatively weak-seeming Israel. Of course, Arab oil played a large part in that romance.

By the early 1950s, relations with the United States had begun to move to a more practical basis. My feeling is that American politicians had not, deep down, believed that Israel would survive the War of Independence; they thought of us as they thought of the European Jews, who, they believed, had passively succumbed to the monstrous evil of Nazi Germany, but there was a major difference. Palestinian Jews had lived through a revolution. They had been prepared for battle for years and were ready to fight to the death to establish a homeland. They were even ready for the Nazis. When Rommel approached Egypt, the British turned to the Haganah, which was more than ready to resist militarily.

Israel's relationship with the United States developed because of mutual need. It became clear early on that we would not succeed in our efforts to receive military aid from the Soviet bloc. We had received Messerschmidt fighter planes from Czechoslovakia and some equipment during our initial honeymoon period with the bloc—they were eager to support any national movement fighting colonialism—but the relationship soured quietly. We were ideologically opposed, and when we were turned down by the Czechs and Russians in our bid for surplus armor and equipment captured from Germany, it became clear that we must make a major effort to move toward the Western bloc.

At this point, Yadin felt that we were on the verge of a breakthrough with the Americans. We needed a strong defense representative in Washington, and I finally realized he was talking about me. I was to do for our military relations what I had done for Israeli intelligence: organize it, promote it, and get it on a long-range track.

I arrived in the United States in April 1950. In Washington, D.C., I found a comparatively small embassy headed by Eliahu Elath, our highly respected first ambassador to the U.S., who had represented Jewish Palestine in Washington. There was a small economics division and an even smaller military department, which I headed. More than the excitement, more than the worthwhile work, more than the thrill of working right smack in the middle of the world's political arena, what I remember most about my first months in America was the intolerable Washington summer. The city in July and August is as hot and humid as Basrah in Iraq, and the military attaché's office was in the stuffy, airless attic of a building on Massachusetts Avenue. Air-conditioning had not yet made its appearance and, as a result, I felt as if I were working in a sauna. Indeed, in many countries, their Washington embassy was considered a hardship post in those years.

Israel's faith that America would be our military savior soon proved just a bit exaggerated. For one thing, dealing with Washington's bureaucracy, particularly the Pentagon, is a staggering task. For another, it was almost impossible to overcome the American obsession with communism. I heard accusatory rumblings about Jews immigrating to Israel from Communist countries. It didn't seem to matter that they were leaving because of the repressive government; the mere fact that they were from Bulgaria or Romania made them suspicious. I heard rumors of Israeli deals with the Soviet Union. It took quite a few years of public relations maneuverings, political negotiations, lectures, articles, and visits to convince American leaders that Israel could be a major asset as an outpost of democracy in the Middle East.

Toward the end of that long, hot summer, I flew back to Israel to take my bar exams. Hoping for a little relaxation and time to recover, Aura and I sailed back to the States. When our son Joel and his nanny arrived separately in New York, we saw firsthand the implications of McCarthyism as well as the pure and simple stupidity of slavish obedience to bureaucratic rules.

At the airport, all the passengers except our son and his nanny had passed through customs. After much confusion, we finally discovered the problem. Joel, who was traveling on a separate diplomatic passport, had not signed a statement required by the MacCarran Act declaring that he was not then nor had he ever been a member of the Communist Party.

That he was nine months old was of no concern to the immigration officers—if he couldn't sign the loyalty oath he couldn't enter the country.
After serious negotiations, it was agreed that I could sign for him.

WHILE I WAS BECOMING immersed in American politics, I was continually reminded that Israel's survival teetered on shaky ground. The Israeli–
Arab situation remained volatile. Arab leaders were making blood-
curdling statements, and military maneuvers around Israel's borders were
escalating. By 1950, the Arabs had decided to prepare for another round
of hostilities, and Britain was supplying arms. Concerned—and properly
so—lest an arms race develop in the Middle East, the United States endeavored to coordinate with Britain and France, the traditional suppliers
of arms to the region. On 25 May 1950 they came out with the Tripartite
Declaration, which proposed that the balance in weaponry be maintained
while enabling each country in the area to defend itself.

At the same time, the Western powers set up an organization for defending the Middle East against the Soviet threat. On 13 October 1951,
the creation of a Middle East Defense Command was suggested by them.
It ultimately materialized in 1954–55. Known as the Baghdad Pact, it included Iraq, Iran, Turkey, Pakistan, the U.S., and Great Britain and was
the cornerstone of Western, particularly American, plans for a Middle
East Defense Treaty. The treaty was denounced by President Nasser of
Egypt, which initiated a counteralliance, as the division of Arab states
into rival camps hardened.

In endeavoring to ensure Israel's place in the region's defense setup, I
established relations with the munitions division of the State Department, which had to pass on every item, including spare parts for an airplane. I initiated the purchase of weapons directly from the U.S. armed
forces at a reduced price, and by January 1954, fourteen of our nineteen
applications had been approved.

My next step was to develop a campaign for Israel to be included in the
U.S. military aid program, whereby we would receive weapons without
remuneration. To overcome resistance from the State Department—military aid would also have to be distributed to the Arab countries—I began
lobbying in Congress. Senator Jacob Javits, one of the very few Jews in
Congress, acted as the voice of Israel, backed up in many crucial issues by
Senator Stuart Symington.

By 1953, the Senate Foreign Affairs Committee was allotting $20 mil-
lion a year to Israel but only to aid refugee immigration and other social

needs. Greatly helped by Senator Symington, I organized a group in the Armed Services Committee and lectured to officers in the Pentagon, endeavoring to forge a relationship between the U.S. armed forces and the Israeli military industries. Today that $20 million has grown to $3 billion, of which two-thirds is for military use. Our insistence and the effectiveness of the embassy over the years in educating key politicians on the Middle East has borne fruit.

My partner in this struggle was Shimon Peres, who headed the defense purchase mission in New York. His ability and brilliance were obvious, even when he tended to act on his own. He was quite successful in getting defense matériel for Israel but was limited by restrictive U.S. policies. Peres left New York in 1952 to become director-general of the Ministry of Defense under David Ben-Gurion and to leave his mark on the history and development of Israel.

Israel's foresight and emphasis on modern education have given us a clear-cut advantage. In 1950, the first trainees were admitted to courses in the U.S. armed forces, and the Israel air force sent fifty students to a civilian school in Burbank, California, and fifty students to a civilian school in Tulsa, Oklahoma. They returned from their yearlong study of aircraft maintenance, engine overhaul, and avionics with the technical basis to guarantee the nation's survival. And anything that gave hope for survival was not just appreciated. It was essential.

ON 23 JULY 1952, the Officers' Revolution in Egypt greatly affected our relationship not only with them but also with the United States: a group of "free officers," all young majors, seized control of the army and the nation. The new leaders, including Nasser and Sadat and nominally led by General Naguib, exiled King Farouk and his family, inspiring the hope that Egypt might finally enter the twentieth century. The first sign was that they exiled their deposed king rather than simply lopping his head off. The leader of the military, General Naguib, was installed as the figurehead ruler of Egypt.

The "free officers" were against government corruption—the Farouk regime was as corrupt as a government could be—against the cruel, medieval ways of the court, and against the British, who were operating the Suez Canal with Farouk's permission. But they were also totally against the existence of Israel, bitter and furious about their defeat in 1948.

Naguib was soon deposed; Nasser took over, with Sadat as one of his deputies, and the Soviet Union immediately moved to supply arms. Because Israel's Western allegiance was now clear, the Soviets were anxious to build Egypt's power to go to war against us. At this point France, which had been heavily courted by Ben-Gurion and particularly Peres, became our first major Western military ally.

Nasser's reign was a catastrophe. His hatred of Israel had been stoked during the War of Independence when our forces cut off the Egyptian Brigade in Faluja in southern Israel. As operations officer in that brigade, he had been humiliated. His distaste for all things Western and British led him gradually to the Russian side.

In 1958, Nasser entered into a pact with Syria, then took over Syria, and created the United Arab Republic. This bond was a direct threat to the security of Israel. If Arabs could set aside their differences, they could come together in their desire to destroy the Jewish state.

While Naguib was still in power, the United States developed a $12 million aid program for Egypt. The Defense Department was against strengthening U.S. ties to Egypt, and General Omar Bradley vociferously maintained that Israel was the only country in the area worth relying on. But the State Department—ever pro-Arab—held that Naguib would fall if not encouraged, and pushed hard for an American-Egyptian alliance.

I pushed just as hard. Lobbying the White House, the State Department, and the Defense Department, we used any public outlet to educate friends of Israel. The man behind the move to arm Egypt, Assistant Secretary of State for the Middle East Henry Byroade, was incensed at the campaign, lest his backroom maneuverings be exposed to public scrutiny. The Egyptian embassy and its military office in Washington were also disturbed by our revelations and operations against the aid program. Secretary of State Dean Acheson, claiming ignorance of Byroade's plan and agreement with our arguments, decided to reassess the situation. I was soon advised by my contacts in the White House that Egypt would not receive arms unless Israel received an equal amount. President Truman then decided he would not sign the necessary documents granting aid to Egypt.

Although President Eisenhower was not particularly pro-Israel, he followed Truman's lead regarding military aid to Egypt. When nothing came of the program, I was told by the Egyptian military attaché in June 1953 that they credited our activities with their failure. My opinion is that the British, who had a major score to settle with the Egyptians because of their ouster from the Suez Canal, had more to do with Truman's and Acheson's reversal than any other element.

Eisenhower's policy presumed a U.S. attack on the Soviet Union if it encouraged an international conflict on the periphery. This view brought about a change in the American approach to the proposed Middle East Command. The emphasis was now on an upper northern tier—Turkey, Iran, and Pakistan—with Iraq giving support to the alliance and acting as a link with the Arab world. The United States planned to eventually draw Iraq into the official agreement. Once again, fearful of the State Department's Arab favoritism, as well as the consequences of a hostile American-backed Arab entity united against Israel, the Israelis mounted efforts to be included in the Middle East Command. Considering it vital for the United States to have a strong link to the Arabs, Secretary of State Dulles clearly felt that Israel's exclusion would help establish it.

In February 1954, together with Ambassador Abba Eban, I met the chief of staff of the U.S. ground forces, General Matthew Ridgway, who promised to bring our approach before the Joint Chiefs of Staff.

In April 1954, the Americans signed a munitions agreement with the Iraqis, thereby completing the northern-tier defense arrangement. We had failed in our struggle to oppose it, but our fears proved groundless and it never even came close to working. None of the members trusted any of the others, and very little occurred apart from bickering and back-stabbing. The United States simply didn't understand the Arab mentality when it came to the political arena.

While in Washington, I developed many close relationships, but the most important—and surprising—was with the Egyptian attaché, Colonel Abd el-Hamid Ghaleb. Our relationship could and should have been developed more effectively, but it was discouraged by the Israeli Ministry of Defense and the Ministry of Foreign Affairs. It was all petty politics. Everybody in an official position was creating a pet relationship with somebody in the post–Officers' Revolution Egyptian administration. Getting a leg up in the hope of achieving status and power was all that mattered. Because Ben-Gurion did not involve himself in these details, there was no organization or coherent thought given to human friendships. When I explained my relationships with key Egyptians to Moshe Dayan, the armed forces chief of staff, and asked how to proceed with them, he answered, "Tell them if they don't behave themselves, we'll know how to deal with them!"

NOT ONLY DID I DEAL with official government representatives, I was a link to the American Jewish community. Whenever I entered a hall or a synagogue in my uniform, eyes filled with tears as they saw what they believed to be the reincarnation of Zion. American Jews knew that Israel was going through extraordinarily difficult times. They were also influenced by the fund-raising campaign of the United Jewish Appeal, which went straight for the heart, highlighting the struggle for existence, the poverty, the absorption of immigrants in tented camps in Israel. At one synagogue a congregant observed, "They don't appear to be starved. Oh well, they probably give all the food to the army."

Ben-Gurion's unforgettable emotional first official visit to the United States in 1951 to launch the Israel bonds campaign was a brilliant financial and public relations move, allowing Israel to borrow considerable sums over the years while guaranteeing repayment with interest. We also involved non-Jews interested in a sound investment. Over the years, Israel has borrowed billions through bonds—and paid back every cent.

After hundreds of lectures, countless appearances on TV and radio, and meetings in universities with every type of group imaginable, I realized that Israel had to double its efforts to explain itself.

I submitted countless memorandums to the Foreign Ministry about our inability to organize a public relations system in which we could present ourselves effectively, but there was an almost mystical feeling that all we had to do was have one of our leaders make a speech refuting our enemies' arguments. As a result, except for a very short period in the 1970s, there has never been a Ministry of Information in Israel. This narrow and unrealistic approach has cost us dearly. Today, while much of that arrogance still holds, Israeli politicians are able to grasp the concept of public relations, and it is reflected in the work of the prime minister's office and the Ministry of Foreign Affairs. In fact, it has been grasped too firmly, often replacing substance and decisiveness. And no amount of public relations could make Israel look good if its soldiers were chasing after Arab children, no matter how justified such an action might be.

A related flaw in the Israeli government's mentality is a tendency to ignore Israel's basic interests in favor of appeasing various elements, so we can look good in the eyes of the world. Thus, in 1952, when Spain indicated its willingness to establish diplomatic relations with Israel, Moshe Sharett, Ben-Gurion's foreign minister, turned down the approach. I was quite critical of the decision, pointing out that we could not be guided either by events of five hundred years before—the expulsion of the Jews from Spain and the Inquisition—or by the nature of the current government. If we were prepared to establish relations (as in fact we did) with the Soviet Union under Stalin, and would have been prepared to do so with the Arab countries, with their complete absence of human rights, then the fascist nature of the dictatorship in Spain did not warrant our failure to establish relations with a country sharing the Mediterranean and of great geopolitical importance to Israel.

Israel does not have to set itself up as an arbiter of justice. In Saudi Arabia people are still beheaded, but does that mean we should not try to establish relations? A political relationship does not mean condoning behavior or laws. It is a means—a technicality—for establishing communications. Do we press on against countries that violate human rights? Of course. Do we shut down communications with those countries? Of course not. After the fiasco with Spain, we worked to establish relations for years, finally achieving that goal in 1986, following an understanding between Prime Minister Shimon Peres and Felipe Gonzales, Spain's prime minister.

The same mentality undermined our situation at the United Nations. The UN in the early 1950s was prepared to include Israel in the WE&O (Western Europe & Others) bloc. However, Moshe Sharett, our foreign minister, considered this beneath our dignity and insisted on being a member of the Asian bloc. The result? We didn't join any bloc. We have never been a member of the Security Council and are ineligible for various appointments in the UN organization because of the territorial basis on which they are made.

IN 1954, MOSHE DAYAN, our armed forces chief of staff, visited American army and air force installations. After exposure to the American training system, he decided to adopt one requirement for the Israeli army: all combat officers had to be parachutists. Dayan not only instituted this policy but also insisted on going through the training himself. Although he broke his leg on one of his early jumps, the policy proved successful and has been maintained ever since.

Moshe Dayan is a key figure in Israel's history—controversial, much respected, and very much attacked. He contributed much to the modern Israeli army, set the fighting standards, and created the combat attitude. In his later years, he also developed close relations with the Arab leadership in the Gaza Strip and the West Bank. They came to his home to socialize—a very rare occurrence in those days.

Dayan was a totally unconventional man and politician. Part of Dayan's uniqueness was that he had the total backing of the charismatic Ben-Gurion. Left on his own, Dayan became strangely Hamletian—bizarrely unable to make up his mind even on minor issues. He hesitated

on the battlefield, as in the political arena. Politics and his desire to emu-
late Ben-Gurion were his undoing. He never survived the national criticism of his handling of the Yom Kippur War. By the time he died, in
1981, his standing in Israel had plummeted. Ostracized from the mainstream, he wound up in a political party with only two seats in the Knesset. Never the political force he craved to be, he became forlorn, sick, and
depressed.

But in 1954, he was in full glory. At Eglington Air Force Base in
Florida I shared an apartment with Dayan. That was quite an experience.
One definitely has a different view of Israeli politics after seeing Moshe
Dayan walking around in his underwear and without his eyepatch in the
middle of the night. It was there he told me about his difficult experience
with Pinhas Lavon, Israel's minister of defense. It was clear that Lavon
was doing his best to undermine Dayan, at first through petty tricks like
sending open cables that were unflattering to Dayan's American hosts and
certain to be read by them. One evening, Dayan showed me a letter from
Binyamin Gibli, my replacement as chief of military intelligence, that
referred to an operation mounted by Israeli agents in Egypt that became
the centerpiece of one of Israel's most tragic scandals.

Israeli intelligence had very foolishly devised a plan to create unrest in
Egypt and encourage developments that would increase tension between
the Egyptians on the one hand and the British and Americans on the
other. The plan included leaving bombs in cinemas and public places and
creating an atmosphere of mistrust and fear. The operatives, apart from a
few Israelis, were young Egyptian Jews motivated by Jewish patriotism
and fully aware of their fate in the event of failure.

The plan went awry when a bomb ignited in the pocket of a member
of the Jewish network in a cinema, and the entire group was rounded up.
The Israeli leader succeeded in evading arrest, but all the others were
caught. There was an uproar in Israel. Lavon maintained that he had not
given the order for the operation and blamed Gibli, who claimed the operation had been approved by Lavon.

This act of terrorism was compounded by political infighting, lying,
and backstabbing. When the investigation began, Gibli's letter to Dayan
was produced; it said that the bombs had been planted with Lavon's approval. Lavon not only denied that he'd given approval; he accused Gibli
of altering the letter, insisting that the phrases tying him to the bombings
had been forged and added later.

Lavon eventually resigned as a result of the controversy. But Gibli's secretary later admitted that the Lavon connection had indeed been forged, and the complications continued. Ben-Gurion had long wanted Lavon's head on a silver platter and fought for a ministerial commission of inquiry. This political struggle dragged on for years, and Ben-Gurion ultimately left the Labor Party because of it.

This was still not the end of this mess. Gibli's secretary revealed many years later in a newspaper interview that she was the mistress of Levi Eshkol, who became Israel's prime minister after Ben-Gurion.

All of this intrigue not only brought down the Israeli government, but in Egypt two Israeli agents responsible for planting the bombs were hanged, one committed suicide, and the remaining four received long prison sentences.

The entire operation was a cause célèbre and a childish nightmare, a sordid and ill-conceived initiative that served no purpose. Ben-Gurion saw it as a test of Israel's integrity at all levels, and this was the basis of his struggle, which tore Israel politically apart.

The other thing I distinctly recall about my few days of being Dayan's roommate is that the American army, especially the Jewish chaplaincy, went out of its way to ensure that what they assumed were all Dayan's religious requirements were met. Hence we lived on a constant diet of fish (except when Dayan, not wanting to offend his hosts, would escape at night and slip into the nearby town for a good steak). The fine French wine usually served to all honored guests was put aside and special bottles of sweet Manischewitz's kosher wine were flown down from New York. Without meaning to do so, the Jewish chaplaincy and the U.S. army made the chief of staff of the Israel Defense Forces a very miserable man.

DURING DAYAN'S VISIT, I had the thrill of visiting with former President Harry Truman. We spent the weekend in Kansas City, Missouri, and I notified Eddy Jacobson, Truman's former haberdasher partner, of Dayan's presence in the city. Jacobson was certain that Truman would want to see us. He called me on Sunday morning, when we were at breakfast with the leadership of the local Jewish community, to say that President Truman had a cold and Mrs. Truman objected to any visitors coming. Our visit was off. But an hour later he telephoned to say that Truman had called him to say that Bess Truman had gone to church and therefore we could come to visit. So Moshe Dayan, Yitzhak Rabin, Matti Peled and myself, with Eddy Jacobson, went to Truman's home in Independence, Missouri, to pay our respects. We slipped in through the back door and kitchen. I was a little awed being face-to-face with such a very great man. At the end of the meeting, which was quite open and honest and friendly, Dayan said, "Mr. President, give us some advice." Truman looked at him quizzically. "You want advice?" he asked. "Well, here it is. Don't ever trust those goddam sons of bitches in the State Department."

IN JULY 1950 I VISITED a small company led by Al Schwimmer in Burbank, California. An American volunteer during our War of Independence, Al was reconstructing old parts—junk, basically—into operational airplanes and introducing many innovations into plane design. These wrecks were to be among the first El Al planes.

A year later, while inspecting Israeli air force students who were training in California, Ben-Gurion visited Schwimmer's installation. Shimon Peres, always a man of vision, was with him and set out to convince Ben-Gurion to move the entire group to Israel. He had visions of Schwimmer's group becoming the nucleus of an aircraft industry that would be the most important between the Far East and Western Europe. Peres was attacked, ridiculed, and criticized, but Ben-Gurion believed him. Israel Aircraft Industries is now a $1.5 billion industry. We build our own fighter planes and space satellites and are self-sufficient in many aspects of the aircraft industry.

While visiting Jewish communities in 1952, I received an invitation from a strange character known as Sender Kaplan. The central figure in Havana's 12,000-member Jewish community, Sender was the honorary Israeli consul in Cuba and editor of *Die Havaner Zeit*, the Yiddish organ of Cuban Jewry. He invited me to address the so-called Third Seder, which had been inaugurated by the Histadrut, Israel's federation of labor unions, in many communities and was a major fund-raising event.

The Cuba of President Fulgencio Batista was a typical dictatorship, with considerable wealth beside grinding poverty. Nevertheless, it fared well in memory compared to the prison that Castro created.

At this Third Seder, Kaplan waxed enthusiastic and supportive, declaring in Yiddish, "We Cubans stand firm with Israel." Most of the "Cubans" there had escaped from Europe, and their faces bore the sorrow of the Jewish people.

Walking through the busy streets of Havana the next day, we came upon a kosher restaurant. Its name immediately drew our attention—

Moshe Pipik. The owner, Mrs. Weinstein, received us royally. Asked about Moshe Pipik, she countered, "If I had my real name on the window, would you have bothered to come in?"

AT ONE OF THE PARTIES we attended in Washington we met Ambassador John Hearne of Ireland. He knew about my father's association with the struggle for Irish independence, so we had much in common. He was organizing the embassy's traditional St. Patrick's Day party and asked if I would join his receiving line in my Israel Defense Forces uniform. He had no military attaché and feared the omission would affect his standing in the Washington hierarchy. "Nobody will know the difference." Furthermore, I could express myself in Gaelic, which was more than most of the Irish guests could do. As they shook hands with the ambassador, he would say, "Please meet my military attaché."

My Irish origin was undoubtedly an asset, not to mention my slight but detectable brogue. I was in Washington when Robert Briscoe, lord mayor of Dublin, one of the heroes of Irish independence, came to the United States. He was extraordinarily popular and was mobbed wherever he went. One of Briscoe's best comments came in Boston, when he opened his remarks with, "There was once an Irishman and a Jew, and here he is." Years later, when I was ambassador to the United Nations, the Jewish mayor of Cork, Councillor Gerald Goldberg, was entertained by the Irish Tourist Office in New York. He looked at me and said, "I was at your bar mitzvah." I made some fatuous remark in Yiddish, and he replied to me in a few more Yiddish words. The Irish dignitaries surrounding us asked, "What is that?" whereupon I turned on them and said, "You ought to be ashamed of yourselves. Don't you understand Gaelic?" They believed me.

DURING OUR PERIOD in Washington we came face-to-face with the overpowering racial segregation that characterized the South at that time, with its "Whites Only" public rest rooms and seats in the parks.

When our second son, Michael, was born, in July 1952, we brought in a nanny from Jamaica. While vacationing on Martha's Vineyard, we took our two children to the beach in West Chop and, to our horror, were asked to take our black nanny away. We argued, but to no avail, and finally left with her. In Maryland, we stopped at a roadside inn, where our nanny was refused service.

Many prominent Jews supported the blacks' struggle for equal rights. The best symbol of this support was when Rabbi Hecksher of the Jewish Theological Seminary in New York visited the Reverend Martin Luther King, Jr., who was in jail in Alabama. Rabbi Hecksher kept his head covered, and when King asked why, he replied, "You are here and therefore this is a holy place. And by Jewish tradition my head must be covered." It's rather sad that there is distrust between American blacks and Jews today and that many prominent blacks seem anti-Semitic. Israeli society is definitely not racist: we have a large black Ethiopian population, and there is much intermarriage.

We were also aware of anti-Jewish discrimination in Washington, although as diplomats we rarely came across it. A house was for rent in Spring Valley, a very exclusive district, and Aura and I learned that we had been chosen by the owner as the most desirable tenants. While concluding the contract, I told the rental agent that the final arrangements would have to be made with the embassy. "Which embassy?" he asked. "The embassy of Israel," he was told. He began to stutter—there had been a mistake . . . they hadn't really decided conclusively . . . to give us the house. "Do you want to tell me that this is a restricted area, and that we as Jews are excluded?" I asked. He was very contrite and apologetic. But we did not get the house.

Fear of anti-Semitism led many American Jews into the closet. While visiting the Naval Bureau of Ships on a purchasing mission, I was received by Admiral Louis Dreller, one of the navy's top engineers. When I told him that I observed the traditional Friday night service at home, a sad look overcame him. Since he had been in the navy he had not experienced such an evening. He had grown up in New England in a traditional Jewish family and even donned tefillin and phylacteries, ate kosher, and married a Jewish woman. But when he was appointed to Annapolis, he decided that the innate anti-Semitism that pervaded the armed forces would never let him advance—certainly not to flag rank—if it was known that he was Jewish. His exposure to Israel through our meeting made him realize that he had to admit his origins. He could no longer stand the pretense. "Would you invite my wife and myself?" he asked.

A particularly moving story was that of Brigadier General Robert Ginsburgh. He was special assistant to General George Marshall, the secretary of defense, and was an absolutely brilliant man. He was married to the non-Jewish daughter of an admiral and was very much part of the senior military officers' "establishment." We invited the couple to our home, and Mrs. Ginsburgh said to her husband, "Bob, show them how good you are at Hebrew." He thereupon removed a tractate of the Talmud from a shelf and began, with the inevitable singsong of Talmudic study, to read the text and to elaborate on it. It turned out he was the son of a *shochet* in Rochester, New York. He had abandoned Judaism, although he refused to change his last name, which revealed his origin and thereby prevented his advance to higher rank. He had gone so far away from Judaism that he was actually a dignitary in the local Evangelical congregation. Yet he seemed to be drawn, as if by a magnet, to things Jewish in our home.

On the first occasion that the Israel Philharmonic Orchestra visited Washington and played in Constitution Hall, I invited Admiral and Mrs. Dreller and General and Mrs. Ginsburgh to be our guests. President Harry Truman graced the occasion with his presence, together with a galaxy of personalities, the cream of Washington. The orchestra opened this magnificent evening with the playing of the American and Israeli national anthems. Suddenly, in the midst of the playing of "Hatikvah," our national anthem, both Aura and I noticed that General Ginsburgh was beginning to sway. He became as white as a sheet and was obviously about to collapse from emotion. We held his arms and kept him upright until the end of the anthem. Here, perhaps more than anywhere else I've ever been, I saw the unbroken cord of Jewish identity coming to expression, and the tragedy of someone who had cut the cord.

After Marshall resigned and James Forrestal became the secretary of defense, Bob Ginsburgh lost his standing, and retired from the armed forces to become military analyst for *U.S. News & World Report*. On a trip with other military correspondents, he was killed when the plane crashed. When on home leave, I related the story of General Ginsburgh to my father. To my surprise, he had known General Ginsburgh's father, and he said to me, "The general you knew was a sixth-generation descendant of the Sha'agat Arye, one of the greatest rabbinical commentators and scholars of the nineteenth century."

MY SERVICE IN WASHINGTON ended on 30 August 1954, and I came away with insight into what made America tick: the overriding sense that right must prevail. Despite the abominable pressures of McCarthyism and horrible injustices, the courageous individuals who stood up to him during the televised hearings of the Senate Permanent Investigations Subcommittee represented the inherent decency of the American people and proved that the American system knew how to cure and right itself. It was a period of financial, military, and moral growth for both America and Israel. A special bond between the two countries had been established, and continued to grow, but something much deeper had to have been there for it to flourish and develop. Aura and I grew to respect and love America and all it stands for. We had come for two years but stayed for four and left profoundly conscious of its greatness.

CHAPTER 10

———— ⚬⚬⚬ ————

The Jerusalem Brigade

IF ONE HAS never been to Jerusalem, it is difficult to comprehend the influence of its geography on daily life. It had a particular effect on mine as commander of the 16th Brigade (known as the Jerusalem Brigade) and of the Jerusalem District, responsible for West Jerusalem, the Jerusalem Corridor, and the Reserve Brigade. I was appointed by General Dayan and reported to the officer in charge of the Central Command (then Major General Zvi Ayalon and later Major General Zvi Zur). Mine was a historic position. I had joined the long line of commanders of Jerusalem, the capital city of the Jews since King David moved from Hebron to Mount Moriah almost 3,000 years ago.

The front line snaked its way through the city, with the Arab Legion and our forces both at the alert all along the line. We were almost on top of the Jordanians. For example, in the district of Abu Tor a house would be occupied by an Israeli guard, but the outhouse at the back of its small garden, twenty yards away, would be a forward Jordanian position. This was the situation right across the city.

The front line was held by reservists or regular army units that rotated every few weeks. A unit numbered only about 120 soldiers (there were 750 to 1,000 in a battalion and 3,000 to 5,000 in a brigade). I doubt that any capital in a state of war was ever held by such a weak, almost token force. However, our brigade was trained to mobilize in a matter of hours, and the city was comparatively small, so word could get around almost instantly.

The line between the Israeli and Jordanian sectors cut Jerusalem in half. It was officially called the City Line and had been fixed on 30

November 1948, within the framework of a "sincere cease-fire agreement" signed by Lieutenant Colonel Moshe Dayan, Jerusalem district commander, and Lieutenant Colonel Abdullah al-Tall, Jordanian district commander. In the heart of the city, this separation was emphasized by a stone wall designed to prevent sniping. In the no-man's-lands it was a series of barbed-wire entanglements, minefields, and makeshift obstacles.

These no-man's-lands were created because Dayan and Tall had used a thick china marker to delineate the City Line on a map. The line was two to three millimeters wide on the map—which translated to forty to sixty meters on the ground. Their line covered houses and even whole streets indiscriminately. In the heat of the summer, the marker tends to melt and had covered certain areas, thus widening the City Line even further. Neither side could agree on what belonged to whom, and people were killed because of the thickness of a pencil. Guests at the reconstructed King David Hotel sat on the terrace or on their room's balcony overlooking Jordanian sentries perched on the city wall within small-arms distance. The intervening no-man's-land turned into a mass of concertina wire, garbage, and putrefying animals that had been blown up by the mines. Nothing could be rebuilt along the front line—it was simply too dangerous.

To reduce friction between the Israelis and the Jordanians, their governments agreed, in December 1954, to establish direct telephone communications, enabling the two commanders to "discuss and settle questions regarding the maintenance of peace in Jerusalem." The agreement became operative the following April.

My meetings with the Jordanian commanders usually took place at a table in Mandelbaum Square, the main crossing point between the Israeli and Jordanian sectors. We dealt with such practical day-to-day matters as the occasional shots fired from Jordanian positions toward the Israeli positions and the throwing of stones by the Israeli troops. There was also the problem of guerrilla infiltrators. The Jordanians, maintaining that the Egyptians were activating the guerillas, claimed they were doing their best to prevent them. This was a tricky problem for them since public opinion in Jordan heavily favored the Egyptians. I agreed to keep them up-to-date on the infiltrators, and we arranged to eliminate the firing on individuals who had entered no-man's-land and to return people who had lost their way. These meetings helped me understand much of what was going on in the Arab world as well as their feelings about Israel and the world in general. To me, the key is communication: with it I always have a chance to solve a problem or overcome an obstacle.

Growing evidence of opposition in Jordan to King Hussein's rule was reflected in strikes and demonstrations, and I received detailed analyses of what was happening. The Jordanian commander, Lieutenant Colonel Sa'adi, remarked bitterly, "As fate would have it, the country most interested in Jordan's independence is the State of Israel." This was as true then as it has been over the years. It makes perfect sense, though. Jordan under Hussein fought terrorism all along, particularly when sponsored by the PLO. We knew we had to support Hussein, for an extreme Islamic state on our border would be a disaster.

Conversely, Hussein clearly had to support Israel. He has much more in common with us on every level than with other Arab countries. Although he could not muster the courage for years to publicly acknowledge us, he has maintained contact with us since the 1960s. Beginning in 1963, King Hussein discreetly met with Israeli leaders. These meetings were organized by my brother, Yaacov, and included a session with Prime Minister Golda Meir, in Tel Aviv. An open secret over the years, these conferences culminated in the official meetings with Prime Minister Yitzhak Rabin that led to the peace treaty with Jordan in 1994. There are reports that Hussein even warned us about the imminence of the Yom Kippur War.

According to President Anwar Sadat of Egypt, Hussein was not considered a very courageous leader from a political point of view, but, to be fair, Hussein had much to fear and proved to be physically very brave. He was in constant danger from Syrian and Palestinian assassins, and while he has been able to deal with the Moslem extremists who surround him, there are always threats that this element will explode.

But in 1957 our relations were tenuous, and a professional—not to mention cordial—relationship with Jordan's military leaders was unusual. The British officers who commanded the Jordanian army had turned it into the best, most efficient Arab army in the Middle East. The British consuls, who maintained contact with me and acted as go-betweens with the British commanders, were also a very valuable source of information about political developments on the other side of the border.

It is difficult to understand what it is like to live completely surrounded by enemies. That fact seeps into the unconscious, acting as a kind of protective shield, and eventually you are not even aware that it is there. Ultimately, you begin to ignore the fact that you live with the constant threat of danger and even death. You pay attention to it only at the borders, when you see the enemy's guns and soldiers. It's not unlike getting mugged. You become suspicious, you turn when a stranger comes up behind you, you hesitate when turning a dark corner. But you don't stop walking the streets or let your life be dictated by fear. Everyday life in Jerusalem was so connected with our enemies and so reflected our fears that it was impossible to separate them.

As commander of the Jerusalem Brigade, I was in the middle of many things that normally had nothing to do with the military. I was involved in creating reservoirs, landing strips for planes, and developments in the agricultural area of the Corridor, which was a series of mountainous villages linking the coast to Jerusalem. All of them were integral to our ability to defend the city. I had to be consulted on something as seemingly mundane as the erection of a new apartment building; we could not allow a structure to be built that might interfere with a strategic line of fire.

Militarily, we were also kept busy—too busy. Fedayeen guerrillas operating along the border attacked Jewish villages, and we were forced to retaliate without mercy. Ariel Sharon bravely and effectively commanded these missions, devised the plans, trained the men, and led the attacks. It was our only way of protecting the border, and it proved quite effective. Colonel Ahmed Bublaan, commander of the Jerusalem District on the Jordanian side, begged us not to retaliate against Jordanian police buildings and headquarters; that would only help break down their structure of law and order. We held them responsible for everything that happened over the border, but it was obvious they did not control the guerrilla extremists.

At one point, my brigade was involved in a difficult retaliatory attack carried out by paratroopers near the Etzion Bloc in the Hebron Hills. The Arab Legion was in a good position to counter it, and ten Israelis were killed, with many more injured. After this battle I saw Moshe Dayan give rare expression to his emotions. When he learned of our lost fighters, he broke down in tears.

ONE OF THE MOST significant battles in Israel's history, the Sinai Campaign, began on 29 October 1956. I wonder if we would have triumphed in this battle had we not been so under attack by guerrillas coming from Jordanian-held territory, which created the perfect diversion when we finally attacked the Sinai.

Our goal in the Sinai Campaign was to distance the Arab terrorists from our borders, help take back the Suez Canal for the French and British, open up the seaways to Africa, remove the Egyptian navy—and thus the Egyptian embargo—and restore our ability to trade freely with Africa and Asia. To make such an offensive move into Egypt was considered nearly impossible, until we devised a way to conceal our bold intentions. We created the impression that we were moving into Jordan in a mass retaliation against the guerrilla raids. The entire Arab world was caught unawares when we moved on Egypt instead.

Although we did our part, the French and British forces failed miserably in their joint operation against Port Said and the Suez Canal. Their staff work was dismal, their communication and timing were inept, and ultimately they did not accomplish their aim, which was to bring Nasser down and retake the canal.

In Jerusalem, I was ordered to mobilize all our forces. We feared that the Jordanians might launch an attack on the Mount Scopus enclave, which housed the buildings of the Hebrew University and the Hadassah Hospital, the same buildings that had been cut off and surrounded by the Jordanians in 1948. Accordingly, I received orders authorizing me to launch a counterattack if such a move occurred.

But the Jordanians did not intervene or ever give cause for concern. Indeed on one occasion, a Jordanian soldier fired his gun, and within minutes the Jordanian commander called on our direct phone line to apologize and emphasize that it was a stray shot.

As part of the Jordanian diversion, we established a presence at Sheikh Abdul Aziz (now the site of Mevasseret Yerushalayim, near Jerusalem) in the form of an orchard planted right up to the Jordanian border. We awaited the Arab Legion's response. Knowing that we were likely to be attacked, we sent soldiers dressed as farmers to plant the trees. I placed heavy machine guns and mortars on Kastel Mountain (previously a Roman fortress). A battalion commander, Uzi Feinerman, patrolled the main Tel Aviv–Jerusalem road. And to show how haphazard it all was, Feinerman's ten-year-old son was visiting him, and he went on patrol as well—not exactly the safest form of child care.

In due course, we came under heavy fire. We closed the Tel Aviv–Jerusalem road, the Kastel position opened fire, and the Jordanian attack soon stopped. The Jordanians later resumed fire—on UN soldiers who had come to inspect our position. When we finished planting up to the border, our message was clear.

In Sinai all Egyptian telephone wires were cut by Israeli airplane propellers, isolating Egypt's air force and army from any telecommunications. Israeli paratroopers and forces moved quickly and decisively, reaching the Suez Canal and fulfilling our military and strategic goals.

AFTER THE SINAI CAMPAIGN, officers of the Central Command toured the barren area in four-wheel-drive weapons carriers. Passing through stark deserts, deep canyons, moving sands, and bedouin oases we began to appreciate the nomadic way of life and the bedouins' ability to survive, raise families, and eke out a living from the cruel desert in their goatskin tents. The bedouin have always been looked down upon by Arabs, but the bedouin and the Jews have always been close. Their moral rules should be a model for many societies, and their code of justice has been handed down for centuries. Women can wander across the desert and no harm will come to them. Their courts function simply and efficiently. A bedouin tracker can look at a trail of footsteps and tell you if the person being tailed has eaten or is carrying a weapon, or even what his personality is. In the bedouin, I see my ancestors three thousand years ago, as they appeared in the desert after the birth of the Jewish nation.

We passed through a flourishing oasis, Wadi Faran, watered by mountain streams. The bedouins living there made a good living from the soil, growing many different types of fruits. At the head of the wadi we came to St. Catherine's Monastery, the world's oldest functioning building, reputedly built in the fifth century by Helena, mother of the great codifier Justinian. In the courtyard is a thistle bush growing out of a wall, believed by some to be Moses's bush. The monastery has a magnificent library full of priceless icons more than a thousand years old. From here came the famous and priceless Codex Sinaiticus, which now resides in the British Museum. But my two favorite artifacts are in the main library. One is a letter to French troops during their Egyptian campaign, signed by Napoleon, ordering them to do everything possible to preserve the monastery and its inhabitants. The second is a letter from General Moshe Dayan, written when he was Israeli chief of staff. Not to be outdone by Napoleon, Dayan penned a letter with similar injunctions to the Israel Defense Forces. To this day, it hangs next to Napoleon's missive.

While in the Sinai—actually on Mount Sinai—I received a message to travel to America to address the central meeting of the United Jewish Appeal. The American government disapproved of the Israeli attack in Sinai and made no secret of the fact. In the world press the campaign was viewed, incorrectly, as an offensive maneuver, and President Eisenhower and Secretary of State Dulles were angry because they saw the United States as the world's policeman—and Israel had gotten together with France and England to do some policing of our own. Surprisingly blind when it came to Egypt, Eisenhower and Dulles should have gotten rid of Nasser. After all, it was he who brought Communists and communism into the area. Why they used their power to protect him I will never understand. Things were so bad that they were unwilling to receive any Israeli in an official capacity, but somehow I was deemed acceptable. What started as a speech to the UJA ended up as an official visit to the State Department.

Pointing out that I was the second Jew in history to receive a message on Mount Sinai, I explained the background of the Sinai Campaign, our alliances with France and Britain, and our reasoning for going forward into Egypt. Away from the slanted scrutiny of the media and the politically motivated response of government officials, people seemed to accept and understand our position. I made that same case to State Department officials. I spoke to both officials and civilians from the heart and pulled no punches.

My visit was a success. I could return to Israel and report my feeling that our relationship with America would move back on course.

CHAPTER II

The Southern Command

IN MAY 1957 I changed jobs again, moving to Southern Command as chief of staff. Encompassing some 60 percent of Israel's territory but only 5 percent of its population, Southern Command stretched from the area of the coastal plain, in the general vicinity of Ashkelon, southward to include the whole of the Negev Desert, down to and including Eilat on the Red Sea. It was responsible for the border with Egypt in the Sinai Desert—facing the largest Arab army deployed against Israel—for the long border with Jordan from the Dead Sea to the Gulf of Aqaba on the Red Sea, and for the border with the Gaza Strip. The sparsely settled area had development towns, kibbutzim, and farming communities; command headquarters was in Beersheba, set in the middle of the Negev, with a population of 5,000. Beersheba was also the sole urban center for the bedouins, who held their weekly market there, selling or trading cattle, sheep, embroidered clothes—much of which had been smuggled out of Jordan and Egypt.

Eilat, on the Red Sea, was then a group of huts in the wilderness, and Dimona a sordid, miserable collection of huts and the bare bones of some new buildings. These and other desert villages were populated mostly by new immigrants carving out homes and communities on land with little vegetation or even irrigation. But they were starting to build and plant and grow. Beersheba, the "big city" of the area, was a small, frontier-type town. Bedouin who came in from the desert rode through the streets on horseback or camels; Israelis from the desert settlements and the area of the Gaza border invariably were armed, carrying weapons in their holsters. It was like the Wild West.

The military situation was extremely difficult. The northwest border of our command was the Gaza Strip, with its teeming, hostile population. Across from Gaza there were nightly raids and attacks, and Arab fedayeen guerrillas and terrorists would sneak across the border and destroy the new irrigation facilities. They once raided a wedding party and tossed grenades into the midst of the revelers. They attacked a school, shooting children at their prayers, and they raided farms, killing those working the land. The battalion of paratroopers that manned the Gaza border was not always up to strength, and we rarely had the force necessary to truly secure the Negev.

The command was divided into three areas. The Beersheba Area was under Lieutenant Colonel Kuti Adam, whose troops included an infantry company consisting of volunteer Druze soldiers. Adam was an amazing character, with eerily feral instincts. As we were traveling through the Negev, he would alert me that bedouin or Arab infiltrators were observing us from a great distance, hidden in the desert. How could he possibly know this? By the behavior of the birds. He later become deputy chief of staff of the armed forces and was a candidate to head the Mossad. But in 1982, while viewing operations in the Lebanese War, he entered a supposedly abandoned house in a village south of Beirut and was shot to death by Palestinian guerrillas.

In those early years we were almost always undermanned, undersupplied, and underfinanced; the basic problem was a lack of manpower. If our struggling country took people out of the workforce and put them in the army, daily life would grind to a halt. Therefore, our borders were guarded by reserves—amateurs—leaving them much more vulnerable than anyone suspected. The forces available to Southern Command were utterly inadequate, so, as usual, the Israel Defense Forces had to improvise, creating a commando reconnaissance unit known as Shaked.

Because security was so inadequate, terrorists and fedayeen bands had been wandering brazenly around Beersheba, sabotaging, harassing, and keeping the Israel Defense Forces under surveillance. The new unit created to combat them was composed of elite Israeli soldiers led by bedouin trackers, who could describe in detail any individual who had crossed the area, simply by reading the ground. The unit could collaborate with friendly bedouin tribes, whose knowledge of desert minutiae was uncannily accurate.

A bedouin known as Abd el-Maguid Hader rapidly adapted to living with the Israelis and became an officer. This is not so unusual as it sounds. Bedouin serve as volunteers in the Israel Defense Forces and have proved themselves. Israelis tend to respect their way of life far more than their fellow Arabs, who ignore them. Abd el-Maguid regarded the Arabs with disdain, realizing that the bedouin had a much better future if Israel not just survived but flourished. The bedouin are fighters, and few were greater than Abd el-Maguid, who lost a leg and the use of an arm in combat. He had asked to be buried in an area between Northern and Southern Command, so as to emphasize his loyalty to both; his funeral was attended by thousands. A special Moslem corner was established for him in a Jewish cemetery.

Eventually, the activities of this Shaked commando unit began to have their effect. When Egyptian reconnaissance units did not return home— and their replacement units did not return either—the terrorists operating from the Gaza Strip began to realize that the days of the "Wild West" were over.

Southern Command not only defended the borders but covered all aspects of defense, organization, preparation of the command forces for war, rapid mobilization of reserves, and the immediate security of the various settlements. I was responsible for operational activities, relations with the local population and the industrial infrastructure, and discipline, including living conditions, contact with the UN units along the Gaza border, and relations with the bedouin.

This was a heroic beginning of the settlement in the bleak, undulating Negev Desert, in which flourishing farms now abound. We were dealing with a population that had come from the villages of Iraq, the townships of Morocco, and the hills of Yemen, as well as from the shtetls of Romania. Thrust into a foreign background, the new arrivals created an agriculture from barren fields. The army felt responsible not only for protecting but also for improving daily life in the Negev. When I told the great violinist Isaac Stern that an entire segment of the population had never heard him, he gave a magnificent concert for the Southern Command unit stationed along the border of the Gaza Strip. He stood and played there in a cool desert breeze as the soldiers, their arms at the ready, lay all around him in the field. From there he moved to the soldiers' club in Beersheba, where he gave another wonderful concert to a full and appreciative house.

Many of the immigrant soldiers had difficulty adapting to their new country, and I helped them expand their normal educational activities— knowledge is the greatest tool when one is trying to survive. This was an accepted national function of the army. Courses and lectures about the

Middle East were established, and immigrant soldiers were taught history, politics, agriculture, and anything else relevant to their life. Television was not available in Israel until 1968, even as an educational tool. Ben-Gurion had seen it in Oxford and decided it was the ruin of mankind. At times I think he may have had a point.

I DISCOVERED A TRULY fascinating and impressive society in the bedouin. They are organized in tribes, many of which spread across international borders. They respect no national identity: they are bedouin—not Egypt-ian bedouin or Iraqi bedouin or Israeli bedouin—and base their society on an ancient code of behavior. They were nomads then, living in goat-skin tents, with herds of camels, goats, and sheep, moving from water-hole to waterhole after each rainy season. This way of life led to many internal conflicts as well as disputes with Jewish settlements in the Negev. Trying to minimize the conflicts, I proposed extending a water pipeline across the desert from the ruins of the Nabatean city of Ovdat into the area grazed by the bedouin; this would prevent the tribes from moving north and infringing on other areas. In the Negev Heights there were some 4,000 bedouin from Sinai and Jordan. We accepted their presence but realized that they were linked to Jordan and Egypt and, if "activated," could engage in rampant terrorism. Although we could have expelled them—they had Egyptian and Jordanian identity cards—we limited the potential for trouble and maintained peace on all sides by restricting their movement.

We were occupied with the possible effects of the bedouin "frater-nity"—the close relations that existed between the Israeli bedouin and the tribes across the border in Jordan and Sinai. Because of these close ties, trade and smuggling routes had existed from time immemorial. There has always been a steady smuggling of goods and, of greater concern, drugs. The traditional "trading" route linking the sources of drugs in Lebanon with the major market in Egypt crossed Israel and the Sinai desert. Trying to monitor this drug smuggling occupied much of our attention.

One of the bedouin customs was the lavish *sulha* (forgiveness) celebra-tion after a member of one tribe was murdered by a member of another. The two tribes would gather for a huge feast, with extraordinary food: roast sheep in vats of butter, lamb chops, sesame and hummus and fruits, very black pita bread.

Bedouin hospitality was mind-boggling, with the main dish, invariably lamb, served amid piles of rice and sheep butter. The sheikh himself would demonstrate the proper way to enjoy their ultimate delicacy, a sheep's eye: just pop it into your mouth, swallow, and do your best to smile and nod appreciatively. Coffee was then ground to the rhythm of singing, and one had to quaff a small cup of the bitter brew in one gulp without grimacing. If the guests were important, gifts were given. Only after the guests had departed could the men of the tribe partake of the leftovers, which were then shared with the women and children.

I rode with the tribe headed by Sheikh Hamad Abu-Rubeia over much of the Negev, astride their splendid horses and using harnesses made of rope. A colorful character, Abu-Rubeia later became a member of the Knesset and was assassinated by sons of a Druze sheikh. A blood feud now exists, and for years I tried without success to bring about a *sulha* celebration. Another unusual bedouin leader in the Negev was the sheikh of the Al-Huzeil tribe, who was reputed to have thirty-nine wives and numerous offspring and at the same time to maintain a blonde in Jaffa.

We in the West could learn a great deal from this society and civilization. They have a powerful code of honor. They are self-sufficient and live the simple and meaningful life of our biblical forefathers. I regret its passing in so many countries. In the urbanized areas of the Negev in which the bedouin now have houses, they still keep their tent in the backyard; that is where the women of the household sleep.

SOON AFTER I MOVED to Southern Command, Aura was appointed secretary-general of the tenth-anniversary celebrations of the State of Israel; the chairman was Meyer Weisgal, the indefatigable president of the Weizmann Institute.

Aura's contribution was to initiate the World Bible Quiz for Jewish youth, held on Independence Day in Jerusalem. To mark the anniversary celebration, the Irish Jewish community was planting a forest in my father's honor in Israel. We went to Dublin to accept the tribute in his name.

When I returned to Dublin in 1958, my father's health was failing. I knew that he did not have long to live (he died within the year; fifty thousand people attended the funeral), so the trip was particularly moving. We had stayed quite close in Jerusalem, spending the Sabbath with my parents whenever possible. Toward the end of his life, my father became depressed after having foreseen the dangerous and destructive confrontation between Israel's religious and the nonreligious factions. During the War of Independence, as chief rabbi, he gave leadership and moral guidance to the soldiers, and during the siege of Jerusalem, he encouraged people to unload supplies despite the Sabbath and to support their soldiers and country—he was a pragmatist and lived in the real world. Most important, his humanistic views were an integral part of his religious views—which is exactly what the Jewish faith is all about; it is the most humanistic of all religions. But the extreme religious factions, the strict Orthodox, have let their religious beliefs turn them against the very government that is still fighting for their national independence.

My father tried, as chief rabbi, to use his religious influence to coexist side by side with the government. Religion and politics don't mix, but they do need to recognize each other's existence. He realized that the Orthodox sects were moving toward politics, trying to push their religious views into public policy and the courts. This problem has been aggravated, and now the religious parties basically hold the bigger parties hostage in the Knesset. In many countries, including the United States, religious extremists are trying to turn their religious views into public policy. Like the religious parties in Israel, they are a relatively small minority but have enormous political clout.

I doubt that my father would be elected chief rabbi of Israel today. Nor might Ben-Gurion be elected prime minister, for that matter. Neither one would be good on television. They were not subtle or conciliatory; they were truth tellers and leaders. My father used his power for the good of his people, not for personal gain or political motives. Unfortunately, that's not the kind of individual normally elected to public office today.

Soon after our trip to Ireland, I paid the first official visit of an Israel Defense Forces officer to the Bundeswehr, the new army of the Federal German Republic. Soldiers of the German army, who thirteen years earlier would have killed me or thrown me into a concentration camp, stood at attention, saluting me smartly. It was very surrealistic. And then I came to a realization that I've since proclaimed amid much controversy in Israel: it was then and is now a new world. While Jews, especially, can't forget the past, we must live for the future. We must move forward—and that includes forging relationships with Germans and Germany.

After visiting army headquarters near Bonn and an officers training school near Hannover, I arrived at Bergen-Hohne, near the site of the

Bergen-Belsen concentration camp. It was the training center of their new armored force.

On my return to Israel, I submitted a full report and was soon approached by Dr. Israel Behr, who worked in the Ministry of Defense. He was quite close to Ben-Gurion and could often be found hovering around his office. Originally from Austria, Behr was allegedly an Austrian officer and served in the International Brigade in the Spanish Civil War; he wrote extremely well and contributed regularly to the leading daily, *Ha'aretz*. He asked for a copy of my report and cross-examined me about developments and trends in NATO. His requests and questions seemed perfectly normal. But they were not. Soon afterward Behr was caught in a restaurant handing over key documents to the Soviets; he had been betraying Israel all along. I testified at his trial. He received a deservedly long prison sentence and died in jail.

THE MOST IMPORTANT CITIZEN in the Negev during part of my service in Southern Command was David Ben-Gurion. He lived with his wife, Paula, in Kibbutz Sde Boker, overlooking the magnificent Wilderness of Zin and near the site of the Nabatean town of Ovdat.

He moved there following his first resignation from the government, in 1954, which arose out of the abortive intelligence operation in Egypt. Asserting that the Negev was the key to Israel's survival, he settled in an isolated kibbutz to set an example. Sde Boker is a landmark in which Ben-Gurion's home, library, and grave have become the focus for pilgrimage by a grateful people.

In today's multinational, media-dominated world, it is difficult to understand his impact. He led Israel even before it became a nation, guiding it into statehood and preparing it for the future. He made every major decision involved with establishing Israel and keeping it alive. In 1937, when the Peel Commission, set up in 1936 by the British government, proposed partition and the establishment of a small Jewish state, it was Ben-Gurion who took the burden of accepting the proposal onto his shoulders. He believed it was the one way to save European Jewry before World War II, but this recommendation was never implemented.

Ben-Gurion was born in 1886 in Plonsk, Poland. His name was David Green when he arrived in Palestine at the turn of the century. He went to Istanbul (then Constantinople) to study law and then to America, where he joined the Jewish Legion and married an outspoken first-generation

American woman. He returned to Palestine ready to start the move for independence and to begin the process of self-determination for Jews around the world.

Although hardly flawless, he was in his way a prophet, and as a leader and thinker he was magnificent. He studied the Bible and learned Spanish so that he could read Cervantes in the original. But his Messianic side brooked no resistance or opposition, and he could be quite niggardly and small. He had no love for Menachem Begin, who led the opposition to Ben-Gurion's Labor Party once the state was formed. He *never* referred to Begin by name or even met with him until the Six-Day War.

In 1956, two years after his first resignation, he returned to government as defense minister under his successor, Moshe Sharett. It was not a match made in heaven. Sharett was far more dovish than Ben-Gurion, whose ego was hardly adaptable to a secondary role. Later that year Ben-Gurion became prime minister again, retaining that role until 1963, when he acrimoniously left the Labor Party—a split resulting from his demand for a public inquiry into the Lavon scandal in 1954.

In 1965, Ben-Gurion formed a new party called Rafi, liberal socially, conservative economically, firm on security, and intended to avoid the infighting and self-interest that were already downgrading Israeli politics and the Knesset. With Ben-Gurion joined by Peres, Dayan, Navon, Gad Yaacobi, and many other prominent figures of the day—including, I might add, on a far less prominent level, me—Rafi had a chance to resolve many problems in the Israeli system, but it, too, fell prey to political and human nature. By 1968, it had disbanded after failing to establish any kind of substantial power base.

Southern Command was responsible for Ben-Gurion's security during his time at Sde Boker, and a special unit was allotted to protect him. Every day, he insisted on a vigorous walk, and on a number of occasions I accompanied him, wheezing, gasping, and trying to keep up with his pace. What impressed me most were his willpower, stubbornness, and refusal to back down. But he also had a mischievous side. In the late 1960s, on a farewell international tour of Jewish communities, he went to Johannesburg, where the pro-apartheid mayor gave a lunch in his honor to which the Calvinist clergy were invited. Turning to the clergymen, Ben-Gurion asked, "How do you explain the fact that Moses married a black woman?" To say there was total consternation around that table would be a serious understatement.

The Negev has in the meantime progressed and developed. My service in Southern Command had reemphasized to me how important was Ben-Gurion's prophecy about the Negev. Today it is home to a booming capital, Beer Sheva, a thriving port and resort area in Eilat, an arid zone research center, and a university appropriately named after Ben-Gurion, which is becoming a major academic link with the Arab world. I left Southern Command dedicated to the implementation of the prophecy of Ben-Gurion.

———⟨∞⟩———

CHAPTER 12

Intelligence—Phase II

MASADA, HEROD'S ROYAL citadel and the last outpost of the Zealots during the Jewish war against Rome in A.D. 66–70, lies atop an isolated rock on the edge of the Judean Desert. On the east the rock drops sharply some 1,300 feet to the shore of the Dead Sea. Because the defenders— 960 men, women, and children—committed mass suicide rather than surrender, it has become a symbol of great significance to modern Israel; a site of extraordinary heroism rising out of brutal repression. The swearing-in ceremony of armed forces inductees often takes place there. The time had come for my two sons—Joel was nine and Mike was seven—to experience the emotion and power that comes with a Masada visit.

When we reached the nearby youth hostel, there was an urgent message waiting—I was to return to Tel Aviv immediately for a meeting with the chief of staff, General Haim Laskov. When I reached his apartment, I discovered I had a new job.

On 1 April 1959, an embarrassing foul-up occurred. Several officers on the general staff decided, without notice, to execute a mock call-up and mobilization of our reserve forces—on a national level—in order to gauge the Arab reaction. To expedite our mobilizations, we broadcast codes on the radio, creating apprehension and reminding people that they might be facing full-scale war. To do it as an unannounced test is not just foolish, it is extremely dangerous and leaves the nation vulnerable, frightened, and confused.

Ben-Gurion, who was entertaining Queen Elizabeth, the Queen Mother of Belgium, at the time, did not respond well to this little mishap. General Meir Zorea, director of military operations, and General

Yehoshafat Harkabi, director of military intelligence, were immediately removed from their posts and forced to assume full responsibility for the errors of their officers—thus my new job. Ben-Gurion had decided that I would serve my second tour of duty in intelligence. I was Harkabi's replacement, the new director of military intelligence. The new director of operations was the commander in chief of Northern Command, General Yitzhak Rabin.

When I had expressed my appreciation to the chief of staff for the trust shown in me, I decided to return to my *other* job—husband and father. The first step was to fly back to Beersheba, get in a car, and drive down to the youth hostel. Aura and the boys had left to begin the climb up the Snake Path, and I managed to catch up with them. When we reached the top of Masada, the sun was rising across the Dead Sea. Entranced by this breathtaking sight, we listened to the morning news on the radio—and the announcement of my appointment. The children have never forgotten the dramatic ending to their climb.

I HAD BEEN intimately involved in establishing and building Israel's military intelligence organization, but ten years had passed since I had left, and considerable advances had been made. For one thing, the intelligence corps was finally a full branch of the general staff, on an equal footing with operations, logistics, and manpower. There were many more operatives and a much more complicated and comprehensive infiltration of the Arab world. I had always pushed for that, and we needed it then more than ever.

There had been a major upheaval in the Arab world in 1958. The extreme Islamic groups had been growing more and more powerful and were becoming dominant, largely through encouragement and incitement from Egypt. Nasser was the Saddam Hussein of his day, a fanatical anti-West zealot who oppressed the fundamentalists in Egypt while using them for his own purposes abroad. His organization of murderers backed him against anyone who opposed him or the Arab states. His minions tried to kill King Hussein of Jordan several times.

Of course, the rise of fundamentalism and violence is more than the product of powerful, flawed leadership; a lot of it was a direct reaction to the horrific living conditions of the masses. While many people existed in abject poverty, kings and generals drank out of gold goblets. In Iraq, King Faisal and his uncle Abdul Illah were dragged into the streets by angry mobs and torn apart in the most brutal and savage manner. The Iraqi leader Nuri Said was caught trying to escape the country—disguised in woman's garb—and was summarily dealt with by the frenzied mob. Things were so chaotic that an unstable army commander of the local brigade in Baghdad, General Abd ul-Karim Qassem, was able to take control of Iraq. Qassem was stark raving mad—a lunatic. He released political prisoners, even known Israeli sympathizers and spies, for no reason and, just as cavalierly, lopped off the heads of others who opposed him. In Lebanon, civil war broke out; the country was saved only by the arrival of the U.S. marines, who came at the urgent request of the Lebanese president and stabilized the situation. In Jordan, King Hussein was in great danger; British forces were flown to Amman to try to bolster him.

Because relations with the unstable Arab governments and people were impossible, the visionary Ben-Gurion developed and strengthened relations with the non-Arab periphery surrounding the Arab countries: Turkey, Iran, and Ethiopia. For practical reasons, our relationships with those countries thrived. Emperor Haile Selassie of Ethiopia was particularly threatened by Arab extremism along his borders and near his shores. An Israeli military mission was sent there, and Ethiopian troops, with special emphasis on paratroopers, were sent to Israel to train. Our military attaché in Ankara developed a very close relationship with Turkish military leaders, and we agreed to train Turkish troops. In Iran, Reuven Shiloach, Ben-Gurion's right-hand man and, in many ways, the architect of his "periphery policy," had grown very close to the director of military intelligence, General Ali Kia. As a result, we were able to share crucial information, and the Mossad worked closely with the Savak, the Iranian version of the CIA. While none of these countries was, by nature, particularly fond of Israel, our mutual needs overcame prejudice and other obstacles. We needed each other to survive, and the survival instinct is a very persuasive basis for a friendship.

The tension in the Middle East invariably reflected the Cold War between the United States and the Soviet Union. The Sinai Campaign in 1956 signaled the steep decline of British and French influence in the Middle East and the growing increase of Soviet influence. The Eisenhower Doctrine outlined the broad economic and military aid to be given by the United States to Israel and its allies on the periphery, and also provided an understanding that the United States would defend these countries against any Soviet aggression. However, the United States remained inexplicably—to me, at least—passive in its attitude toward Egypt and its pro-Soviet influence in the Middle East. This U.S. passivity was bolstered by the State Department's repeated declarations that the United States would not be the "main weapons supplier" of Israel. Working against that was the fact that the Soviet Union lavishly armed the Arab armies and attached large numbers of Soviet advisors to them. The Soviet Union also established relations with and helped arm Arab underground movements—the FLN of Algeria, and the liberation movements in Eritrea, Somalia, and the southern part of the Arabian Peninsula. As the Soviet Union sent more and more arms to Egypt and other Arab countries and organizations, it also became more and more hostile toward Israel. The Soviets tended to see their political relationships in black-and-white terms—you were a friend or you were an enemy. The U.S. views were always more complex, much grayer. As a result, in those days Israel never enjoyed the same kind of broad and enthusiastic support from the U.S. government that the Arabs received from the Soviets.

ISRAEL'S MILITARY INTELLIGENCE was entering a new age of sophisticated technology and, accordingly, we launched a program to computerize our agency, educate the staff, and bring in trained technicians. We were the first organization in Israel to take this step, and the entire army followed our lead. Soon, all their departments were computerized and prepared for whatever advancements were certain to come. This exemplifies one of the big advantages Israel has always held over many countries in the region. We don't just emphasize education, we consider it the key to controlling our own destiny. As a result of our push for knowledge, we have always been able to embrace change—and that means we've managed to be a forward-looking country. Knowledge is obviously not a be-all and end-all in itself, but it is essential if one is to integrate various elements into mainstream society. Ignorance can never solve a problem; it can only disguise it, ultimately causing it to fester and grow. If Israel stands for anything—and I hope it stands for many things—I believe its struggle to educate all segments of society is one of the most important. Special emphasis was laid on understanding the Soviet Union's goals and means of expansion, and the detailed analyses and studies by Israeli military intelligence were used by many Western intelligence services. In February 1961, I proposed that we expand our intelligence work to include African countries with whom the Arabs were developing relationships, which I considered a direct threat to Israel's security.

Intelligence work cannot rest on its laurels. It must adapt itself to the most up-to-date technological advances and derive much of its progress from the development and strengthening of mutual relations with intelligence agencies of friendly countries. It is essential, in the case of a country such as Israel, with its regional neighborhood problems, that the highest possible standard be maintained and that the organization always guarantee an effective warning system. Furthermore, the machine must always be aware of developments in the neighboring countries, giving adequate warning on the one hand, and on the other hand being sensitive to changes in approaches that could lead to negotiations and peace.

Our top priority, after the United States, was France, which had become Israel's main supplier of arms. The two countries had many mutual interests, and militarily we were very much on the same wavelength. France was heavily involved in Algeria and saw Israel as a Western bastion in the Middle East, an ally against the United Arab Republic and Arab organizations.

An Israeli involvement with France raised certain problems. Efforts were being made to conclude the emigration of Jews from North Africa, and in the Maghreb countries, particularly Algeria, the friendship was looked upon in a very hostile manner. In the long run, the Algerian FLN extorted a great deal of money from the Jewish community and the Moroccans also placed obstacles in the path of Jews wishing to emigrate. The French, whenever possible, supported our emigration policies.

My opposite number in Paris was Conte de Loustalle, the chief of the Second Bureau (Intelligence). I was also in close touch with the SDECE, the French intelligence service, and its head, General Grossin. In one conversation Grossin told me that each day he prepared a file exclusively for the eyes of General de Gaulle. We eventually came to a unique arrangement: Grossin agreed that anything I considered important enough to bring before the general would be included in this file. Our main purpose was to block the spread of Nasserism in the Arab world. The French services worked hard to save North African Jewry. In exchange, we kept a very close watch on activities in Arab countries in support of the Algerian FLN.

In January 1960, Yitzhak Rabin, then chief of operations, Uzi Narkiss, our military attaché in Paris, and I were invited for an extensive visit with the French armed forces, including a trip to the combat area in Algeria.

Our trip to Algeria was preceded by an operational-level meeting in Paris. At that session, Rabin gave a presentation detailing the threats against the State of Israel, our response to such threats, what we still needed in order to stand up to such threats, and what France could do to help us with equipment, preparation of infrastructure, and operations, should we be attacked on land, on sea, or from the air. The French chief of operations, General Jean Niko, led the discussions on the French side, and General Meurice Challe, who was commanding the forces in Algeria, sent his deputy for naval affairs, Admiral Duget, to represent him at the talks. Rabin and I also prepared a joint position paper for the French chief of staff, General Paul Ely, in preparation for a discussion with General de Gaulle on the need for the French supply of Mirage fighters to Israel.

On our way to Algeria, we stopped to visit a commando and naval reconnaissance base at Perpignan, a small seaside resort just north of Spain, and viewed the latest developments in commando warfare, both on ground and underwater. We then flew to Corsica, where we stayed at one of the French army's main parachute and commando training centers; from there we flew to Algiers.

On our arrival, we called on General Challe. He was supposed to entertain us at dinner that night but while we were in his office he received a telephone call from Paris. We watched him turn pale. The call was to inform him that the Massu Affair had begun.

General Massu was the commander of the army corps responsible for the city of Algiers. In a moment of weakness or frustration or sheer idiocy, Massu had given an interview to a German correspondent maintaining that the French army no longer understood de Gaulle's withdrawal policy. Moreover, he said, it was unlikely the army could or would follow such a policy. Massu went on to characterize de Gaulle as left-wing and, most damning of all, said that he, Massu, and most of the other French officers bearing the responsibility of command would not carry out orders from the head of state. He was called to Paris immediately and de Gaulle dismissed him on the spot. We had arrived just in time to witness a near revolution of French army officers, many of whom were vehemently opposed to de Gaulle's policy of withdrawal from Algiers. General Challe excused himself as politely as he could. He had to fly to Paris immediately. General Jil, the commander of the parachute forces, became our new host.

We visited the Casbah in Algiers, Constantin, Bone, and the Ligne Meurice on the Tunis border. The most memorable visit, however, was to the 10th Parachute Division, which until very recently had been under the command of General Massu. The troops were positioned high up in the Kabilye Mountains; we could reach them only by helicopter. The snow on the ground was three meters high. Standing on a hilltop, Rabin and I watched as the 10th Division did battle with the rebel FLN forces in the valley below. The French forces were far superior and wiped out the resistance facing them. It was quite obvious that the French had developed new and effective guerrilla-type methods of winning such a battle. They were precise and efficient in their use of helicopters on the battlefield.

The officers we spoke to expressed great support for General Massu. We heard, over and over again, that if de Gaulle handed Algeria over to the Moslems, they would face three choices: to leave the army, to migrate from France to another country, or to engage in open revolt. I honestly believed that France was heading toward a possible military dictatorship.

The French Liberation Front (the FLF) declared a general strike that week. Bloody rioting followed in its wake. The extreme French elements were determined to force de Gaulle's hand, determined to make him give up his plan to "abandon" Algeria. It was an impossible problem, one that tore France apart. Frenchmen were actually killing Frenchmen. It was a tragedy on a human as well as a political level.

Soon after we returned to Israel, de Gaulle appeared on television, in uniform, and made a speech to the nation, clearly setting out his policy of leaving Algeria. Subsequently, most of our friends in the French military, including Generals Challe and Niko, were removed. With all the internal upheaval, with so many political, military, and diplomatic changes being made, it became imperative that Ben-Gurion meet directly with de Gaulle. France's pulling out of Algeria strengthened the Arab world, creating another Arab stronghold. We obviously had to prepare ourselves for the day when the Algerian War would conclude—and we needed to emphasize the very special link between Israel and France. We had to make sure that link was over and above the volatile diplomatic and military situation.

One evening I was summoned to Ben-Gurion's home. He had read my report about our visit to France and Algeria. He was particularly interested in my meeting with General Grossin, the head of the SDECE, and the fact that Grossin was prepared to communicate directly with de Gaulle on our behalf, bypassing all diplomatic channels. Ben-Gurion swore me to secrecy, then said he wanted me to request a meeting with de Gaulle—but no one else was to know about it. De Gaulle was about to meet with Nikita Khrushchev, and Ben-Gurion wanted to see the French president before the Soviet leader got to him. I instructed a young officer to go to Paris with a letter I had prepared. Grossin made good on his word and Ben-Gurion's visit with de Gaulle was approved and arranged.

On 13 June 1960 Ben-Gurion arrived in Paris accompanied by

Shimon Peres. Their discussions with de Gaulle lasted a number of days. At the end of their sessions, France was not only our number-one supplier of arms and our chief military backer but also our intelligence cooperation was cemented, and perhaps most important, we had new arrangements to cooperate scientifically. The only drawback to this meeting of two great men was the fact that Ben-Gurion, for security reasons, had arranged his trip through me instead of through the proper channels. This heightened the tension between the Mossad and military intelligence, typical of the mindless rivalries between intelligence services in many countries throughout the world. Israel was no exception.

As stable as our relationship was with France, that's how erratic it was with the United States. Our conversations were often tense and reflected no small measure of mutual mistrust. The U.S. embassy had an almost obsessive interest in the Israel Defense Forces, Israel's military planning, and our defense potential, and its almost clandestine form of collecting intelligence was totally opposed to the normal procedures and behavior of diplomatic personnel, especially of friendly countries. The Americans were obviously determined never to be caught napping again, as they were at the outbreak of the Sinai Campaign, and their ties to Egypt also complicated their relationship with Israel. At one point, we learned from Egyptian sources that secret information about Israel was being leaked to Cairo from U.S. sources.

While remaining leery of what they perceived as our leftish leanings, the Americans presented a position of impartiality as to the Middle East situation. We had applied to the State Department for a grant of weapons in 1949, in 1951, in 1955, and again in July 1960, and the reply was invariably the same. They never acceded to our request and requested top-secret material about our military. Any policy breakthrough on supplying arms to Israel seemed dependent on two factors: the Pentagon's strengthened influence in the State Department and a president strong enough to overrule the latter's decisions. My evaluation proved correct. The arms breakthrough finally occurred during John F. Kennedy's presidency.

In January 1960, Syrian shelling from the Golan Heights on Jewish villages in the valley became more intensive. As a response, Israeli forces attacked the village of Tawfik, which overlooks the southern end of the Sea of Galilee. This, in turn, caused the United Arab Republic to fear an impending Israeli attack on the Heights. Egyptian forces thus moved into Sinai to the Israeli border. That move was followed very carefully by Israeli intelligence; we covered them by aerial reconnaissance and photography. Some days later, several hundred Egyptian tanks were photographed in the vicinity of the Israeli border. Intelligence work gave us four days to prepare for an attack, more than enough time. Israeli forces were reinforced, the Egyptians withdrew their armor. The averted crisis showed that indeed the intelligence system was working.

Meanwhile, our periphery policy was progressing. Relations with Ethiopia and Iran were quite strong, relations with Turkey somewhat less so. As a member of NATO, Turkey had access to modern technological developments, which tempered their need for what we had to offer. Nonetheless, mostly due to their disappointment with U.S. tolerance of Nasserism, our relatively solid ties showed signs of getting stronger. Furthermore, while Israel had no formal relations with any Arab country, some contact was maintained. The Jordanian-Israeli committee was the most active arm of the Armistice Commission, and as commander of the Jerusalem District I conducted regular meetings with the Jordanian commander. That relationship would lead to an astonishing development.

On 28 August 1960, a bomb exploded in the Jordanian prime minister's office in Amman. It was planted by the United Arab Republic intelligence, based in Damascus (the United Arab Republic comprised the union of Egypt and Syria). The explosion killed the prime minister, Al Hazza el Majali, a close confidant of King Hussein, who was reportedly due in the office at the time; the bomb could well have been directed at him. Soon after the news broke, I was informed through our representative on the Armistice Commission that the Jordanian chief of intelligence wished to meet with me surreptitiously.

To my surprise, I was met instead by Colonel Emil Jamian, an aide to King Hussein, who explained that Hussein was determined to put an end to the United Arab Republic's terrorist activities. Accordingly, he had moved three operational brigades to the border, intending to invade Syria and settle accounts. They wanted to let us know their intentions and also to ensure that their flanks and rear would not be in danger. In other words, they wanted Israel to look after their border while they went to war with another Arab nation. Such an alliance made enormous sense from a practical point of view, and that's why I've always felt Israel could eventually come to some sort of peaceful arrangement to exist in the Middle East. As a rational man and a moderate, Hussein trusted Israel—certainly more than the Syrians, who had tried to assassinate him several times. He turned to us, and it was in our best interest to listen. We knew that at some point our help and trust would be reciprocated.

Ben-Gurion instructed me to guarantee the Jordanians that we would take care of the border and do everything possible to ensure their security.

This was all carried out amid great secrecy. At that time it was absolutely out of the question that an Arab, particularly a leader like Hussein, could publicly acknowledge any sort of relationship with or sympathy toward Israel. It would have been, quite literally, the kiss of death. Despite these extraordinary negotiations, King Hussein was talked out of his risky adventure by the British and American ambassadors, who sat with him into the early hours of the morning and convinced him of the inadvisability of his plan.

They were probably right to avert this particular war, although it is intriguing to envision what might have happened if, back then, Israel had been on the same side as Jordan in a major battle. Ten years later, in 1970, Syria and Jordan did go to war when Syrian forces invaded Jordan. This was during the so-called Black September, during which a PLO terrorist group began hijacking BOAC and Swissair planes and landing them in the desert and blowing them up. A hijacked Pan Am Boeing 747, which was too big to land in the desert, was diverted to Cairo and blown up. Hussein had always been anti-PLO and very much against the terrorist extremists, and he was nearly as much a target of their wrath as Israel. After all, the PLO had created a state within the Jordanian state and threatened Jordan's existence as an independent entity. Worried not only that these terrorists would attempt to take over his country but also that their actions could bring about serious and damaging repercussions with the U.S., Hussein declared war on the PLO, and that led to the Syrian invasion. Israel came to Hussein's aid, mobilizing and activating our air force along the Syria-Jordan border and holding the Syrian forces at bay long enough for Hussein's army to seize control of the battle. Syria withdrew and that's where Hussein's moderation ended. In the struggle with the PLO, thousands of Palestinians were slaughtered. The hatred was extreme and Palestinian losses were heavy. If Israel ever retaliated in such a fashion, there would be an international uproar of unprecedented proportions.

To this day, Hussein and Arafat dislike each other, but they must get along. And so they do, the strangest of bedfellows. In a way, it's a matter of survival.

BECAUSE THE ARAB WORLD was so volatile and, in many ways, irrational, we had to keep many of our dealings secret. Any friendly gestures toward us from a periphery country—not to mention an Arab country—could result in anything from a political freeze-out to a full-scale attack. Countries were reaching out to us, but in the quietest way imaginable.

Our most intensive and far-reaching contacts at that time were with Iran, and we had an unofficial office that, in many ways, acted as an embassy. Cooperation was kept absolutely secret by both sides, but the Mossad had contacts with the Savak, the widely feared Iranian secret service headed by General Teymour Bakhtiar. Bakhtiar had a reputation for extraordinary cruelty and ruthlessness. When some of his former colleagues and friends from the military academy were suspected of disloyalty to the shah, they were shot by a firing squad and the shah allegedly laughed publicly as he watched them being shot. Lusty, greedy, immoral, and even savage, Bakhtiar was warm, friendly, and charming to me. The shah, who was not a strong man, was easily influenced by Bakhtiar, who ultimately paid the price for such manipulation. On a hunting expedition in Iraq arranged by the shah, he was shot and killed.

Before I took over, military intelligence had established relations with General Ali Kia, head of Iranian military intelligence. Following his World War II experiences as military attaché in Berlin and Stockholm, he went out of his way to help refugees from Iraq's Jewish community cross into Iran and make their way to Israel. He felt he was in some small way atoning for the Holocaust. As different as we were culturally and politically, there was a bond, and in a frank and open discussion he made it clear even then that he intended to achieve normal diplomatic recognition. As we mapped out various possibilities, with a view to creating precedents, it struck me that in some ways it was easier dealing with an Iranian military man—someone not considered a natural friend—than with the American State Department. It's all a question of mutual need and what you want to accomplish, and Kia and I knew what we wanted: a relationship that would help both countries survive. When I raised the question of establishing formal relations with Abas Aram, the Iranian foreign minister, Aram answered me in the most evasive manner, practically in the words he had used when talking to our own foreign minister, Golda Meir, in New York two months before. In the midst of Aram's obfuscation, Kia intervened angrily. "Who are you afraid of? The Arabs? What can they do to us?" he asked angrily. They argued bitterly until the foreign minister backed down and acknowledged that he would consider a mutual appointment of consuls.

My work began with an introduction to the joint Iranian intelligence committee, known as the Supreme Security Committee. It was housed on the grounds of the shah's marble palace, where I had my first audience with him. We met in a huge hall with a magnificent carpet worth many millions of dollars; at the entrance were displayed scrolls of pure gold and silver, thousands of years old, discovered in archaeological excavations at Persepolis, once the Persian capital.

The shah greeted me in a very friendly manner. His English was perfect, and he could have passed for a Western dandy. He looked young and relaxed—all of which belied the nature of his regime. I was disturbed to see the slavish demeanor of the generals and officials who attended that meeting; some of them prostrated themselves on the floor, and all of them exited walking backward, bowing and facing the shah. The shah was very bitter about Nasser, whom he considered an enemy of the West as well as of Iran. He kept returning to the question of why the Western powers were so obtuse and blind as to strengthen our common enemy, Nasser, militarily, which he believed was the case. He would be open to any suggestions from Israel, he said, provided they did not conflict with Iranian interests.

"Iranian interests" meant, of course, the shah's interests. His regime was very corrupt, and no business could be done without payoffs to the royal family. Human rights did not exist. The laws were medieval, enforced by torture and executions. The only right that seemed inviolable was the royal family's right to get richer.

By the end of his rule, I believe, the shah had become eccentric. To celebrate the three thousandth anniversary of the monarchy in Persia, he flew in jetloads of guests and had Parisian couturiers design gowns and costumes and fly them to Persepolis. He spent tens of millions of dollars on party after party, while his people were starving to death outside his window. After that anniversary celebration, the Israeli ambassador, Uri Lubrani, told the Americans that the shah would be overthrown within a year. But the American ambassador did not accept this. Had they not ignored our warning, the Americans could possibly have stopped Khomeini's ascent.

Politics is a strange and sometimes confounding business. The shah was an indefensible leader, and what he did to his own people was morally repugnant. And yet he was our ally—and much needed. His moral bankruptcy was replaced by Islamic fundamentalism, one of the greatest threats to the security of the modern world. Sometimes that's what politics seems to boil down to: the choice of a rational evil over an irrational one.

During my first up-close look at this rational evil, and under the prodding of General Kia, Iran decided to lift the veil of secrecy surrounding its relations with Israel—a supremely courageous act. The shah, to my surprise, had no fear in letting the Islamic nations know that he had not just an Israeli option but a full-fledged relationship with the Jewish State.

When I returned to Israel, I showed Ben-Gurion a joint declaration that I had prepared with the shah's approval. The proposal laid out our common goals and ways for cooperation and reaffirmed a desire to establish normal diplomatic relations. Ben-Gurion embraced me. Realizing that Iran had come over to our side, he decided to make our "periphery" relations with Iran, Ethiopia, and Turkey official. That document, signed by order of the shah, was a huge step forward in establishing Israel as a permanent force in the Middle East.

Once a relationship becomes official, new problems emerge. In this case, they revolved around ridiculous internal politics.

The first thing I now needed to do was appoint a military attaché as quickly as possible. My candidate was Lieutenant Colonel Yaakov Nimrodi (in later years an astute businessman on the international scene; he became a friend and partner of Adnan Kashoggi), the perfect attaché. He had served in the Mossad in Iran, spoke Persian and Arabic fluently, and was completely at home in Iran. But Isser Harel, head of the Mossad at the time, objected vigorously, maintaining that we should send somebody with a European background to represent us.

Harel was a tough character who did not brook opposition or criticism, and his attitude reflected the inevitable clash between intelligence organizations. A strong and difficult opponent, he enjoyed considerable support from the prime minister and members of the government.

Ben-Gurion, apprised of Harel's objections, came up with a diplomatic way of pushing Nimrodi through—if Kia would help. At our meeting with Ben-Gurion, the prime minister asked what qualifications were needed in an attaché to Iran, and Kia detailed every attribute of Nimrodi's (which I'd had him commit to memory). Ben-Gurion asked me if we had a suitable candidate, and I said yes, and Ben-Gurion authorized me to appoint Nimrodi, who went on to serve for ten years with the greatest distinction.

Over the next three years, I met several times with the shah in the marble palace, in his lavishly appointed home in Teheran (where I also met Queen Farah Diba and their children), and in the Darvand Palace, in Shimran, on a mountain overlooking Teheran. Surrounded by a forbidding wall, that huge complex housed not only the shah's palace but also the homes of members of the court and of the shah's family. The Peacock

Palace housed the Peacock Throne, encrusted with diamonds and precious stones. All of these houses and treasures bespoke unimaginable opulence, even as most of his downtrodden countrymen lived in dire poverty.

Traveling freely throughout Iran, I saw firsthand the virtually uncontrolled expenditure of funds for achieving an almost obscenely showy military grandeur. To the shah, appearance and style were clearly not only expressions of power, they were power. I also witnessed the power of Islam and its hold over people, a subject that obsessed the shah. He discussed it freely and, with rare insight, recognized its threat to his rule. It would ultimately lead to his downfall.

On a vacation with General Kia, I traveled to Rasht, on the Caspian Sea, and I shall never forget our drive along the Soviet border. At regular intervals were high sentry posts with armed guards who surveyed us and trained their weapons on us as we passed. The implications of this wicked empire were terrifying: on one side, a nation of starving people ruled from golden thrones; on the other, an oppressed empire under a dictatorship whose money was poured into an enormous military and security machine.

The shah, always able to act on a dictator's whimsy, liked to shake up his military organization to keep it all in line. So when Kia's enemies—he had many—complained about a road to his country estate built at the government's expense, he found himself on trial along with three other members of the Supreme Security Committee. They were held in what can only be characterized as a golden cage, the officers club of the military police. I considered Kia a friend and I knew he was quite depressed about his incarceration, so I arranged to see him. It was not a simple arrangement. Kia had a son, Feredoun, known as "Freddie," who was married to a very attractive Swedish lady, Amy. Freddie applied for Amy's "brother" to visit the general, the application was granted, and I showed up at the officers club, one of the least likely Swedes ever. But the ruse worked. Kia was moved to tears that I had taken such a risk, but, as I told him, I was always willing to take a risk for a good friend of mine and of Israel's. His detainment was little more than a slap on the wrist, and he was released after the trial with no damage except perhaps to his ego. But when Khomeini came to power, the damage was much greater: Kia was forced to escape to Paris, leaving behind his fortune, estimated to be approximately $50 million.

On a trip to Abadan, the great center of oil refineries on the Shatt-el-Arab River, I saw the confluence of the Persian and Arab cultures. At every turn, the Iranians made a point of emphasizing their hatred of the Arabs, who had tried to annihilate their culture over the centuries. In Khorramshahr, adjacent to Abadan, the strength of the Arab culture and tradition was quite powerful. (This area would be bitterly fought over from 1980 to 1988—and an estimated one million people would die—when Saddam Hussein tried to nullify a 1975 border agreement.) On my last official visit to Iran, in 1961, with General Zvi Tsur, our chief of staff, we had the inevitable audience with the shah, in whom we had invested a lot of time and energy—as had the Americans. They had bolstered him with arms to the tune of $20 billion, but their time, energy, and money would prove useless. Indeed, it was dangerous. After the Khomeini revolution, much of the equipment and arms sent to the shah fell right into Khomeini's hands and Iran's relationships with the West came to a rude conclusion. The danger facing the world from the rise and spread of Islamic fundamentalism, powered by the revolution in Iran, is incalculable. To religious fanatics, death is a meaningless deterrent; freed from fear, there is nothing that fundamentalists will not do. Unfortunately, the West was given only two choices of leaders. There is a direct link between the fanatic extremism of Islamic fundamentalism and the shah's abuse of wealth and power. Although the dangers of such abuse were manifest, the implications of what would develop in its wake were not.

The Khomeini revolution ended the Israeli-Iranian association, and many of us followed with trepidation the inhumane excesses of the fundamentalist regime. Our ambassador, Joseph Harmelin, and his staff barely escaped a grim fate, but many friends who had helped and supported Israel were executed in the cellars of Teheran prisons.

Now an implacable enemy of Israel, Iran has become officially committed to our total destruction—indeed, to the destruction of all "enemies of Islam." Israel's true and devoted ally has emerged as one of the great dangers to world stability. And it does not seem to be going away.

WITH MAJOR CHANGES taking place in Africa and the Middle East, as one country after another achieved independence from colonial powers, Ben-Gurion suggested that I monitor our operations in Ethiopia and assess the situation at the opening to the Red Sea.

Ethiopia's soldiers and policemen were being trained by Israelis, and in Addis Ababa it was easy to see the nation's potential for wealth and growth. Our programs were helping them develop their resources and overcome handicaps and deficits in agriculture, water resources, medicine, and the military. As with so many of Israel's actions, there was a duality inherent in these good deeds. As a humanitarian nation, we feel a legitimate duty to contribute to the needy. On the other hand, there were great political advantages to helping Ethiopia. Their goodwill could help protect our shipping lanes, and permission to use their airspace en route to South Africa, which housed a major Jewish community, was particularly important to the growth of El Al. Thousands of Israeli instructors have traveled throughout Africa, living in the bush with the local inhabitants and improving their lot. Africans and representatives of other developing countries in the Caribbean, South America, and the Pacific area have come to Israel to study and acquire skills. In the past thirty years, half of the eye operations carried out in black Africa were performed by Israeli doctors, primarily from Hadassah Hospital in Jerusalem. Many African political, labor, and civil service leaders are familiar with Israel and can even speak a smattering of Hebrew. Were it not for the Arab economic boycott of Israel, Israel could have helped to transform much of the Middle East, eliminating a legion of human and social problems.

For one night in Ethiopia, my host was the chief of the security services, whose name was unpronounceable, so we called him Gaby, an amalgam of the first two letters of his name. Gaby was handsome and extremely personable, and a gracious host. Soon after I left Ethiopia, Israeli intelligence got wind of an internal plot to assassinate Haile Selassie, who was then in Liberia on a state visit. Our people, who participated in his security arrangements, reached him to warn him, the revolt was put down, and the emperor returned safely. Two weeks later, an Israeli military advisor in Ethiopia, "Zonick" Shaham, wrote that I might be interested to see my dinner host in his present condition. Enclosed with the note was a photograph of the main marketplace in Addis Ababa. My gracious friend Gaby was hanging by his neck.

I CONCLUDED MY SERVICE as director of military intelligence in January 1962. My final task was to present the annual national intelligence evaluation for the coming year to Ben-Gurion and the general staff. I estimated that the Arab armies would be ready for war in five years' time, 1967. This proved to be correct.

Before leaving my post, I asked for a meeting with Foreign Minister Golda Meir. Haim Yachil, director-general of the Foreign Ministry, had told me that the ministry very much wanted to appoint me to an important ambassadorial post, but, to their amazement, had come up against stiff opposition from Golda. I was surprised because my relationship with her had been strictly businesslike and uneventful. There were a few minor problems with her when I was director of intelligence, and I once went to Ben-Gurion to ask him to help me. "No, you deal with it," he told me. "She is a great woman, but she is a woman!"

I told Golda that I was not interested in a job in the Foreign Ministry and had already made arrangements to head an industrial concern. But I wanted very much to know what she had against me and why she had turned me down for the job. "The head of the Mossad is against you, and whatever he says is right," she said, before lecturing me on his honesty, accuracy, and healthy instincts. Speaking with equal passion, I pointed out that I had weathered a head-on attack based on interservice rivalry thanks to backing from Ben-Gurion. In my view, Ben-Gurion was now reassessing his attitude to the Mossad.

A few weeks later, Dr. Haim Yachil told me that I had done the impossible. Golda *never*—ever—changed her mind, but she had just instructed him to offer me an ambassadorial post. I refused politely, but I felt good. I had warned her of a problem that they would soon have to confront.

Sometime after I left, Isser Harel, the head of the Mossad, issued dire warnings about assistance being given to Egypt by German scientists, fearful that rockets would be created that could destroy Israel. The issue came to a head, and Harel resigned amid a storm of controversy— daggers drawn with Ben-Gurion. Golda Meir found that the Mossad chief, whom she considered never to have made a mistake, had just made quite a grave one.

Several years later, while in New York to address an annual United Jewish Appeal lunch and rally, I ran into Golda Meir. As we parted, she said, "I have never forgotten that conversation of ours. You were right and I was wrong."

WHEN I CONCLUDED my term of office in January 1962, I embarked on a three-month tour abroad. First I went to America to address the Israel Bonds organization, then to Canada to visit with Yaacov, who was Israel's ambassador there. Then I flew to Japan, where I spoke to the Japanese military establishment and intelligence organization about the Middle East. From there, via Hong Kong, I went to address the University of the East in Manila in the Philippines. Even then, I felt very uncomfortable there; it appeared that law and order almost did not exist. When I took a taxi from the embassy to the hotel, I was actually obliged to phone the embassy to report that I had arrived safely.

From there I flew to Vietnam. The U.S. military had not yet entered the country in force, but the Americans were training soldiers in the military schools. I had a lengthy session with President Ngo Dien Diem, who had a propensity for lengthy sessions. He questioned me not only about our settlements along the frontiers but also about the Israeli military educational system and even about the quality of the runways in the small feeder airports that we had established around the country. He was curious about the smallest of details. It was very strange.

While I was in Saigon, there was an attack on the palace. An air force lieutenant bombed it, attempting to kill Madame Nhu, the president's sister-in-law, who many felt had too much power. Diem himself was, of course, later assassinated. In fact, I believe that the most serious mistake the Americans made in their Vietnam debacle was apparently to acquiesce in the murder of President Diem. He may have been a very difficult character for them to handle, but he was the people's leader. After his murder, the American government was forced to ally itself with leaders who really weren't of the people. They were backing a corrupt regime that, in fact, had no real support *except* the American government. If a watershed has to be noted in the Vietnam War—the point of no return, so to speak—I would say it was the murder of President Diem.

I spent a short period with the Fifth Vietnamese Division in Bien Ho, not too far from Saigon. I met with the various ambassadors and military attachés, and left with a reasonably clear picture of what was going on there, although I was not fully aware of the degree of corruption which was eating away at the body politic of the country.

Within a few years, Haim Bar-Lev, who was to become our chief of staff some years later, visited Vietnam. He was followed by Moshe Dayan, who was visiting as a military correspondent. His analyses at that time were very telling and indeed prophetic. Their perception was that America was involved in a war that couldn't be won.

The next few weeks were a blur of worldwide travel. From Vietnam I went to Bangkok. From Bangkok to Vientiane, Laos, and thence to Rangoon, Burma. This was at the height of the honeymoon between the Israeli forces and the Burmese. It was before Burma went over to an extreme form of socialism and cut itself off from the world. My next stop was Calcutta; the poverty was horrifying to me. I could never forget it. I was told that approximately two million people were born, lived, grew up, and died in the streets there. What I witnessed there and in Bombay is a horrible commentary on the human race. One night I came out of my hotel room and stumbled against something, which moved. It was one of the servants in the hotel sleeping in the outside corridor.

From Calcutta I flew—in a Nepal Airlines DC-3, which seemed to me to be tied together with string and stuck together with spit—to Katmandu, and from there to New Delhi, and finally home to Israel.

In August 1962, I was formally released from the Israel Defense Forces. I had been offered a job as manager of an industrial development firm called GUS-Rassco, whose shares were publicly traded. I sensed an imminent industrial explosion in Israel, and I wanted to be a part of it. I wanted economic independence, particularly because I had thoughts of going into politics. I had run a large and very complicated organization, and it was time to turn that experience to my own advantage. And it was time, once again, to have a private life.

The Six-Day War

IN 1962, AFTER concluding my military service, I went to "Chera" Tsur, chief of the general staff, to discuss an appointment to the active reserves. Tsur had decided to introduce changes in the command staff structure; each command headquarters would now have a military government section equipped to handle civilian governance in time of war. As a reserve officer I was entrusted with the task of creating and heading a military government branch in the headquarters of Central Command.

Problems with the bureaucracy made allocating personnel, administrative requirements, transportation, and communications nearly impossible. But I managed to create a somewhat primitive organization by mobilizing the top people who were not allotted to fighting units in every department of government. When war did come again, in 1967, I felt that our team was far more impressive than any existing government. We studied Jordan quite closely—I arranged for regular delivery of Jordanian newspapers, Arabic and English, so we could keep abreast of everything that was happening there, and in the West Bank in particular. In addition, we had regular lectures and courses on Jordan and the West Bank. The idea was to make my entire administrative team comfortable and familiar with all things Jordanian. But it was clear that we were not considered anywhere near a top priority, and my new job as managing director of an industrial investment group was keeping me busy.

The period following the 1956 Sinai Campaign was one of relative quiet along the Israel-Egypt border, but the Middle East was far from quiet or calm.

In 1958, Iraq's King Faisal was assassinated and mobs in Baghdad tore

Prime Minister Said to pieces. The weak revolutionary regime that followed, led by General Abdul Karim Qassem, enabled the Soviet Union to take hold in that oil-rich state and establish a foothold in the Persian Gulf. Arabs were turning against Arabs everywhere; because Nasser was constantly fomenting unrest in Lebanon and Jordan, civil war broke out in Lebanon. United States marines arrived there to stabilize the situation at the same time the British army came to bolster King Hussein's regime. In 1958, Egypt and Syria united to establish the short-lived United Arab Republic, and Syria became Nasser's northern center for activities against Israel. By 1961, when Syria revolted against what was in effect Egyptian occupation and became independent, antipathy toward Israel had exploded. The Syrians shelled Israeli settlements from their advantageous positions along the Golan Heights, laid mines and waged a war of attrition along the frontier, and regularly attacked fishing boats in the Sea of Galilee.

In 1964, at the Casablanca Conference, the Palestine Liberation Organization was established, backed with over $1 billion from Arab sources. Its objectives included the destruction of the State of Israel and, by implication, King Hussein's Jordan. In 1965, when the Fatah organization, headed by Yasser Arafat, took over the PLO, it embarked on a policy to create a situation along the Israeli border that would draw every neighboring Arab state into a war with Israel.

Israel had long declared that the closing of the Strait of Tiran in Sinai, in the south, or the diversion of the Jordan waters in Syria, in the north, would be considered an act of war. As work on the diversion of the sources of the Jordan River was stepped up, Prime Minister Levi Eshkol responded by ordering long-range artillery and tank fire against the diversion work. The Syrians realized that to continue would mean a full-fledged war, which they were not prepared for, so their work was halted. Dominated by extremist elements in the Ba'ath Party, the Syrians continued to send terrorist raiders into Israel. When Israel retaliated, the Syrians stepped up their attacks. By April 1967, escalating tension between Israel and Syria had been critically aggravated by the involvement of the Soviet Union.

Encouraged by the Russians, Nasser paraded his forces in full view of the world and through Cairo, en route to the front in Sinai. The Arab world now mobilized against Israel, and the Arab media promised daily that Israel's population would be thrown into the sea. Succumbing to pressure by Nasser, UN Secretary-General U Thant withdrew the forces that for ten years had been a buffer between Israel and the Gaza Strip and

Sinai. With Israel now ringed by some 250,000 Arab troops, over 2,000 tanks, and some 700 combat planes, Prime Minister Levi Eshkol reorganized his cabinet and brought in the farther right, more militaristic Menachem Begin of the Herut Party as minister without portfolio. Moshe Dayan, who had joined the Rafi Party, became minister of defense.

Perhaps one of the most rational leaders Israel has ever had, Eshkol needed all the help he could get. Amid this external crisis, he was under attack from within. Ben-Gurion, our first prime minister, had appointed Eshkol as his successor but, unable to accept his assertion of independence, gave him no support. Eshkol was no puppet. He had great courage and in 1967 he needed every ounce of it.

Every political and diplomatic development pointed to an imminent Arab attack, and even King Hussein signed an agreement to join in it, letting Egypt assume joint command of his own Jordanian army. It was an incredible miscalculation. He was then in control of the West Bank and East Jerusalem but would almost certainly have been ousted by either Nasser or the PLO if the Arabs had won the war. The Arabs never would have trusted Hussein, as did Israel—until he aligned himself against us in 1967. Hussein's failure in this campaign would return to haunt him in 1973. As a result of his defeat and loss of land in 1967, he didn't join the Arab attack in the Yom Kippur War, when we were extremely vulnerable. If he had, we could have been in very great trouble.

Neither side particularly desired the 1967 Six-Day War. It came about because of Russian urging and interference—which caused a series of military escalations and miscalculations.

On 22 May 1967, Nasser announced the closing of the Strait of Tiran. I realized that this was war and that Israel was in great danger.

On 5 June General Mordechai Hod, commander of the air force, led what is perhaps the most brilliant operation in Israeli military history. Surrounded by Arab troops and tanks poised to attack, the air force made a preemptive strike. Timed to coincide with the hour when most Egyptian pilots would be en route after breakfast from their home to their base, Israeli planes attacked nineteen air force bases, flying in low under radar screens, taking everyone completely by surprise. In one fell swoop, within three hours, the Egyptian air force was destroyed.

Unaware of the catastrophe and believing false reports of victory emanating from Cairo, the Jordanian, Syrian, and Iraqi air forces began operations. By that evening, the Jordanian air force had been wiped out, two-thirds of the Syrian air force had been destroyed, and the Iraqi air force had also been badly mauled. By nightfall of the next day, 416 Arab aircraft had been destroyed, 393 of which had never gotten off the ground. Twenty-six Israeli aircraft had been downed.

On the first day of the war, Nasser telephoned Hussein. Neither of them knew that their conversation was being monitored by Israeli intelligence—this one was later broadcast to the world. Unaware that his air force no longer existed, Nasser lied outright, telling Hussein that Egypt's armored forces had attacked and were halfway across the Negev. Therefore, he said, Hussein should attack from the West Bank across the Negev and meet up with the Egyptians, cutting Israel in half. Levi Eshkol, privy to the conversation, immediately sent a warning through the UN to Hussein not to become involved, assuring him that he would not be harmed by Israel. Unfortunately for Hussein, he believed Nasser, and the City Line in Jerusalem erupted with artillery shells as the Jordanians moved their forces forward along the border. Totally in control of the air, Israeli forces destroyed the Jordanian armored reinforcements on their way to Jerusalem and captured the Old City of Jerusalem and the whole of the West Bank. After six days, Israel also controlled the Sinai, the Gaza Strip, and part of the Golan Heights, captured from Syria.

In 1962, I BEGAN to appear on Israeli radio (there was still no television in Israel) and the BBC as a military commentator. Over the years, I would comment on military subjects such as the China–India struggle in the Himalayas, the India–Pakistan War, and the Vietnam War.

In the tense waiting period before the Six-Day War, with our borders surrounded by Arab soldiers, the Holocaust was still fresh in the minds of many Israelis and the potential for total destruction was very much a reality. Preoccupied with national survival, the government had little time for its citizens' individual problems and concerns. One Friday afternoon, some ten days before the start of the war, Hannoch Givton, the director-general of Israeli radio, called me. He said, quite plainly, that the public was in a panic and that the government was cut off from the people. So I agreed to translate the military events into the language of the people.

On a Sunday evening, I appeared at the radio station. The first item that evening was a speech by Prime Minister Eshkol, whose staff had done a horrendous job of preparing him—and public speaking was not his forte. His speech was a disaster. Panicked by his perceived indecision and weakness, people wept openly in the streets and even in the military units. Immediately after Eshkol's fiasco, my first broadcast began.

I hit the jackpot.

Logically and strategically, I explained Egypt's strengths and weaknesses, enumerating our difficulties and theirs. Putting things in perspective, I concluded that Egypt would be facing nearly impossible problems if it attacked us.

The reaction was electrifying. Three hours later I was still answering calls from citizens, kibbutzim, soldiers, and rabbis.

Encouraged by this reaction, I began a nightly series devoted to various aspects of the Arab military threat. Expecting a Warsaw- or London-type blitz, people were digging slit trenches in the parks and in their back gardens. The fear, though legitimate, was brought home when I found Aura taking down our art and taping up the windows—the civil defense had recommended it.

On the fifth night, I broadcast an in-depth analysis of the air force situation, concluding that there was no danger of a blitz. I ended with a declaration that has lived on in the national consciousness: "If I had to choose tonight between being an Egyptian pilot attacking Tel Aviv and being a citizen in the city of Tel Aviv, I would in the interests of self-preservation prefer to be in the city of Tel Aviv."

To MY AMAZEMENT, I had become a source of support for Israel's people, and my broadcasts turned their terror aside.

They continued nightly until the outbreak of the war. From then until the war ended, I spoke three times a day in Hebrew and once in English.

During the war, Israel made very smart and manipulative use of the media. Unlike the Arabs, whose false bombast claimed success after Day One, we said nothing. We assumed that if the world thought Israel was doing badly, there would be no international reaction—and we were right. Only after the great Egyptian debacle was made public did the UN and various powers start condemning the war.

As SOON AS the Jordanians moved into combat, the military government was mobilized.

As its head, I drove to Jerusalem on 6 June 1967 and was handed my appointment as governor of the West Bank, with an Arab population of 800,000, by Moshe Dayan and Rabin. "Moshe," I asked, "what is our policy to be?" He replied, "Let the Arabs rule themselves under our control. I want an Arab to be born, raised, and live in the West Bank, and never to see an Israeli official. It's bad enough that we have to suffer from our bureaucracy. Why should they?"

I joined the convoy led by Dayan, Rabin, and General Uzi Narkiss, chief of Central Command, and drove through the silent streets, the quiet punctuated by exchanges of fire, accompanied by Meir Shamgar, the judge advocate general and later Israel's chief justice. "If we have any sense," I said, "we will assemble the Palestinian leadership and offer them autonomy under Israeli sovereignty." Shamgar relayed this idea to Prime Minister Eshkol, but the reaction was not favorable because of the intricacies of coalition government.

We reached the Lions Gate overcome by emotion. I had been to the Old City with my father during the British Mandate, but now it was ours. The dream had come true. For 2,000 years, every day, three times a day, observant Jews had prayed, "May our eyes see Your return to Zion." The longing for the Old City and the Wailing Wall was palpable.

On the main square, facing the Mosque of Omar, on the Temple Mount, the brigade of paratroopers who led the way into the city was drawn up in honor of our convoy. An Israeli flag had been hoisted in celebration—and Dayan's first order was to haul it down. He did not want to offend Moslem sensibilities.

We passed through the Maghreb Gate, leading down to the Wailing Wall. To the sound of the shofar, hardened paratroopers who had never prayed in their life, who knew little about Jewish tradition or religious education, stood against the wall in tears. Dayan, in accordance with tradition, put a little note into a crevice between the ancient stones, a written prayer for peace. We had come home to this hallowed spot, he declared, never to leave it again. We were walking back to the Lions Gate when Dayan turned to me. "It's all yours now," he said. "Do your best."

I realized that now that I was military governor, it was time to end my broadcasts. My immediate task was to make sure children had milk, people had food, and all the bodies were buried. On Thursday of that week, I concluded my final radio speech by saying, "I am broadcasting these words from Israeli headquarters, which but three days ago was Jordanian headquarters. From my window I look out upon the Temple Mount and once again the armies of Israel guard the city wall adorned by the flag of Israel. A burned-out Israeli tank lies on its side before a gate in the wall, silent testimony to the price which our people paid. May we be worthy of this price."

⸺ ⟨⟩⟩⟩ ⸺

CHAPTER 14

Military Government

As THE NEW military governor of the West Bank, I had jurisdiction over the city of Jerusalem. General Shlomo Lahat, who later became mayor of Tel Aviv, was appointed commander of the eastern part of Jerusalem, which was populated by Moslem and Christian Arabs. Our first order of business was to announce a general curfew except for those in charge of vital services. This was martial law and we needed a period of calm and order. Our second proclamation made Jordanian law fully valid, if it did not clash with the authority of the Israeli forces. Yes, we now controlled Jordanian or Palestinian territory, but as Dayan had specified, we did not want to control another people. We also had to keep the demarcation line between Israeli and Jordanian territory hermetically sealed—not an easy task with a naturally curious Israeli population eager to see districts it had known so many years ago.

In the midst of this, the mayor of Jerusalem, Teddy Kollek, stormed into my office. The Arab children in East Jerusalem had no milk, and he insisted we help distribute it to every child. Within three days, municipal services—water and electricity—and civil order had been restored throughout the city.

On 8 June I invited the leaders of Jerusalem's fifty-odd Christian churches and denominations to our headquarters at the Ambassador Hotel in East Jerusalem: Greek Orthodox, Armenian, Syriac, the Latin, Lutheran, Anglican, Copt, Abyssinian, Chaldean, the apostolic delegate of the Vatican, and many more. "I know many of you from my father's home," I said, pointing out that we, the Jews, who had not been allowed even to reach the holiest place in Jewish belief, the Wailing Wall, during two decades of Jordanian rule, were more sensitive to this problem than others would be. On behalf of the government of Israel I guaranteed complete freedom for all religions and sects.

My words were well received, and several Christian leaders extolled the Israel Defense Forces' respect and consideration for the security and sanctity of the holy places during the war. Frequently this concern had come at no small cost to our soldiers' security.

Having won not only the battles but also the war, we were inundated with visitors; everyone wanted to see and be a part of the Jerusalem that had been cut off for two decades. Golda Meir, now secretary-general of the Labor Party, arrived en route to address major rallies of American Jewry. Golda wanted to be—or at least be seen as—the mother of us all. She believed that she had the common touch and was one of the people. The fact is that as prime minister, she was very much out of touch with the ordinary citizen. Doctrinaire and obsessed with the trappings of power, she believed that only she was right about any subject under discussion. Her stubborn blindness to outside influences cost Israel much in 1973, leading up to the Yom Kippur War. At times removed from day-to-day reality, she allowed herself to be misled by the Egyptians and Syrians, and, as on many other occasions, refused to listen to those trying to tell her the truth. Yet, despite her personal flaws and shortcomings as prime minister, she was quite remarkable and made tough decisions during the Yom Kippur War, though she had never held a rifle in her life. And make no mistake—the decisions were hers, and she gave the orders to the minister of defense and the generals.

On 9 June Ben-Gurion and I went to the Wailing Wall. With his head covered, he faced the wall, the prayers and dreams of centuries reflected in his face. Ben-Gurion believed unequivocally that Israel should return to the Arabs all of the territories taken in the Six-Day War, except for East Jerusalem and the Golan Heights. In exchange for such concessions, we should demand complete peace with our neighbors. "This city will never be united, will never be one," he told me, "unless you tear down the ancient walls." I was startled, because he meant the physical destruction of those four-hundred-year-old walls, built by the Ottoman sultan Suleiman the Magnificent. But he insisted that this was the only way that Jerusalem would ever become an undivided capital. While I did not agree with his proposal I realized that as a genuine visionary, Ben-Gurion was foreseeing the very peace process that, with all its problems, is today approaching reality.

That evening, Anwar al-Khatib, the Jordanian governor of Jerusalem, called on me to pay his respects. He recounted his nation's experiences during the war. As he was advancing armored forces to Jerusalem from the Jordan River, King Hussein assured him that help was on the way, an empty promise. Al-Khatib had begged the Jordanians not to store their shells and high explosives on the Temple Mount, in the caves beneath the mosques of Omar and Al-Aksa, but to no avail. (The holy area of the Temple Mount could have been blown to the heavens.) In the divide-and-rule Jordanian system of government, King Hussein did not allow a central administration on the West Bank. It was divided into five districts, each headed by a governor who reported directly to and received orders from Amman. In other words, there was no single Palestinian ruler of the area, no unity, and no vision. Eager to help us set up a central West Bank administration, Al-Khatib asked for permission to attend a conference of foreign ministers of Arab states that was being convened and to "tell them in the name of the Palestinian people some of the facts of life." I liked the idea of an autonomous Jordanian area under Israeli sovereignty, but Dayan had his doubts and it never happened.

During the war the Arab consuls had fled to Jordan, their families left stranded in Jerusalem. The families of Jordanian officers who had withdrawn with their forces had also been abandoned. Accordingly—and humanely—buses were immediately made available at the Damascus Gate for everyone who wished to leave via the ruins of the Allenby Bridge on the Jordan River. They could take whatever they could carry on the sole condition that they sign a document attesting that they were leaving of their own free will. Approximately 100,000 people crossed over to the East Bank of the Jordan.

A month later, when tension had subsided, the Israeli government permitted those who had left to return, and somewhere between 40,000 and 70,000 did.

Two days after meeting with Al-Khatib, I received the Moslem religious leaders. They were not nearly as forthcoming or as friendly as the Christian community leaders had been, but I still reiterated our guarantee of freedom of religion for all. This was an uneasy alliance, but at least it was a beginning.

Anwar Nusseibeh, who had been Jordanian ambassador to the Court of St. James and the Jordanian minister of defense, came next. He was in many ways the lay head of the population in the West Bank and in later years was to become what could be called an unofficial ambassador of Jordan to Israel. We had negotiated together—although we had not met—during the War of Independence, attempting to achieve a cease-fire in Jerusalem. He gave me a rundown of Palestinian thinking in the light of developments and invited me to meet with the West Bank Arab leadership in his home. He was both rational and realistic and I accepted the invitation.

On Saturday, 10 June, I attended Sabbath prayers at the Wailing Wall with General Narkiss, General Lahat, and Teddy Kollek. Built against the Wailing Wall, under the Maghreb Gate, was a public latrine, and we decided that it had to be removed. Although the Wailing Wall, the holiest place on earth for Jews, was now open, there was barely room for a few hundred people in the space before it. And with Shavuot, a festival traditionally requiring Jews to come on pilgrimage to Jerusalem, only four days away, we expected that tens of thousands would flock to it.

The Mughrabi Quarter, which faced the Wailing Wall, thus creating a narrow passage for those who wished to pray, was now empty. There was no alternative. Only by removing the Quarter could we create enough space to accommodate the huge crowds. If we waited for bureaucratic approval, there would never be a decision. So we made it there and then.

That night, after the Sabbath, the bulldozers rolled into action, and by the next morning a huge open area had been created, covered by dust and rubble. At midday the cabinet, headed by Prime Minister Eshkol, arrived by bus at the Mandelbaum Gate and drove to the Wailing Wall. They were quite surprised, to say the least, but only one minister commented. In his view we had contravened the law. Perhaps . . . But the area was completely clear in time for the mass pilgrimage, and our estimates had been a little low. Over 200,000 people crowded into the Old City to pray.

Meanwhile, the administration of the West Bank was slowly being created, and within a week we were a functioning and efficient government —or at least as efficient as any government can ever be under such circumstances. The experience and ability of our department chiefs, each one a major figure from industry, economics, or higher education, enabled us to solve most problems. Eliezer Zurabin, who controlled one of Israel's leading public relations and advertising groups, handled the international media and achieved one of our greatest successes. The military government staff disseminated an international image of what *The New York Times* called "the most humane occupation ever." It helped that the reality of the situation matched the image.

That great image-maker, Moshe Dayan, came to the Wailing Wall, where he reiterated his oath never to leave this holy place. The emotion and affection that greeted our national hero, accompanied by several of our military leaders, were overwhelming. Dayan strode through the cheering crowd like Caesar entering Rome after a military victory.

We were received at the Temple Mount by the Wafd (religious property administration) of the Moslem community. We entered Al-Aksa Mosque, removed our shoes, and sat on the floor. There was slight damage to the cupola of the mosque dating from the Jordanian occupation, and Dayan asked if Israel could contribute to the cost of the repair. The reply was firmly negative—they received resources from the Arab and Islamic world. Their only request was that we authorize them to reactivate the Moslem police force responsible for the security of the Temple Mount. Many of those who dealt daily with the Moslem population were not too happy that Dayan agreed to reinstate the police, but his word was a writ. For years opinion was divided on his decision.

Next on the agenda was to gauge the atmosphere in the West Bank and among religious groups and leaders, and to advise Dayan on new problems and activities with possible political overtones. Dayan wanted a team that would lay down relevant principles for other areas under Israeli control, such as Gaza and the Golan Heights.

Our preliminary recommendation was the carrot-and-stick attitude: firm action against those beginning to resist Israeli rule, total noninterference in internal Moslem problems, and absolutely meticulous relationships with the holy places.

Prime Minister Eshkol did not like a committee reporting to Dayan on these problems, and the intense rivalry between the two powerful personalities again came to the fore. Eshkol replaced the committee with his own team, subordinate to him and given the typically Israeli long-winded moniker Special Inter-Ministerial Committee for Political Negotiations in the Occupied Areas.

On 20 July, two weeks later, we recommended to Eshkol that regardless of whatever political decision might be reached, the Jordan River should be Israel's eastern military border; no Arab military presence would be tolerated to the west of it. Our approach was geared to an intensive political move forward with a view to achieving a lasting peace agreement with King Hussein. Should it fail, we proposed that the West Bank be controlled as a separate organizational and economic administration under direct Israeli rule.

Absolutely nothing developed out of all this, because King Hussein refused to come forward to negotiate. Had he done so, he could have achieved a great deal. By 19 June 1967, the Israeli government had agreed

ABOVE: My maternal grandfather, Rabbi Samuel Isaac Hillman
(second row, center), at prayer in the Hurva Synagogue in Jerusalem,
the morning the news came of the Holocaust. BELOW: *From left to right*:
My cousin Rosette, my paternal grandmother and grandfather, Miriam and Joel
Herzog, my cousin Annette, and my aunt Esther, at their home outside Paris.
Annette was later deported to Auschwitz, where she was killed.

My father, Dr. Isaac Herzog,
the chief rabbi of Israel, at work in his study.
(Burt Glinn/Magnum Photos Inc.)

ABOVE: With my
mother, Sarah Herzog.
I'm about six months old.

BELOW: With my
younger brother, Yaacov,
in Dublin, sometime in the
late 1920s. We are wearing
our school uniforms.

ABOVE: The very model of a London barrister in 1940.

BELOW: In 1943, soon after I became a British officer.

Visiting the tank production unit at the Ford Motor Company
in Detroit in 1954, when I was the defense attaché at the Israeli Embassy.
From right to left: Yitzhak Rabin (then director of training for the
Israeli Defense Forces), Moshe Dayan (then Israeli chief of staff),
our host at Ford, and me. *(Courtesy Ford Motor Corporation)*

ABOVE: Israeli President Zalman Shazar *(center, in suit)* with the victorious generals of the Six-Day War. I'm standing, second from the left. *(Government of Israel Press Office)* BELOW: Escorting Chief of Staff Yitzhak Rabin *(extreme left)* through the Old City of Jerusalem in the aftermath of the Six-Day War. *(Government of Israel Press Office)*

ABOVE: At the Wailing Wall with David Ben-Gurion, after its liberation during the Six-Day War. I was military governor of the West Bank at the time. *(Government of Israel Press Office)*

BELOW: Doing one of my famous radio broadcasts during the Six-Day War. *(Israel Broadcasting Service)*

ABOVE: With Prime Minister Golda Meir and Zev Birger in 1973.
Birger now runs the Jerusalem Book Fair. *(Ross Photo)* BELOW: October 1975,
at the beginning of the "Zionism is Racism" debate at the United Nations.
At the extreme right is the Iraqi representative. *(United Nations/M. Tzovaras)*

in principle to return Sinai to Egypt and to return the Golan Heights to Syria in exchange for peace and demilitarization. Appropriate arrangements were prepared separately for Jordan. These proposals were passed on by the Americans, and King Hussein was ready to talk. Warned by Nasser against any attempt whatsoever to negotiate or reach an accommodation with Israel, he was told to await the Arab summit conference in Khartoum. The reply to all the Israeli advances was given there: "No negotiations with Israel, no recognition of Israel, no peace with Israel."

Because of intransigence and shortsightedness, a major opportunity to reach an accommodation between Israel and the Arab world was lost.

Soon after the Khartoum dictum, I met with the young Arab leaders of the West Bank and some members of the Arab Higher Committee, the old guard who had led the Arabs under the British Mandate. I told them that I did not need any better witnesses as to the causes for the Six-Day War; they had been there and had seen for themselves. They were still laboring under a misguided unwillingness to compromise and meet Israel at the negotiating table. I told them not to put their trust in the Arab nations that had betrayed them—they were being manipulated as political pawns. Some old-timers proposed a completely unrealistic return to the UN proposal of 1947, which the Arabs had rejected at the time out of hand. The proposal would have cut the State of Israel in half, giving us no land in the Negev and in much of the Galilee. They had been offered that once, turned it down, and went to war to destroy us rather than allow us such meager holdings. They failed then, and they failed again. They had to face reality, I insisted. In a few days the walls—figurative as well as barbed wire—dividing the new (Jewish) and the old (Arab) city would be removed. They would then be free to travel and see that time had not stopped. What they were remembering was a country they had not seen since 1948.

The debate raged on. Many young members of the audience, who are now important leaders of the Palestinians, berated the older members for their wrongheaded policy, missed opportunities, and outdated attitudes and perceptions. The discussion was an eye-opener: a lack of realism commingled with the first awareness of a new situation. This surprising openness was a remarkable change. Considering Israel their ultimate enemy, Palestinians had for years been determined to annihilate us. Had we lost the Six-Day War, Israel could well have faced a second Holocaust.

While the official Arab approach of total negativity and rigidity reflected the desperate situation in the Middle East, human initiatives on both sides created new hope. Colonel Zeev Shaham, governor in Nablus, and his agricultural officer inspired a great leap forward in the Israeli-Palestinian relationship. Realizing that the rotting harvest of fruit and vegetables could not be sent to markets in the Arab world, he authorized the Arabs to ford the Jordan River with trucks loaded with produce. It was worth the risk, he decided; otherwise, the farmers and their families would starve. Gradually, this tacit supply of produce from the West Bank to Jordan and, later, to other countries in the Arab world grew as hundreds of trucks forded the river. Moshe Dayan, with his clear, incisive instincts, approved and adopted this policy, which relieved the economic situation of the Palestinians and helped establish an ongoing link with Jordan. The bombed-out bridges were reconstructed and served as crossing points. Due to Shaham's initiative and power of improvisation, the passage of goods and people across the Jordan River has remained a major human and economic element in relations between Israel and the Arab world.

One of the most intelligent and impressive Arab leaders, Sheikh Ja'abari of Hebron, was the father-in-law of Anwar al-Khatib (the former governor of Jerusalem) and became a close confidant of Dayan's. Only too aware of our mutual problems and difficulties, he was basically a moderate man, mindful of the danger inherent in Palestinian extremism. He outlined a viable situation that has proved to be, in many ways, prescient and anticipated the Israel-PLO agreement of September 1993. Ja'abari hoped for a federation that would include Israel and the Palestinians and, ultimately, Jordan as well. Unfortunately, in 1967 not many Palestinian leaders had his vision or courage. Not many Israeli leaders did either, for that matter.

I have always felt that we missed major opportunities after the Six-Day War. Had Hussein been able to come forward and negotiate, we could well have achieved peace. It was a mistake not to create immediate autonomy for the Arabs, under Israeli sovereignty, thus enabling the two peoples to get along independently and cooperatively, and learn to work with each other. There was much talk about that, but the only practical proposal put forward over the years was the so-called Allon Plan, created by Yigal Allon. It would have left an Israeli presence along the Jordan River and would have established Palestinian autonomy or Jordanian rule in the densely populated Arab areas. Because of the various Knesset factions and pressure from the hawkish right, the plan was never adopted. This was a major error.

My work as military governor was coming to an end, and the structure was sound. I now entrusted it to Brigadier General Raphael Vardi. Being the first Jewish governor of the West Bank for so many years allowed me to have an important encounter with the basic realities of the Palestinian problem. It made me very aware that much needed to be done before this problem could possibly be transformed into peace. In the meantime, the reservists mobilized for the Six-Day War were gradually returning to civilian life, and I was eager to get back to work.

———— ∞∞∞ ————

CHAPTER 15

Commerce, Industry, and Law

ONE OF THE great failings of the Israeli political scene is that many politicians are afraid. Because they generally need their job to make a living, they frequently will avoid doing anything courageous or controversial that might compromise it. The law forbidding a politician from earning anything apart from his salary in the Knesset sounds as if it should keep politicians honest. But it doesn't work that way. It tends to encourage corruption and under-the-table deals; it often discourages capable people from running for the Knesset. It also insulates politicians from the real world. Why shouldn't they work and mingle with real society? I'd be much less courageous if I were dependent on someone's favors.

I returned to my job with GUS-Rassco, working under Sir Isaac Wolfson. The Wolfsons were longtime family friends and Sir Isaac was a particularly unusual character, a brilliant businessman and great philanthropist. He spoke with a broad Scottish accent and never tired of telling the stories of his youth in Glasgow. He began in a small picture-framing business run by his father, and later, when the Great Universal Stores, a struggling mail-order business in which he worked as a salesman, was in trouble, he offered to buy the company. He went to the bank to get a loan and when the bank manager asked him what his collateral would be, he brought in his wife and son and simply pointed at them. The bank manager was right to give him the loan, no matter how unorthodox the guarantee, because under Sir Isaac's leadership, the Great Universal Stores became the largest mail-order service in the world outside the United States. Over the years, Sir Isaac's interests expanded into industry, banking, and finance. He also established the Wolfson Foundation, which has benefited great projects in the fields of medicine, economics, science, and education in Britain, Israel, and elsewhere. It was estimated that at the height of "IW's" career, 25 percent of the population of Great Britain were his clients.

Army life may have been more dangerous, but it was not nearly as cruel as the business world I returned to. Despite my experience running government organizations and army formations, not to mention my legal training, I was a babe in the woods of capitalism, with grown-up responsibilities as managing director of GUS-Rassco, a medium-size, publicly listed industrial investment company. Controlled by Sir Isaac Wolfson and Rassco, an Israeli building conglomerate headed by Mordechai Stern, the enterprise bought small businesses and developed them into larger, more productive ones. One company made small motors for appliances, others made lace, elevators and air-conditioning equipment, and carpets. My job was basically to make sure these companies all ran smoothly and profitably (I was so inexperienced, *after* I had the job, that I had to be tutored by my father-in-law, Simcha Ambache, in the art of reading a balance sheet!).

I learned how to structure a company financially from the bottom up and, because we did so much business overseas, how countries deal with business and negotiations. All of this would later prove invaluable. I learned the ins and outs of loaning and borrowing and the cost of money —so many political issues are steeped in economics—and soon found myself at home with such matters. A new world was opening before me.

One of the interesting things I learned at Sir Isaac's side was that international business dealings can, because of mutual need, overcome political entanglements and differing viewpoints—not always, but surprisingly often. Doing business can be a means of communicating and, in fact, of establishing relationships that might otherwise be impossible to form. For instance, I went with Sir Isaac several times to his sisal estates in Tanzania, where we were guests of President Nyerere. We toured industrial concerns, diamond mines, and sisal-processing plants. Nyerere's extreme leftist views made him extraordinarily hostile to Israel, but we were able to talk and negotiate on a business level. Both business and politics do indeed make for strange bedfellows—but that's not always such a bad thing. Compromises and negotiations do not always result in losing something. They often bring about important gains and long-term trust, which ultimately is what any relationship—personal or political or economic—is based on.

One of my proudest moments was as chairman of the Keter publishing house when it produced the monumental *Encyclopedia Judaica.* Mammoth and comprehensive, this great sixteen-volume political, social, and religious reference work was a landmark of scholarly publishing. An outstanding team had worked for years to produce it and I was privileged to present it not just to the leaders in Israel, Ben-Gurion, Golda Meir, Shazar, Dayan, and others, but to leaders around the world. Pope Paul VI received a copy at a ceremony at the Vatican, with a dedication in Latin and Hebrew. He read it aloud without too much difficulty—his Hebrew was definitely superior to my Latin.

Yitzhak Rabin, the victorious chief of staff in the Six-Day War, was ambassador to Washington when we presented a set to President Nixon. Every volume had to be vetted by the Secret Service. Don't ask me what they were vetting it *for*—I suppose explosives. Perhaps they also feared some subliminal message cleverly planted to influence Nixon's Israel policy. In the Oval Office ceremony Nixon looked at the volumes, turned to me, and asked what he should read. I suggested that since he was about to make his historic visit to China, he could read about the ancient Jewish community in Kaifeng. Clearly taken aback, Nixon said, "What? There, too?"

Though he was considered something of a political pariah—particularly in light of his unequivocally anti-Semitic statements in the Haldeman diaries—did his personal attitude have any effect on his dealings with Israel and with Jews? None. He supplied arms and unflinching support when our very existence would have been in danger without them. Let his comments be set against his actions. His words may have raised eyebrows—but not his actions. And I'll choose actions over words any day of the week.

We can be much too serious about labels, nasty words, and sporadic outbursts. Senator Daniel Patrick Moynihan, a devoted friend of the Jewish people, once muttered to me his humorous definition of an anti-Semite: "Someone who dislikes Jews more than absolutely necessary." All races and religions have foibles and shortcomings and you have to see them—along with the good. Otherwise neither side has any validity.

No RECOLLECTION OF these years could be complete without mention of Pinchas Sapir, the indefatigable minister of trade and industry, and later minister of finance. A dynamic force and genuine visionary, Sapir was the driving power behind the construction of immigrant townships, creating all educational and recreational facilities. Without his initiative and drive,

Israel would have been hard pressed to achieve its present industrial success. Regrettably, many Israelis are unaware of this phenomenon named Sapir, who knew everything that was happening. He broke the restraints of bureaucracy without hesitation, involved himself in our problems, and usually helped solve them. One of Israel's greatest builders and promoters, Pinchas Sapir deserves to be remembered and hailed as an important personality.

After ten years with GUS-Rassco and Sir Isaac Wolfson, it was time for me to move on; I had always wanted to become independent and not work for others. In April 1972, with Michael Fox, I opened the law firm of Herzog & Fox. I hadn't become a rabbi or a doctor, but I was now finally the next best thing for a nice Jewish boy.

Although I'd been called to the bar in 1950, this was the first time I'd practiced. Again, gearing up for a life in politics, it seemed the logical next step. I felt sufficiently well schooled in business and economics, but a politician may also be a legislator, and I looked forward to using my legal training at last. Michael had considerable experience in England and at a leading Israeli law firm and was an outstanding lawyer of the utmost integrity and intelligence. After a few months, we took in Yaakov Neeman, a brilliant young professor widely acknowledged as one of Israel's leading tax-law authorities (and, in later years, minister of justice in Netanyahu's government). Herzog, Fox & Neeman has since grown from a small office to one of the country's leading firms, and my third son, Isaac—whom we call Bouji—is now the firm's Herzog.

Our first big case was on behalf of the companies that had insured the Pan-American jet blown up by Palestinian terrorists in the Cairo airport in 1970. We argued that the blowup was the result of a warlike act and that a state of war existed. This would refer responsibility to Lloyds, which insured against acts of war. Although we lost the case in the federal court in New York, it received much attention, and as a result we were in great demand.

My most famous case before the Supreme Court of Israel involved Lady Yvonne Cochrane, daughter of a vastly wealthy Palestinian Arab family in Beirut. Her property included a major portion of central Jaffa and the area occupied by the Baha'i Temple on Mount Carmel in Haifa. Most of it had been confiscated during the War of Independence. Thanks to her marriage to Sir Desmond Cochrane, the Irish honorary consul-general in Beirut, Lady Cochrane was a British subject, but her family's insistence that she retain her Lebanese nationality made her an absentee landlord. After a long battle Lady Cochrane received partial compensation for her land from the State of Israel. This landmark case set a precedent.

My brother, Yaacov, and I had remained very close and got closer still after he returned from Canada to run Prime Minister Eshkol's office. He had become a very influential behind-the-scenes worker on the political scene, advising Sharett and Ben-Gurion, Eshkol, and finally Golda Meir. He was never too happy with Golda as prime minister, largely because she was not happy with intellectuals around her—and Yaacov was a genuine and brilliant intellectual.

Toward the end of 1971, he fell ill and was hospitalized. For several weeks he struggled for life, but it was clear that he was dying. He was due to travel with Golda to see President Lyndon Johnson and, even in his weakened state, was desperate to make the trip because he felt Golda needed him. "What a terrible tragedy," he said. "For the first time she really wants me to accompany her. But now that she really needs me I can't do it."

In the course of his brilliant career, he had been responsible for the maintenance and development of relations between Israel and the Vatican. He was highly respected in the Vatican. When Yaacov took sick, Cardinal Casaroli, the Vatican secretary of state, asked me if we would object to prayers being offered up for Yaacov's recovery. I said of course not, and expressed my deep appreciation for this gesture. Despite all our prayers, Yaacov died two months later, in March 1972.

His able widow rose to prominence in the World Health Organization; two daughters, Shira and Eliezra, and a son, Yitzhak, all attained success in their fields. But I had lost my closest confidant, and his passing left a void in my life. And Israel had lost a phenomenal mind and an important man.

⊸⊷⊶⊷⊷⊸

CHAPTER 16

The Yom Kippur War

In October 1972, our oldest son, Joel, married Marguerite Gaon, a charming girl from Geneva, the daughter of parents from Egypt and Sudan. Her father, Nessim Gaon, a prominent businessman, was the president of the World Sephardi Union.

Israel was in the midst of a joyous period as well. Since the end of the 1967 Six-Day War, we had experienced a period of unprecedented economic growth. However, unlike the joy Aura and I experienced with the expansion of our family, Israel's was a bit of a false front. With our economic success came a certain military malaise. Lulled by Moshe Dayan's assertions that the Arab armies were incapable of threatening our security, and encouraged by Golda Meir's motherly optimism, we believed that all was right with the world.

As we would soon learn, in the Middle East rarely was all right with our world.

In May 1973, we received word that Egyptian troops were being mobilized. Expecting them to cross the Suez Canal and attack, Defense Minister Dayan countered by approving a mobilization of Israeli forces on the recommendation of General David Elazar, the chief of staff. We were ready for anything—but nothing happened. It was a false alarm.

Almost five months passed. Then, in the first week of October there were signs that both Egyptian and Syrian forces were massing for a possible attack. Although some alarms were sounded, Golda and Dayan tended to ignore them with a sense of déjà vu, strengthened by the failure of our intelligence to assess correctly the Arab intentions. As a result of that overconfidence, Israel was to face its grimmest hour.

A week before the October warnings, after attending a meeting of the Socialist International, Golda was in Austria, where a train carrying Russian Jewish refugees had been hijacked. In all probability, the hijacking had been initiated by the Syrians and carried out by their proxies to divert our attention. When she returned home, all discussion in her cabinet centered on the events in Austria; Israel's prime minister, the Knesset, and various ministers were totally unaware of the scope of the action taking place on our own borders.

On 6 October, the first day of Yom Kippur, I was in synagogue atoning for my sins, like the rest of Israel. People were leaving in groups, and the congregation was emptying. Gradually, I realized what was happening. Our troops were being mobilized. We were facing attack.

Israeli intelligence had received word of an imminent attack that evening, but it came at 2 P.M., and we were caught with our pants down. We did not have nearly enough reserve forces or arms on the banks of the Suez Canal. As Egypt's armies crossed the Suez Canal into Sinai, and as the Syrian forces advanced through the Golan Heights toward the Galilee, it was obvious that we were facing a very serious situation.

Summoned to general headquarters, I was asked to go on the air because of the success of my broadcasts in 1967. This time, I was given access to military information and freedom to come to "the pit"—the underground military headquarters. I began broadcasting in Hebrew and English, on radio and television, along with the noted Arabist Professor Shimon Shamir, later our ambassador to Egypt and Jordan. Our job was to assuage people's fears when possible, and alert them to danger when necessary.

Our counterattacks were at first unsuccessful. The so-called Bar-Lev Line along the canal crumbled, and the strongpoints fell. Overall, we would lose approximately 2,500 soldiers, a heavy price for a country our size. Not one city, town, or village escaped losses. As the real truth and the scope of the losses penetrated the public consciousness, the nation experienced a nightmare. But we dug in and the momentum gradually shifted. The Israeli bank of the Suez Canal was the site of the biggest tank battle since the battle of Kursk in World War II. We followed this victory with a series of successful counterattacks, as the division under Ariel Sharon crossed the canal. Within days, we had surrounded the Egyptian Third Army on both banks of the Suez Canal.

At the very moment that the Egyptians were attacking, the Syrian army assaulted the Golan Heights. By sheer guts—and, I'm forced to say, a miracle—our forces managed to stop their advance. No one knows why the Syrians advancing toward the Galilee at one point stopped surging forward, but we took advantage of it. On 11 October our troops were moving toward Damascus.

On my daily broadcast of 19 October, I made a correct guess. Realizing that the Egyptians were totally under siege, I evaluated that the Egyptian war room was probably the scene of bitter debates and recriminations. General Saad al-Shazali, the chief of staff, was pressing to save his army by withdrawing it back to Egypt on the west bank of the Nile, even as Sadat was pushing it to fight on in the hope of a political victory by holding on to the foothold on the Sinai east bank. That is exactly what happened: at that very moment, Shazali and Sadat were quarreling and Sadat, backed by his minister of defense, Ahmed Ismail, dismissed the commander of his troops. In the final analysis there is no doubt that Sadat's instinct was the correct one.

The Soviets and the Americans now got involved. Kissinger's shuttle diplomacy was at work, and a cease-fire was negotiated. Egypt agreed to a mutual withdrawal of troops, and in May 1974, a UN force was set up on the Syrian border in the Golan Heights. To this day, that agreement is being meticulously observed.

THE YOM KIPPUR WAR had wide-ranging ramifications.

In Israel, there were political shock waves throughout the country, and Moshe Dayan was never the same again. The shock of the war caused something to snap inside him, and he sank into a morass of pessimism and self-pity. Until the last possible minute, he had tried to dissuade Golda Meir from a total mobilization of our troops. Had she listened to him, we could well have been in serious danger. My only explanation for his decision making, or lack thereof, is that the Arab attack did not jibe with his theories and public pronouncements. He had said that the Arabs could not and would not attack, and dammit, if he said so, there would be no attack. And even as the Egyptian army was invading, he was incapable of admitting his mistake. Despite the strength he projected, Dayan was a Hamletian figure, torn by doubt and often incapable of making a decision or imposing his will.

Mrs. Meir, on the other hand, had no such problem. Although her nearsightedness had nearly caused our defeat, once the war began she showed great strength of character and enormous composure. In peacetime, her ad hoc system of governing—there were no checks and balances on her or her kitchen cabinet—was nearly disastrous, but her inflexibility proved to be an enormous asset in the war. She used common sense to make military decisions, often opposing the choices made by lifelong military men—and her choices were usually correct, as witness her wise decision to call in Haim Bar-Lev at the outset of the war. But the public uproar against the government, and those responsible for the careless way we were led to a very serious military situation, caused protests and demonstrations against her. While no blame was ever officially laid directly on them, the nation never fully forgave either Dayan or Mrs. Meir, and the war led to their eclipse as political leaders. It was the beginning of the end for the Labor government, which had been in power for twenty-five years. Apart from the upheaval within Israel, the war forced the leadership to seek a new political approach and a realistic policy which would lead to a political solution.

In Egypt, the defeat had a great effect on Sadat, who realized that he could never reach Jerusalem with tanks; he had to find another way. And so the Yom Kippur War ultimately led to the historic Sadat-Begin peace conference at Camp David and set much of the peace process in motion.

For me, as for many others who served in Israel's battles, the Yom Kippur War was a new experience. Instead of my being in the field, our two elder sons were serving. Mike was mobilized with an infantry unit which was sent to the Sinai to the area of the Suez Canal to do battle with the Egyptian army. I worked out a complicated system of codes with him whereby he could write and tell us roughly where he was, but even so we were without news of him for weeks on end. One friend serving with him managed to get leave because he was slightly wounded and he called us, reporting that the unit was having a very hard time. I visited the underground headquarters of the armed forces every day for my broadcast briefing. There I saw parents like myself, senior officers anxiously searching out the location and fate of the units to which their sons were assigned, without appearing to do so. No one wanted to show anxiety or fear, but none of us could really hide what we were feeling.

At the conclusion of the hostilities, Joel and Mike arrived home safely. Mike had grown a scraggly beard, and was utterly exhausted and traumatized. He was basically shell-shocked. Fortunately, he was assigned immediately to officers school, where the regime and discipline helped him regroup psychologically and emotionally. But I shall never forget his return from the front. As I opened the door, he staggered in and said softly, "Father, war is a terrible thing. It is no picnic."

That is the understatement of my lifetime. And I can only hope that my grandchildren never have to make it.

CHAPTER 17

———— ⊗∞∞⊙ ————

The UN Years:
Stepping into the Hornet's Nest

ON A MISTY August dawn in 1975, I stood on the deck of the *QE2* as she slipped under the Verrazano Bridge at the entrance to New York Harbor. All around me on deck was the usual pre-arrival bustle: sailors preparing to dock, children excitedly pointing toward shore, harassed parents trying to control them. Out of the mist loomed the twin towers of the World Trade Center, and as the majestic ship glided past the Statue of Liberty, I thought of Wordsworth as he looked at London from Westminster Bridge:

> *. . . This City now doth, like a garment wear*
> *The beauty of the morning; silent, bare, . . .*

The muted sounds of Manhattan coming to life wafted across the water: the revving of motors, the hum of traffic, somewhere in the distance the strident wail of a police car siren as it rushed to answer a call. They mingled with the deep blast of the ship's horn as it answered the impatient hoots of the accompanying tugs.

Warmed by the rising sun, I wondered what this city had in store for me.

Almost nine months earlier, I had been offered the job of ambassador to the United Nations, and a crucial period was now coming up. Because all indications were that, in the upcoming General Assembly, a determined effort would be mounted by the Arab countries to suspend Israel, we were under diplomatic siege. Furthermore, Foreign Minister Yigal Allon believed it was vital that American Jewry have an Israeli figure in New York, to which it could relate and with which it could develop a common language.

Israel was greatly dependent on American Jews to fight and lobby for financial support. Israel is distinguished from other small nations by its centrality to Jews throughout the world. That role is essential to the unity and strength of the Jewish people everywhere and not least to our political clout. And nowhere is that clout more essential than in America. More than half of all U.S. aid to Israel is military. It not only gives us strength, it is acknowledged as a great investment for the U.S. In essence, the United States has an effective allied army in the Mideast without risking its own soldiers.

From the very beginning, American financial assistance reflected major involvement and commitment. Always interested in political debate, American Jews are now much less starry-eyed about Israel; their involvement is based more on reality than on fantasy—a much healthier situation.

On 19 August 1975, I presented my credentials to Secretary-General Kurt Waldheim. His nickname in the UN corridors was "the Viennese Headwaiter," and that fit his demeanor exactly. He was a hard worker but essentially not a very strong personality. When I criticized him for some aspect of the UN behavior toward Israel, he would explain to me that while it was true that in a way I was his boss, he had to take into account the feelings and desires of his 143 other bosses, and this wasn't easy. Our relationship was perfectly friendly and professional, and I had absolutely no idea about his background or connections to the Nazis—no one did. Everyone at the UN had access to his files, but it never occurred to anyone to check up on him. Not until he ran for the presidency of Austria did the missing chapter of his life make headlines. I was unhappy about the public outcry raised against him. I felt that it would work against Israel and that our protests would help his campaign. They did.

Another individual who would have an important impact on Israel made quite an impression when we met.

I found myself very much in demand in the American media, and on my first TV show I was introduced to another guest, Georgia governor Jimmy Carter. During the interview, he launched into one of the most forceful pro-Israel statements I'd heard in a long time. A strong Israel was essential to American security, he said; America had to support Israel. It was not even a choice—it was a necessity.

After the show, I learned that "Jimmy Who?" was running for president. I can't say that I took the news very seriously; he seemed like quite a long shot. But a week later, on another talk show, he reiterated his pro-Israel statement verbatim. A few days later I appeared in Boston on yet another show. Who should be there but my new best friend? Once again his encomium was propounded flawlessly.

Carter struck me as a man of steel: very cold, extremely cautious, tremendously determined. He was also clearly quite moral with great and unbending strength of character.

It's funny that Carter first appeared to me as so strongly pro-Israel. Although he led the negotiations that culminated in the Camp David agreement with Begin and Sadat—no one can take that away from him—we don't recall him all that favorably. He was supportive, but frequently with reservations—I can't really put my finger on it. Carter was and is deeply religious and very much a Christian. My preference is for someone who leaves his religious fervor outside the office, whether it is an oval one in Washington or a square tent in a Middle East desert.

Carter may not have been America's best president, but he is a great ex-president. He has involved himself with great success in international diplomacy, and his foundation does important and superb work both domestically and internationally. He has emerged as an effective public servant.

Soon after my arrival I met my new colleague. Daniel Patrick Moynihan, America's newly appointed ambassador to the UN, was not only erudite and sophisticated, as well as a genuine intellectual and an effective political manipulator, but also a great friend to Israel. As with previous threats to Israel's UN membership, the United States threatened to end its own participation in the General Assembly if Israel's was not approved. It was quite a gesture, and Moynihan made it effectively and convincingly.

My debut at the UN was a speech at a special General Assembly convened to discuss the economic problems of the have and have-not countries. Emphasizing Israel's eagerness to improve the economic atmosphere in the Middle East, I created a stir by offering Jordan—and any of our other Arab neighbors—the use of our port facilities on the Mediterranean. That kind of open-arms policy was then unheard of, but the speech was not out of character for Israel and certainly not for me. I was always extremely respectful in the UN toward the Arabs, who did not always reciprocate in kind. In all fairness, though, they couldn't. The Jordanians and Egyptians were always polite but terrified of the terrorist tactics of the PLO. Any Arab politician who was visibly friendly toward Israel faced serious, often fatal, repercussions.

I knew I couldn't buck or change either the Arab system or the UN system, which was a morass of political infighting and treachery, but I had a case I believed in and a forum in which to present it effectively. While the extraordinary advancements in modern communications have many drawbacks, they were a godsend. Media coverage offered an unofficial meeting ground for those who had poor or no relations with Israel. I could explain our positions in detail and lay the groundwork for a meeting of the minds. My reasoning proved sound.

THE UN IS a strange and wondrous organization. Sometimes effective, often maddeningly ineffective, it is always bogged down by special interests, pettiness, and political ineptitude. The principal organ of the United Nations is the General Assembly. This is the only body in which all the UN members are represented. It convenes annually and works through a structure of main committees, procedural committees, standing committees, and subsidiary and ad hoc bodies. The important committees in the General Assembly include the Special Committee, which deals with political matters; the Second Committee, which deals with administrative matters; the Third Committee, which deals with human rights problems; the Fourth Committee, which deals with the trusteeships of colonial and former colonial territories; the Fifth Committee, which deals with the financial problems of the UN; and the Sixth Committee, which deals with legal matters.

Under the General Assembly are the Security Council, the Economic and Social Council, the Trusteeship Council, the International Court of Justice, and the Secretariat. Election to these councils is organized on a regional basis. Hence Israel, which officially belonged to no region because of Arab and Communist opposition, could not be a member of *any* of these bodies.

The UN building in Manhattan, rising to a height of thirty-eight floors and overlooking the East River, was built in 1951. It has, in addition to the office space, an impressive General Assembly Hall capable of seating—in the days in which I was active there—the delegations of some 144 countries, each delegation allotted six seats. Today, the hall has been extensively enlarged to seat more than 180 member countries. The main councils—Security, Economic and Social, and Trusteeship—have appropriate meeting halls at their disposal, together with the necessary areas for administrative and secretarial backup. The various committees are allotted halls, most of them in a horseshoe form, capable of accommodating all the representatives on the committees.

Inside the UN's serene and commanding New York headquarters, emotions run deep and seem to seethe into the streets below. In 1975, Israel was facing one of its most difficult periods in that organization. The Arab bloc wanted us removed from the premises; the Soviet bloc and so-called nonaligned group of more than one hundred nations were equally hostile. Despite their appellation, nothing was more aligned than the nonaligned group—usually on the side of the Soviet Union.

Israel was under constant attack. Half the time of the General Assembly, which was supposed to deal with the world's problems, seemed to be devoted to maligning Israel. We thought that the UN had reached the nadir. Little did we know.

MANY OF THE developing, or have-not, Asian and African countries, which had recently liberated themselves from colonialism, banded together against what they called the First World, namely the haves, and were supported by the Arab bloc. This was a convenient way to escape responsibility and blame for their failure to administer their affairs effectively. Their frustration and dissatisfaction gradually spilled over into the General Assembly, giving new impetus to anti-Israel sentiments.

An additional impetus came from Egypt, whose influence led many of the have-nots to break off relations with Israel. During this period, oil was first used as a major political and economic weapon. The Arabs' control of so much of it gave them strength and power: oil could be utilized for political blackmail.

Not all of Israel's problems came from external sources. We had plenty of infighting and bickering between the UN delegation and our embassy in Washington. In an effort to establish diplomatic relations between them, I told Ambassador Simha Dinitz that a smoother relationship would help our common purpose, and he promised every cooperation. I still had my doubts.

The UN of the 1970s was a fine and exclusive club in which your fellow members were your sworn enemies as well as your true friends. It's a thrilling group, many of whom have been heads of state, prime ministers, or foreign ministers. Over the last ten or fifteen years, the UN has lost much of its effectiveness by assuming too many functions, and Secretary-General Boutros-Ghali has overcentralized the bureaucracy. Judging by

Bosnia, Somalia, and Rwanda, the UN troops are failures, and as a governing body, the UN has lost a lot of clout.

AT THE OPENING of my first General Assembly, during a long, boring speech by the foreign minister of Brazil, Tap Bennett, the number two in the American delegation, introduced me to Secretary of State Henry Kissinger. He had spoken to Andrei Gromyko, foreign minister of the Soviet Union, and Gromyko was prepared to meet with Foreign Minister Yigal Allon. I was told to call the Soviet delegation and set up the meeting.

Before our session with the Russians, we met Kissinger for breakfast at the Waldorf Towers. Kissinger launched into a long tirade about the Israeli press and an apologia about statements attributed to him by *Ha'aretz* and *Yedioth*; he had apparently been quoted as praising Peres, our minister of defense, while declaring our prime minister, Rabin, to be colorless, and he was very disturbed by this. It was quite striking to see a man of such standing concerned with journalists' innocuous remarks. I evoked some mirth when I said that he was the only person in the world to take the Israeli press seriously. His mirthless reply was that he did not take the Israeli press seriously, but some of the American press had the habit of quoting them.

Kissinger spoke quite openly and freely about the problems created by various congressmen and senators, and he was surprisingly contemptuous. "This one is an idiot," he would say, "that one is a fool . . . That one can be handled . . . So-and-so is in our pocket, the other one is impossible." Henry Kissinger is probably the most brilliant contemporary statesman, and his brilliance is matched by his ego. He understood the corridors of power as well as any statesman I've ever met, and he moved freely within them.

Our breakfast meeting continued with discussions about Syria and the Interim Agreement in Sinai. Allon insisted that new ideas propounded by the U.S. State Department on the Middle East be cleared with Israel first. An angry Kissinger immediately went red in the face, and there was tension in the air. Kissinger peevishly offered to stop the discussion altogether, but somehow the matter was glossed over and we moved on. Clearly feeling that we were muscling in on territory that was his alone, Kissinger told Ambassador Mordechai Shalev, who was about to leave Washington, "You are the only Israeli whose motives I do not suspect."

Later that afternoon, we met with Gromyko at the Soviet Embassy. Across the street was a synagogue, and I later learned that an unsuspecting believer, who had gone to the evening service, came out of the synagogue and saw the Israeli convoy draw up to the Russian Embassy. He was sure that the man he saw getting out of the car and going into the embassy was Yigal Allon—but dismissed the idea as preposterous and went home.

But we were, in fact, there. The area was well covered by American security personnel. We entered the large embassy entrance hall and were ushered from one official or security man to the other, until a folding door opened and revealed an alcove in which we could hang our coats. We stepped into what looked like a locker room, and there were our hosts—Gromyko, Dobrynin, the Soviet ambassador in Washington, and Viktor Sukhodrev, their well-known official interpreter. Allon, Eliyahu Hassin (Allon's aide), and I sat on the one couch in this sparsely furnished room, while the other three sat in armchairs. Our conversation was clearly being recorded.

After asking about the weather in Israel, Gromyko turned to Allon. "What have you got to say?" he asked. Allon began by talking about the Geneva Conference, of which Gromyko was joint chairman. The Geneva Conference was run jointly by the United States and the Soviet Union; its purpose was to promote peace in the wake of the Yom Kippur War. It didn't make sense for the country of one of the joint chairmen—the U.S.S.R.—not to have diplomatic relations with one of the parties to the Yom Kippur conflict—namely Israel. Without diplomatic relations, Allon explained, it was impossible for us to trust them. Gromyko countered that the Soviet Union had *always* been in favor of the existence of the State of Israel. Recalling his role at the 1947–48 UN debates, he held up his hand and said, "This hand was raised to support the establishment of your state." Turning to the Palestinian issue, Allon offered to give Jordan back all the heavily populated Arab districts in the West Bank and to open negotiations with the Arabs. Gromyko found this a definite move forward but could not agree with it—he wanted Israel to give everything back. During the ensuing talk about resuming Soviet-Israeli relations, Gromyko admitted that Russia was seriously considering it. Tension rose only over the issue of Jewish emigration from Russia.

The meeting created quite a sensation in Israel. Rabin asked Allon to cable him a full report, which Allon had been trying to avoid. For good reason. We had agreed with the Russians to keep quiet about our conversation and I was determined to keep my word. To the annoyance of the

Russians, as soon as the cable was sent, news of the talk leaked. I was approached by the Israeli media to reveal details, an act that might prejudice the fate of Soviet Jews. I kept mum.

As the UN debate over Israel's ouster continued, Allon threatened to remove the United Nations peacekeeping force from Israel; there would be no Geneva Peace Conference, the only hope for peace in the Middle East. President Anwar Sadat of Egypt declared that "Israel must be present in the United Nations if it is expected to comply with its resolutions." Kissinger, on behalf of the United States and the European Nine (Great Britain, France, Germany, Italy, Ireland, Denmark, the Netherlands, Belgium, and Luxembourg), took a very strong stand, and a Senate resolution avowed that if Israel was expelled from the UN, the United States would seriously reconsider its own membership.

World opinion, however, was clearly against us, and the clouds of hatred and bigotry were gathering. An international women's conference held in Mexico under UN auspices, though allegedly nonpolitical, became political enough to pass a resolution condemning Zionism.

On 1 October we learned that those three great bulwarks of democracy, Cuba, Somalia, and Benin, had submitted an amendment to the Human Rights Committee's resolution attacking racism and apartheid; they wanted to add Zionism, by equating it with racism. This was the first attack in the United Nations on an "ism." Nobody had ever attempted to attack communism, socialism, or capitalism, but now Israel's beliefs, our national liberation movement, and our very existence were being lined up before the firing squad.

At the Third Committee's meeting on 3 October, Leonard Garment, the U.S. representative, attacked the resolution as "an obscene act," and Piero Vinci, the Italian representative, announced the opposition of the European Nine. "What we are witnessing," I declared, "is a scurrilous attack on an established religion which has given to the world the Bible, with its Ten Commandments, the great prophets . . . the great thinkers of history. . . ." As the representatives of many of the black African countries were taking a second look at the problem, any feeling of optimism disappeared. The committee's chairman, a Czech named Smid, a blatant anti-Semite and anti-Zionist, spoke up vehemently in favor of this vile resolution.

Three days later I asked, "Does anybody in this hall . . . believe that this is the manner whereby one can achieve understanding and advance toward peace?" We were facing the severest attack on the Jewish people since Hitler, yet the silence of the U.S. Jewish community was deafening, and not one voice of protest was heard in the American media. "Where are your bloody Jews?" Pat Moynihan asked in his usual abrupt manner. The German ambassador, Rudiger von Wechmar, who was strongly on our side, added tactfully, "It would be helpful if the Jewish community were to react." Moreover, there was little or no response from the Israeli media, politicians, or academia. How to explain it? I can't. Except to say that perhaps people didn't realize the danger.

On 17 October, the committee met to vote on the resolution. Our extensive lobbying had created serious doubts about it. In my remarks I said:

> We have listened to the most unbelievable nonsense on the issue of Zionism and from whom? From countries who are the archetypes of racism.
>
> . . . How dare you talk of racism to us, we who suffered more than any other nation in the world from racist theories and practices, a nation which has suffered the most terrifying holocaust in the history of mankind.
>
> . . . This is a sad day for the United Nations. The Jewish people will not forget this scene nor this vote.
>
> We are a small people with a proud history. We have lived through much in our history.
>
> We shall survive this shameful exhibition, . . . and I thank the delegations who have expressed themselves against this pernicious resolution. We shall not forget those who voted to attack our religion and our faith. We shall never forget.

As I shouted out the last words—"We shall never forget"—a hush fell and there was absolute silence.

It was clear how the vote would go. I instructed my delegation to show no signs of emotion when we lost—and I knew we would—and to behave with dignity and not enter into an argument with the Arab delegations.

The vote was taken, and the resolution was indeed passed with a majority. When the vote was announced, the Arabs broke into long and mocking applause; indeed, they seemed on the verge of a war dance. As our delegation gathered up its papers, Pat Moynihan got up, the blood rushing to his face. He straightened his tie and buttoned his jacket. As he came toward me, I rose to greet him. He took my hand, pulled me to him, and embraced me in front of the entire hall. His gut reaction spoke more than anything else. I was very moved indeed.

The British critic Goronwy Rees described the moment in *Encounter*:

> There were ghosts haunting the Third Committee that day; the ghosts of Hitler and Goebbels and Julius Streicher, grinning with delight to hear, not only Israel, but Jews as such denounced in language which would have provoked hysterical applause at any Nuremberg rally. . . . And there were other ghosts also at the debate: the ghosts of the 6,000,000 dead in Dachau and Sachsenhausen and other extermination camps, listening to the same voices which had cheered and jeered and abused them as they made their way to the gas chambers. For the fundamental thesis advanced by the supporters of the resolution, and approved by the majority of the Third Committee, was that to be a Jew, and to be proud of it, and to be determined to preserve the right to be a Jew, is to be an enemy of the human race.

In *A Dangerous Place*, Moynihan describes the scene:

> These last words ["We shall never forget"] were shouted, and the room for a moment fell silent. Then, as if the others were rallying their ranks, the stirring commenced again, rising to a frenzy. The vote came, racing across the computer screen. 70 in favor, 29 against, with 27 abstentions. . . . A long mocking applause broke out. The Israeli delegation, clearly on instructions, showed not the least emotion.
>
> I rose and walked over to Herzog and embraced him. "Fuck 'em," I said.

Three weeks after the resolution was introduced into the UN Human Rights Committee, I was finally invited to address the Conference of Presidents of Major American Jewish Organizations. Pulling no punches, I reviewed Israel's relationship with the UN and surveyed the anti-Zionist history of the UN:

> My friends, I tried desperately in the two weeks in which the debate was going on to bring home to the Jewish community the gravity of the situation. I cannot say that I was encouraged by the Jewish reaction.
> . . . While the Jews were comparatively passive on this issue, and in my view failing in their duty as Jews because they did not apparently appreciate the dangers to the Jewish people inherent in this Resolution (and you only have to read it carefully to realize the dangers it harbors).
> . . . My friends, you can be proud of your delegation to the United Nations . . .

But I ask, can we be proud of the Jewish reaction? Here in this city, in the midst of the largest Jewish concentration in the world, with a small Israeli delegation fighting desperately against the heaviest possible odds to defend Jewry from a major anti-Semitic attack against Jews wherever they may be . . .

Can you honestly say that the dangerous significance of this development has penetrated American Jewish consciousness?

Remember, it did not begin yesterday. We have been waging the battle for three weeks now. . . . And yet, where were the Jewish people?

The essentials of my speech were reported in the next day's *New York Times*. The headline was "Herzog Says Jews Let Israelis Down During UN Debate."

All hell broke loose. I had insulted the American Jewish leadership and, by implication, the Israeli embassy. My criticism had obviously hit home. Some members of the Conference of Presidents, apparently not used to such criticism, telephoned Prime Minister Rabin to complain. Minister of the Interior Yosef Burg asked for an explanation of the uproar, and Minister of Justice Haim Zadok asked that I be called home to explain myself.

But I would soon find myself a hero with the rank and file of American Jewry and the Israeli public. The mail I received was strikingly disapproving of the American Jewish leadership.

Sometime later, I asked Rabbi Israel Miller, president of the conference, to explain their lack of reaction. He went to the Israeli embassy in Washington, he said, but the only advice he received was *"Azov, shtuyot"* ("Forget it, it's nonsense"). Can I explain that? No. Was I enraged? Yes.

The final vote in the General Assembly was set for 10 November 1975, and my speech this time had to be significant. At a dinner of the United Jewish Appeal shortly before the vote, Ernest Michel, who managed the New York branch, told me about his father, who was taken away on 10 November 1938 by the Nazis on Kristallnacht. "Ernie, thank you," I said. "You have given me the opening of my speech."

Pondering tactics, I realized that even a good speech would not be enough. I needed something dramatic and unforgettable. My father, as chief rabbi of Palestine in 1939, once stood in front of the Jeshurun Synagogue in Jerusalem. Before the thousands gathered, he dramatically tore up into little pieces the British White Paper which called for a severe restriction of Jewish immigration to Palestine and virtually banned Jews from buying land in the country. *That* was unforgettable.

In the morning, as I prepared to leave for the UN, Aura said to me, "I was thinking—do you remember what your father did with the British White Paper?" Without giving anything away, I replied that I did, and said I would consider it. When I arrived at my office, David Afek, a first secretary and one of the ablest members of the delegation, came in and said excitedly, "Can you think of something dramatic, like tearing up the resolution?" I replied noncommittally that I would indeed think about it. By now, the debate was big news: President Ford had deplored the committee's vote "in the strongest terms," and Moynihan had condemned it on *Face the Nation*. Paul Johnson, the brilliant editor of the *New Statesman*, wrote:

> Indeed, the U.N. is rapidly becoming one of the most corrupt and corrupting creations in the whole history of human institutions. . . . The melancholy truth, I fear, is that the candles of civilization are burning low.

In Moscow, Andrei D. Sakharov, the renowned physicist, declared, "If this resolution is adopted, it can only contribute to anti-Semitic tendencies in many countries by giving them the appearance of international legality."

At the General Assembly, the atmosphere was tense and charged, and the house was packed. The Jewish organizations in New York had encouraged members to attend the session, and the galleries were full.

Walking down the long aisle to the podium, I mumbled the prayer from the Yom Kippur service, "Almighty God, inspire the mouths of the emissaries of your people, Israel." My heart was pounding as I opened my remarks:

> It is symbolic that this debate, which may well prove to be a turning point in the fortunes of the United Nations and a decisive factor as to the possible continued existence of this organization, should take place on November 10. Tonight thirty-seven years ago has gone down in history as Kristallnacht or the Night of the Crystals. This was the night, on 10 November 1938, when Hitler's Nazi storm troopers launched a coordinated attack on the Jewish community in Germany, burned the synagogues in its cities, and made bonfires in the street of the holy books and scrolls of the Holy Law and Bible. It was the night when Jewish homes were attacked and heads of families taken away, many of them never to return. It was the night when the windows of all Jewish

businesses and stores were smashed, covering the streets in the cities of Germany with a film of broken glass which dissolved into millions of crystals, giving that night the name Kristallnacht, the Night of the Crystals. It was the night which led eventually to the crematoria and gas chambers, Auschwitz, Birkenau, Dachau, Buchenwald, Theresienstadt, and others. It was the night which led to the most terrifying holocaust in the history of man.

. . . It is indeed ironic, Mr. President, that the U.N., which began its life as an anti-Nazi alliance, should thirty years later find itself on its way to becoming the world center of anti-Semitism. Hitler would have felt at home on a number of occasions during the past year, listening to the proceedings in this forum, and above all to the proceedings during the debate on Zionism.

. . . It is sobering to consider to what level this body has been dragged down if we are obliged today to contemplate an attack on Zionism.

For this attack constitutes not only an anti-Israeli attack of the foulest type, but also an assault in the United Nations on Judaism— one of the oldest established religions in the world, a religion which has given the world the human values of the Bible. . . .

I do not come to this rostrum to defend the moral and historical values of the Jewish people. They do not need to be defended. They speak for themselves. . . .

I come here to denounce the two great evils which menace society in general and a society of nations in particular. These two evils are hatred and ignorance. These two evils are the motivating force behind the proponents of this resolution and their supporters. These two evils characterize those who would drag this world organization, the ideals of which were first conceived by the prophets of Israel, to the depths to which it has been dragged today.

. . . Zionism is the name of the national movement of the Jewish people and is the modern expression of the ancient Jewish heritage. . . . Zionism is to the Jewish people what the liberation movements of Africa and Asia have been to their own people. Zionism is one of the most dynamic and vibrant national movements in human history. Historically it is based on a unique and unbroken connection, extending some four thousand years, between the People of the Book and the Land of the Bible.

. . . How sad it is to see here a group of nations, many of whom have but recently freed themselves of colonial rule, deriding one of the most noble liberation movements of this century, a movement which not only gave an example of encouragement and determination to the peoples struggling for independence but also actively aided many of them either during the period of preparation for their independence or immediately thereafter.

I stand here not as a supplicant. Vote as your moral conscience dictates to you. For the issue is neither Israel nor Zionism. The issue is the continued existence of this organization, which has been dragged to its lowest point of discredit by a coalition of despots and racists.

The vote of each delegation will record in history its country's stand on anti-Semitic racism and anti-Judaism. You yourselves bear the responsibility for your stand before history, for as such will you be viewed in history. We, the Jewish people, will not forget.

For us, the Jewish people, this is but a passing episode in a rich and event-filled history.

We put our trust in our Providence, in our faith and beliefs, in our time-hallowed tradition, in our striving for social advance and human values, and in our people wherever they may be. For us, the Jewish people, this resolution based on hatred, falsehood, and arrogance is devoid of any moral or legal value.

Taking the resolution in my hand, I tore it up in front of the UN General Assembly, and said, "Thank you, Mr. President." Grasping the torn pieces in my hand, I walked back to my seat as the hall erupted into tumultuous and sustained applause. Soaked in sweat, I sat down, exhausted. The speech—like Khrushchev's shoe—would live on.

The vote was seventy-two for the resolution and thirty-five against, with thirty-two abstentions. We assumed that seventy biased nations would always vote against us; we had only lost four undecided votes. We did not win the war, but we had made friends during the battle.

THE EFFECT OF the resolution on Jews throughout the world was electrifying. Our dignity and honor were being assailed, and the fight had clearly touched a nerve. I was inundated by cables and phone calls from Israel, and the embassy was swamped with mail. Jews everywhere wore buttons declaring I Am a Zionist or I Am Proud to Be a Zionist. Most amazing of all, I was lavished with praise by the Israeli press.

One of the great shocks was Mexico's vote in favor of the resolution. There was no logic to it; Mexico had always been friendly to Israel and home to a prosperous and influential Jewish community. The reason for the vote was simple: President Echeverría's ambition to become secretary-general of the United Nations. He encouraged the nonaligned and hostile countries to vote against Israel, with a view to winning their votes. But there were repercussions. Without a word about retribution, without any directives, 60,000 American Jews canceled their vacations in Mexico that week. The economic damage was enormous. Mexico's foreign minister, Emilio Rabassa, rushed to Israel and, on his return to New York, urgently requested me to come to the Mexican embassy. The visit had opened his eyes, he said. What could he do to make things right? Votes were coming up on Israeli-related issues, I told him. He assured me that Mexico would vote as Israel wanted. I did not know—no one had bothered to tell me— that Rabassa had *already* reached an agreement with Yigal Allon on how Mexico would vote. My ignorance of that agreement would cause quite an uproar.

In the next vote relating to Zionism, four anti-Israel resolutions were proposed. Mexico voted against us. Four more resolutions on Israeli practices in the occupied territories followed. I spoke against them, citing the Bible as the basis for our stand. Again, Mexico voted against us—after assurances from the foreign minister that everything would be all right.

In the meantime, all hell again broke loose in Israel. In his meeting with Rabassa, Allon had agreed that Mexico could continue to vote against us on these issues, then gradually change its votes in the future. Why Allon gave away the store, as it were, when we were dealing from strength was beyond me. I felt abused, both personally and for my country.

Agitated to a degree out of control, the director-general of our ministry, Eppie Evron, called me. What did I mean by telling *The New York Times* the Mexican vote was regrettable and disappointing? The Mexicans had kept their word, he said, they had honored their agreement. Only then did he realize that the ministry had forgotten to let me know about Allon and Rabassa's understanding.

As the story emerged, enraged Jews everywhere continued their boycott of travel in Mexico, and Mexico panicked over the loss of tourist dollars. A week later, Rabassa resigned, and Mexico fell into line on future votes.

AFTER THE EXCITEMENT of the Zionism-racism battle and all that followed it, I settled down to the daily grind, and at times drudgery, of my job. The obsession with Israel seemed never to abate in the UN. We belonged to no bloc, and therefore were fair game for the bullies. It was a constant battle. Resolutions were automatically brought up on the Palestinian problem, on Israel's relations with South Africa, on the nuclear problem in the Middle East, on alleged abuses of human rights, and almost anything else you can imagine.

One of the main problems facing Israel was the increasing vociferousness of the PLO, which enjoyed observer status in the General Assembly. The delegation was led by Labib Terzy, a mild-looking man whose appearance belied his hostile, vicious, and devious behavior. In early December, I was in battle again over the PLO because of the so-called Middle East resolution, which had been forced upon the General Assembly by the Syrians. Again, we endured a week of severe infighting, and again we lost. A special Palestine Committee of twenty was established to ensure that all resolutions concerning the Palestinians—and their "legitimate national rights"—were carried out. The resolution eliminated any mention of compromise, and the handsome budget provided for the committee gave it a solid basis for attacking Israel.

That week, Israeli aircraft attacked Palestinian terrorist camps in Lebanon. The Security Council was called into emergency session by the Lebanese and the Egyptians. This time they insisted that the PLO be invited to the meetings on this issue. The seating of the PLO at the Security Council was a dangerous precedent, and I asked for instructions from home. I wanted to attend the meeting, but I also wanted the option to leave should the PLO be seated. However, I received instructions not even to attend, and thus let our case go by default.

I asked Moynihan to support us by blocking the invitation to the PLO and vetoing the hostile resolution that had been submitted. I maintained that the invitation of the PLO was in violation of Article 32 of the UN charter, which limits such invitations to states, whether or not they are members of the UN. I warned him that if Palestine was admitted to the Security Council, Puerto Rican nationalists would be demanding the same rights.

Moynihan was very concerned about the Swedes, who were a real problem. Olaf Rydbeck, the Swedish ambassador, was prepared to abstain, which would have been fine for us, but Prime Minister Olaf Palme decided that Sweden would vote in favor of the PLO. Rydbeck's conversations with Stockholm had obviously been to no avail. Had they abstained, the PLO would have been eliminated from the Security Council. We felt as if we had been stabbed in the back by a friendly country that wasn't even supposed to have a knife.

—

ONE OF THE ENCOURAGING aspects of the struggle in the United Nations was the attitude and backing of the United States. Along with that, I got to know Henry Kissinger very well.

Every session with Kissinger was an overwhelming intellectual experience. At one luncheon in early January 1976, he was asked about international affairs and launched into a long speech about the impossibility for America to conduct foreign policy. Foreign policy, he said, is a function of strength; foreign policy is a function of being able to do something; foreign policy could not be a function of paralysis. In his view, the weakening of executive authority and the strengthening of Congress—this was soon after Congress had turned down President Ford's appeal for help for Angola—would have disastrous effects on America's ability to conduct any form of effective foreign policy. Kissinger not only believed in crisis control, he believed that any time a strong country was attacked or threatened or muscled, it had to be prepared for instant and massive retaliation. Kissinger pointed out that he'd done that in 1970 when Jordan was invaded by Syrian troops; he'd saved Jordan by using the threat of Israeli troops and the U.S. Sixth Fleet. He had responded the same way in 1973, in the Yom Kippur War. We had come to the United States asking for Galaxy planes to carry weapons and arms to Israel. Nixon okayed the request and Kissinger responded immediately, getting them from the Pentagon. Those planes *saved* Israel. And he had also come through for us when rumors were flying that Russian ships had gone down the Bosphorus, in Turkey, carrying nuclear weapons on board. Kissinger reacted instantly, letting the Russians know that they were not the only ones with nuclear weapons at their disposal.

Kissinger felt that one's reaction must always be so massive that the other side will not be prepared to match it; you have to be prepared to use power when necessary; and, because of that show of strength, you will not have to use it. His example was that because Nixon had convinced the Russians that he was crazy enough to carry out his threats, none of them ever had to be carried out.

Israel's only hope for survival, Kissinger believed, was in a strong America. It didn't matter that America might not always be as friendly as it should be to Israel; what mattered was that the Arabs would talk about peace with Israel only when they were convinced that there was no hope of defeating Israel militarily—and they could come to that conclusion only if they knew the United States would always back Israel. If that backing became questionable, the Arabs would step up their pressure, and Israel would become a free-for-all. His evaluation was a correct one, as proven by the last twenty years of Middle East history.

Kissinger worried that America's willingness to use its military might had been greatly weakened as a result of Vietnam and Watergate. It would take a long time for the United States to recover and the world to believe in America's strength. By then, it might be too late. The natural tendency of any country attacked by the Communists would be to surrender if there was no hope of help from the Americans.

I will say that America's backing of Israel was not a one-way street. We stood by the United States any time America was maligned. Even when it meant going against our principles—as it did when we voted against admitting Vietnam to the UN—we felt we had to back our one true friend.

As U.S. AMBASSADOR to the UN, Pat Moynihan had become a personal as well as a political friend. So I was upset when, in the course of a meeting with him, he produced a copy of the *Washington Post*. There was a front-page story in which Ivor Richard, the British ambassador, criticized Moynihan, likening him to Wyatt Earp, the avenging cowboy, running amok in the UN. Richard also made the damning criticism, which I had heard before, that Moynihan put off the Third World countries by his frank and outspoken manner.

Moynihan had been around long enough to realize that this article was damaging to him. He did not believe that it came only from the British. He felt it was no accident that it was published in Washington, that the British would not have done this without knowing they had the backing of the State Department, indeed of the secretary of state. A few days later, Leonard Garment called and told me that Moynihan was about to resign. The full story had now run in *The New York Times*, and Moynihan believed it was definitely Kissinger-inspired. On my way to the UN, I met Norman Podhoretz, editor of *Commentary*. I said to him that it would be wrong for Moynihan to resign; the opponent was the wrong opponent, namely, the British ambassador. I didn't think they could pin this on the State Department, certainly not on the secretary. Podhoretz felt that once a person began to go down in Kissinger's eyes, there was no stopping the sinking and the sooner one faced reality the better. I insisted that wasn't the case. Moynihan was strong publicly, I said, and Kissinger could break his neck on him. Podhoretz just laughed at my naiveté. For six years now, he said, all those who had predicted that Kissinger would go too far and would stumble and fall were either in jail or put out to pasture, while Kissinger was still secretary of state. There was no one as nasty as Kissinger when it came to political infighting, Podhoretz said. There was no question that these articles and the campaign against Moynihan came from the great man himself. Moynihan obviously agreed. In February 1976, he went through with his plan to resign. It was a sad moment for his friends.

Moynihan was replaced by William Scranton, former governor of Pennsylvania, and onetime candidate for the Republican nomination for president. Scranton's past was not without controversy, at least as far as Israel was concerned. He had, after the Six-Day War, made some remarks which ruffled many feathers in Israel; he talked about evenhandedness after the aggression of the Arab forces. I was a little suspicious at first, but as I got to know him as a colleague I grew to admire him.

He found himself, however, a complete novice in the intricate web of the United Nations hypocrisy, and he was thrown into the cold waters of the Middle East issue with little or no preparation.

In March 1976, an Israeli magistrate in Jerusalem dismissed a charge, on technical grounds, against a group of Jewish extremists who had attempted to pray on the Temple Mount. The Arabs maintained, falsely, that this was tantamount to authorizing the Jews to pray in the Al-Aksa Mosque. I approached Feredoun Hoveida, the Iranian ambassador, and pointed out that what had happened was that Israel was actually *protecting* the rights of the Moslems; the fact that the UN was now once again moving against us over this issue was an attempt to incite religious feelings for political aims. Hoveida was unmoved by my explanation, however, and once again we were in the middle of a Security Council debate.

It was decided that I would appear this time even if the PLO was seated at the Security Council. It was clear that we had to defend ourselves; we could not let debates go by default. Oddly enough, the question of seating in the Security Council chamber created new problems. There were only four available seats for nonmembers. It was obvious that one seat would have to be permanently occupied by Israel, but the Arabs quarreled among themselves as to who would occupy the other seats. The Jordanians did not see why they should allow the PLO to be the only ones seated whereas the Egyptians would not agree that the Syrians should be seated at all. Finally, after a delay of an hour and a half, they compromised: the PLO was the only Arab delegation seated full-time; all the other Arab participants rotated. This was the kind of decision that could take up all of one's time at the UN.

The Temple Mount debate was William Scranton's initial appearance at the Security Council on behalf of the United States. The Pakistanis led off in the attack, producing as usual a resolution condemning Israel (which had been discussed three days before the debate began by all the members—so much for the objectivity of the Security Council). The Egyptians opened the Arab attack with a volatile and extremist speech, threatening war. It was typical of the one-upmanship struggle between the Arabs; they were all attempting to prove they were more extreme than any of the *other* Arabs.

I spoke next. I had researched the subject in great detail and thus spoke for an hour, making, I felt, a very strong case proving that the entire accusation about the Temple Mount was "a damnable lie." As the debate continued, it became clear that my words had had their desired effect; there was a tendency on the part of everyone concerned to switch over to another complaint. They left the subject of the Temple Mount and concentrated on the West Bank. Baroody of Saudi Arabia launched into one of his horrible diatribes, meaningless, irrelevant, and shameful, denying that Anne Frank ever existed, and spewing nonsense about Auschwitz and the Holocaust. I in turn delivered a violent attack on the Soviet Union, which had based its arguments on utter lies. The Russians, in their right of reply, attacked me for not attacking the Chinese. Just a typical UN free-for-all.

I made further responses to many of the allegations, and it was clear I was getting under the Arabs' skin. They were beginning to have second thoughts about raising issues in a forum where I had the freedom of speech to say whatever I wanted in response.

And then it was Scranton's turn to speak on behalf of the United States. As he rambled on, I was left utterly speechless—he was officially buying into the Arab point of view, hook, line, and sinker. It was a shock to all of us and was a very serious and disturbing development. Dinitz, our ambassador in Washington, tried to use his contacts to find out what the hell had happened. I called Scranton directly and expressed my extreme disappointment and anger. His speech had no precedent, I told him. Then, surprising me even more, he told me that he too was disappointed by the speech. In fact, he was horrified by parts of it—but he only grasped what was happening when he was actually speaking. That speech had been put in front of him moments before he delivered it, sent word for word by the State Department. He said he was truly embarrassed, and I believed him. I was advised later that it was Kissinger who had approved and authorized the speech. It was the ultimate in political maneuvering; it was pure Kissinger. He didn't want to appear too anti-Arab, so apparently he had his representative take a pro-Arab stance and then, when the Temple Mount resolution came up for the vote, he had the United States apply a veto.

DURING THE DEBATES on the Middle East, some panacea for attaining peace was invariably offered. The solution now was to reconvene the Geneva Peace Conference.

Established after the Yom Kippur War by the United States and the Soviet Union, the conference was attended by the foreign ministers of the Soviet Union, the United States, Israel, Jordan, and Egypt. Although nothing concrete developed, it became a symbol of the possibility that something could. The main stumbling block to its resumption was the Arabs' insistence on including the PLO, whose sworn mission was to destroy us. Pressure to reconvene the conference came from the Russians, who hoped to assume the central role in Middle East negotiations.

Since the break in official relations in June 1967 following the Six-Day War, Israel had had little contact with Russia, which was rearming the Arabs, particularly Egypt, and preparing them for a new war with us. Insisting on Israel's complete withdrawal from the territories acquired in the Six-Day War, the Soviets were striving for preeminence in the Middle East, maintaining that the region was close enough to be of vital strategic interest. They saw Israel as their main stumbling block to control of the region, since we were so closely allied to the United States. Above all, they wished to avoid the creation of Western-based military pacts in the area directed against them.

Israel, for its part, had to walk a fine line with Russia. We did not wish to abandon millions of Soviet Jews, so we went out of our way to develop some kind of dialogue. One of the few places where this could occur was at the UN.

When I came to the UN, the Soviet ambassador was Yakob Malik, a Communist of the Stalinist school who fervently believed in the philosophy that he was representing. When I first called on him in his capacity as president of the Security Council, he burst out in rage, pointing at a carafe of cold water on the table, shouting, "That is all the UN allows itself for members of the Security Council!" Turning to Malik, I said, "As soon as I return to my office, I will send you a case of Israeli vodka."

Malik glowered and said, "Only the Czechs can make beer, only the Scots can make whiskey, and only the Russians can make vodka—and don't ever let the Poles tell you otherwise." The barriers between us immediately began to break down. A few weeks later, I felt free enough to ask, "Mr. Ambassador, why do you hate us so much? What have we ever done to you to make you feel this way?" He replied, "I hate you? Of course not. Some of my best friends at Kharkov University were Jews. But if you raise the issue, I'll tell you what annoys me. I don't believe in God, but if you are right and there is one, by what right will you, when you go to heaven, sit nearer God than me? Who chose you to be a chosen people?" I laughed and said, "Mr. Ambassador, after what we have suffered for over four thousand years because we are a chosen people, I am quite prepared to hand the privilege over to your people so that you can learn what it is like."

THE MOST IMPORTANT Russian in the United Nations was Arkady Shevchenko, undersecretary general for political and security affairs. His eleven years in the United States had profoundly affected him, and he was much freer and more amenable than other Russians. He was highly intelligent and we developed a good relationship. In Security Council matters, I found to my amazement that he was helpful and willing to ease problems for me. We began to meet regularly for lunch, and he would consume respectable quantities of vodka. He was always available for a dinner party at my home, and always brought his attractive Polish-born wife. I suspected her of being Jewish, although she never admitted to it. But I had in my library an old Sefer Torah presented in 1904 to the Czar of Russia by the Jews of a town called Suvalk, and her reaction and excitement when she saw it and realized what it was seemed to betray her identity. At one point, after a considerable helping of vodka, Shevchenko admitted that he had had a Jewish grandmother—to which I attributed his openness and willingness to discuss life in the Soviet hierarchy. He was obviously jealous of Dobrynin, the Soviet ambassador to the U.S., and felt that he deserved that job.

Very nervous and suspicious, Shevchenko saw enemies lurking behind every door. One day while lunching at a nearby restaurant, he was particularly nervous, suspecting two attractive women at the next table of spying on him. I said to him, jokingly, "Here we see the basic difference between your world and mine. My assumption is that they sat near us because they are interested in two attractive young men." Shevchenko didn't find it amusing and went to make a phone call. He returned satisfied that they had no hostile motives. Shevchenko's strange behavior was explained in later years when he became the most senior Soviet diplomat to defect to the United States.

It soon became clear that the Russians were seeking in a very gauche and heavy-handed manner to bridge the gap with Israel. By severing the relationship, they had backed themselves into a corner. Historically, Russia was anti-Semitic and particularly anti-Israel. But we weren't going away, and they needed to deal with us.

The Soviet ambassador had indicated in an off-the-record interview that their foreign policy was moving toward normalizing relations with Israel. The Russians were looking for an opening and wanted a dialogue. It was a policy of self-interest: they could not be major players equal to the Americans without having normal relations with both sides. They were not concerned about our welfare—I had no illusions about that—but an opening was an opening. And for the first time, we could deal from a position of strength. I was greatly in favor of establishing a dialogue with Russia—I am usually greatly in favor of establishing a dialogue with almost anyone—but our Foreign Ministry seemed incredibly inept, unprofessional, and dogmatic on this issue and wanted no part of the Soviet Union. Human foibles always get in the way of progress.

Nowhere was that more obvious than when observing the hypocrisy and cowardice of the Arab representatives. In February 1976, I was invited to attend a lunch at John and Peter Loeb's. John Loeb was head of an important Wall Street financial house, and Peter Loeb, his wife, was New York City commissioner of city affairs. A large and distinguished crowd of diplomats and politicians was filling their elegant apartment, and I noticed among them, out of the corner of my eye, the Egyptian and Lebanese ambassadors, with their wives. As we sat down to the table, I saw that they had disappeared—in protest at my being invited, as I later learned. Such foolish, childish, and ill-mannered behavior was typical, particularly of the Egyptians. It opened many eyes and helped people like the Loebs to understand my position and the problems facing Israel.

THE UN, I FELT, had a very hypocritical approach toward Israel's relationship with South Africa. Much attention was paid to our minuscule trade with that nation; very little to its enormous trade with Britain, the European Community, and the United States; and none whatsoever to South Africa's trade with Black Africa. All of them assuaged their conscience by attacking Israel. After producing details of trade with Black African countries, I was asked by President Julius Nyerere of Tanzania through their ambassador to stop attacking their clandestine relationship with South Africa. I was prepared to reach a mutual agreement: if they stopped attacking us, I would keep quiet.

In general, Israel had a double-edged relationship with the African countries. Thousands of Africans had trained in Israel in agriculture, medicine, business, and science. Thousands of Israelis had worked with Africans in the bush and helped to advance them. It was not unusual for me to meet Africans at the UN who addressed me in Hebrew. One Ethiopian ambassador would sidle up to us in the General Assembly and in fluent Hebrew whisper, "Be careful, the bastards are preparing a trap for you."

That pretty much summed up my view of the UN at the end of my first year: Be careful, the bastards are preparing a trap for you.

CHAPTER 18

The UN Years:
Labor's Downfall

IN THE SUMMER OF 1976, one of the great heroic moments in Israeli history occurred.

An Air France plane was hijacked by Palestinian and German terrorists. After landing in Greece, it was flown to Benghazi in Libya and then to the city of Entebbe in Uganda. Jews were separated from non-Jews, a horrible reminder of the days of the Nazi "selections." All non-Israeli passengers were released and flown to France. The one hundred or so Israeli passengers and the French crew were herded into the Entebbe air terminal and held as hostages. The terrorists demanded the release of a long list of imprisoned international terrorists. At the UN an emergency session was called.

When I arrived, the celebrations to mark the two hundredth anniversary of the birth of the United States had already begun. On the Fourth of July, the "tall ships," magnificent sailing ships from the many countries coming to celebrate the occasion, were to sail past President Gerald Ford as he stood on the deck of the aircraft carrier *Forrestal* in New York harbor. In the evening of 3 July, I received an urgent call from the switchboard operator at the embassy. She was choking with emotion as she spoke, barely able to control her voice. Between sobs, she informed me that the hostages had been rescued by the Israel Defense Forces. Together with every single Israeli and every single Jew—and, I like to think, every decent person in the world—I uttered a prayer of thanks. It was a proud moment indeed. And as the information poured in and we got a fair picture about the amazing rescue which had been carried out, it became even prouder.

The raid was carried out under the instructions of Prime Minister Rabin, his minister of defense, Shimon Peres, and Israel's chief of staff, Motta Gur. The officer in charge of the operation was the chief of infantry and paratroopers, General Dan Shomron. Israeli elite units were surreptitiously flown in a number of Hercules aircraft to the Entebbe air terminal. Taking the Ugandan guards and the terrorists by surprise, the Israelis rescued the hostages and rushed them to the Hercules planes. The Ugandan fighter planes sitting on the airstrips were blown up so that they couldn't follow. Several of the German terrorists and some of the Ugandan forces were killed in the break-in. Less than an hour after landing in Entebbe, the Israeli planes were airborne, with every hostage but two safe and sound. (One hostage made the mistake of standing up when the raid began; he was shot and killed when the terrorists were shot. The other, an elderly woman named Dora Bloch, had earlier been moved to a hospital in Entebbe, where she was subsequently brutally murdered.) The Israeli planes landed to refuel in Nairobi, Kenya, and came home to Israel to a tumultuous welcome and the adulation of the rest of the world. One Israeli officer, Lieutenant Colonel Jonathan Netanyahu, the very able and outstanding elder brother of the current prime minister, Binyamin Netanyahu, had been killed. Yoni, as he was known, became an instant national hero, the symbol of Israel's great fighting spirit.

Early in the morning of the Fourth of July, Aura and I drove to Brooklyn, where we boarded a tugboat that took us to the *Forrestal.* The *New York Times* had given expression to the feelings of all free men and women in a very moving editorial about the rescue, and I doubt that Israel has ever stood taller in prestige than on this special occasion. As Aura and I went on board the *Forrestal,* along with the 4,000 other guests, we found ourselves the center of attention. In many ways, Entebbe had stolen the show on this, America's bicentennial. To a degree, it was an eloquent reflection of the great ideals of the liberty of man which the bicentenary represented. Hundreds came over to congratulate us.

At midday, President Ford rang a replica of the Liberty Bell to mark the anniversary of the United States, then took the salute from the passing ships. Ford never commented publicly on the raid—as crazy as it seems, the public outcry in Africa and the UN would have been too great if he took Israel's side officially on such an aggressive military mission— but privately he told me how thrilling it was. Ford was a hard man—and president—to read. He was quite remote and difficult to get to know well. He did, however, know a lot about Israel because of his years in Congress.

THE ARAB DELEGATIONS, correctly gauging antiterrorist and pro-Israel feeling in the aftermath of Entebbe, decided not to lead a UN attack against us. However, they were inciting the Africans to take action against Israel for this "act of piracy." Many Western countries warned them against this, but Benin, Libya, and Tanzania nevertheless introduced a resolution to the Security Council criticizing Israel for "violation of . . . Ugandan sovereignty and territorial integrity," demanding that Israel offer Uganda full compensation for damage and destruction inflicted during our raid.

At the Security Council meeting of 9 July 1976, the Arabs wisely kept in the background; the African attack was led by Sir Harold Walters of Mauritius, who chaired the Organization of African Unity.

After his opening, I spoke:

. . . From a purely formal point of view, this meeting arises from a complaint brought against the Government of Israel.

However, let me make it quite clear that sitting here as the representative of the Government of Israel, as I have the honor to do, I am in no way sitting in the dock as the accused party.

On the contrary, I stand here as an accuser on behalf of free and decent people in this world . . .

I stand here as an accuser of this world organization, the UN, which has been unable, because of the machinations of the Arab representatives and their supporters, to coordinate effective measures in order to combat the evil of world terrorism.

I stand here as an accuser of those delegations to this organization which for reasons of political expediency have remained silent on this issue . . .

Addressing the Soviet Union, I said:

It is not enough to raise your voice in horror when it affects only you. If terrorism is bad, it is bad for everybody, in every case, on every occasion, by whomever it is committed, and whoever the victim might be. It must be eliminated . . . In many ways this is a moment of truth for this organization.

In reply to the Tanzanian representative, I asked:

> Would Africa have looked better with the blood of those innocent
> victims bespattering the soil of Africa?

I hit out against all those who attacked us:

> The representative of the Soviet Union talked about aggression and
> the inviolability of territorial integrity and national sovereignty. On
> these subjects I defer to him, considering the Soviet Union's very con-
> siderable record in these respects in Hungary, in Czechoslovakia, and in
> other countries in Eastern Europe. My colleague from China could
> doubtless elaborate on this subject.

As the debate continued, I called on the United Nations to break away
from the grip of despots and to reassume its rightful role in behalf of humanity and international peace. Following those remarks, the Libyan representative made a hysterical attack on me. In exercising my right of
reply, I quoted the rational Arab leaders such as President Sadat—who
had declared that Qaddafi, Libya's leader, was a certifiable lunatic—and
President Numeiry of Sudan, who was totally opposed to Libya's terrorist
policies. Refuting the allegation that I hated Libya, I added laconically,
"Indeed, some of my best friends are Libyans." The Security Council dissolved in laughter.

In the final vote, the resolution was not adopted; the Africans failed to
mobilize the necessary nine votes. It was a rare triumph for Israel in the
Security Council. Ivor Richard, the British ambassador, sent me a note:
"This is a famous victory."

AFTER THEIR EMBARRASSING loss, there was much gnashing of teeth
throughout the African delegations as well as serious internal squabbling.
After the operation at Entebbe, Israeli planes had landed in Kenya, at
Nairobi airport, to refuel. This had been previously coordinated, and we
had also made arrangements to treat the wounded, in case there should
be any. At the Security Council, Kenya, maintaining the stand of African
unity, denied any connivance with Israel; Foreign Minister Waiyaiki
never exchanged a single glance with me and criticized Israel quite
strongly. The Ugandans, for their part, accused Kenya of collaborating
with Israel. The Kenyans denied it and complained of the massacre of

hundreds of Kenyan citizens by Ugandans. Throughout the entire debate, Israel and Kenya formally ignored each other, and Waiyaiki insisted there had been no contact or collaboration.

Immediately after the final session of the Security Council, I went with Ambassador Sofer of our delegation straight to Waiyaiki's apartment. He opened the door, we embraced, and then we raised a glass to victory.

TWO WEEKS AFTER the Entebbe debate, I flew with Aura to attend the FEDECO Conference in San José, the capital of Costa Rica. FEDECO is the representative body of all the Jewish communities in Central America, and I was to address the convention. We flew via Pan Am from New York. En route, we made a stop in Guatemala City, and were allowed off the plane to stretch our legs and to purchase souvenirs. The stopover was uneventful and then, right on schedule, we took off for San José.

Twenty minutes into the second leg of our flight, the chief steward came over and asked me, "Are you the ambassador of Israel to the UN?" I replied in the affirmative, and then he said, "Because of you, we have been advised that there is a bomb on the plane." He was quite unpleasant, making it clear that I shared a good part of the blame for this horrible situation. We sat there, Aura and I, knowing that we had left our children behind on their own, not knowing if we would ever see them— or anyone else—again. It was the longest twenty minutes in our lives. As we approached San José, an announcement was made to the passengers that the moment the plane landed and the engines were switched off, everyone was to rush out as rapidly as possible from the plane, taking no luggage with them. As we approached the airfield, we saw that it had been cleared, and was lined by firefighting equipment and ambulances. We lined up at the door immediately after the landing, and as it opened, ran down the steps and got away from the plane as fast as we could. When we reached the terminal, several hundred yards away, we found a distraught group of Jewish community leaders and representatives of the Costa Rican government. For the rest of my stay in Costa Rica, I was surrounded by a small army of security people. However, no bomb was found on the plane. It turned out that I had apparently been spotted at the Guatemala airport by someone hostile toward Israel, who then and there telephoned the bomb warning to Pan Am. Whoever it was must have recognized me because I'd spent so much time on television during the aftermath of the Entebbe raid.

—

By 1977, for the first time in Israel's history, the Labor Party was in danger of losing the election. They had held absolute power for almost thirty years and, in addition to their accomplishments, had proved that absolute power corrupts absolutely. From top to bottom, the Labor government was replete with scandals and corruption. The director-general of the ministry of trade and industry was caught taking bribes and went to jail. The nominated head of the Bank of Israel was indicted for corruption and convicted. The party had bogged down in a morass of greed, incompetence, and self-interest.

Shimon Peres, as minister of defense, was trying to win control of the Labor Party from Yitzhak Rabin. The party had experienced many key defections. Golda Meir was retired and Moshe Dayan, as always very conscious of the political situation, was about to make a controversial switch to the Likud government after the elections. Peres suggested that I stay on at the UN—hinting broadly that I stood a very good chance of becoming a minister in the new administration. The Labor Party could not win, he believed, without new faces; if he was nominated to lead the party, he wanted me to be one of them.

I knew Peres's intuition was right. "Yigal," I told our foreign minister Yigal Allon, "you are all living in a fool's paradise. You have no idea how the public feels about you as a government. I have been here for some ten days. I have lived in a hotel and talked to all the employees. I traveled everywhere by cab and talked to all the cabdrivers. I met with many of my friends, including most of the principal figures in the media. During my entire visit, I have not heard one good word about the government, only condemnation. Labor is heading for disaster." I was right. Rabin fought back Peres's challenge and retained control of the party, but not for long. That summer, the Likud won the elections, which were a debacle for Labor. Rabin had resigned before Election Day.

In the meantime, Jimmy Carter had been elected president of the United States and appointed a new ambassador to the United Nations, Andrew Young. An outspoken member of the black community, Young had tremendous energy and the enthusiasm and arrogance of someone used to working outside the system. He obviously thought he could introduce a new style into U.S. representation in the UN, and Jews were initially thrilled with his appointment. He said all the nice things they

like to hear, but I was a little wary of him. He was in a very difficult position, basically pro-Israel but also something of a black crusader. Many of
Israel's problems were with countries whose populations were dominated
by people of color—and not with the people themselves but with their
government. That put Young squarely in the middle. He was quite naive,
particularly when it came to dealing with the African delegations: because
they were black they were good and he could deal with them. He didn't
take into consideration just how corrupt so many of their regimes were.
They didn't care whom they were dealing with—they were unreliable.
Color had nothing to do with it.

Young, of course, was taking his orders from Carter, and Carter was
very empathetic toward the Palestinians, seeing them as oppressed. Many
Palestinians had been living in wretched conditions, but Carter did not
realize—or would not acknowledge—that many of their problems were a
result of self-oppression and an irrational unwillingness to compromise
or attempt to coexist with Israel. We were anti-Palestinian not by nature
but by self-preservation: the expressed goal of their leadership was to destroy Israel and drive us back into the sea.

Carter's ultimate great Middle East triumph was the groundbreaking
negotiations he maneuvered between Begin and Sadat at a later stage. The
summit at Camp David was Carter's idea all the way, and he cashed in on
it politically, just like everyone else involved. It was an outstanding strategy and he manipulated it brilliantly. Sadat and Begin disliked each other,
yet Carter locked them up in negotiations for two weeks.

Labor was greatly in favor of the Camp David meeting. Much of the
Likud, even though Begin was their leader, was opposed to it; to his
credit, Begin held firm. It was not dissimilar to when Nixon opened up
U.S. relations with China. No Democrat could have done that; people
would have been suspicious and wary that any Democratic line would
have been too soft. In the same way, only a hard-line rightist could have
done something as dramatic as making an accord with Egypt.

Carter's role was invaluable. He was the most powerful man in the
world, and when he spoke, the world had to listen. It would never have
happened without him. But it was also a publicity and political gimmick.
Carter needed the glory and he got it—the same way Clinton soaked in
the glory of the now-famous Rabin–Arafat handshake on the White
House lawn. They were both grandstand players—but very effective ones.
Politics at any level is a game. The higher the level, the higher the stakes.
But there was much ground to cover before the parties would reach the
cruicial negotiations at Camp David.

Soon after his face-losing apology to Britain for very undiplomatic comments about their racial policies, Young did it again. People should not be paranoid about seeing a Communist behind every tree in Africa, he declared, the Cubans had brought stability to Angola. This defied common sense. As William Safire pointed out, "When one has a bayonet at one's throat, that does create a certain degree of discipline."

As a result of Young's outbursts, Vice President Walter Mondale took charge of enunciating Carter's African policy. Young continued to carve out an important political niche, his policy reflecting the Carter administration's rather blatant move toward accommodating the Third World and away from the subtle but firm pro-Israel policy of Henry Kissinger.

The administration's policy was made quite clear when President Carter addressed the UN General Assembly and attended a reception that was not only for members but for observers as well, and thus receiving representatives of the PLO, in direct contravention of the declared U.S. policy. I tried to intervene with Andrew Young, but to little avail. The Americans apparently hoped that a signal of moderation would elicit one from the Palestinians. Young, who was very pro-PLO, was responsible for Carter's decision to receive them. (Young was ultimately fired for meeting with their representatives, in violation of U.S. policy.)

I was instructed not to attend Carter's reception but was horrified by this approach. This would not only underscore the PLO's victory but would also cause an unnecessary split with the administration and would insult the president of the United States—all of it covered extensively by the world media. It was hard for me to understand the Israeli government's lack of understanding. Like so many governments, they were obsessed with symbols rather than reality and practicality; a reaction to this symbol would be a disaster. In desperation, I told Allon that he was laying himself open to ridicule, that it would be a public relations catastrophe for Israel, and that we were handing an unnecessary victory to the PLO. He finally relented and issued a statement that only because of respect for the president of the United States would we attend.

Because of the presence of the PLO, no photographers were allowed at the reception and there was no handshaking. Many Jews waited until the last minute to see what I would do, before coming to the reception after the speech; others called me that day to ask if I was going. Most of them followed my lead; the party was quite well attended. Carter received the PLO but the controversy was diffused. Carter's national security advisor, Zbigniew Brzezinski, told me that Israel owed me a debt.

Of all the scandals that had hit the Labor Party, the question of Mrs. Rabin's financial misconduct was the most devastating. A journalist had discovered that she was maintaining an account in Washington, in violation of Israeli currency laws. We in Labor thought that the matter would blow over—the transgression was that of Rabin's wife's, not his—but Attorney General Aharon Barak thought otherwise. Proceedings were instituted against Mrs. Rabin, and suddenly the prime minister resigned, replaced as leader of the party by Shimon Peres. But it was too late to salvage Labor's reputation, and Peres had the misfortune to preside over its debacle in the June elections.

A political earthquake had hit Israel. Menachem Begin and the Likud gained an overwhelming majority; Labor, which had always held between forty and sixty seats in the Knesset, dropped to thirty-two. The reaction, particularly in the United States, was very unfavorable. The new government was described in terms of hard-line hawks and terrorist leadership. *Time* magazine headlined the story "Begin Rhymes with Fagin"—a Dickensian reference with anti-Semitic overtones.

A freedom fighter who had struggled hard against British rule, Begin was one of the underground leaders who fought against the British rule in Palestine. He was a firebrand who, his critics believed, would not change just because he was prime minister.

Did I think we'd had a revolution in Israel? Yes. For the worse? Absolutely. I was concerned but decided to wait and see; after all, Begin was a patriot. I was on the other side politically, but you can't let ideology blind you to the truth. And the truth was that he was our prime minister, chosen by the people of Israel, and worthy of support. So I did my best and managed to do him some good. Early on, I suggested he come to the UN. In typical Begin fashion, with a chip on his shoulder, he asked, "Why should I?" Because everyone would expect him to spew fire, and instead he'd talk peace. That is exactly what he did, in a remarkably successful move from every point of view. *Newsweek* even put him on the cover, with the caption: "A Charmer Called Begin."

I was soon inundated with invitations to explain the new regime on TV, but the Foreign Ministry, still under the old administration, had forbidden any statements.

Furious at the government's shortsightedness. I complained to Shlomo Avineri, director-general of the Foreign Ministry in the Labor government, that I should be visible to American Jewry, explaining how the democratic process had been at work. We couldn't hide from this forever. I was due to debate George Ball, former undersecretary of state, and would have to acknowledge and deal with Arab comments about Begin. After a long and bitter argument, I got the green light and appeared on three TV shows and briefed *Time, Newsweek,* and the *Christian Science Monitor.* Mine was the first voice in the United States to defend the election process and decry attempts to call Begin a terrorist.

American Jewry was in a near-panic, fearing a probable confrontation between Carter and Begin; both were inflexible and hardly of the same mind. Begin had no idea at first how to play the game of politics. Our friends demanded that we take a hawkish position, while creating the most dovish possible image. We had to talk all day about negotiating a peaceful solution, knowing full well that the Arabs would not do this. Some might call this position cynical, but politics is largely about image and flexibility. A politician can say no, or he can say yes, but . . . One leaves room for negotiation; the other does not. It's an essential tactic, one we feared Begin might not use.

The election result—much like the Republican sweep of 1994 in the United States—was more a condemnation of one party than a mandate for the other. Cut off from the people, the Labor Party existed in a political ivory tower sunk in the bedrock of mediocrity. Israel was getting used to mediocrity and tending to expect it. The change could prevent politicians from getting lax and smug and insulated. Politicians exist to serve, not to preserve their job or their hold on power.

I hoped that the new leaders who would emerge would abandon not the Labor ideology but its pettiness, system of governing, and isolation from reality. I had hoped that the slap in the face it had received would result not in a knockout but in Labor's determination to fight the good fight.

In late June 1977, I flew to Israel, to find it adjusting hopefully to Begin's strong and authoritative leadership. The newly appointed minister of foreign affairs, Moshe Dayan, had been a stalwart of the Labor Party, a standard-bearer of its aims and principles. He had been quietly negotiating with Begin before the elections, having seen the writing on the wall. After Begin's ascension, Dayan almost gleefully abandoned his party in its hour of defeat, to face violent accusations of political prostitution. He later made quite a convincing case for his belief that he could move Begin toward peace negotiations with Egypt and possibly other Arab states. Depending on one's point of view, he was either treacherous or extremely brave and imaginative. In the final analysis, he was a major force in bringing about the peace agreement with Egypt.

From my standpoint, Moshe Dayan was not the ideal boss. My book, *The War of Atonement,* pulled no punches about his leadership—or lack of it—in the Yom Kippur War as well as his involvement in the failures that led to it. Although he had a valid reason to resent me and to remove me from my UN post, he asked me if I wanted to stay on, and I said yes. Although Dayan dismissed my views that the Russians were interested in opening talks with us—his ego wouldn't allow him to meet with them unless they came to him—Begin for his part made it clear that he would meet with Gromyko anywhere, at any time.

The task of rebuilding the Labor Party had fallen on the shoulders of Shimon Peres, who appeared to be a broken man. Although not responsible for Labor's defeat—Rabin had not been a very effective prime minister—Peres had obviously been through a tremendous trauma. He had considerable stamina and was extraordinarily brilliant, but the task of rebuilding the party was formidable.

On his first visit to the United States as prime minister, Begin performed brilliantly at rallies of Jewish organizations, UJA dinners, and gatherings for Hadassah and Israel Bonds—smiling, affable, and making the same winning speech. Not since Ben-Gurion's triumphant 1951 visit had anything like this been seen.

Perhaps more than anything, Begin seized the diplomatic initiative, giving Israel the public relations advantage in the battle for the United States. The Arabs were extremely concerned. But on the only real issue of substance, we had a setback. Begin's combativeness eventually came out over the settlement issue.

A considerable area of state-owned land in the West Bank and Gaza, known as Crown Lands during the British Mandate, comprised terraced hills that were not settled or generally farmed. The Labor administration had concentrated on settling those areas which fell in line with the plan devised by Yigal Allon, whereby the Jordanian government would take over the heavily populated Arab districts, while many of the remaining empty areas would be reserved for Jewish settlement. The Labor government tried to maintain this policy, although it was not always successful because of pressure from more extreme settlers. No public issue was made of settlement; the policy was to talk as little as possible about it. It seemed that we could build settlements in the barren areas with little or no Arab population, as long as we merely did so—without announcing future plans.

This policy changed under the new Likud government, which began highlighting plans for settlement even before a single stone had been turned. Settlement was established in populated Arab areas, a policy that aroused severe antagonism in the American administration; Carter saw it as a major issue and hit the ceiling in September 1977 over Minister of Agriculture Ariel Sharon's announcement about future settlement.

When Begin announced, on the occasion of his U.S. visit, a decision to establish three new settlements, the UN General Assembly also decried the move. It was the first of several self-defeating moves by the new government.

Soon after Begin returned home, I learned from Arkady Shevchenko, the Russian undersecretary-general of the UN, about an upcoming joint American-Russian declaration on the Middle East, supporting the reconvening of the Geneva Conference. I cabled this crucial information home, but there was absolutely no reaction. Begin told me later that they simply had not believed the story Shevchenko had passed on to me and thus they ignored it, to their great regret when the declaration was made on 1 October 1977. The joint statement meant that the United States, having kept the Soviets at arm's length during the Kissinger era, was now moving toward cooperation with regard to the Middle East—a definite shift in favor of the Arabs.

Shevchenko proposed that we organize a meeting between Dayan and Gromyko. Knowing what Dayan's response would be, I explained that Dayan ought to be *invited* by Gromyko. The meeting never happened. Once again, a false sense of pride dictated our policy—not expediency or self-interest.

Months later, Yossi Sarid created an uproar in the Knesset by questioning if the Soviets had really suggested a meeting between the foreign ministers and Dayan had turned it down. Dayan's spokesman denied this in a blatant lie. Two Soviet approaches for a meeting of foreign ministers had been rejected, by Allon and by Dayan. Now it was being lied about, typical of the shortsighted policies of the Foreign Ministry.

Dayan's ego was out of control. He insisted that every meeting with a foreign country be initiated by the other foreign ministers, and that it be announced that they had asked for it. I think Dayan was bored by these meetings and didn't want to have them. He did not care about the niceties of diplomacy.

Then came the day I was dreading. In September 1977, Dayan made his first trip to the U.S. as foreign minister. I was advised in advance that he would have no meetings in the evenings, that he would not attend any dinners or receptions, and that he would concentrate entirely on talks with the United States to the exclusion of any of the other problems facing us. It was an ambassadorial nightmare. A representative of Tass emphasized the importance of a meeting with Gromyko, and again, the same response: if the Russians wanted a meeting, they could officially ask for it. Once again, there was no meeting.

Waldheim was the next to ask for a session with Dayan, who was simply uninterested in many issues the UN had to deal with. A meeting with Waldheim would be insignificant, but a refusal to have it would create an international diplomatic incident. Miraculously, logic won out and the meeting took place without a hint of the preexisting antagonism.

THE GROUND WAS prepared for a major attack on Israel in the General Assembly. The Arabs felt they could begin to lean on us very heavily because of the erosion in the American position and Carter's willingness to partner with the Soviets. On 29 September, Syrian foreign minister Abdul Hamid Khaddam made a speech and, in effect, called for the destruction of Israel.

On 4 October 1977, President Carter again spoke to the General Assembly. His speech was a great disappointment, an obvious attempt to avoid treading on toes. He talked at length about the "legitimate rights" of the Palestinians. After the president's speech I was interviewed on several television shows. My position was that I regretted that the issue of human rights had been ignored, and I wondered if Carter was pandering to the Soviet Union. My comments didn't seem to endear me to anyone, certainly not to the Carter White House.

That evening Dayan and I were invited to dinner with President Carter at the United States mission to the UN. The president was fairly friendly but made some caustic remarks about the opinions that some of us held. I had more than a vague suspicion that he was referring to my statements made earlier that day.

After dinner, Carter retired with Dayan and Secretary of State Cyrus Vance. At 2:30 the next morning, Dayan announced a new joint Israel-American working paper, emphasizing that the previous Soviet-American statement was not binding on either side. In essence, this let Carter off the hook for his pro-Soviet stance on Middle Eastern matters, and Dayan took a lot of heat for it. The Likud was furious; they felt Dayan had taken a soft Labor-like stance and sold out. Begin was very upset, feeling that Dayan had put his government on the spot.

Under siege from all sides, Dayan seemed uncertain, trying too hard to explain himself—particularly to supporters in his own government—and to ward off heavy criticism.

Dayan was due to speak at the UN on 10 October. Instead of being well rested and well rehearsed, he was worn-out and disorganized. His command of English was not good enough for major public appearances. His limited vocabulary could not always convey his intended meaning. The day before, he had appeared on Barbara Walters's show *Issues and Answers*. Half the show was devoted to Ismail Fahmi, the Egyptian foreign minister, and half to Dayan. Dayan's appearance was not as good as it should have been. Fahmi, although somewhat transparent, came over much better. Dayan just faded beside a consummate operator like Menachem Begin. Following the press conference, for some unfathomable reason he went to address a UJA luncheon, and from there came to the General Assembly. I had begged him to rehearse his speech with me, but he refused. His presence a day earlier at Fahmi's UN speech would have stolen the show, highlighting the contrast with the Arabs' negative attitude. But Dayan would have none of it.

The hall was packed for his appearance, and Dayan was extremely nervous. His delivery was not good, his English was halting, he stumbled over words, and made mistakes. The speech was an obvious attempt to protect his flank when he got back to Israel, and it did not go over well at all.

This was not the man people imagined Moshe Dayan to be. But although Dayan was perceived as a charismatic leader, he was actually torn by doubt, uncertain of himself, and dependent on a strong figure behind him. He was very critical of the government in which he was serving, yet also very subdued and concerned. He knew his public image was not dependent on his success as foreign minister. Success—or the perception of success—seemed to be more important to him than any result. As always, Dayan was very self-involved.

However, during this seemingly erratic behavior, Dayan knew something I did not—in fact, he was a driving force behind it. On 19 November 1977, much of my criticism would suddenly seem irrelevant.

CHAPTER 19

The UN Years:
Sadat, Begin, and Carter

IN THE MIDDLE OF November 1977, in a speech to the National Assembly of Egypt, Anwar Sadat said that if he could avoid ever having another Egyptian soldier wounded, he would go to the ends of the earth. He would even go to the Israeli Knesset to address it. This came after Dayan had had a clandestine meeting with Sadat's envoy Hassan Tuhami in Morocco in September. Prime Minister Begin immediately invited the Egyptian president to make good on his pledge.

Sadat proved to be a great man. He had grown and put past prejudices behind him, and he had the vision to overcome centuries of religious and political entanglements. As history clearly proves, he had an incisive political instinct.

Sadat knew he could not get to Jerusalem by the military road. Despite his vast preparation for the Yom Kippur War, he could not defeat Israel militarily. So he had to take the political road to get where he wanted to be.

He began to use the media brilliantly. He reached out via the airwaves to Begin and to Israel, going over the heads of the Egyptian people and the Arab world. He appeared on television with Barbara Walters and Walter Cronkite, preaching reason and peace. The Cronkite show was a landmark in using the media for international diplomacy. Begin and Sadat were *both* on that show, via satellite, and it was then that Begin indicated that he would officially issue an invitation to Sadat to visit Israel. On 14 November the Knesset issued the formal invitation.

At a luncheon given by the ambassadors of the European Community, I suggested that the UN put off any debates and resolutions on the Middle East so as not to prejudice and endanger Sadat's historic trip. The Egyptians were certainly in favor of my suggestion, but the Arabs, particularly the Syrians and the PLO, insisted on a debate. So in the theater of the absurd that was the UN General Assembly, as a world-shattering event was about to take place in the Middle East, the Arabs and their allies continued to act like buffoons.

The excitement surrounding Sadat's trip truly made one's heart beat faster. It was all so hard to believe, one wondered whether one was dreaming. Then, on 16 November, I received a cable from the Israeli chief of protocol, asking me to get Egyptian flags of different sizes and sheet music and a recording of the Egyptian national anthem. Not only was it not a dream, there were details to attend to.

I called the chief of protocol at the UN, a Spaniard, and told him what I needed. He began to explain somewhat lamely that he had to maintain neutrality in this conflict. I cut him off. It was obvious that he did not have the vaguest understanding of the importance of what was happening, and I was not interested in his bureaucratic excuses. So for this historic event, the Israeli government bought some Egyptian flags in the UN souvenir shop and more from an establishment in New Jersey which specialized in flags. We also managed to get hold of a recording of the Egyptian anthem. In the meantime there was a frantic rush by all the Israelis who were in America at the time—Shimon Peres, Golda Meir, Yitzhak Rabin, and others—to get back in time for Sadat's visit. Adi Amorai, a member of our parliamentary delegation to the UN General Assembly, carried the flags and record back with him. Barbara Walters called me to get various telephone numbers, as she was planning to leave for Israel.

Two days before Sadat's arrival in Israel, I was interviewed on the *MacNeil/Lehrer NewsHour* on PBS. Robert MacNeil asked why Sadat had decided on this move. I analyzed what Sadat had been saying and doing over the past six months. In July 1977, a mere four months earlier, he had said that if Jesus and Mohammed were resurrected, they would not be able to open Egypt's borders with Israel. And I'm sure he believed that. Relations between the two countries seemed an absolute impossibility. In my view, the straw that broke the camel's back and pushed Sadat to this extreme and courageous measure was the Soviet-American statement. It was such an act of American ineptness, in his view, to bring the Soviet Union back to center stage in the Middle East. The Egyptians were very hurt. They had finally managed to free themselves from under the Soviets' thumb and then Carter had to bring that intrusive digit right back in. In my view, what Sadat was saying to the Americans and Europeans with his direct overtures to Israel was "To hell with you all, you brought back the Russians whom I expelled, you let me down, you are trying to build up the PLO and tear me down." He was emphasizing the fact that Egypt was *the* major power in the Arab world, that without Egypt no peace could be made, nor could any war be waged.

President Sadat arrived in Jerusalem. Aura and I watched the historic ceremony on TV in New York at the home of Billie and Larry Tisch, with whom we were spending the weekend in the country. Aura, a native of Egypt, wept, and I was moved beyond words. Jews everywhere, I believe, were thrilled and filled with hope. Not so, however, in the Arab world. In Israel they were raising the Egyptian flag with full honors. In New York, the Libyan ambassador, Mansur Rashid Kikhia, burned the Egyptian flag in front of his embassy. On 22 November the Middle East debate opened at the United Nations with a speech by the Syrian ambassador, Muaffak Allaf, who launched into a violent tirade against Sadat, accusing him of stabbing the Arab nations in the back. Two days later, I replied that after Israel's four wars with the Arab nations it was time to set out on the fifth struggle, the struggle for peace, together. Esmat Abdel Meguid, the Egyptian ambassador, looked at me and smiled. This was picked up by the media and actually made the headlines. A sign of how things have changed: in those days, an Egyptian smiling at an Israeli was front page news.

Five days later I met for the first time with Meguid, at the apartment of Johan Kaufman, the Dutch ambassador, who had arranged the meeting in an example of skillful behind-the-scenes diplomacy. I got there exactly at 5:00 P.M., the first to arrive. Kaufman wanted to bring out a bottle of champagne, but then suddenly recalled that Meguid, a Moslem, would not drink. There was a knock at the door and then Meguid came in smiling. I said to him, "Mr. Ambassador, I have been privileged to live to see this moment, and I am grateful for the privilege of it happening to me." He replied in heavily accented English, "Me too. I am really happy that we are at last together."

We talked at length about problems in the Arab camp and Egypt, and about my wife's childhood in Egypt and our engagement in Cairo. Meguid handed me a formal invitation for Moshe Dayan to attend Sadat's Cairo Conference to help cut through all the procedural problems. "There is no problem in being together," he said. "From now on we talk." We agreed not to publish a word of our conversation; we would leave that to Cairo and Jerusalem as they saw fit.

The next morning, Prime Minister Begin informed the Knesset of our meeting and the conference invitation. But in Begin's version, I met Meguid at the home of our Dutch colleague to hand him our official acceptance—and handed him an ultimatum. Either we were going to behave normally as friends, without this surreptitious procedure, or we would not meet. Meguid agreed; on all public occasions he would greet me, shake hands, and behave naturally.

Moreover, this progress in overcoming enormous barriers was greeted by a cable from the Foreign Ministry. On no account was I to initiate a meeting with the Egyptians or accept an invitation without prior approval. The only thing I could do was follow my conscience—and ignore such instructions. If they then wanted to take action against me, so be it.

On Friday, 2 December, Andrew Young gave a party for Warren Christopher, the U.S. assistant secretary of state. Here, for the first time, Meguid greeted me publicly, shook hands, and exchanged words of public greeting. Despite Israel's Foreign Ministry, the barriers were finally beginning to break down.

ON 16 DECEMBER 1977 we joined Begin in Washington on his surprise visit to the White House for a private discussion with Carter, and the official presentation of Begin's plan on the Sinai and the West Bank. It soon became clear that Begin's plan had not been prepared in full detail, and many questions were raised about its legal aspects and open-ended nature. Nevertheless, Begin was clearly elated after his sessions with Carter and the American delegation. I did not totally share his euphoria.

AT THE END OF December, Begin went to Egypt. The proposal had many changes from the original that had been discussed with President Carter. A new problem, inherent in the times, now began to crop up: the media. Both leaders were on television every day, and it was becoming ridiculous. Barbara Walters could pick up the phone—and often did—to call Sadat. She'd wind up talking to him about a subject that she did not ever truly grasp or master, and her interpretation would then air in America and have worldwide media pickup; the same thing was happening with Begin. TV diplomacy was becoming very dangerous, with incorrect information being disseminated and correct information being diluted and

interpreted. Dayan seemed pessimistically aware of the developing problems; Begin seemed optimistically oblivious. The obvious solution was to
begin to negotiate quietly, to take the negotiators off the TV screens and
get down to tough, brass-tacks bargaining. By not doing so, Israel was
making a serious mistake. We were placing all our cards on the table—a
very visible table—forgetting that we were in the Middle East, where negotiations are a way of life and where very little can be taken at face value.
While we were living through one of the great moments in history with
this astounding breakthrough, we were also in the midst of a potential
tragedy, with both sides gradually becoming captives of their own slogans
and losing any form of flexibility in negotiation.

I returned to Israel at the end of 1977, and to a minor crisis created by
a member of the government. Ariel Sharon, the minister of agriculture,
had reportedly given a story to Israel Radio—he later denied it—about a
government plan for twenty new settlements in the Rafah salient in Sinai,
four of which would be established immediately. This went right to the
heart of Begin's negotiations with Sadat and was a particular sticking
point with the Carter administration. The proper step was to postpone
settlement activity in order to give peace negotiations a chance. A superb
general but a politician with an insatiable desire for power and attention,
Sharon had dropped a bomb—with the fuse lit—right in Begin's lap.

On 18 January 1978, the Egyptian delegation to the peace talks in
Jerusalem was instructed by Sadat to return to Cairo, and the talks were
suspended. Andy Young believed that Sadat was trying to mend fences in
the Arab world, and I tended to agree.

The move was understandable. Sadat was out on a limb. He was not
gaining the support from Arab moderates that he had counted on. Saudi
Arabia was not going along with the peace talks, nor was Jordan. Sadat's
public admission that the Arabs would have to take what they could get
in the negotiations did not find a warm reception in the Arab world.

Sadat was clearly disturbed by the settlement issue, particularly by its
effect in the Arab media. How could Sharon thumb his nose publicly at
him while Begin was negotiating with him? The Arab leadership was suspicious. Apart from other considerations, it made them lose face. Sharon
and, to some degree, Begin had insulted Sadat and put a serious crimp in
any hope for peace.

President Sadat had often said that 90 percent of the problems between Israel and the Arab countries was psychological. He was definitely
on target as far as the latest round was concerned.

We had just handed over not only the psychological edge to Sadat but also the public relations battle on a platter. News that Israel was reestablishing settlements turned sentiment overwhelmingly against us. At this stage of such delicate negotiations, why alienate the United States on an issue that could easily have been avoided or certainly postponed? *The New York Times* published a devastating editorial implying that we were being tricky and dishonest.

On 7 February Moshe Dayan arrived in New York, ostensibly for a UJA fund-raising operation but also to counteract Sadat's positive public relations effect. I was not quite sure that it was the right move. Dayan did not match Sadat's ability to cope with or manipulate the media. For instance, he had recently advised an Israeli newspaperman that Israel had been selling arms to Mengistu's Communist-dominated Ethiopia, not a smart thing to reveal. Because the African nations were so afraid of Arab reprisals, we kept our relationships secret. Dayan's attitude, however, was that whatever he said or did was right. It was inept and shortsighted that some haphazard question at the Zurich airport could cause him to reveal classified information that nobody had ever admitted.

In New York, Dayan went from one public relations blunder to the next. He told *Time* how difficult it was to be so dependent on U.S. military aid and talked about the erosion of Israel's military stamina. On *Meet the Press* he was sullen and did not respond well to the openly hostile questions about Israeli policies.

The settlement problem was really getting out of hand, especially because it was totally unnecessary. We had not deposed a single Arab from his land. Apart from historic claims and in keeping with what we'd inherited from the British Mandate, we had every legal right to do what we were doing. But this was not a question of right and wrong but of perception. The Israeli government believed we were right, the world perceived us as wrong. Rather than recognize the problem and try to solve it, we were charging forward, cloaked in the arrogance of moral and political superiority.

When our position was presented fairly, reaction was quite positive. I spent many evenings talking to writers and intellectuals, trying to get the word out. At an appearance before the Council on Foreign Relations in New York, I explained to an amazed audience that not one single settlement had actually been established since the creation of the Likud government. We had refortified and strengthened settlements, but we had not actually expanded. But the world was under the impression that a juggernaut was sweeping over the land, seizing anything in its way.

The perception was having a serious effect. A congressional debate about reducing the number of F-15 and F-16 warplanes supplied to Israel was coupled with an increased number of planes sent to Saudi Arabia and Egypt. In one public opinion survey, 65 percent of those polled were against giving planes to Israel and felt that Egypt was more sincere about peace than Israel was.

In the midst of this, Minister of Defense Ezer Weizman came to New York, and his TV appearances helped eradicate the adverse impression that Dayan had made. Meanwhile, Sharon was back in Israel trying to convince Begin to initiate new settlement projects in the West Bank, and when word reached Weizman, he threatened immediate resignation. Picked up in American papers, the story underscored the irrational behavior of Sharon and the apparent indecisiveness of Begin.

MEANWHILE, AT THE UN, business continued as usual. President Carter had spoken strongly in the General Assembly on his support of human rights but the reality was that Israel's voice—not the United States' voice—had been the only one raised in the UN against the holocaust perpetrated by the Pol Pot people in Cambodia, in which millions were massacred. I was publicly maligned by the East German, Czechoslovak, and Chinese representatives for even daring to raise this issue in the Special Committee, while all my colleagues from the West, including the U.S. representative, were absolutely silent. Six months later, the British delegation finally raised the issue—and even then not a single representative of any other Western country spoke up. William Safire wrote a superb column in *The New York Times* pointing out that I was the only one in the United Nations to raise the question of the Cambodian holocaust.

EACH YEAR, THE Gridiron Club in Washington, D.C., holds a white-tie dinner for its membership—limited to fifty members of the working press stationed in Washington—and a large number of their associates and guests. The club has been holding these dinners since the end of the nineteenth century. At the first, John Philip Sousa conducted the United States Marine Band, and ever since then the Marine Band has performed during the evening. I was invited to the 1978 dinner by my friend Arthur "Punch" Sulzberger, the publisher of *The New York Times*.

The Gridiron dinner is a great tribute to American society. The journalists prepare and put on scathing and often bawdy skits which primarily make fun of the president and his White House staff. Those unfortunate souls are skewered in the most hilarious way. Each group that is attacked then gets to reply, and those replies often outdo the initial attack in wit and ribaldry. Senator Robert Dole replied the night I was there in the name of the Republican Party, and he was absolutely brilliant. He can be as sharp and caustic as they come. The Democratic Party reply was given by Robert Strauss, a Jew from Texas and Carter's roving ambassador. Brzezinski and Kissinger were raked over the coals. President Carter even got into the act, giving almost as well as he was forced to take. It was a tremendously impressive expression of the ability of the American leadership to laugh at itself, which of course, in the final analysis, is an expression of freedom, of democracy, and of a healthy nation.

At the pre-dinner party and during the dinner itself, I spent time with many of the American media and the leading power brokers: Andrew Heiskell, the publisher of the Time Inc. magazine group; Otis Chandler, the publisher of *The Los Angeles Times*; all the leading network commentators and newspaper columnists throughout the country; all the members of the cabinet; the present and former heads of the CIA; the heads of the armed services; *The New York Times* group, which included Max Frankel, head of the editorial page, Sydney Gruson, my friend from childhood in Ireland and then vice chairman of the *Times* group, and Hedrick Smith of their Washington bureau. All the key White House staff were present, as were a large percentage of the leaders of the United States Congress. Begin was due to arrive in D.C. the next day, and the consensus of that extraordinary group was that there would be a volatile confrontation with the Carter administration. The feeling was that Begin's back was to the political wall and he would not be able to fast-talk his way out of his dilemma. They all seemed to think there might be a change of government in Israel. Weizman had publicly taken a more moderate—and more popular—line on the settlements than Begin's.

In the middle of dinner, Zbigniew Brzezinski, the head of Carter's National Security Council, took me aside and asked if I had received any news from Israel. I didn't know what he was talking about and said so. I had been cut off from my office all day, so it was then that in the midst of the frivolity I first heard of the terrifying massacre that had been carried out by Palestinian terrorists on the Tel Aviv–Haifa road. After landing from the sea, the Arabs shot and killed an American girl who was photographing wildlife, hijacked a bus, and ordered the driver to head to Tel Aviv. Israeli soldiers intercepted them, and a battle ensued. The terrorists had all been killed—but not before burning the bus, where the thirty-five passengers also died.

It was a sobering and painful reminder. In the white-tie world of Washington there was a lot of laughter, even among adversaries. But between enemies in the Middle East there was only suffering and death.

SEVERAL DAYS LATER, Israeli forces moved into Lebanon, beginning the so-called Litani Operation. The terrorist attack on the bus gave us a justification for the move on Lebanon, in addition to other ample and legitimate reasons. The Litani River was ten miles from the Israel-Lebanon border. The PLO had encroached on that area, using the space to set up a base for terrorist operations against northern Israel. Our forces went in and swiftly cleared out the PLO.

Begin and Dayan were due to arrive in New York to see Carter at the White House, but they had postponed their trip because of the tragedy on the coastal road and the incursion into Lebanon. Neither Carter nor the powers at the UN were very supportive of our position. I was even assailed by my friend Meguid, the Egyptian ambassador. The Security Council wanted Israel's immediate commitment that it would withdraw from Lebanon; Dayan was not prepared to say anything of substance. I obtained approval from Begin of the line I proposed to take: we had made our move for one purpose, had succeeded in that purpose, and would leave only after a guarantee that the terrorists would not return to this area of southern Lebanon.

The Security Council adopted a resolution setting up a UN force for Lebanon, UNIFIL, empowered to forbid the entry of unauthorized persons into the area. Obviously this was aimed at the PLO. The Americans backed down from this interpretation, but I kept fighting. During these battles, I found Dayan to be a shadow of what he had once been. Only Defense Minister Weizman seemed willing to make a difficult decision and to be in control of the Lebanon question.

The big surprise was that the Lebanese ambassador did not want us to withdraw—he was the only one on my side. The Lebanese in no way wanted the PLO occupying their land but were too afraid to do anything about it; as it is today, the Lebanese government was weak and ineffectual, content to let Israel do the dirty work—though they would never admit it.

I was stuck between a rock and a hard place. On one side was the UN, pressuring us to make a commitment for the withdrawal of Israeli troops.

On the other side was the Begin government, frozen in indecision. Eventually, we got what we wanted, as matters were taken over by the Defense Ministry.

Begin and Dayan were once again in New York—at separate hotels.

The picture from Washington was not pretty, and there was a serious divergence of views between Carter and Begin. Thinking he could sweet-talk Carter, Begin got the firm word that if he didn't stop the "nonsense" with the settlements, he could no longer count on U.S. arms, aid, or money. Carter had called Begin's bluff, giving him no other choice than to fold his tent, and the pressure was getting to Begin. He looked frail, weak, and tired, under siege from the U.S. government, the worldwide press, and Moshe Dayan.

In Israel, Weizman was calling for a national peace coalition that would include the Labor Party, which turned it down. They saw what was happening within the Likud and the world's response to its leadership. The conservative revolution was already starting to swing back, so Labor busied itself rebuilding the party and waiting for the power to shift.

Inside the Likud, there was talk of a change; Weizman was an obvious choice to take over from Begin. But Begin was a very smart politician, who had outmanuevered all other alternatives, controlled the party machine, and did not hesitate to use it. Any opponent within his own party had been crushed. Begin was a survivor, determined to surmount this latest crisis.

I was less concerned with Begin's survival than with the erosion in Israel's international standing.

UNLIKE MANY RUSSIANS, Viktor Lessiovsky, special advisor to the UN secretary-general, who so terrified Shevchenko, the Russian UN deputy secretary-general, had no qualms about meeting with prominent Americans in public and was usually surrounded by members of the media and leading opinion makers. He was a small, fat man, aggressive and exuding self-confidence. He never admitted his connection with the KGB, however, even after *Newsweek* "outed" him as the head of that organization in the United States.

In early June 1978, Lessiovsky told me that Anatoly Sharansky, the prominent Soviet refusenik charged with "treason against the motherland" and passing secret information to foreign correspondents, was facing the death penalty. But mounting pressure in the Jewish world, particularly in the United States, was beginning to embarrass the Russians. I told Lessiovsky that the Jewish people, and indeed free men and women throughout the world, could not accept this situation, and that Israel would make every effort to save Sharansky.

At a second meeting, a month before Sharansky's trial, Lessiovsky told me that his "inquiries" in the Soviet Union had brought forth an assurance that Sharansky would not be sentenced to death: he would receive a stiff prison sentence, and he, Lessiovsky, believed that halfway through the prison sentence the matter would be reviewed. Thus, I knew that Sharansky would not face the death sentence approximately a month before he learned of it at the conclusion of his trial, and I immediately cabled the information home. On 14 July, Sharansky was sentenced to thirteen years in jail; nine years later, in 1986, he was released.

Sharansky's triumphant reception in Israel—his new home after his release—was a most moving event. Just to see his wife, Avital, by his side was enough to make anyone weep; they had been married and together *one night* before his arrest and in the intervening years she had fought fiercely and bravely to save his life. Jews everywhere rallied around this small, rotund, bald-headed man, today a minister in Prime Minister Netanyahu's government.

MY THREE YEARS at the United Nations were extraordinarily difficult for Israel—indeed, the UN had become a beehive without honey but with plenty of stings. At least half the General Assembly's time was devoted to condemning Israel, even though sensible members realized that this mass attack on a small nation was destroying the UN's image. I learned the attackers' special code: "imperialists" meant the Americans; "hegemonists" was used by the Chinese to vilify the Russians; "a true and lasting peace in the Middle East" implied the ultimate destruction of Israel.

Strangely enough, the more Israel came under political attack, the more I sensed a feeling of guilt from many representatives, who quietly expressed their discomfort at their country's behavior. I heard many lame explanations about "only following instructions." Many of those who attacked me and Israel in public were assuaging my feelings and assuring me of their friendship in private. A member would often descend from the podium, having maligned Israel viciously, and engage in a conversation that was as friendly as one could imagine. Many Western representatives held dinner parties in our honor, expressing shame and disgust at the General Assembly's conduct.

Unlike most of my UN colleagues, I had great freedom and generally did not have to get approval for my speeches. I was free to give as good as I got—to hit back at the small and the great alike, to condemn dictatorships and autocracies and describe their regimes with a complete lack of diplomatic restraint. In this theater of the absurd and make-believe, adorned by diplomatic niceties, my abrupt and truthful descriptions had great effect. Though at times frustrated by the hypocrisy of my surroundings, I thoroughly enjoyed the freedom to hit back with no holds barred, and I took great pride in my blunt, outspoken remarks, which reflected the dignity and pride that Israel now contributed to the Jewish consciousness.

As we were leaving New York on 15 August 1978, I recalled my hesitation in accepting Yigal Allon's offer of the post of ambassador to the UN. Despite the craziness and pettiness, the pressure of being on the world's stage, I had no regrets. I am grateful for the privilege of having represented my people and my country and of helping to lay the groundwork for peace in the Middle East.

CHAPTER 20

———— ∞∞∞ ————

Membership in the Knesset

OUR MOVE BACK to Israel was a transition to a comparatively relaxed society, with little outward concern about military urgency, busily going about life's daily chores. The struggle against an alarming inflation and the inevitable rise in prices exercised the man on the street far more than Arab threats or international political problems.

Paradoxically, there was a greater sense of security than in New York. Though besieged on all sides, one could walk the streets without fear or meet a friend in an East Jerusalem café, smack-dab in the Arab section. In New York, I could not have ventured up to Harlem to dine casually with a black friend.

As part of getting settled in, I rejoined my law firm and began to plan the next stage of my political career. Part of that plan involved becoming more active in public and political affairs. I soon began organizing the Labor Party members who originated from English-speaking countries. I also headed the public relations and information campaign of the Labor Party in the 1981 Knesset elections. I like to think that my efforts helped Labor rise from thirty-two seats to forty-seven.

THE ISRAELI ELECTORAL system is inadequate in a modern political society. Basically introduced by Yitzhak Greenbaum, our first minister of the interior, it combined that of the Polish Sejm, of which he had been a member, and that of the World Zionist Organization, which strove to broaden representation within the councils of the organization. The entire country is one district and the public votes for a party's list and not for individuals. Candidates to be included in this list are elected by a system of primaries. Party members nominate their preferred candidates in the order of preference. The very low threshold that a party must cross to enter the Knesset, 1½ percent as opposed to 4 to 5 percent in many European countries, guarantees a multiplicity of small parties. Thus, according to the system before 1996, the voter voted for a party, and not—as in the United States, Britain, and other Western countries—for an individual.

The system not only placed a premium on small parties but also guarantees a multiplicity of them, even though over 80 percent of the votes in the Knesset were usually controlled by the two leading parties, Labor and the Likud. Thus, to ensure a majority, both major parties required the support of the smaller parties. Since a majority government by either major party is most unlikely without creating a coalition government, horse-trading—and, indeed, political blackmail—took and continues to take place. The degree of parliamentary power wielded by the small parties bears no relation whatsoever to their parliamentary strength.

After the elections and after consultation with the parties, who recommended a candidate to form the government, the president invited one member of the Knesset to do so. The candidate will invariably do this if, after the horse-trading, he can muster a majority of the members of the Knesset. The net result did not contribute to stability. The peace process was carried by a small majority in the House, a situation that obliged the government to yield to various forms of pressure applied by would-be recalcitrants.

The new electoral law provides for direct election of the prime minister, who will have considerable powers, and if there is a majority unfavorable to him in the Knesset, he is empowered, in consultation with the president, to dissolve it and call for new elections. This was expected to reduce the tendency to engage in political horse-trading, as members would not want to run to the polls too frequently. There has been much criticism of the new law since the 1996 election. The two major parties lost power while the smaller parties grew larger, with the inevitable fragmentation.

The obvious solution is a constituency system, as in the United States or Britain, or a mixed system, as in Germany, with half the members elected from constituencies and half from a national list. But change will come slowly—if ever—with the two major parties reluctant to antagonize the small parties.

Despite the shortcomings of the Knesset, I decided to run for it in

1981. Placed fairly high up on the Labor list, I won election and appointment to the party's Central Committee and Leadership Bureau.

Because my position was strong on election reform, I decided to practice what I preached. A Knesset member represents his party, but I told the people in my chosen district that *they* now had a representative in the Knesset who would be happy to solve *their* problems. At first distrustful, the public soon inundated me with the very real concerns of everyday life. In many cases, a letter on official stationery solved the problem— whether a hassle with a public utility or a question about a landlord's responsibility.

I pressed the leadership of the party to adopt the system I had introduced to the Sharon area. I felt that if we did this throughout the country, Labor could only gain in stature and in votes. The party leaders concentrated mainly on issues of defense and foreign affairs, over which they had little or no influence, but which were the "glamour" issues. They provided prestige. I kept hammering away that the heads of the party had to become more involved in domestic policies. International affairs got one's name in the paper and got one invited overseas to speak to American Jews, but people in Israel wanted help in economic and social affairs.

While Shimon Peres was minister of communications, I headed a high-powered committee to examine Israel's telephone service—it could at the time take up to ten years to have a phone installed. The Herzog Report advocated the creation of a telephone corporation owned by the public and the government but independent of government interference, which would mobilize funds for investment on the stock exchanges in Israel and abroad. Israel now boasts one of the world's more modern, efficient, and up-to-date telephone systems.

I fought for the reconstruction of the railroad system, suggesting a monorail linking Jerusalem with the coast. I proposed turning the railroads into an independent government-owned corporation or an agency, giving them the chance to raise their own financing and develop the whole system. I fought to create toll roads, which of course would pay for themselves, and which exist in most advanced countries in the world. I also proposed the creation of bicycle paths wherever possible, trying to alleviate the heavy traffic on the roads and also improve the health of the citizens. I concentrated on what affected people on a day-to-day, even minute-by-minute basis.

I was very active on the issue of tourism, knowing how crucial that was for our future. And it was directly tied to our daily quality of life. As I said in one of the Knesset debates, addressing the minister of tourism:

"The question of quality of life in the country is a subject which should affect you and your office directly. Tourism will never succeed by combining luxurious hotels with broken-down roads and filthy beaches and restaurants."

I was quite active on the subject of higher education as well. I felt that there was a great deal of waste in our existing system. We faced very serious cuts in the budgets for our universities, yet academic staffs benefited from what seemed to me to be extraordinarily expensive arrangements for sabbatical years. I campaigned against duplication in our higher education system. There were three to four different faculties in the country, each teaching Ugaritic or Akkadian or Ancient Egyptian, but each course catered to only three or four students. Taking into consideration the expenses of the various professors and the staff around them, I came to the reasonable conclusion that it was time to check out what was going on in this field. I also tried to expand our range and the subjects in which we granted degrees, particularly in the field of technology. I was at the time president of the World ORT Union, the Jewish organization devoted to modern technological training—the largest of its kind—an organization which was very active throughout the world, helping developing countries everywhere. ORT and a number of other organizations had very successful technological colleges in Israel, but the universities objected to allowing them to give degrees. The net result was that a large number of students were leaving the country on the basis of their college training to obtain a degree abroad. This led to a brain drain of no small proportions.

I raised the matter in the Knesset, a special committee was set up, and after years of lobbying, pressuring, and proving that the colleges were of an adequate academic standard, a system of technological colleges authorized to grant degrees, such as exists in most Western countries, was introduced in Israel.

As a member of the Law, Constitution, and Judiciary Committee, I attacked the heavy load placed on the courts; it was creating a system whereby a citizen could not get justice. Frequently, when someone's problem finally reached the courts, it was too late to solve the problem. The system was absurd and totally counterproductive. I suggested an overall examination of the entire legal system, something which still needs doing today.

Some of my causes became reality, others did not. Some are still ongoing issues—simple resolutions can take years to pass through and be approved by the system. In 1981, I introduced a law giving a vote in the national elections to all official Israeli representatives abroad. Israeli seamen abroad could vote in public elections, but Israeli diplomats could not. I introduced a bill enabling diplomats, state employees, and all representatives of national institutions who were living abroad to vote in elections for the Knesset. This law finally passed, in 1992.

One of the most frustrating issues I've ever been involved with was the publication of the name of a suspect before he was arraigned in court. My proposed law forbidding this aroused a great deal of interest, and I was assured of a majority in the House. Newspaper editors came to meetings of the Law, Constitution, and Judiciary Committee, and vociferously opposed the introduction of such a law—it meant more work for them, and who cared about the ordinary citizen's right to his good name? In the course of this legislation I was elected president of Israel and asked two committee members to see that the bill became law. Six months later no advance had been made; threatened by the press, committee members realized they were endangering their political lives and let the matter drop. It has never been satisfactorily resolved to this day, and grave injustices are still perpetrated. After the tragic murder of a young Israeli at a demonstration in favor of peace with the Arabs, several suspects were arrested and saw their names in headlines before the real murderer was finally sentenced to life imprisonment. A totally innocent suspect left the country when life became unbearable for his family. Headlines were more important than the truth, but the Knesset would do nothing about it.

In addition to the daily Knesset battles—not all that different from life at the UN—three events are indelible.

The first was quite personal and quite moving. In January 1981, Aura and I returned to Egypt for the first time since our engagement.

Cairo at the end of World War II was a city of some two million. We now found a city with five times that population but no changes in the infrastructure of roads, bridges, or telephones; there didn't appear to be any traffic regulations whatsoever. Soon after we checked into our hotel I noticed that we were being shadowed, and I became somewhat concerned; the relationship between our two countries was still rather turbulent and who knew what could happen. I called the Israeli embassy and told the security officer that I was being shadowed. Within five minutes there was a knock on our door. The gentleman who had been shadowing us politely excused himself; he was an Egyptian security agent whose duty was to protect us. Egyptian telephonic surveillance worked very effectively.

In Cairo, we retraced our steps to all the places we recalled so nostalgically. We went to 12 Kamal Mohammed Street in Zamalek, where I first met Aura. We wanted to go inside to see what had become of the house, but we were not allowed in. It had become the Saudi Arabian embassy residence in Egypt, and Israelis were not welcome.

The most chilling moment came when Aura got in touch with a very old friend, an Egyptian woman, the daughter of a former prime minister, with whom Aura had been very close. The woman acknowledged the fact that she remembered Aura and recalled their close friendship, but she refused to meet with her; she was afraid of what might happen to her if word got out that she had entertained us. Aura did not insist, but it was quite clear that although the countries were officially at peace, normal relations still had a long, long way to go.

In Aswan, a small, attractive desert town on the banks of the Nile, famous for its waterfalls, I was taken to meet President Sadat by Anis Mansour, editor of the magazine *October* and our host in Egypt. There had been a lot of talk about the tension between Sadat and Vice President Hosni Mubarak, who was present during the interview, but did not once open his mouth or participate in the discussion.

Sadat revealed a profound understanding of the political groupings and factions in Israel. In talking about the prospects of long-term peace with Israel, he was evidently content with the relationship he had established with Begin, not on a personal basis but on a political level. Asked why he did not include King Hussein in the talks on autonomy in the West Bank and Gaza, he said that King Hussein had no courage; if Hussein came to such negotiations he would be looking over his shoulder every second to gauge the feelings of President Assad of Syria or Yasser Arafat, the leader of the PLO. "He has no independence of thought, and I have my reservations about him," Sadat told me.

The Iran–Iraq War had broken out about four months earlier. I asked Sadat how he saw the resolution of that war. He replied that within the year, "the people of Iran will have overthrown Khomeini and the people of Iraq will have overthrown Saddam Hussein," and then for good measure he added, "Assad's regime is very shaky too." Unfortunately, though a great statesman, he was not much of a political prognosticator. The only national leader in the area to be eliminated that year was President Sadat himself, who was assassinated in October 1981.

The second event that still reverberates was not anything personal. For the first time in Israel's history, the government made an offensive military attack across foreign borders.

For some time, Prime Minister Begin had been under pressure from Minister of Defense Ariel Sharon to go into Lebanon and clean out the

PLO. Northern towns and villages in Israel had been subjected to attacks by the PLO's terrorist groups, including a Katyusha rocket bombardment. An uneasy cease-fire had been negotiated, thanks to U.S. mediation, but Israel still faced a major security problem. For the first time in quite a while, we had a reasonably peaceful period, and the border had been quiet for most of 1981 and 1982. But Sharon still wanted to invade, believing that Israeli forces would move into Lebanon, link up with the Christian elements there (about one third of the population), and return the country to a Christian-dominated state friendly to Israel. The problem was that we had absolutely no excuse to make such a move.

The excuse came in May 1982, when Shlomo Argov, Israel's ambassador to Britain, was shot and paralyzed by Arab terrorists in London. This was immediately seen as a casus belli.

Israel invaded and there was very heavy fighting with many casualties. In the final analysis the invasion was a disaster for Israel—physically, politically, and morally. A limited entry in order to destroy terrorist bases would have been justifiable. Begin expected the depth of our penetration to be no more than forty kilometers. However, the ground forces went far beyond that and many believed that Begin and the government had been misled by Sharon.

Inching their way into the country, the Israeli forces ultimately reached Beirut and linked up with the Christian forces, who proceeded to do absolutely nothing. They had lied to Israel and declined to help us in any way. Contrary to the understanding achieved before the invasion, they reneged on all their undertakings and expected Israelis to do their dirty work for them.

During the battles, I went twice to Beirut and visited the Christian "capital" of Junieh, where I saw the terrifying anomaly of Lebanon. Our Lebanese hosts took us to a magnificent yacht club. I sat amid expensive boats while bikini-clad women, equipped with the best that nature and Dior could offer, served us drinks or lay around the pool. And as I sat, I looked across the bay, north of Beirut, and saw the western part of Beirut enveloped in the smoke and dust of the brutal battles. I asked our hosts if this did not move them and their answer was a most definite "no." Their hatred of the Moslems was intense and immovable and very disturbing. There was no trace of compassion or humanity in their words.

The plan had been to besiege Beirut and reach Arafat and his cohorts, who managed to leave, thanks to international mediation—i.e., Israeli acquiescence to considerable political pressure—and escape to Tunis. Unknown to Israel's forces, the Lebanese Christian forces attacked two camps of Palestinian refugees and massacred the inhabitants. The sound of the shooting reached Israeli troops stationed nearby, but not knowing the scope of the massacre, they did not move.

Begin learned about the developments on the BBC, and an international uproar ensued. A public inquiry commission reported that although no Israeli forces were involved in the massacre, they should have moved to stop it.

As a result of the inquiry, several people found derelict in their duty were transferred or dismissed; Minister of Defense Ariel Sharon was removed from his position.

The failure of the invasion had an overpowering effect on Begin, who became more and more despondent as the number of Israeli casualties grew. Finally, in September 1983, he resigned as prime minister, seriously affected and depressed by the pressure of his failure in Lebanon. He was never the same again.

Yitzhak Shamir replaced Begin and in 1984 set up a national unity government. Yitzhak Rabin, who was minister of defense, obtained a bare majority in the Unity government empowering him to withdraw all Israeli forces from Lebanon except for a narrow security zone on Israel's border, and to make arrangements with the South Lebanese Army immediately north and adjacent to the Lebanese border. Bashir Jemayel, the leader of the Lebanese Christians, was assassinated by Christians sent by Syrian intelligence. With his death, the myth of our true Christian allies in Lebanon evaporated.

The war in Lebanon was an unfortunate chapter in Israel's military history. It proved that no matter how just the cause, it is wrong for a nation to damage that cause by grasping for more power. It also impaired Israel's deterrent posture, cost many lives, diminished our self-confidence, wasted years which could have been devoted to developing the new peace with Egypt, and, most serious of all, broke a heretofore national consensus on our ability to wage war and the moral basis for doing so.

The third event came in November 1982. I was stricken by a very serious heart attack, but six weeks later was back at work in the Knesset. A month after I returned, Yitzhak Navon, the president of Israel, announced that he would not run for a second term.

The next thing I knew, I was running for president.

CHAPTER 21

The Presidency—1983

THE PRESIDENCY OF Israel is a greatly misunderstood job. In some ways it is intensely political with much backroom negotiation and deal-making; in other ways it is a ceremonial position requiring manners and decorum. It helps define moral guidelines, can greatly aid in the everyday life of the average citizen, and symbolizes and represents Israel for world Jewry.

The president is the head of state, Israel's number one citizen. His political power is limited, stemming from the rivalry between Chaim Weizmann, Israel's first president, and Ben-Gurion, its first prime minister. Ben-Gurion fought for as much control as he could muster and greatly limited Weizmann's clout—and the clout of future presidents. (During the term of office of the second president, Yitzhak Ben-Zvi, the Knesset approved amendments that increased the president's authority.) But while the president's power may formally be narrow, it is still far more considerable than is popularly appreciated. He formally appoints ambassadors and judges, the board of the Broadcasting Authority, the governor of the Bank of Israel, and the president of the Israel Academy of Sciences. He alone in the State of Israel has the power to pardon, represents the state abroad on worldwide public occasions, and receives the credentials of all foreign ambassadors. Until 1996, he chose the candidate for prime minister who he believed could put together a majority coalition in the Knesset. Now under a new law the prime minister is elected directly by popular ballot.

The president is quite possibly Israel's best-informed citizen, briefed regularly by the prime minister, by government ministers, by the Foreign

Ministry, by the intelligence agencies, and by the general staff of the armed forces. He has access to all top-secret information.

The moral power that comes with the title is out of all proportion to any formal power. The president consults with the prime minister and the ministers as the voice of the people and wields considerable influence behind the scenes. All of Israel's presidents have enjoyed an intimate relationship with the public, which instinctively turns to him in difficult times. The presidency is an exhilarating experience that is not easy to describe.

When President Navon announced in early February 1983 that he would not run again, my candidacy, which had unexpectedly for me been proposed in some of the media and by public figures, seemed like the natural conclusion to an eventful life. I felt I could do some good, bridging the ever-widening gaps between Jews and Arabs, the religious and nonreligious factions, and even between the political parties. I had a reasonably strong sense from the media and from the man in the street that I would be a popular candidate, and I had already gone as far as I could within the normal political party structure.

After consulting with Aura and our children, I decided to take the plunge.

My first act was to call on Shimon Peres, chairman of the Labor Party. The way the system works is that a party nominates its candidate, and then one candidate must be agreed to by a majority of the Knesset in a secret ballot. The Likud was thinking of putting up Dr. Yosef Burg, the minister of the interior. I told Peres that I had made a provisional head count that indicated that I could get the vote of the Tami Party (an Oriental group with three seats in the Knesset) and part of the Liberal vote, even though they were gradually being absorbed by Begin's Likud group. If the race was between Burg and myself, Peres thought I had a 90 percent chance of winning. If the Likud put up a candidate of Oriental background, Peres thought I would lose a lot of the non-Labor votes, and it would be better for Labor to nominate someone else. Peres finally agreed that I would be considered as a candidate. I don't think he was convinced that I could win.

The behind-the-scenes maneuverings were fast and frantic. The Likud was in total disarray on this issue and couldn't find a candidate. In Labor it came down to a choice between me and Shlomo Hillel, of Iraqi origin, a former ambassador and later speaker of the Knesset. He had been active in smuggling the Jewish community out of Iraq. I gradually emerged as the Labor favorite, Hillel withdrew on the morning of the ballot in the Labor Party, and Labor made me a unanimous consensus candidate. The Likud picked Menachem Elon, a brilliant Supreme Court justice, a tough opponent, and a worthy candidate. Our political differences were minimal.

Two colleagues in the Knesset, Uzi Baram, later minister of tourism in Rabin's government, and Avraham Katz-Oz, later minister of agriculture, managed my campaign brilliantly. Baram was already considered a king-maker, having managed President Navon's election campaign five years earlier.

Labor was still the minority party, but signs gradually indicated that I could put together a winning coalition of Knesset voters. People in and out of the Knesset were worried about a totally Likud-controlled govern-ment; at one point, Begin was told I could win and that he had a chance to steal credit from Peres and run me as a two-party consensus candidate. But he rejected the proposal.

The election was held on 22 March 1983. If party lines held, I was a loser. I needed not only luck but also voters to cross the floor of parlia-ment and go against their own party in the secret ballot.

That morning I went as usual to the meeting of the Foreign Affairs and Defense Committee. Geula Cohen, one of the most right-wing members of the Likud—she later bolted to set up an extreme right-wing party—sent a very polite note singing my praises, telling me how much she admired me, but apologizing for the fact that she would have to vote against me. Party discipline would not allow her to vote for a Labor can-didate. I respected her honesty.

Baram did not want to wake sleeping dogs, and as he realized that I could win, he encouraged the party faction to exude pessimism, thus throwing the Likud off their guard and reducing their lobbying, and en-couraging them not to run scared. At 10:30 A.M., a short meeting of the Labor Party caucus took place. A general feeling of pessimism was again encouraged at the meeting. At 11 A.M., the full Knesset was called to order.

When the voting was over and the counting of the votes began, I was escorted to the office of the clerk of the Knesset. It suddenly hit me that my ultimate goal in life depended on a handful of Knesset members mak-ing backroom deals and promises and forging interparty alliances. Within that political morass, how many people would vote according to their conscience?

Suddenly there was a commotion outside the office and Moshe Shahal, leader of our parliamentary faction, rushed in. "Mr. President, we have won!" he called out. I had wound up with sixty-one votes, Elon had fifty-seven, and there were two abstentions. Thus at least seven members had crossed party lines and coalitions to vote for me—which was unheard of.

Basically, my victory represented a revolt against Begin within his own party, a terrible shock to him that he took very hard. Our prime minister was declining, getting old not just in years but in spirit. He had been growing increasingly morose and depressed since the fiasco of the Lebanese War. He had been let down not only by the Lebanese Christians but also, he believed, by his own ministers, particularly Sharon. For all his faults, Begin had an intrinsic honesty, and the actions of Sharon and others in his intimate circle shattered him. He had been failing to preserve control of the government ever since; my election confirmed that he had lost control. It was a hard slap in the face to the Likud and they did not take it well.

I was in a trance. My mind flashed back to Dublin, where my father had imparted such a love of Jewish tradition and history. And now I was head of the Jewish State. My only regret was that my parents and my brother had not lived to see it.

Peres came in, beside himself with joy. This was the first victory that the Labor Party had had in any race for public office since the 1977 debacle. Aura, the children, Suzy Eban, Aura's sister, and my brother-in-law, Abba Eban, the press, TV and radio, friends—all crowded into the office of the speaker of the Knesset. We raised a glass of champagne and then I was called out to receive a telephone call from Begin. He graciously offered congratulations. He said that now I was the president of *all* the citizens of Israel, regardless of political identity. In return, I expressed the hope that we would be entering a period of close cooperation for the benefit of the country.

After a celebratory lunch, I returned to the Knesset. A bodyguard suddenly appeared, the first inkling of how much our lives were about to change; this new shadow almost never left my side for the next ten years. My election was greeted with approval in many parts of the world. The Irish were proud of their son of Ireland, the British recalled my service in World War II, and the Egyptians did not hide their approval that the First Lady of Israel was a native of Ismailiya.

At 11 A.M. on 5 May 1983, the speaker of the Knesset, Menachem Savidor, with representatives from every party in the Knesset, came to our home. With all the formality he could muster, Savidor informed me that the delegation had come to advise me officially that I had been elected president of Israel. It was time to be sworn in.

Before going to the Knesset, I went to the Wailing Wall and uttered a prayer; at moments of destiny, only religion and prayers offer refuge. From there I went to the cemetery in Sanhedria in Jerusalem and visited the graves of my parents, my grandparents, and my brother. It was a strange and lonely feeling. Here I was, by virtue of my office connected to all Jews the world over, but I was forever separated from the people who had shaped me and whom I had adored. I stood with Aura alone in the cemetery, and across my inward eye there flashed their images and their stories. My father had been dead twenty-four years, his last years plagued by trouble with the ultrafanatic Neanderthals of Israel's religious factions. My father had wanted so much to bring religion into the twentieth century, to keep it relevant to everyday life, but he was blocked and thwarted at every turn. In the fifties, worn down from the battle, he became depressed and remote, even from his family. His death was a big loss to the country and an even bigger loss to me, one that I still feel. With my father's death, I felt as if my childhood died as well.

My brilliant brother, Yaacov, had been dead for eleven years, having served Israel as right-hand man to the country's prime ministers. No one knows exactly what happened to Yaacov. We knew he had a stroke and we knew he fell but it was never determined which had come first. All we know was the result: a hemorrhage, a coma, and then death at the tragically young age of fifty.

My mother continued on as a grande dame, even as she lost her husband and her younger son. She was fully in charge of her senses and clever to the very end. She had even been offered—several times—the opportunity to run for the Knesset, opportunities she wisely turned down. She devoted her life to Israel—starting schools, helping immigrants, and setting up the largest mental and geriatric hospital in the Middle East, which is named after her. She died at age eighty-two, in 1979. As I stood by their graves, I so wished they could have witnessed this day.

That afternoon, Aura and I were driven, with a motorcycle escort, to the Knesset. A police honor guard, mounted on white horses, was drawn up to lead our car the final stretch to the ceremony. Aura told me that years ago, in 1967, when I was appointed governor of the West Bank, my mother told her that her own father, my grandfather Rabbi Samuel Isaac Hillman, had revealed that he had dreamed I would one day enter Jerusalem on a white horse. Here the dream was coming true.

Cheering children greeted us as we reached the building. Once inside, I was escorted to the speaker's office, to await the arrival of the outgoing president, Navon. As we entered a packed Knesset, the traditional shofar was sounded and all present stood. After Navon's farewell speech, I was called to rise, in accordance with Jewish religious tradition covered my head, and took the oath of office with one hand on my mother's Bible— as the sixth president of Israel. I then spoke to the nation, emphasizing that the main danger lay not across the borders but within our own society's lack of tolerance, its internal strife, and its division. The entire assembly rose, the speaker called out in accordance with tradition, "Long live the president!" and the audience answered three times, "Long live!" *("Yechi, yechi, yechi!")*

Led by the sergeant at arms to an overcrowded reception in the Chagall Hall, I was still in a dream. Hearing "Mr. President," I instinctively looked around to see whom they were addressing. Surely they were not speaking to me.

The change in my life was enormous and immediate. The first disruption was our move into the Presidential Residence in Jerusalem, which we found broken-down and dilapidated. Pipes had burst in bedrooms, soaking the electrical wiring; paint was peeling away from chipped plaster—a disaster. We spent the first few weeks of my administration in a hotel and then in the home of our friend Mrs. Gitta Sherover, as plumbers, carpenters, and electricians reversed the effects of the maintenance authorities' negligence.

I HAVE TRIED to give an overview of what the president of Israel is. What he does will become evident.

In ten years in office, I addressed over 11,000 events and meetings, an average of over five events every working day. We visited more than thirty countries, on every continent except Antarctica. I addressed more parliaments than any Jew in history, opened every annual Knesset session and addressed it after every election when a new government was installed. I visited towns, villages, kibbutzim, and factories on an average of six times a month. Through the President's Fund we solved thousands of social cases annually. I went to mosques, churches, and synagogues; sponsored operas, plays, and concerts; and hosted numerous state dinners.

My presidency covered the terms of four prime ministers, Begin, Shamir, Peres, Rabin, and Peres again. It was a busy time and required amazing energy. A typical day would be like this:

Awake at around 6:00 A.M., with a half-mile swim at a public pool, with much security, at 6:30.

Breakfast with Aura, and then the newspapers: the *International Her-*

ald Tribune, the *Economist,* all Israeli dailies, and several international Jewish papers. At 8:00 A.M. in my office, meeting with my chief of staff.

If a visiting head of state was in the country, I'd receive him, and dinner that night would be an official state reception. If a prime minister was visiting Israel, we'd have a formal lunch. I also lunched regularly with ministers and members of the Knesset and media. Lunch with our prime minister or foreign minister was a regular affair.

Issue meetings concerned the latest strike or health care crisis. Regular sessions with mayors and representatives from the settlements revealed local problems. I'd meet with representatives from organizations for the infirm, sick, and handicapped, and help them where necessary. I met with members of academia and with artists, and at least one day a week I'd visit a town, city, kibbutz, factory, or new immigrant town or center, and frequently inaugurate public projects.

After lunch, I'd try to rest for an hour or so, and work would resume at 4:00 P.M.

Every Sunday, after the weekly cabinet meeting, the cabinet secretary gave me a full report, and I was regularly briefed by the head of the Mossad, the head of Shin Bet, and the head of military intelligence.

Throughout the ten years, our family would return home to Herzliya whenever possible on weekends and try to live like normal citizens. Even one day a week away from meetings and maneuverings was a much-needed connection to reality.

IMMEDIATELY AFTER ASSUMING office, I invited Prime Minister Begin to be the first to meet with me in the Presidential Residence. As he came in he handed me a document, the text of the agreement which had been negotiated—but not yet signed—with Lebanon. He sighed as he gave it to me, mournfully remarking that it was probably not worth the paper it was written on. I told him that in my view, that approach was very destructive. Even if there was nothing of substance in the agreement, the mere fact of an Arab country's agreeing to sign a document with Israel was of great symbolic importance. It was crucial that another Arab government was coming into line following the Egyptian treaty. But Begin was depressed and totally pessimistic.

During our regular meetings over the next few months, his depression deepened. He became more and more remote and agitated, clearly still tortured by the results and effects of the Lebanese War. At one meeting, he emitted a loud sigh and said to me, "Every time that my military aide knocks on the door and his head appears from behind the door, my heart seizes up, because I am immediately gripped with a fear that he is going to tell me that yet another boy has fallen in Lebanon."

SHIMON PERES called on me. As leader of the Labor Party, he had rebuilt it under the most adverse circumstances. He felt that the tide was changing and that Labor was making a comeback. One of Israel's leading statesman, Peres has unfortunately developed something of a Nixonian image. Because he is so brilliant and so adept at behind-the-scenes maneuvering, he is perceived by some as not reflecting integrity; but, of course, reflection is not reality. Peres does what he has to do to achieve his goals, which are lofty. But his methods, like those of any true politician, cannot possibly be. Peres often quoted François Mitterrand, who said it best: "A politician who doesn't promise before an election is not a politician. A politician who keeps his promises after an election is not a statesman." I don't endorse Mitterrand's cynical view, but many people do, and that is why they are so disgruntled: they don't believe in their government. In a recent poll at Tel Aviv University, the professions receiving the lowest rating for honesty and trustworthiness were politicians and the media. I find this extraordinarily depressing—these are the two groups most essential to a healthy democracy.

THE FIRST STATE visit to Israel during my period of office was that of Liberian president Samuel K. Doe, who arrived on 27 August 1983. Zaire had reestablished diplomatic relations with Israel, and accordingly many of the nations in the area now tended to look to Israel for support. President Doe needed support since Colonel Qaddafi, the Libyan dictator, had spent millions of dollars hiring assassins to kill him. Doe called Qaddafi a madman who had dreams of an empire throughout North Africa. It is fascinating how enemies become friends when threatened by a greater enemy. The Libyans' invasion of Chad had undoubtedly prompted many African countries to renew or establish relations with Israel. We were by far the lesser of two evils.

At the dinner for President Doe, it was clear that Begin was a very concerned and worried man. But I was unprepared for his intention to resign. Disloyalty and internal party bickering had weakened him; he was sick and tired of the whole business and he felt he was no longer up to the job. His colleagues failed to talk him out of his resignation. His min-

isters, who only hours before had been tearing him apart and destroying his government's credibility, now begged him to stay. He refused,
and there was an immediate struggle for leadership of the Likud between Yitzhak Shamir, the foreign minister, and David Levy, the deputy
prime minister and minister of housing. Israel now needed a new prime
minister.

Begin's choice as his replacement, endorsed by his ministers, was
Yitzhak Shamir, the minister of foreign affairs. Though generally perceived as a lackluster politician, the Likud obviously felt that he would
continue Begin's policies and, because of his noncontroversial nature,
would give the country time to rally around him. It made perfect sense,
but of course it didn't go as smoothly as envisioned.

Among my official responsibilities was that of designating a member
of the Knesset as the one invited to form a government and become
prime minister. Labor was still the largest party in the Knesset, and its
representatives were the first I consulted. Moshe Shahal, who led the delegation, maintained that Labor had seventy votes for a coalition in the
Knesset, although he had no proof of those numbers. At my meeting
with the Likud, David Levy produced a document with sixty-four signa-
tures supporting Shamir personally and sixty-two supporting his government. That made it clear that Shahal's coalition was held together mainly
by wishful thinking. The figures being what they were, I invited Yitzhak
Shamir to form the government. Peres and the Labor Party were not
happy with my decision.

During this transition period, Begin gradually became a recluse, immersed in melancholy memories. He died in March 1992 and was
buried, at his request, on the Mount of Olives in Jerusalem, in the section reserved for those executed by the British. He wanted to be buried
next to the two boys who, in 1947, had blown themselves up in jail with
a smuggled-in hand grenade rather than die on the British gallows.

The reaction to Begin's death was extraordinary. Tens of thousands of
mourners came to pay tribute. The Oriental population had always had a
near-mystical feeling for him—they felt he'd raised their dignity—and
their grief was palpable. Begin got so little pleasure out of the last few
years of his life, it was sad he was never able to see this outpouring of affection and love.

ON 10 OCTOBER when Shamir gave his first speech as prime minister,
Israel was in an economic crisis. Inflation was rampant, imports were

rising, exports were way down, and we had the largest unemployment figures in history. In anticipation of a major devaluation of the shekel, the
public began to sell stock and buy dollars, resulting in a stock exchange
crisis as prices plummeted. With the public buying hundreds of millions
of dollars, banks had to borrow from abroad. With our banks in danger
of collapse, the top bankers came to the Ministry of Finance for help and
received none. An immediate devaluation could well have solved the
problem. The public would have stopped buying dollars and reconverted
them into shekels. However, Yoram Aridor, the minister of finance, who
was aware of and condoned the support given by banks to their shares in
the stock market, obstinately refused to do this, and panic developed.
The stock exchange closed for a week, as Israel tottered on the brink of
economic collapse by mid-October 1983.

The government began to restructure the banks, which had been operating under a system whereby the banks supported their shares on the
stock exchange with the knowledge and acquiescence of the Treasury and
the Bank of Israel. In other words, there was no backup system, no insur-
ance against loss, and no protection for the buyer if a bank mismanaged
its money. All the banks, with a few notable exceptions, had mismanaged
their money. The government now agreed to guarantee the banks' stocks,
in effect as debentures linked to the dollar, provided those shares were
held for five years. The shares represented the savings of people who were
left high and dry, as their money was frozen.

The government finally agreed to a 23 percent devaluation and greatly
reduced many taken-for-granted subsidies. The Histadrut, the federation
of labor unions, was up in arms. Aridor had to resign as minister of
finance when the third phase of his plan, dollarization, became public; it
would have abolished the shekel and adopted the dollar as Israel's currency. The story, leaked before Aridor was ready to release it, created a national uproar. Shamir denied any knowledge of the plan, although Ezra
Sadan, director general of the ministry of finance, told me that he had
spent four hours explaining every detail to the prime minister. As soon as
Aridor resigned, the government beat a hasty retreat from dollarization,
and Yigal Cohen-Orgad became Shamir's new fiscal savior. I prayed that
Shamir would put us back on course, but he was not off to a very good
start.

⊸⊷

The Presidency—1984

IN NOVEMBER 1983, I met with President Ronald Reagan in Washington to discuss the military situation in the Middle East, particularly the SA-5 ground-to-air missiles that Russia was supplying to Syria. The Syrian army was one of the largest in the world, and Hafiz al-Assad, Syria's president, had a very clear vision of Lebanon, Jordan, and Israel one day becoming part of Greater Syria. Because the only real deterrent to a serious Syrian attack was Israeli-American unity, it was important that it be demonstrated. Above all else, the nonfundamentalist Arab world is pragmatic. If it was convinced that the U.S.-Israel partnership was unbreakable, it would adapt.

At that time—as opposed to later—I found Reagan alert and pleasant, with a good sense of humor, and much better versed in the Middle East than I had imagined. By his second term, "alert" no longer described Ronald Reagan, who actually used cue cards during our conversations— private conversations, small meetings. His handlers did not want him making mistakes. He literally read questions to me, I answered, he'd flip to another card and read another question. It was extraordinary.

While in the United States I addressed the UN General Assembly, the first Israeli head of state to do so, and also spoke to the annual general assembly of the Federation of Jewish Communities in Atlanta, Georgia. My trip received a lot of positive publicity in Israel. I was seen as much more of an international presence, and this international reputation redounded to Israel's advantage. So much of politics is perception. As with politicians, so with political systems. As African nations were attacked by the PLO and other terrorists, they flocked to Israel, perceiving our strong relationship with America. Thus, they thought we could help them in Washington, where they were under attack for their human rights policies and other transgressions. Much of the running after Israel that happens today is because of our perceived clout in Washington, even though it is somewhat exaggerated.

IT WAS EXHILARATING to watch countries that had long regarded Israel as their enemy come quickly into the fold. There are no cultural gaps that can't be crossed in time, with patience, using rational thinking.

In Zaire, Aura and I were greeted by (quite literally) a million people on the orders of President Mobutu or, to give him his full title, Citoyen Fondateur President Marshal Mobutu Sese Seko. He arranged a review of his honor guard and took the salute from his goose-stepping troops, groups playing tom-toms and drums, dancers, musicians, singers—many of them singing Hebrew songs—and hundreds of thousands of people holding Hebrew signs and banners, screaming out welcome. I have never seen anything quite like it. Nor have I seen anything quite like the People's Palace in Kinshasa, a slightly scaled-down replica of Beijing's People's Palace, given to Zaire by the Chinese government.

Mobutu is tall, domineering, obviously hard as steel, very concerned for his people, and even more concerned that he should be loved by his people. He is also an absolute despot.

Mobutu spoke that night about how Zaire had paid heavily for reestablishing relations with Israel. The country had suffered attacks and threats from the PLO and Arab terrorists as a result, but he did not regret the action, despite the resulting violence. He spoke strongly in favor of recognizing the rights of the Palestinians. I dwelt on the changing relationship between Israel and the African countries.

Several days later, we stayed at Mobutu's magnificent private estate in Gbadolite, the town where he was born in equatorial Africa. It is in a vast park with exotic fruit trees, organized and run by Israeli experts. He again brought up the dangers of doing business with Israel, but this exchange was not nearly so statesmanlike.

That morning, he had received word that the Libyans were planning to kidnap his children, to protest his relationship with Israel. He then tied this in to our arms policy. We were providing arms to Zaire, and for that he was grateful. But we were not providing them for free, we were insisting on payment or barter. In light of the threat to his children, how could we justify asking for payment?

This was my first diplomatic crisis, for Mobutu became quite vehement as he raised this issue, and he was also trying out a little blackmail. Thanks to my extensive briefing, I knew much about Mobutu, who had stacked away a fortune in private bank accounts. He was ruthless and tough, as of course he had to be as a onetime army sergeant who was now running a country whose raw materials made it one of the world's richest nations.

I did my best to cope with Mobutu's tirade against Israel (apparently this was a fairly standard outburst—I'd also been briefed on that by Avi Primor, a deputy director at our Foreign Ministry, who accompanied us). I stayed calm and explained that over eighty countries in the world had trade and diplomatic relations with Israel and that none of them bombarded us with complaints about how dangerous it was to do business with us. We managed to survive, I pointed out, even though the Arabs didn't much care for us either.

Mobutu and I held a joint press conference later that day, and there was no hint of tension. The Zairean press peppered me with questions about Israel's relations with South Africa. I explained that we were antiapartheid but we could not abandon or endanger our large Jewish community there. I also struck back, accusing the African nations of hypocrisy. Less than one-fifth of one percent of South Africa's trade was with Israel. Other African nations—not to mention the United States and the European Community—did the most trading with them. Mobutu said it was time that people stood up and talked to the Africans as honestly as I had done.

One of the things that most impressed me was the close and friendly relations between the wives of the Zairean officers and the wives of the Israeli officers. One reason for our success there was that Israelis did not frequent white clubs or associate with white missions. Israelis, who liked and identified completely with Zaireans, were often the only whites at Zairean parties.

In Lumumbashi I met with Moise Levy, chief rabbi of Zaire for some fifty years. The Jewish community there was established by immigrants from the Mediterranean island of Rhodes in the early 1900s. A Sephardi community, it was once 8,000 strong but had dwindled down to approximately eighty. It was sad to see the remnants of a once proud community. We were received at their magnificent synagogue. A choir sang beautifully, and Levy made a moving speech and then opened the Ark to show us the beautiful Torah scrolls housed within.

Rabbi Levy broke down with emotion in the middle of our visit and his tears showed me exactly what it meant to be president of Israel. He was crying not because *I,* Chaim Herzog, was there. He was crying because there, in the middle of the jungle, he was being visited by the man who represented and symbolized the independent State of Israel. There really is an extraordinary bond among Jews the world over, one that can cause such open emotion. I suppose it's because Jews have been so oppressed over the years; we tend to move toward each other as family members would. The closest I've seen to this bonding is the Irish. They react much the same way when they meet another Irishman in a strange and foreign location.

In Liberia, I met with President Doe and our talks went a long way toward cementing our countries' relationship. He, too, stressed that our trading position with South Africa was working against us throughout Africa, as was the constant threat of Arab terrorism. There were the usual state dinners—already becoming somewhat of a bore; and only nine more years of them to go!—and colorful parades and receptions and a ceremony in which I received an honorary doctorate from the University of Liberia, then 130 years old, the oldest university on the African continent. Its president, Mary Antoinette Sherman, was a black woman who had graduated from Radcliffe and received her doctorate from Cornell. At that ceremony, a local student choir sang "Hatikvah" in Hebrew. We also had a fascinating visit to a Firestone rubber plantation. It covered 90,000 acres, had 10 million rubber-bearing trees, had a self-contained community of 100,000 people living on it, and was absolutely self-sufficient agriculturally, with its own hospital services and schools as well. It was the largest plantation of its kind in the world and its production netted over $50 million a year.

However, perhaps the most memorable part of this portion of the trip came right before we departed Kinshasa for Liberia. We were plagued by an extremely unpleasant and overwhelming smell in the plane. After a search, it was discovered that the Liberian ambassador to Israel, who was accompanying us, had suffered considerably during his time in Israel because of the unavailability of his favorite food—monkey meat. He had therefore acquired a large supply in Kinshasa and loaded it on to the plane, expecting to take it back to Israel with him. In the oppressive heat and humidity, his hidden delicacy became all too unpleasantly evident and was removed from the plane. I'm afraid the ambassador had to make do without his monkey meat when he returned to Israeli shores.

ON MY RETURN, I went back to the daily issues and routines of being president. I began a series of meetings with visiting dignitaries: the foreign minister of Australia; the head of the Domei, the second-largest trade union federation in Japan; the chairman of the trade union federations in Asia; and quite a few others. The most interesting session, and probably the most controversial, was with the German chancellor, Helmut Kohl.

There is and always will be controversy whenever Israel and Germany confront each other. Germany perpetrated on Jews the greatest crime in history; there is no way to minimize that. However, it is also in the past and it does no good to dwell on it. Remember it? Yes. Use it as a reminder of the dangers of evil run amok? Of course. But use it as an excuse not to deal with the German people? Absolutely not. Many Jews still won't go to Germany or won't buy German goods. I can understand their feelings. However, Israel and Germany now have very good and strong relations. They began when Germany paid the Jewish people $1 billion in reparations after the war, money that allowed Israel to create a new infrastructure. At the time of Kohl's visit Germany was our second-largest trading partner, second in joint scientific research, first in sending tourists to Israel, first in Mutual Youth Visits, and first of any nation in establishing Twin Cities. Kohl's visit was controversial, however. Despite our friendly relations, the past still haunts memories, and Kohl was not always sensitive to them. He was dismissive of Israeli suspicions and at times even rude on the subject. Our private conversations went well indeed, but his public dealings were much less successful.

Because of the horror at the center of the Holocaust, there is no way to intellectualize it. In a sense, it is beyond human comprehension; it can only be dealt with emotionally. It must be felt because it cannot be understood. To reduce what happened to an intellectual conversation is, in a way, to trivialize it, and I worry that this is happening. I have fought against a proliferation of Holocaust memorials. I fear that it will become institutionalized and cheapened and thus lose its power and meaning. The central memorials should be at Yad Vashem in Jerusalem, the Holocaust memorial of the Jewish people, and the Washington, D.C., Holocaust Museum.

Steven Spielberg's superb film *Schindler's List* has done more to keep the Holocaust alive and in perspective than anything since Leon Uris's *Exodus* or Herman Wouk's *War and Remembrance*. Like Wouk, Spielberg made it a human rather than an abstract experience. The most moving depiction of that experience I have ever seen was an East German movie called *Jacob the Liar*. It was about a Jew in the ghetto who befriends a little girl. She comes up to his attic to listen to his radio, which is a fake; he, behind a curtain, is the announcer. He uses the radio to broadcast only good news; he lies to make people happy. The movie reduces what happened to a simple and human tragedy for so many innocent individuals.

In 1983, there was a demonstration in Jerusalem by the left-wing group Peace Now against the government's settlement policy and in favor of opening negotiations with the PLO. A bomb was thrown and Emil Grunzweig, a young Peace Now activist, was killed. The bombing shocked the country. In due course the perpetrator, Avraham Avrushmi, a right-wing activist, was apprehended, tried and convicted, and jailed for life. In January 1984, on the first anniversary of Grunzweig's death, I addressed a memorial meeting, making a strong speech which attacked the atmosphere of division and violence in the country. I called for everyone to wake up and confront the dangers facing us internally. My early childhood recollections were of internal strife and civil war in Ireland, and the developments in our society were disturbingly familiar.

Several days prior to the memorial, Moslem guards at the Temple Mount had seen suspicious figures and challenged them. The intruders disappeared and the guards discovered they had left behind a cache of weapons, explosives, and grenades. These saboteurs were obviously Jews embarking on a holy war. If their attempt to destroy the shrines had succeeded, it could have been a tragedy of almost unbelievable proportions. The lives of tens of thousands of Jews in the Moslem countries would have been endangered. There would certainly have been a bloodbath in Jerusalem as retaliation, and Israel's international standing, precarious at best, would have been severely jeopardized.

The lunatic fringe of the extreme right wing was as dangerous then as it is today. It was only a stone's throw from the violence of the 1983 Grunzweig bombing to the 1995 assassination of Yitzhak Rabin. Ten years ago, the far right was composed mostly of American misfits. Their "Messiah," Rabbi Meir Kahane, urged violence against, and advocated driving out, the Arabs. He was basically attempting the creation of a fascist state.

The big change in Israel today is that the far right is no longer just a bunch of crackpot American immigrants; it now includes Israelis. We are in danger of destroying ourselves, working in an undemocratic manner against our own government. A Jew killed his prime minister—all in the name of protecting Israel! It's insane. What's worse, it seems to be a worldwide epidemic of insanity. The justification for slaying Rabin echoes almost verbatim the twisted logic of the Oklahoma City bombing. We murder our kind to save our own kind? It is sad and terrifying. The only benefit I can see coming out of it is that *good* people will rise up against such mindlessness, and politicians who throw around with ease such words as "traitor" will realize the impact of their bombastic negativity.

JUST HOW DIFFICULT is it to operate rationally and democratically in a country experiencing fundamentalism—not only Arab but also Jewish fundamentalism?

Noam Semel, director of the Haifa Municipal Theater, had a problem. The theater had put on *The Messiah,* in which the Lord is cursed by a female character. This created a major scandal. Public outrage was such that the Aguda faction in the Finance Committee of the Knesset blocked approval of any budgets for the entire Haifa municipality. But moral outrage was not the only problem. Under the Israeli Penal Code inherited from the British Mandate, anyone who offends the religious susceptibilities of a citizen, either in writing or verbally, is liable to one year's imprisonment. The law is usually ignored, but in this case it was not—and blasphemy in Israel is a serious crime.

Noam Semel was headed for jail until I worked out a compromise. He agreed to delete the offensive words—there were only three. I was immediately attacked by prominent left-wing citizens, in the cause of freedom of expression. I had saved the actors from a probable jail sentence—and at the theater's request. But they did not have the guts to defend me when the left criticized the decision. I was hung out to dry and take the brunt of the criticism.

OF ALL THAT Israel has accomplished, perhaps nothing is so impressive as what we've done agriculturally. We have very little land; what we do have is desert. We had to figure out a way to turn it into a supplier of food (other than oranges, which is all we had). Our scientists and researchers, hand in hand with farmers in the field, began to work on the problem. Using genetic engineering, they adapted Israel's produce to the requirements of foreign markets. By means of biotechnology we invented new fruits and vegetables; a cross between a tomato and a potato was developed, hard enough to be shipped by sea and not by air to Europe. We changed the growing seasons, with strawberries that ripened in November in order to be available for the best season in the European market. We changed the face of nature, turning the desert into lush gardens and exporting three million flowers a day to Europe and the United States. When exporters found that gladiolus were too heavy for air shipment, and therefore not economically feasible, our scientists developed a new gladiolus with a short stem. It was astounding to think that for official ceremonies celebrating the creation of the State of Israel, just thirty-six years before, flowers had to be imported from Cyprus. Our advances have not been simply for our own use: Jordan, via the West Bank farmers, has successfully copied our irrigation systems, and a joint research project with Egypt will turn even more of the desert into useful land.

AT THE TIME of my first official visit to England, in March 1984, no British monarch had ever been to Israel. Prince Charles later told me, "Israel is the one country I want to visit, but the Foreign Office won't let me." I have only one explanation for this strange and irrational behavior: the residual effect of British–Israel hostilities from the time of the British Mandate. In 1994 unofficial British royal visits to Israel began.

I met with Margaret Thatcher at 10 Downing Street and liked her enormously. I still do. I was most impressed with her strength and belief in her own strategies, policies, and opinions. One could not help but be somewhat intimidated by her. I subscribed to Thatcherism, which basically is just free enterprise, but her country clearly needed her powerful personality to pull it off. Reaganism was much the same way; without the sway of Reagan's personality to hold America in economic check, George Bush, as president, could not keep Reagan's economic policies viable. John Major, Thatcher's successor, does not have her kind of personality, and Britain is suffering for it. Once again we see, for better or worse, how much of politics is perception.

The day after my meeting with Mrs. Thatcher, Aura and I drove to Windsor Castle. We entered at the Sovereign's Entrance, both like excited tourists as we passed the famous buildings with all their historical connotations, the huge pastures and fields and the royal horses grazing in them, the cricket ground and golf course. Not to mention that the road we were driving on, a three-mile avenue leading into the Great Park, was planned by Charles II in 1685. There was a royal residence in Windsor in Saxon times (the ninth century), which was enlarged by William I, the Conqueror, two hundred years later. Henry II (1154–89) built the stone round tower that still stands today. The mausoleum of Queen Victoria and Prince Albert is also within the park. It *is* a little overwhelming.

The Palace was aware of the fact that I had served in the Guards Armored Division in World War II, and as a gesture, as we drove through the George IV gate, a guard of honor of the Grenadiers drew up and presented arms. The senior members of the queen's staff and of the royal household then met us at the entrance to the castle.

As we came up the winding steps it was difficult to fathom that someone actually lived there. The furniture, the china, the table settings were all extraordinary museum pieces, not to mention the magnificent art on every wall. But someone did live there, and the queen and the duke of Edinburgh were waiting to greet us at the head of the stairs.

The royal couple had just returned from a state visit to Jordan. While they were there, BBC television had used directional microphones, which picked up, from a distance, some private remarks made by the queen, and those remarks gave rise to some public criticism. The queen had been caught making a comment about King Hussein's father, who was clinically insane. He was never allowed into public view and it's something Hussein keeps very quiet. The king's brother, Mohammed, is also kept out of sight.

The queen was visibly disturbed by the attitude of the British media. I certainly don't think she is above criticism, but I also think that the media is much too invasive. She shouldn't be criticized publicly for private remarks—no public person should. With the media as hungry and sharklike as it is, there really *is* no privacy anymore. I believe it's one of the things that are destroying the quality of the people who choose to become public servants.

The queen and I discussed quite a few political issues: the Jordanian political approach, which she had just seen in person; Israel's parliamentary system, our judiciary, and our form of government; and her recent meeting with Lebanese president Amin Gemayel, in which she could not get a word in edgeways because he insisted on totally dominating the conversation—in an atrocious English that she could not understand.

During lunch, the queen's famous corgis gathered around her, and she tossed biscuits to them from time to time. After the meal, while touring the castle's artwork, the private secretary to the queen, Sir Philip Moore, took me aside to say that he hoped we would not formally announce the invitation to the queen to visit Israel. From the level of their obsession, it would have been a lot easier for her to just come to Israel and get it over with, but that clearly was not their intention. I replied to Moore that his approach would be counterproductive; after all the publicity, to actually announce that no invitation had been given would be construed as an insult to the queen. Instead, I proposed that we use the statement worked out by Sir William Heseltine, the queen's deputy secretary, which said that "the President told Her Majesty that were she able to accept an invitation, she would be a most honored and welcome guest in Israel. Obviously it was a matter to be dealt with through the customary government channels." He reluctantly agreed, and that's what was released. Of course, she has so far not come to Israel, but other members of her family have.

BACK IN ISRAEL, life was not quite as jolly as in the queen's country palace. I quickly found myself stuck in the day-to-day reality of politics.

As always, the turmoil between Israel and the Palestinians was at the forefront of daily life. I had been very impressed by the recent writings of Jemil Hamad, a Palestinian journalist, who regularly criticized not only Israel but also the Arab leadership; in their restrictive society, it was unusual for a Palestinian to have the courage to say quite so publicly what he thought. I asked him about the effect of our democracy on Palestinians in the West Bank and in Gaza, and his response surprised me. The impression made by Israeli democracy was a very deep one, he said. While they hated being ruled by us, they would never want to live without us. They would never be able to go back to the kind of autocratic regime that existed in the West Bank when Jordan occupied it. The Arabs in the territories had, despite their resentment and opposition to Israel, tasted freedom of expression. They were used to Israeli TV and radio and newspapers. They were familiar with Israeli culture and politics. In many ways, they were closer to Israeli society than to Arab society, and they would not readily give up the things they'd come to take for granted. Hamad felt that the Arab countries were afraid of the effect that Israeli democracy would have on their societies. That was, he believed, the main reason Egypt refused, at that time, to allow Egyptian tourists to come freely to Israel.

He described to me a rather shocking conversation he'd had a year earlier with Libya's prime minister, Abdul Salam Jalloud. Jalloud was asked if

Hamad had, while in Israel, visited the large prison built by the Israelis in Ramallah. Jalloud said that the prison housed 3,000 Arab women prisoners, and that Israeli soldiers were permitted to enter every evening to perpetrate whatever they wished on these women. Hamad responded that there was no prison in Ramallah, for women or for anyone else, and that there was no prison for Arab women anywhere in the territories. In Israeli society and under the Israeli legal system, it would be impossible for anything untoward to happen to prisoners without legal steps being taken in defense of anyone who was wrongly attacked. Jalloud's response was to accuse Hamad of being an Israeli agent. In Hamad's view, this attitude—truth is irrelevant compared with hatred—was true of many leaders throughout the Arab world. Until the Palestinian Arabs, who recognized the truth of their own situation, took their fate into their own hands, there would be no negotiations and no peace.

A few days before I met with Hamad, the nation had learned that a Jewish underground operating in the territories had emerged—and in a terrifying way. Bombs timed to explode at peak rush hours had been placed on five Arab buses. If they had exploded, they would have caused hundreds of Arab—and possibly Jewish and tourist—deaths. Our security service, the Shin Bet, saved the nation from a catastrophe. Their informers leaked word of the plan, and the perpetrators were caught red-handed. Approximately thirty suspects, in Israel and in the territories, were immediately arrested. Many members of this group were highly trained professionals serving as officers in the reserves. This was not a senseless, Kahane-type fringe group but a dangerous underground organization of intelligent men who had decided to carry on their own Messianic war. In addition to the bombs in the buses, large caches of ammunition, military equipment, and explosives were found.

The head of the Shin Bet, Avrum Shalom, told me he had difficulty in getting to the bottom of the terrorists' thinking. They seemed rational and even patriotic, yet their mental makeup was flawed. Their terrorism differed from that which brought about Prime Minister Rabin's assassination in 1995. This terrorist group operated within the restraints of the Arab–Israel struggle but not against the leadership of the state. Twenty-nine people went on trial and were sentenced to imprisonment. In due course, some of them broke, signed confessions, and even worked against their former colleagues. They were obviously a disturbed element. One of the conspirators, a reserve officer in the Golan Heights, had lifted a minefield designed to protect Israeli villages from a possible Syrian attack, and had used the mines to extract explosive material. It was an act of treason.

I wanted to discover the Arab response to this near-disaster, and it was as complicated as I'd expected. The official word was to attack Jews as a people who wanted to kill Arabs. Privately they were thankful, recognizing that most Israelis did not support such extremism. It was typical of the problem between Arabs and Jews.

THE COUNTRY MOVED toward elections in July 1984. The Likud had still not recovered from Begin's abrupt resignation, and no one had assumed a clear-cut leadership role. In a Central Committee vote for party leadership, no one was really expected to oppose Shamir, but Sharon had thrown his hat into the ring. He was expected to receive 10 to 20 percent of the vote but instead received 42 percent, with Shamir carrying only 58 percent of the party. In the popular elections, however, Sharon did not fare nearly as well. When the elections had taken place for the Knesset candidates on the Herut List, the major component of the Likud Party, Moshe Arens, minister of defense, had come out on top (Shamir, as prime minister, did not have to run as a candidate for the Knesset). Arens suddenly had a very strong base for the future leadership of the party. Sharon, on the other hand, was badly defeated, finishing ninth on the list. With the man on the street, Sharon still had a lot to overcome. He was perceived as one who had singlehandedly hijacked the cabinet and led the country into a disastrous war.

Labor was rocked by yet another financial scandal when Yaakov Levinson, chairman of Bank Hapoalim, one of Israel's two largest banks, committed suicide amid rumors of irregularities and conflicts of interest within the Histadrut, which controlled Bank Hapoalim.

As the election campaign warmed up, Shimon Peres's top priority was to restore the public's confidence in the government. Aside from Ben-Gurion, Israel owes more to him, defense-wise, than to any other politician in its history. Like any great statesman, he is morally ambiguous. All great statesmen, I don't care who—Churchill or Mao or Roosevelt—are morally ambiguous. What makes them different from the normal citizen is their ability to rise above that ambiguity when the situation calls for it. Most statesmen today tend to sink down to a challenge rather than grab it by the throat and conquer it. Perhaps that is the price for a lifetime of compromise: when the time comes to act with passion and moral belief, there is none left.

On election day, 23 July 1984, twenty-seven parties participated. Labor, lulled into a false sense of security by its pollsters, got only forty-four seats against forty-one for the right-wing Likud. The great surprise was the new Shas Oriental movement, which won four seats. It represented the revolt—a justified revolt—by the Sephardi religious establishment against the Aguda monopoly.

A much less pleasant surprise was the election of Rabbi Kahane, leader of the Kach movement, to the Knesset. His campaign, including troopers wearing yellow shirts, was horribly reminiscent. He rejected Western democracy and the Israeli Declaration of Independence, in which equality is granted to all races, religions, and sexes, as irreconcilable with Zionism as he saw it. His racist campaign advocated the creation of a Jewish movement that would settle accounts with the Arabs; his main platform called for the expulsion of all Arabs from Israel and the territories. The Elections Committee had disqualified Kahane's list, as well as the Arab-backed Progressive Movement for Peace list, because their platforms were both, in the view of the committee, irreconcilable with democracy and Zionism. However, on appeal to the Supreme Court they were both reinstated. It was an all too familiar scenario: totalitarian organizations using democratic processes to destroy democracy.

The results of the Israeli elections were a disappointment to many who believed in mainstream politics. Both Labor and the Likud lost seats to the smaller parties. The nation's youth was shifting to the right, a development due in no small measure to the growing influence of the Oriental groups, who originated in the repressive Arab countries. They had no reason to harbor affection for the Arabs, whom they mistrusted and often hated. Looking as if he had been through a terrifying trauma, Shimon Peres told me that he was concerned by the rise of fascism and clericalism in Israeli society. As usual, he was optimistic about the possibility of the various parties aligning with the Labor philosophy, but by now it was clear that the party's big mistake had been to retain its parliamentary alignment with the far-left Mapam Party. When people thought of Labor, they still conjured up such extreme left-wingers as Yossi Sarid, who was believed by many to be very much to blame for the failure of the alignment in the election campaign. He is extremely articulate with great ability and a surfeit of self-confidence, but he is also extremely self-important and very ambitious. Many of our political leaders have feared him, and Labor has tended to kowtow to him.

I had to bring together the diverse elements instead of allowing a dangerous fragmentation to develop. Accordingly, I approached Shamir and Peres, who agreed to go ahead with the idea of setting up a national unity government. Kahane then threatened to force his way into the presidential residence. He came to the gate and was escorted off by the police. I was president of a population of whom 17 percent were Arabs and Druze. I was not prepared to insult their honor by consulting with a man who was openly campaigning to drive them out of the country and publicly rejected the idea of democratic government. I felt it my moral duty to lead a public protest against everything Kahane represented.

The public's reaction, not what I expected, was interesting to me. Professor Ephraim Urbach, president of the Academy of Sciences, called to congratulate me. He said one word, "Hindenburg," referring to Hindenburg's hesitations about whether or not to receive Hitler, a symbol of the lack of courage that too often characterizes public servants. But nobody from the media, no kubbutzim or left-wing groups encouraged me to stand up to this violent, dangerous, and irrational man, and much of Israel seemed afraid to speak out against him.

Shimon Peres came to the meeting with me with the leadership of Labor, Yitzhak Navon, Yitzhak Rabin, and Haim Bar-Lev. I explained to them that I was acting in reaction to a tremendous public demand for a unified government and that every effort had to be made for the two big parties to get together so as to limit the capability of the small parties to blackmail and cripple the government. The leaders of the big parties, those who represented the beliefs of mainstream Israel, must be the ones to determine priorities, the first of which had to be a solution to the still crippling economic problems we were facing. Peres made, as usual, a very convincing presentation for Labor leadership and Labor solutions. Rabin talked about the problem of Lebanon and the effect that the Lebanese War, the product of Likud policy, was still having on our national morale and economy. They all maintained that because they had the largest group in the Knesset, they had the right to be the first party to be called upon to form a government.

They were followed by the Likud group, composed of Prime Minister Shamir, Deputy Premier Levy, Minister of Health Eliezer Shostak, and the leader of the Liberal Party and minister of energy, Yitzhak Modai. The best presentation was made by Modai, who appeared clearly to be the most articulate person in the delegation. He emphasized the extreme danger inherent in the current economic crisis. In a tactical move, Shamir invited the Labor Alignment for a meeting, and the leaders of the two groups met at the King David Hotel the next day.

Ezer Weizman, who controlled three seats, was the key figure now. With his support, Shamir could form a government: without him, it would be difficult. But Weizman had an account to settle with his old party. He had resigned from the Likud government under Begin because he felt they were abandoning the peace process with Egypt. He had been expelled quite acrimoniously from Herut, and yet the Likud were now coming to him on their bended knees asking him to come home and telling him that all would be forgiven.

Serious negotiations began as the parties trooped in one after the other. Shinui, a progressive liberal party led by Professor Amnon Rubinstein, had gained very considerable support in the Druze sector. (In general, it was interesting to note the breakdown of Arab voting. Nine thousand Arabs voted for the Likud, and some 7,000 for the National Religious Party. There were even some Arabs who voted for Kahane's Kach Party, believing that the strengthening of Kahane would embarrass Israel and bring about a much stronger Arab nationalist reaction.)

Weizman's group, Yahad, supported a national unity government, and proposed giving the mandate to Peres as leader of the largest party in the Knesset.

The religious Aguda Party, as was its wont, could not reach agreement among its members, and asked for a postponement of our consultations. The left-wing, pro-Palestinian, and pro-PLO Progressive Movement for Peace was composed of both Arabs and Jews. Their official aim was to create a Palestinian state side by side with Israel. As this group increased in strength, a major battle was developing between it, the Communists, and the Labor Alignment for control of the Arab sector. They did not favor a national unity government. The Tami Oriental Orthodox group, led by Aharon Abuhatzeira, gave me their mandate to use as I saw fit.

Yigael Hurwitz, the representative of the center right-wing Ometz faction, which had achieved just one seat, expressed his view that the nation was on the verge of a national economic catastrophe. He believed that if events continued as they were going we would have riots in the streets, with cars being burned and stores being destroyed. Surprisingly, he abandoned his longtime pro-Likud stand and now came out unequivocally in favor of Peres.

The result of the consultations was that fifty-nine members of the Knesset recommended Peres, and fifty-four recommended Shamir. Five members representing the National Religious Party and Tami handed over their mandate to me to decide, as I saw fit, to add their votes to the total. Thus, the total result could be a clear-cut and decisive majority for Peres to put together a government.

There could be no delays—the public wanted prompt and decisive action—and I made it clear that at the first opportunity I would announce my decision. Peres could do what needed to be done and it was up to me to give him that opportunity. I told Shamir of my decision, and he quietly accepted it.

Having devoted his entire life to reaching this moment, Peres seemed stunned. He asked Shamir to join him in creating a new government and, as he left my office, embraced me. He had no illusions about the difficult task ahead. After a statement to the press, he went to the Wailing Wall and inserted a small note with the prayer "Put our hearts together."

ISRAEL'S YOUNG PEOPLE reacted to the turbulent political facts of life with expressions of deep mistrust and, occasionally, hatred of political parties and their maneuvering. Deeply critical of the blackmailing ability of the small religious parties, they wanted a change in an electoral system where a few small groups could hold the nation hostage. I was on their side. If the United States had Israel's electoral system, the Ku Klux Klan and black anti-Semite Louis Farrakhan would be represented in Congress.

Under the law, Peres now had twenty-one days to form the government, and I had the option to extend it by another twenty-one days. Then I would have to offer the position to another member of the Knesset. The Knesset opened without a government's having been formed, as the political jockeying continued and the country approached total economic failure. According to the law, Israel was run by a transitional government until the Knesset voted in a new one—not a good situation but, in Israel, politics as usual.

On 26 August 1984, Shimon Peres presented himself to ask for a twenty-one-day extension. As usual, he was very optimistic about forming a unity government, although he acknowledged that the task of unraveling the intricacies of the Israeli political map was almost unsurmountable. He had come to an agreement with Shamir in their private talks on the economy, Lebanon, the approach to King Hussein, and Egypt. One big obstacle was the establishment of new settlements, but Peres would agree to a simple majority in the cabinet as a way of deciding the issue.

I agreed to give Peres another twenty-one days; failure would mean an opportunity gone forever. By the end of the week it was obvious that Peres was going to give in on what he had opposed most of all, the rotation of the prime minister's job between the two parties. There would be a cabinet of twenty-four with twelve places to each party. Peres, however, insisted that Rabin be made minister of defense for the entire four years.

**UN
Assembly
Is a
Yawn**

ABOVE: This photograph was selected by *Time* magazine as one of the most memorable of 1978. The yawn came while the Libyan representative was speaking. *(United Nations)*

BELOW: Being sworn in as president of Israel in 1983. *(© David Rubinger)*

ABOVE: Addressing a joint session of Congress on 10 November 1987. *(United States Congress)* BELOW: Praying at the Birkenau concentration camp in Poland. *(Government of Israel Press Office)*

ABOVE: At the Auschwitz Wall of Death, where prisoners were executed by firing squad. *(Government of Israel Press Office)* BELOW: Presenting the *Encyclopedia Judaica* to Richard Nixon in the White House in 1972. I am at President Nixon's left. Facing him is Yitzhak Rabin, who was then Israel's ambassador to the United States. *(The White House)*

ABOVE: With Margaret Thatcher in front of 10 Downing Street in 1985. *(Government of Israel Press Office)*

BELOW: With Anwar Sadat and Hosni Mubarak in Aswan, Egypt, in January 1981. *(Government of Israel Press Office)*

ABOVE: Arriving at the Presidential Palace in Bonn with
President Richard von Weizsäcker in 1986. *(Government of Israel Press Office)*
BELOW: My wife, Aura, and I with Mikhail and Raisa Gorbachev during
their visit to Israel in 1992. *(Government of Israel Press Office)*

ABOVE: With Ronald Reagan at The White House in 1983. *(The White House)*
BELOW: With George Bush at the vice president's residence in 1987.
(The White House)

ABOVE: With President Clinton and eleven other heads of state at the opening of the United States Holocaust Memorial Museum in Washington, D.C., in 1993. *(The White House)* BELOW: With Prime Minister Shimon Peres. *(Government of Israel Press Office)*

ABOVE: With Aura *(© Photo "Noy")* BELOW: The Herzog family, April 1996.
Standing, from left to right: Mike, Alexandra, Marguerite, Joel, Ariel, Ami,
Michal, and Isaac (Bouji). *Middle row, from left to right:* Shirin, Aura,
Chaim, and Ronit. *Bottom row, from left to right:* Renee, Nathaniel, Matan,
and Noam. *(Government of Israel Press Office)*

Ben-Gurion had long ago maintained that our electoral system would bring catastrophe on the nation. It seemed that his prophecy was coming true.

In the midst of all this, Meir Kahane announced that he was going to a large Arab township, Umm el-Fakhm, to arrange for the villagers' expulsion from Israel. Dr. Burg, the minister of the interior, came up with a ridiculous compromise, forbidding Kahane's cohorts and followers to enter the village but allowing Kahane himself as a member of the Knesset to go in—even though it is illegal for a member of the Knesset to use his immunity to create bloodshed and unrest. In an extraordinarily wonderful display, thousands of Jews swarmed to Umm el-Fakhm to protect the Arab population against the proposed entry of Kahane, who had instructed his aides to come armed. At the last minute, the district chief of police forbade Kahane to enter the village, despite Burg's ruling, and Kahane was taken away in a police car, his Knesset immunity notwithstanding. Stones were thrown and injuries inflicted but the damage was minimal—considering what might have occurred.

As the negotiations to bring into existence a national unity government bogged down, I arranged for the creation of a junior negotiating team, with two new representatives from Likud and Labor. I was desperate to move things forward to achieve a national unity government, and time was running out; the deadline for Peres to form a government was 16 September.

Three days before that date, he succeeded. The new government was presented to the Knesset on 13 September by a man who had exhibited extraordinary resilience, nerves of iron, and unusual staying power in the political arena. As minister of defense, he was responsible for creating and establishing Israel's aircraft industry and much of its electronics industry and had convinced the government to build two nuclear research stations. He was responsible for our alliance with France, and he developed binational research projects with America, France, and Germany. Maligned and upbraided publicly, he had rehabilitated the Labor Party after its resounding defeat in 1977. Now he was prime minister—at least for two years. At long last, after a major struggle, Israel had a government. That left one big question: Would the new leadership have the strength to carry the country out of its deplorable economic situation?

The answer was a resounding yes. With the help of Yitzhak Modai, a very effective but somewhat erratic minister of finance, Peres succeeded in one of his most impressive achievements to date. In July 1984, our rate of inflation was 450 percent; three months later it was 20 percent.

Unparalleled negotiator that he is, Peres worked out a social pact among the government, the trade unions, and industrialists in which the unions accepted a 30 percent cut to save the economy and solve the unemployment problem. Ironically, Labor, always perceived as the more socially conscious major party, was the more effective capitalistic party. Under Labor, in power from 1992 to 1996, our gross national product grew to some $90 billion a year—more than those of Jordan, Egypt, Syria, and the Palestinian Authority combined. And it is still growing, because our infrastructure is finally sound.

WITH A GOVERNMENT in place, I could now return to the routine of being president.

To develop closer relations with the Israeli Arabs, I decided to visit Nazareth, the largest Arab town in Israel, which is governed by a Communist-run municipality. My reception there was surprisingly dignified and at times enthusiastic. Visits to schools—in some cases the physical facilities were inadequate—and leading families gave me insight into the difficulties inherent in the relations between the Jewish and Arab communities in the Galilee. But I also saw that, as I deeply believe, those relations can work and even thrive when dealt with on a one-to-one basis. It is ignorance that creates problems; with knowledge comes solutions.

MUCH BITTERNESS AND heated discussion attended the upcoming swearing-in of a Druze *qadi* (judge for the religious courts). The candidate, Sheikh Naim Hinnu, had been an Israeli army officer and was acclaimed as extremely well qualified, but the spiritual head of the Druze community, Sheikh Amin Tarif, did not find him religious enough. Of course, it was not that simple. Sheikh Amin Tarif wanted to appoint his nephew, who was not considered suitable for the post by the people in the Ministry of Religious Affairs. If the nephew didn't get the appointment, the sheikh was threatening to move to Nabatiya, in Lebanon. In the final analysis, qualifications won out over nepotism; Sheikh Hinnu was appointed *qadi*, and the furor eventually died down. This controversy was no aberration, however. It only served to highlight many of the problems in the Druze community.

The Druze are concentrated in Lebanon, Syria, and Israel, and the martial tradition is of great importance among them. They serve in the armies of these three nations, and troops of all three armies are commanded by Druze generals.

A long-standing friendship links the Druze and the Jews in Israel. In our War of Independence, many Druze fought side by side with the Jews to repel the Arab invasion. The Druze broke away from Islam in the eleventh century and for centuries enjoyed a partial autonomy in their three countries. Their religion—originating in an extreme branch of Shiite Islam and considered by most as having seceded from Islam—is a cult, its secrets fully known only to the religious heads of the community. They stress moral and social principles rather than ritual or ceremony. Their legendary patriarch is Jethro, Moses's father-in-law, reputedly buried at Nebi Shueib in the Galilee.

From the problems of the Druze, I went to the problems of the Jewish settlements in the Gaza Strip. The Gush Katif group of villages, then composed of seven settlements, enjoyed good relations with the Arab population. Sadly, this was to change. In December 1987, the so-called *intifada* (an Arab grass-roots revolt against the Israeli occupation) broke out and ultimately led to the Oslo agreement, giving autonomy to the Palestinian Arabs. From a strategic point of view, there were advantages of having Israeli settlements in the area: a barrier between the Egyptians in Sinai and the Arabs in the Gaza Strip. But the violence that eventually erupted raised serious questions about the wisdom of settling in an area with such a large Palestinian refugee population. We were making a point, but at what cost?

ONE OF THE Arab leaders I met with was Hikmat el-Masri, head of a distinguished family in the West Bank and a leading, relatively moderate figure. We had, by this time, proposed to enter into conversations about autonomy for the Palestinians, who had refused to talk to us. El-Masri did not agree with me that their refusal was a mistake. In his view, our proposal was an insult. His dogmatic approach was totally different from that of the younger Palestinian leaders, who were prisoners of their own slogans. The Palestinians did not appreciate the fact that the Israeli public was basically quite moderate. In an opinion poll published the day El-Masri and I met, approximately 89 percent of the Israeli population favored withdrawing from Lebanon and quite a few favored leaving without any preconditions at all.

I invited for a talk the Arab headmaster of a large school in East

Jerusalem and a well-known Arab political writer had spent many years in the Jordanian desert prison of El Jafar, near the Saudi Arabian border, for having been active members of the Ba'ath Party. It was not easy or pleasant to oppose King Hussein's views, and they had paid the price. Both said that new winds were blowing among the Palestinians and that the Arabs themselves were primarily to blame for the missed opportunities of the Palestinians, who were never prepared to accept anything less than 100 percent of what they wanted—"We always wanted the whole cake and so got none of it." In their eyes, the ideal solution would be a Palestinian entity or state linked to Israel rather than to Jordan. Israel's democracy was its source of strength, and the absence of democracy in the Arab world was its source of weakness.

Even then, there was an undercurrent among Palestinians in favor of negotiating with Israel and, in some cases, of coming closer to us. But that was only the feeling of the Palestinian man in the street. It would not come to practical expression until the gradual change in the approach of the PLO and the attitude of a growing number of Israelis toward the PLO culminated in Peres's and Rabin's peace plan in the early 1990s. By then, Yasser Arafat had gone from hostility to partnership in a working relationship, one of the more astonishing relationship shifts in history.

FOR QUITE SOME TIME, there had been a secret operation in place to bring Ethiopian Jewish refugees, some 15,000 of them, into Israel. The need for secrecy was indeed great; for one thing, we did not want to embarrass the Ethiopian government, which could not appear to be cooperating with this exodus because of what it would do to their relationship with the Arabs. More important, many of these refugees had crossed into Sudan before being brought "home," and if the Sudanese government got wind of this massive operation, they would imprison and possibly even kill them. Once again, this was Middle Eastern politics as usual: saving face and coping with the Arab mentality—even with so many lives at stake. As long as we could do this quietly, we could pull it off. The Israeli press kept a lid on the story; *Time* and *Newsweek* published nothing until the refugees were safe. But there was a leak in *The New York Times,* and the paper broke the story early.

With the help of George Bush, then vice president, and the U.S. air force, thousands of refugees were airlifted to Belgium and on to Israel. In October 1984, a planeload of refugees arrived at Ben-Gurion airport, while a long line of ambulances waited to take them to the hospitals.

The passengers were remarkably subdued and docile, debarking without a murmur. Most of them were emaciated, with clear-cut signs of malnutrition. All the children were naked except for shirts that had been provided them, and most of the passengers presented the same terrifying scene from the Ethiopian hunger camps that the world had seen on television.

This encounter across a bridge of 2,500 years was with Jews who lived to this day by the written law of their people. They had no knowledge whatsoever of the oral law as propounded in the Talmud or in subsequent theological developments. This was a Jewish community emerging from the post-Solomonic era; from the point of view of their tradition, nothing had changed since then. They had resisted all other religions that surrounded them and had adhered strictly to their own traditions. They observed the Sabbath and holy days and maintained family purity exactly as it was laid down in the Bible. Since the average life expectancy was no more than forty years, there were very few old people in the group.

Many refugees had engaged in a primitive form of farming in Ethiopia. Many of them had great difficulty coming down the steps from the plane; it was only the second time that they had negotiated steps. The first time was when they boarded the plane.

They brought with them many diseases, some of which were no longer present in Western society. These were people emerging from a time capsule, and they presented an obvious burden to the state, but in the final analysis we had to be proud of what we were doing. The operation vindicated the existence of the State of Israel, homeland for every Jew throughout the world.

The children would be easily absorbed, but the adults would constitute a major problem. They had to be taught everything—how to use a toilet and bathroom, how to use a toothbrush and soap, how to eat with utensils. They received their introduction to electricity and to electrical appliances. It was indeed a great challenge, at a time of great national crisis and economic weakness. Nonetheless, we met it and would do so again. With all our flaws, despite our weaknesses, Israel could still be a moral compass for the world.

⤙⤚⤛⤜

The Presidency—1985

THE YEAR 1984 came and went, and fortunately the dire prognostications of George Orwell did not materialize. However, what he described in his famous book was, unfortunately, all too relevant still. Side by side with the most unbelievable scientific advances, human misery and man's inhumanity to man broadened and deepened.

In the midst of such insanity, I found a peaceful refuge in my family. Our children were grown by this time but Aura and I still spent much time with them. During my ten years in office, we never thrust them into our public, presidential lives, but we spent weekends with them at our real home in Herzliya whenever possible, doing our best to live a normal family life. Three of our four kids were married during my presidency, and the wedding ceremonies were private affairs in our garden. Weddings were not official business, they were pure pleasure, and that's the way I wanted to keep them. Three grandchildren were born during this period and they were invited—to either house—whenever they wanted to come. We had two historic first ever *brit mila* ceremonies, for Noam and Matan, Bouji's sons, in the President's Residence.

Of course it is never possible to keep one's family completely out of the public eye, not with the media as ravenous as they are these days. When our second son, Mike, got a divorce, one Israeli paper treated it as the biggest scandal of the century. They ran one headline that said, "Divorce in the Presidency." Even I had to double-check to make sure that Aura hadn't left me in the middle of the night!

I tried to take my reverence of family and translate that to my role as president. In a certain sense, the president of Israel is much like a national father. He is an authority figure but an approachable one. He cannot force anyone to obey the government's guidelines, but he can act as a moral compass and a role model. And much as a father does his best to bring all the warring factions of a family in line, I tried to act as a binding force among Israel's various populations.

Along those lines, I continued meeting with influential Arabs and began to appreciate that while the extremist view tended to rule—it was backed by guns and bombs—the moderate view was predominant. The Palestinian population was fed up with the continued conflict with Israel. Many of them felt that turning down autonomy was a grave error. We had established a military rule because if we annexed the Palestinian land—as we had a right to do, having taken it in the Six-Day War— we would have had to establish a democracy. But if we did that, we would have been creating a binational state, thus endangering our own existence.

The Arabs greatly resented the military government; they felt they were treated in a demeaning and offensive manner, and on occasion they were probably right. Oddly enough, the Arabs trusted the Israeli Supreme Court and our democratic system. This conflict has, obviously, changed quite a bit today, in large part because the Palestinian police have clamped down on their own extremists. Unfortunately, the wisdom and moderation that had begun to characterize many opinion makers in the West Bank and Gaza did not spill over to the youth of the region. The older population was prospering under our rule, and they remembered the restrictive and cruel Jordanian regime. The students, on the other hand, saw only the limitations that we put on them; they had nothing to compare their situation to, and it fit the classic pattern of youthful rebellion. They resembled the youth of America who rose up and rebelled against their government's policy in Vietnam. Young people can sustain their anger and keep fighting, but you seldom see a Middle Eastern terrorist over the age of twenty-five. The older generation sees that life is improving. The younger generation sees only what needs to be improved and won't let anything stand in the way.

Meanwhile, life in Israel had definitely improved. Our economic problems were being corrected; the cabinet had, after much debate, finally voted to withdraw from Lebanon; and the religious right-wing extremists had been defeated on their "Who is a Jew" legislation in the Knesset. The religious battle had centered on the Law of Return, which allows any Jew to come to Israel, become a citizen, and receive full benefits. The religious parties were insisting that a converted Jew be legitimated only by

Orthodox procedure. The more liberal view was that a Jew is anyone who declares himself a Jew.

Prime Minister Peres was solving problems at an almost superhuman rate. The only blot on his political horizon at this point was with his so-called partner in the new government, Vice Premier and Foreign Minister Yitzhak Shamir. Mistrusting Peres and his policies, Shamir did not care to advance our peaceful relations with Egypt and resented the positive reception greeting the prime minister as he made his dynamic changes.

But Peres was not the only one in the midst of a spectacular political recovery. Ariel Sharon returned from his libel case in New York against *Time*, which had accused him of being directly involved in the 1982 massacre of Palestinians by the Lebanese Christians. He was not directly involved; he had simply turned a blind eye to the savagery. He was not responsible for the bloodshed; he had just done nothing to prevent it. An American jury found that *Time* had indeed lied, but the magazine technically won the case because no malice was proven, and therefore, according to the court, there was no libel. Nevertheless Sharon declared it to be a major victory, and back in Israel he was greeted as a hero.

IN FEBRUARY 1985, I paid an official visit to the European Community, the European Parliament, Luxembourg, and Belgium. In temperatures of thirteen degrees below zero, Aura and I were met in Luxembourg by Grand Duke Jean of Luxembourg and Grand Duchess Marie Astrid, the sister of King Baudouin of Belgium. The grand duke had been my contemporary at the Royal Military College in Britain in 1943. He had graduated two months ahead of me. Later we had served together on the staff of the 32nd Brigade of the Guards Armored Division in Western Europe. This common background developed into a close personal relationship over the years of my presidency. We stayed at the Grand Ducal Palace, a magnificent sixteenth-century building. In our private conversations with the grand duke and the grand duchess, it became obvious how deeply she felt that a great injustice had been done to her late father, King Leopold III, in connection with his behavior in World War II. Leopold's actions as commander in chief of the Belgian army during the German conquest of Belgium (1940) aroused opposition to his rule, eventually leading to his abdication in 1951.

In Strasbourg, I was the first president of Israel ever to address the European Parliament. My host was Pierre Pflimlin, president of the parliament and a former prime minister of France. In Brussels, we were the guests of King Baudouin and Queen Fabiola and I addressed the foreign affairs committees of the House and Senate of the Belgian Parliament. I still remembered some Flemish from my days in the army in Belgium during World War II, and created a very friendly atmosphere everywhere by opening my speeches in Flemish and continuing in French.

EARLY IN 1985, President Hosni Mubarak of Egypt called for a peace conference involving Egypt, Jordan, Israel, the United States, and, within the Jordanian delegation, Palestinians who were not members of the PLO. Mubarak made his proposal in *The New York Times* in a very effective public relations move. Mubarak and other Arab leaders obviously wanted to take advantage of Peres's two-year term to move things forward. It was just as clear that Mubarak was using the *Times* to influence Washington. After Israel, Egypt is the single biggest recipient of U.S. foreign aid, and Mubarak was just about to ask for a huge increase. Shamir and other Likud leaders closed ranks and attacked the initiative, calling it a public relations ploy; I told Peres that we had to make the right noises. It cost us nothing to respond positively and only improved our image. One thing was clear: the Arab population in the Middle East was getting used to its leaders talking about negotiations with Israel, and even though nothing much occurred at the meetings, they set the stage for the groundbreaking peace negotiations that Rabin and Peres pushed through almost ten years later. Politicians must be patient and have long-range vision. Nothing happens overnight, and sometimes the most innocuous conversation can pay off years later.

Shamir was critical about the "euphoria" surrounding Mubarak's proposals. In his view, Mubarak and King Hussein just wanted to bring the PLO into negotiations through the back door—via the Americans. Shamir and Peres both wanted to get the peace process under way but were unequivocal about not negotiating with the PLO. Their differences were mainly political game-playing and responses to the need for worldwide public relations.

In April, Ezer Weizman, minister in charge of Israeli–Arab affairs, arranged to be invited to Egypt. Peres was not happy about the trip, which, in a way, was upstaging him. He had only recently come to an agreement with Mubarak about the terms for their summit conference and did not need Weizman's intervention. Shamir, the foreign minister, was very upset about this expedition, seeing Weizman as intruding on his province. Learning that the discussions with Weizman would be of a substantive nature put his back up. The visit came to a normally perfunctory vote in the government, and the Likud rose up as a bloc to vote it down. Peres threatened to resign, seeing the vote as an issue of confidence in his leadership. Luckily, Dr. Burg of the National Religious Party changed his vote from an abstention to a favorable vote, and Weizman's trip was approved. The incident was petty, demeaning, and ridiculous and did no good for Israel's image.

Weizman returned triumphant, announcing that he had come to certain agreements with President Mubarak. Officials in the Foreign Ministry and the prime minister's office began to work out final arrangements for the summit conference. I was sure it would never take place, and I was right.

As THE FORTIETH anniversary of the defeat of the Nazis in World War II dawned, President Reagan decided, to the horror of Jews around the world, to lay a wreath at the German military cemetery at Bitburg, where a number of SS soldiers are buried. It was a stupid move and his advisors had to be idiots or extraordinarily naive not to have known this would cause such a stir. But the Jewish people, by their violent reaction, were putting Reagan in an impossible position. The German government was insisting that he carry out the visit exactly as planned, and Reagan could not appear to be giving in to pressure. I knew him as one of the greatest friends Israel had ever had—he and Clinton are the two most pro-Israel presidents of my lifetime—so I trod very softly on this Bitburg issue. After all, our future is much more important than our past. And Reagan was essential to our future.

The controversy didn't fade away. Perhaps the most noble gesture that came out of the whole sorry affair was made by German president Richard von Weizsaecker, who courageously sent me a note indicating his displeasure with the developments surrounding Reagan's visit. Despite his political office, he did not attend the ceremony and ordered Germany's ambassador to Israel to lay a wreath in his name at Yad Vashem on the anniversary of the German surrender. In a most unusual and moving speech, he emphasized the nation's guilt, pointing out that all Germans knew about the Nazis' hideous crimes. He pointed out that they had seen the synagogues burning, had seen the Jews forced to wear the yellow badges, had seen the deportations, and they knew about the concentration camps. He told the German people the bitter truth, which at long last they needed to hear.

I LIKE TO THINK that Israel's government is basically a moral governing body and that our system works because it lives up to the high standards expected of it. But the individuals who make it work seem increasingly to fall well below those standards.

In 1985, the American ambassador to Israel, Sam Lewis, resigned amid a major controversy. A week earlier, he had revealed on television—in a perfectly calculated and planned manner—that in December 1981, six months before the outbreak of the Lebanese War, Ariel Sharon had disclosed the plans for the incursion to Philip Habib, the U.S. ambassador-at-large. Several representatives of our Foreign Ministry were at the meeting, Lewis said. Sharon emphatically denied the allegation, but Habib and Yehuda Ben-Meir, the former deputy foreign minister, confirmed that the meeting had taken place. Representatives of the Foreign Ministry had reported it to him and to Shamir with great concern. In other words, Sharon had given representatives of the American government details of a planned military operation before the Israeli cabinet knew anything about it.

Sharon immediately launched an unpleasant counterattack on Lewis. However, an action that could—and probably should—have brought down a minister and a government in another democratic country had almost no effect on the ordinary Israeli public. No one cared. We had become inured to a lack of moral standards, even at the ministerial level.

The lowering of standards was brought home when Vice Premier and Foreign Minister Yitzhak Shamir met with the wives of several Jewish underground radicals awaiting trial. These prisoners had set off a bomb, causing the Arab mayor of Nablus to lose his legs, in an illegal and repugnant act of violence. The wives were on a hunger strike to get clemency for their husbands, and Shamir gave them his word that it would be granted.

Horrified by Shamir's action, I made a statement on this issue the next day to high-school students in the town of Kiryat Shemonah. The target of extensive shelling by Katyusha rockets from Lebanon, the town understood violence only too well.

Asked about Shamir's attempted rapprochement with the Jewish underground, I replied that any attempt to bend the rule of law to the will of a group would bring catastrophe and destroy our democratic system. Only the president could grant pardon; nobody else had the right to make commitments on that issue. I can't say Shamir was too thrilled, but I had no sympathy for him. A politician's job is not just to curry favor with popular choices but to provide moral leadership.

One of my more controversial decisions as president was to reduce the sentences of two convicted members of the bomb plot after they expressed full regret in writing for what they had done and condemned the activities in which they had been involved. One of them, Dan Beeri, declared unequivocally that even if the government decided to remove settlements or settlers from the West Bank, he would never again lift a finger against a legally elected government of Israel. Such a statement had more effect than all the speeches of well-intentioned politicians against the terrorist underground.

I chose to lighten their sentences because of the Likud's attempt to pass a bill granting amnesty to all members of the terrorist underground, which I believed posed a great danger to our democracy. My actions both split the underground organizations down the middle and headed off the amnesty law. It was one of my more effective bits of politicking.

THE SENSELESS MURDER of two Israeli teachers in a picnic area near Afula gave rise to another outburst of anti-Arab rioting. Meir Kahane and his mob instigated the violence, attacking innocent Arabs who had been working in the town for years. Things quickly turned ugly when Kahane announced his intention of driving the Arabs out of Israel and called for the death sentence for terrorists. His cry was taken up by many Likud leaders, even though Israel had abolished the death sentence with the establishment of the State and had long resisted calls to reinstate it. There were Israeli prisoners in Lebanon; if we put Arabs to death, they would surely retaliate in kind. Much of our population tends to be hysterical in times of crisis, and many politicians were trying to cash in politically, creating insurmountable problems. Peres, to his great credit, was a steadying influence, speaking out strongly against Kahane and his mindless violence. I began to fear for democracy in Israel—and not just the angry mob mentality. The Histadrut, our federation of labor unions, was blocking Peres's plans to salvage our economy, using what seemed to me to be corrupt tactics.

Intermittent strikes by electric corporation workers and telephone engineers penalized the poor, the weak, and the sick. Carried away by a feeling of power, the unions were deliberately pushing the country to disaster, and the Histadrut was trying to set itself up as an alternative government without responsibility. In mid-July Peres was scheduled to appear on television and explain the government's policy. The Histadrut ordered communications workers to block out the broadcast. This move to muzzle the prime minister convinced me that democracy in Israel was in serious danger. After many sleepless nights Peres worked out an agreement with the Histadrut and the industrialists, and the economic indicators finally began to be positive.

IN JUNE 1985, Aura and I went on a state visit to Ireland. As can well be imagined, it was of particular significance to me. I invited our niece Shira, Yaacov's daughter, to accompany us. In preparation for my trip, I decided to open every speech in Ireland with some remarks in Gaelic. It is an impossible language, and although I passed my exams in Gaelic as a boy, I had forgotten most of it. All our efforts to find suitable candidates to help me, particularly among the nuns in the churches and monasteries in Jerusalem, were unsuccessful. In desperation, I phoned General William Callaghan, commander of the Unifil forces in Lebanon, invoking the bond of friendship among all natives of Ireland, and asked him to help me. He sent me a colonel and a lieutenant colonel, who translated the opening remarks of seven speeches, prepared phonetic texts and recorded them on tape.

It was a wonderful visit, with dinners, speeches, and trips to the very beautiful area of Cork and Kerry in the south. In Cork the former mayor, Gerald Goldberg, welcomed me in Hebrew, translating each sentence for all the city council as he went along. In Dublin, I attended a service in the Adelaide Road Synagogue, where I was bar mitzvahed. I addressed the congregation from the same pulpit from which my father had addressed me. I talked about my youth and my bar mitzvah and my father, and before I was done, the entire congregation was in tears. The community had the lectern on the pulpit inscribed, indicating that it had been my father's and that I had spoken from it on the occasion of my state visit. and gave it to me as a memento. Also in Dublin, I inaugurated the Jewish museum. Some years later the Dublin municipality established a park named Herzog in my honor.

In an editorial at the conclusion of my visit, the *Irish Times* wrote: "The President was a welcome visitor; Ireland and Israel know each other better; the exercise has to be recorded as a genuine success."

ON A HOT DAY in August 1985, I managed to escape briefly from the web of violence and political intrigue that seemed to be spinning out of control, when Aura and I married off our third son, Yitzhak (Bouji), to Michal Afek, in a beautiful ceremony at our home in Herzliya. The religious service was on the roof and dinner was served in the garden. It was a very moving occasion for me. Bouji had become a very close friend over and above the normal parent-child relationship. His bride was beautiful and intelligent; she was studying law with him. Although it was an elegant wedding, it was also quite modest. We were not oblivious to the hard times we were living through. No ministers and only two members of the Knesset, one of them my brother-in-law, Abba Eban, were invited. The cabinet came on the next Sunday to Beit Hanassi, after the cabinet meeting, to drink a toast to the bride and groom. As usual, Aura's imagination, energy, and good taste made the whole occasion a success.

Reality returned with a vengeance in September, with a new growth in terrorist activities. Two Israeli reserve soldiers were stabbed in Hebron, where the Tehiya Party, unfortunately backed by the Likud, had been forcing the issue of settling Jews in the heart of the Arab population. Settling Jews in densely populated Arab areas meant assigning troops for their protection, creating a serious defense burden that would in turn prevent the Israel Defense Forces from carrying out their job. Reserve soldiers were not up to the job of fulfilling their police duties, and their lives were being unnecessarily endangered because of the idiosyncrasies of the settlers and the politicians who were backing them. Jews certainly have the historic right—in principle—to settle in any part of the country. That is not the issue. The issue is the political wisdom in implementing this right in certain instances. In this instance, settling in Hebron, in a sea of Arab hostility, was self-destructive.

The settlers in the West Bank initiated a vigilante operation, sending out armed patrols into major cities like Ramallah and Hebron. The campaign of terror by the PLO and particularly by Fatah continued. Two yachts—filled with terrorists hell-bent on destruction—en route from Algeria and bound for Israel were apprehended by the navy. The gulf was widening between Jew and Arab, yet there was hope.

Near the Trappist monastery of Latrun on the road to Jerusalem is the joint Arab-Jewish village of Neve Shalom, established six years earlier in 1979. The citizens leased land from the monastery for farming, and a dozen Jewish families and a dozen Arab families lived together as an integrated community; the schools were—and still are—bilingual. The settlers were probably naive and Utopian: Israel could never be turned into one big Neve Shalom—it was not human nature, at least not on a grand scale. But the experiment was a step in the right direction; we needed to start small and grow from there. Dedicated people had planted the seed that could one day bring forth the fruit of peace.

ISRAEL HAS A small community of Circassians, approximately 3,000 souls, located in two villages. I visited the very beautiful village of Kafr Kana near Mount Tabor. Circassians, Sunni Moslems in every way, are Caucasians who came from the Caucasus, and who moved to the Ottoman Empire at the time of the Crimean War, in the mid-nineteenth century. The Moslem Circassians spread over Syria, Jordan, and Palestine, and were partly assimilated by the Arabs. In Jordan many of them serve in the army, and in Israel too, they are subject, on their insistence, to mandatory army service. Israel is one of the few countries where their language (Circassian) is preserved, and it is taught in the schools with the approval of the Ministry of Education. It is the language they speak. In addition, they are all Arabic speakers, and the children learn the Hebrew curriculum and attend Jewish schools. They are a handsome people, and on the occasion of my visit I was regaled by the Caucasian dancing of boys and girls dressed in their traditional robes.

In the course of my next official visit, to the city of Petach Tikvah, I met with children from the senior classes in the secondary schools. The first question posed to me was about Kahane and Kahanism. I lashed out at Kahane and his movement, explaining the dangers to our society and to our democracy. Kahane's desired confrontation with the Arab population would, in my view, make us another version of Belfast, Cyprus, or Beirut. I maintained that it was a stain on the history of the Jewish people that such a philosophy could even have supporters in our public life. I asked my audience what sort of a youth we had, if they were prepared to follow a man who, while our boys were giving their lives for the country—not only Jews but also Druze and bedouin boys—was acting, according to published reports, as a paid informer for the FBI? My remarks were the first really major public attack on Kahane and they were relayed all over the world, arousing a tremendous reaction. The youth reacted most favorably, and the feedback in Israel was very positive. Somebody in authority was speaking in a clear, unequivocal manner about this unpleasant phenomenon.

My attack on Kahane was having its effect. His speech at a mass rally in Givatayim was greeted by 20,000 protestors who drowned out his words with whistles. Kahane retaliated with vituperation directed at me, the police, and the kibbutzim; when he came to power he would destroy Givatayim, he promised. Kahane's speech was an incitement to riot and hatred. This was not the time to don kid gloves; the offense was covered by law, and without much ado the government should demand the removal of his parliamentary immunity and send him to jail. They didn't —but it was clear he had declared war on his own government. Unfortunately, the government's reaction was totally inadequate.

ON TUESDAY, 8 OCTOBER 1985, there began the first state visit of a German head of state to Israel. At noon, a German military plane, with the word *Luftwaffe* emblazoned on it and the insignia of the German air force landed. The insignia—a huge iron cross—is, of course, associated with the horrors of Nazism, and it seemed out of place. I often wondered why they insisted on maintaining these symbols and the national anthem "Deutschland Über Alles." The Germans maintained that these symbols represented Germany before Nazism and had nothing to do with the Nazis, which is true—but that still didn't change public perception.

President and Mrs. Von Weizsaecker landed with an entourage of over thirty people, including Hans-Dietrich Genscher, the foreign minister; members of the Bundestag; and a large press contingent. They were met by a 21-gun salute and a receiving line headed by the prime minister, the speaker of the Knesset, and many of Peres's ministers. Following the welcoming ceremony, Aura and I entertained the Von Weizsaeckers and their son at a private luncheon.

I traveled with the German president to Jerusalem and acted as tour guide, describing the various historic sites along our route. We held a dinner that night in honor of our visitors, a dinner that was interrupted by a number of demonstrations mounted by right-wing Israeli youth. The demonstrations both infuriated and baffled me. Why would anybody want to demonstrate against a German who had had the courage to say about German guilt what Von Weizsaecker had said in the Bundestag on 8 May. In general, I cannot understand people who demonstrate against Germany and then, as so many of them do, get into their Volkswagens and drive to the university to benefit from the facilities made available by grants from the German government.

This hypocritical attitude was highlighted by the Hebrew University senate. There had been a proposal that Von Weizsaecker receive an honorary degree, but the Hebrew University Senate refused, proving that academic knowledge was not necessarily compatible with a measure of common sense. They did not turn down German grants, just the award of honorary degrees. The Weizmann Institute immediately offered to give the president a doctorate, and I agreed to be present for the ceremony. I wanted to make my position absolutely clear. Having fought Nazism in the field of battle had made me feel free to take a stand on such issues.

The state dinner was a magnificent affair, of special importance because the event and the speeches were broadcast live by satellite to Germany, where they were watched by millions of people.

The presidential itinerary included a visit to the Holocaust Memorial, Yad Vashem, where it was evident how very moved Von Weizsaecker and his wife were by what they saw. I stood by the president as he laid a wreath in the Hall of Remembrance, where the names of all major Nazi concentration camps are inscribed. Seeing tears in this man's eyes, I was struck once again by the extraordinary contradictions of history.

The visit had done much to contribute to a rapprochement between our countries.

NOT LONG AFTERWARD, terror struck again, reaching its climax when an Italian cruise ship, the *Achille Lauro,* was hijacked in Egyptian waters by four terrorists. The world was horrified by the news that Leon Klinghofer, an American Jewish passenger confined to a wheelchair, was shot in cold blood and thrown overboard. The attack was organized with Arafat's knowledge by a terrorist known as Abu al-Abbas. Forbidden to land in Syria, the hijackers sailed back to Egypt, where they surrendered. A deal struck with the terrorists allowed them to fly back to PLO headquarters in Tunis. To cover their role in the bargain, the Egyptians became involved in a series of lies. President Mubarak announced that the terrorists had left Egypt, when they had not. He maintained that he did not know that a passenger had been killed, when the captain's report of the murder had been broadcast around the world well before the terrorists arrived in Egypt. En route to Tunis in an Egyptian plane, they were intercepted by U.S. planes and forced to land at a NATO base in Sicily, where they were placed in Italian custody to be held for trial. The Americans demanded their extradition, but the Italians flew them to Yugoslavia, which did not honor their extradition treaty with the United States. The killers and their leader were never brought to justice. The irony of history was emphasized in 1996 when Israel permitted the very same Abu al-Abbas to return to Gaza to attend the meeting of the Palestine National Council which voted to amend the Palestine covenant that cancelled those provisions which called for the destruction of Israel.

TOWARD THE END of November, the Jonathan Pollard case broke. An American Jew working for U.S. naval intelligence, Pollard was apprehended by the FBI and arraigned for passing to Israel highly classified information relating to Arab armies. Pollard's wife was also arrested.

Peres was very concerned about the ramifications of the case. Rafi Eitan, who activated Pollard to transmit the information, had been Peres's advisor on counterterrorism and was still associated with the Ministry of Defense. With this operation he apparently wanted to out-Mossad the Mossad, despite clear instructions forbidding any form of intelligence gathering from any Western country. The prime minister, the minister of defense, the vice premier and foreign minister, and the Mossad maintained that they knew nothing about this operation; those apprised of it must have considered it routine, without assessing the political implications and ramifications for American Jewry and Israel's relations with the United States.

The case had all the earmarks of amateur mismanagement, but one particularly disturbing element did not make sense: how could an operation with such direct bearing on Israel's relationship with the U.S. government be mounted without formal ministerial approval or at least tacit acknowledgment? Something seemed very wrong in the workings of our government. As the investigations continued, it became clear that the head of the Mossad had not been put in the picture, either.

Pollard maintained that the information was strictly Arab intelligence; it was not being transmitted by the U.S. authorities to Israel, and in no way had he endangered U.S. security. Pollard was motivated by his knowledge of America's obligation to hand this information over to Israel. The unit that had been involved was terminated, after enormous damage to international relations.

In December, the Israeli government issued a public apology; Pollard was sentenced to life imprisonment. At his trial, Secretary of Defense Caspar Weinberger called the episode the worst case of espionage ever perpetrated against the United States. This, of course, is absurd; Pollard's crime had no adverse security effect on the United States, and the severity of his punishment was ridiculous. I made a personal plea to Bush and Clinton on different occasions to release Pollard. Both of them promised to consider it; neither one did anything.

RIGHT BEFORE THE END of the year, I received a letter from Meir Wilner, the secretary-general of Israel's Communist Party, formally inviting me to attend the party's quadrennial conference. I hoped that this invitation indicated a change in the attitude of the Communist world toward recognizing Israel. I could not ignore the fact that the bulk of the membership and support of the Communist Party in Israel came from the Arab population. So I took this as a positive sign and decided to attend. The invitation—the first of its kind ever given to an Israeli president—could mean something important in the diplomatic parlance of the Communist world. My instinct has always been to look for these tiny openings and then try to exploit them. I might not be able to, but in this instance I intended to express my views without reservation; with Communist Party delegates coming from many countries, it wouldn't hurt for them to hear what I had to say in the name of the people of Israel.

When I arrived at the opening of the Communist Party conference in the Shavit Hall, in Haifa, there was tremendous media interest. Response in general was mixed, but the public reaction was reasonably favorable. Editorials in *Davar*, the *Jerusalem Post*, and *Ma'ariv* were all complimentary. In Haifa, however, there were demonstrators with placards criticizing my move.

There were delegates from sixteen countries, including the Soviet Union, Cuba, Bulgaria, Romania, Czechoslovakia, East Germany, Mongolia, Cyprus, Greece, Italy, the United States, and Canada. My entrance to the hall was greeted by a demonstration of approval; 1,000 delegates rose and cheered. It was surely the first time in history that a Communist Party conference had risen in honor of a Zionist, much less the president of Israel.

The meeting was a typical Communist conference, a copy of those we saw broadcast from the Soviet Union. Strict party discipline was in evidence at every point. Everything was orchestrated. Delegates applauded together, stopped applauding together, and rose together, as they did when the Russian delegation entered.

Tewfik Toubi, the veteran Arab member of the Knesset, opened the conference in Arabic and Hebrew. When it was my turn to speak, I took advantage of the occasion to bring home some hard truths and gave the young Arabs what must have been a very rude lesson in the history of relations between the Soviet Union and Israel. I quoted at length Gromyko's pro-Zionist speech in the UN on 29 November 1947. I recalled that not only had the Red Army played a major part in saving humanity from the Nazis in World War II but also the fact that in Israel's own War of Independence, when we were suffering from an embargo on the part of the Western countries, it was the Soviet Union and the Eastern bloc that supplied us with our arms and thus saved us. I told them that we would never forget this. I reminded them that they were signatories to Israel's Declaration of Independence (Meir Wilner, member of the Knesset, was the signatory). I declared that we were a nation seeking peace, one prepared to make great sacrifices for that peace. I raised the issues of Soviet Jewry and our relations with the Soviet Union and talked about our refusal to negotiate with any organization that adopted terrorism as a weapon or did not recognize our right to exist.

The speech was well received, even punctuated at times by loud applause, although there was a polite silence when I deviated from the party line. I don't know how much good I accomplished. I do know that the Russian Jewish reaction to my participation was very positive. *Pravda* highlighted my attendance, as did the important press in the East European satellite countries. All in all, I felt good about attending. The only thing I think is truly dangerous is a *lack* of communication between people and a hypocritical approach—whether it's from the left or the right— about selecting whom to communicate with.

DURING THE FIRST years of the State of Israel, a call went out for families to adopt children from the refugee camps (*ma'abarot*). My parents took in a twelve-year-old boy called Shalom from Yemen, who later set up a bakery in Petach Tikvah, and a little black girl from the Hadramaut Desert in southern Arabia, who was completely ignorant of modern Western customs. She lived with us for over half a year.

At a reception years later, she introduced herself. She now had a daughter in the university, a son in the aircraft industry, another son in the army, and a third son studying at a yeshiva.

A typical Israeli story, of which we as a people could be proud; it vindicates our dedicated efforts over the years.

The Presidency—1986

ON 10 FEBRUARY 1986, dissident Anatoly Sharansky was released after nine years in a Russian jail and labor camp, freed in an exchange of convicted spies between the West and the Soviet Union. Sharansky had been through a horrendous ordeal, tortured mentally as well as physically, but, mostly through the activities of his wife, Avital, his name had become a household word, a symbol of all those oppressed behind the Iron Curtain. Avital worked nonstop, demonstrating unbelievable faith and energy, mobilizing large sums of money, and traveling around the world leading demonstrations, seeing heads of state, and rousing public opinion. She was so visible, so relentless, that when, after Natan (as Sharansky is called in Hebrew) and Avital had been in Israel for some time, I introduced them to Mikhail and Raisa Gorbachev at a state dinner, Mrs. Gorbachev actually recognized Avital from her demonstration activity against them. What made her efforts even more moving was that when Sharansky was arrested, he had been married to Avital for only one day.

A strong and impressive personality, Sharansky was living evidence that the human spirit can be stronger than great powers. He was dignified, quiet, spoke excellent English, and passable Hebrew for a beginner. Very soon after they arrived in Israel, the Sharanskys were our guests. Their biggest complaint about their new life was that they were so very exposed; people would not leave them alone and were trying to exploit them for political reasons. In his mind, Sharansky was simply an ordinary man who wanted to go back to an ordinary life, but to the outside world he was a hero.

Sharansky asked detailed questions about the Lebanese War, having learned about it by reading *Pravda* throughout his imprisonment and by listening to Moscow Radio. Of 4,000 letters written to him over the years, only about 10 percent ever reached him. Avital wrote him twice a week but he received only a total of nine letters from her. He could not believe that Israeli prisons do not have forced labor and that many prisoners even get leave to go home. Appropriate arrangements were made for the Sharanskys to be spirited to a hideaway where they could relax without being persecuted by well-wishers. Ten years later, Sharansky led a party representing Russian immigrants to success in the 1996 Knesset elections, and achieved a ministerial post. What better example of the Jewish saga—from the darkness of a KGB prison to a high political position in the Jewish state.

The nature of the dangerous world in which we live, a world so much in the shadows of terrorism, was highlighted by two assassinations in the beginning of March 1986. One was the murder of Olaf Palme, the Swedish prime minister, shot in the streets of Stockholm, assailants unknown. As once again the world was rocked, there was much lip service about the need to fight the extremists. But very little was done. A country like Sweden was caught in a dilemma. What could the Swedish people do? Historically, they had been overly liberal in their attitude toward extreme organizations. Now they experienced the violence firsthand, but they couldn't just renounce their collective social conscience.

The second assassination struck nearer to home, when the newly appointed mayor of Nablus, Zafer el-Masri, was shot to death. He had been appointed to his position some two months earlier by the Israeli military government, with the tacit approval of Jordan and the PLO. His murder was a direct move against King Hussein and probably against Arafat. Immediately afterward, candidates for the post of mayor in other West Bank towns withdrew from their races. The world was learning what a tremendous influence the assassin's bullet wielded in the West Bank and Gaza. Israel had begun a policy of devolution of powers to the Arabs in the territories, in the hope that a local leadership would emerge, but one bullet was already endangering this process.

The internal struggle for leadership in the Herut Party, the predominant element in the Likud, came to a head in early March at the fifteenth annual Herut conference. David Levy, campaigning heavily to unseat Yitzhak Shamir for the leadership, had his delegates organized in groups with placards, flags, and prepared chants in the style of American political conventions. Every time Levy's name was mentioned, a tremendous cheer rose. Despite this raucous behavior, Shamir clearly had an edge over

Levy, whose supporters stormed the platform, threw down the microphone, knocked over the podium and the table, and began pushing and shoving. All of this was recorded for the nation on television, and it did not help his cause. Not a single discussion of policy took place, nothing of substance was brought up. After a three-day struggle between power blocs, the convention broke up in utter disorder.

In the Labor Party and the media, voices were raised against honoring the rotation agreement reached in 1984, by which Peres and Shamir would rotate as prime minister every two years. To this group, to which Peres was instinctively drawn, it was inconceivable that the affairs of state should be handed over to the stars of the disturbing exhibition witnessed at the Herut conference.

Peres was disturbed at the idea of Shamir's replacing him in accordance with the agreement. He maintained that Shamir had never opened his mouth on the economic issues and had broken his silence at cabinet and government meetings only to say no, on every constructive approach to peace or peace moves. To gain public support, Peres would need a major issue, such as the electoral system, on which he would have much backing from the development towns and much of the Likud. But Peres felt that the electoral system was a nonissue in the eyes of the public. Unfortunately, this was typical of his tendency to engage in wishful thinking when it suited him. It was clear that he would ultimately have to honor the rotation agreement, and he might as well do it in good grace.

Knives were being sharpened for the Labor Party conference, scheduled for 8 April. Early that month, Minister of Finance Yitzhak Modai, in two newspaper interviews, seriously insulted the prime minister, insisting that he did not understand economics, attacking his economic proposals, and accusing him of robbery and "sucking the blood of the nation." Peres decided to fire Modai, and the Likud announced that in such a case all their ministers would resign. This put Peres, as head of a unity government, in an untenable position. He postponed firing Modai until the Labor Party conference, over which he was presiding, concluded.

This being Israel, there were political negotiations between the two main parties, and Modai was finally transferred to the Ministry of Justice, and his position at the Treasury was taken by Moshe Nissim, the minister of justice. Neither Modai nor Nissim nor the Israeli public was happy with the solution, but Peres could not suffer Modai any longer as finance minister and would not be held hostage by the rotation agreement.

Peres believed that we had to get out of Gaza; it was essential that the more than half a million Arabs there be kept out of Israel. Economically, we could not handle their absorption as citizens, and we certainly did not want them voting as a bloc. Peres wanted to push the concept of autonomy in Gaza but was very concerned that the Jewish settlements in the Gaza Strip, comprising about 1,500 people at the time, would block it.

While speaking to delegations to the Labor Party conference, I received a most interesting insight from Boutros Boutros-Ghali, the Egyptian minister of state for foreign affairs, later to become the secretary-general of the United Nations. There still was strong and vocal opposition in Egypt to the peace with Israel. Egypt had basically been taken out of the Arab world and wanted to rejoin it, but this would be very difficult without compromising the agreement with Israel, Boutros-Ghali said. We had to understand the Egyptians' problem. It was a very disturbing situation (they were later readmitted to the Arab League and assumed their rightful role as leader of the Arab world).

Boutros-Ghali described in disturbing detail the situation in the Sudan. The Libyans were very active there, pouring arms into the south of the country, which was in the throes of a major revolution. As a result, a vital project to build a canal to drain swamps that lay in both the Sudan and Egypt had been stopped and could not be resumed because the French engineers were being kidnapped by the rebels. This was the second important agricultural project to be put on hold. The canal would be held up for ten years; in that time, Egypt's population would have grown by another 40 million people to be fed. Because they had not succeeded in adding several million acres of cultivable land—which both projects were supposed to do—feeding Egypt's masses was becoming a near-impossibility.

A complete reign of terror imposed by the Libyans existed in the Organization of African Unity, Boutros-Ghali added. Nobody would stand up and attack Libya for fear of terrorist-style revenge. And not only the Organization of African Unity was being terrorized.

In early April 1986, a bomb exploded in a TWA plane over Greece, killing four, but the plane landed safely in Athens. A week later, a bomb exploded in a Berlin discotheque frequented by American servicemen. Two soldiers were killed and several hundred other people were wounded. The signs pointing to Libya were strong enough that U.S. planes bombed Tripoli, including Qaddafi's home. Miraculously, he emerged unscathed. Typically, except for Britain, the European Community did not back Reagan's decision to attack.

The Arab terrorist attacks continued. A Syrian agent used an Irish girlfriend as a carrier and a human bomb. She was due to travel on an El Al plane to Israel with five kilos of explosives in the false bottom of her suitcase. Fortunately, an alert El Al security guard saved a whole jumbo plane-load of passengers. The Irish girl was apprehended; so was the terrorist who had sent her. It was a little unnerving that the girl had passed British security without anything being noticed.

ONE OF THE PROBLEMS I was forced to deal with was Israel's "open arms" policy for new immigrants under which they were welcomed with overwhelming love and affection on their arrival; unfortunately, that warm spirit did not seem to last long. When they really needed a helping hand —when the reality of everyday life hit them—they faced problems. At Ben-Gurion airport, in Lod, immigrants waited to be interviewed and processed, obviously nervous and tense, concerned about their children and the problems confronting them in a new country. Meanwhile, youth groups and yeshiva students incongruously performed Israeli folk dances all around them to make them feel welcome. These dervish-like ceremonies were not exactly what new immigrants were short of after days en route from some remote town or village in Russia. A month later, would any more helpful attempts be made to please them? Even most so-called do-gooders prefer symbols and public displays of effort to behind-the-scenes work that might do some real good.

The flaws of our immigration policies were emphasized by what happened to the Sharanskys. After arriving to a hero's welcome, with almost everyone of any prominence clamoring to be photographed receiving Natan and Avital at the airport, Sharansky was having trouble finding and keeping an apartment. In prison he had spent sixteen months under interrogation and was threatened with execution; but he was offered the opportunity to emigrate to Israel if he would incriminate his contacts and admit his crimes. He refused, even though agreeing would have meant instant freedom. Having fulfilled his dream of settling in Israel with no strings attached, he was being undone by the bureaucracy. I intervened on his behalf successfully. But we have the same problem frequently today. Morally, our policy is impeccable; practically, we have a long way to go to make it work, although in recent years there has been a marked improvement.

In May 1986, Margaret Thatcher paid the first visit by a British prime minister to Israel. Aura and I had her to lunch, along with various ministers, newspaper editors, and a delegation of prominent British Jews. In my welcoming remarks, I emphasized the unique association between Britain and Israel: the historic occasions; the names of the great supporters of Zionism—Lloyd George, Churchill, Balfour, etc.—the debt we owe to Britain for many of our systems, including our judicial and parliamentary systems. I expressed the hope that Mrs. Thatcher would be more objective about Israel after she'd seen us close up, and quoted Abba Eban's explanation of objectivity in Israel as "acceptance of Israel's case 100 percent."

Mrs. Thatcher was very moved by a visit to Yad Vashem, as well as one to the British Military Cemetery on Mount Scopus. She also went to the ORT Technical Training College in Jerusalem and in her speech linked the significance of these three places together, emphasizing the sacrifice of youth.

She was most impressed by the beauty of Israel and on her return to Britain launched a clean-up campaign of the United Kingdom, such as she had witnessed in Israel.

Her visit was an outstanding success; the Israeli people just took to her. She visited Ben-Gurion's grave, which touched the hearts of many Israelis, was mobbed in Ashkelon, and was honored by 40,000 people in the main square in Ramat Gan. She exuded friendship everywhere.

In the spring of 1986, we seemed to be facing new crises practically every day. One crisis had very serious ramifications. I found myself facing possibly the most difficult decision of my presidency.

Two years earlier, a bus en route from Ashkelon had been hijacked by four Arab terrorists. They threatened to kill all the passengers, and one girl was shot dead. The bus was stopped and surrounded by Israeli security forces in the Gaza Strip, and two of the terrorists were killed on the bus. The other two were reported killed in the exchange of fire but were photographed by a journalist while being taken off the bus alive. Nothing came of an inquiry into the affair by a senior army officer, but following complaints by three senior officers of the Shin Bet, our general security services, Attorney General Yitzhak Zamir announced that there was prima facie evidence indicated that Avraham Shalom, the chief of the Shin Bet, was involved in a cover-up. Maintaining that security considerations should prevail, Prime Minister Peres did not want the Shin Bet exposed and compromised by agreeing to an inquiry.

The Shin Bet was probably Israel's most effective organization, and

Shalom was a tough disciplinarian. It could be dangerous to remove this man, no matter what his indiscretions, when we were in a bitter and crucial struggle against terrorism. The previous year, 301 terrorist groupings had been apprehended or wiped out by Shin Bet—almost one organization for every working day. The public was unaware of the terrorist attempts foiled by the Shin Bet; for them to be most effective, much of their work was kept secret.

To attack and expose this organization would have been a national tragedy. The job of a government is to govern. On an issue of major security—and the struggle against terrorism was surely such an issue, with thousands of lives at stake—the government must have the final say, even though that does not sound very democratic. Reason and logic sometimes had to win out over political dogma.

But the Shin Bet affair did not disappear, it escalated. The two surviving terrorists had been severely beaten by military personnel in an attempt to force them to reveal whether the explosives in the bus were wired and detonatable. They were handed over to the Shin Bet, looking very much the worse for wear, and then it was announced that these terrorists died in the shoot-out. Obviously, there were serious discrepancies in the story. During the initial inquiry, there was collusion between a member of the inquiry panel and the Shin Bet, in order to cover up the wrongdoing. The Shin Bet then maintained that their treatment of the terrorists and the subsequent cover-up were approved by Yitzhak Shamir, who was prime minister at the time of the hijacking. The matter was clearly out of hand, and the police investigation would have to take its logical course.

I had been thoroughly briefed by Avraham Shalom in May, when the issue was made public. However, in late June, Shalom sent an urgent request to see me. I agreed and he came toward evening. His world had collapsed and he was a broken man. He was more concerned with the Shin Bet's stability and future than with his personal problem. A police investigation, he feared, would give rise to inquiries into many incidents that had occurred as part of the normal workings of a national security service. There could be no security once the hearings took place, he said, even if they were held behind closed doors; the cumulative effect would destroy the Shin Bet. His proposal, therefore, was that I grant pardons in advance of legal proceedings and thus take the security services out of the public debate.

I saw only one way out: he had to tender his resignation. At this, he burst into tears. By this point it was clear to me that there had been a cover-up. This was not just a case of overzealousness in the cause of national security; laws had been broken. An outstanding and successful career was about to end, as Shalom prepared to resign.

Shalom then asked permission for the lawyers Ram Caspi and Yaakov Neeman to join us. Caspi then produced a body of legal opinion proving that as president, I had the discretion to grant a pardon even before a person was arraigned. That was the only way to save the Shin Bet from destruction. I was convinced, but I wanted the cabinet to recommend this step to me through the minister of justice. I was not asking them to make a decision in my place—I would do that and bear full responsibility—but I wanted to gauge their opinion and the depth of their feeling. I also wanted the attorney general, Yosef Harish, whom Peres had just appointed to replace Zamir, to be directly involved. Toward midnight, Minister of Justice Yitzhak Modai arrived with a recommendation from the cabinet to grant the pardons. There had been only one vote against it.

The next day, Modai and the cabinet secretary, Yossi Beilin, arrived with the documents relating to clemency. As I signed, I said to Modai, "Now the heavens will fall down on us. I can take it; can your colleagues in the government?" "I doubt it," he replied with a smile. I had told Peres the evening before of my decision. I also said that I would publicly condemn the Shin Bet's behavior and insist that Shalom resign. I called for the appointment of a public commission to examine the Shin Bet's procedures for interrogating and handling prisoners, and to provide guidelines for future behavior. All my conditions were met: Shalom resigned and the commission was created. In the evening, I went on television and made a statement to the nation, explaining that I had put an end to a national witch-hunt that was threatening to destroy the security services, but the media, especially the TV commentators, were heavily weighted against me.

In an interview I mentioned that President Gerald Ford was attacked with equal ferocity by the media and by the legal community for granting a pardon to Richard Nixon before impeachment proceedings ever began. Ford was right. Nixon, like Shalom, was punished by his resignation from office and his public disgrace. Further recriminations in the Shin Bet case would have served only to paralyze the Israeli security services and whet the media's sharklike appetite for revenge. Those responsible were punished, steps were taken to make sure that such actions would not be repeated, and the security services survived intact.

The debate on the Shin Bet pardons continued for months. The left-wing element in the media refused to drop the matter. My decision was presented, over and over again, in the worst possible light by the media, but I stuck by my decision. I had found myself facing the problem of judging between the rule of law and overriding security considerations. The vast majority of the public did not want to hear any more about it, and yet the media's obsessiveness was making Shin Bet a dirty word, creating an atmosphere in which it was viewed as a bunch of criminals. That in itself was a miscarriage of justice. A group of dedicated boys was saving us day in and day out from terrorist attacks. Indeed, had all the planned attacks been executed, Beirut would have looked like a quiet holiday resort compared with Israel.

Eventually the reactions in the press and from the public gave me reason to feel that the tide had turned on this issue. The Supreme Court upheld my authority to pardon, ruling that when the rule of law and national security considerations vie for priority, the president is authorized to decide. I had acted within the law. Shamir was later exonerated of dishonesty in connection with the Shin Bet affair. The accusing finger pointed to Avraham Shalom.

In July 1986 Vice President George Bush visited Israel. We gave a dinner party in his honor. When Bush's advance staff turned up at the presidential residence to examine it before the dinner, I issued strict orders forbidding any inspection of our building by foreign security or protocol personnel—nobody would dare request permission to scrutinize the White House before a visit. It caused a stir but they backed down, acknowledging that Israel's security precautions would be sufficient.

At the request of the Americans, a team from Bezeq, the Israel telephone corporation, was sent to install two telephone lines in the house, including the famous hot line, in the building. I forbade this, too, allowing the hot line to be installed in the police guardhouse at the gate.

Our dinner took place in the garden—without any speeches. I told a few jokes about Texans, and Bush replied in kind, reminding us that the difference between a Texan and a pigeon was that a pigeon could still make a deposit on a Mercedes. That night, everybody saw a Bush relaxed and at ease.

Although I had an excellent relationship with George Bush, as vice president as well as president, Shamir did not get along with him at all, insisting that Bush and his cronies, Jim Baker in particular, were hostile. That was not the case at all. Bush and Baker were members of a rich, elite, country-club society and simply did not know many Jews or Israelis. If they looked down on them, it was because basically they looked down on everyone outside their small, insular, very particular world.

In July 1986, Peres advised me that he was leaving the next day for Morocco to meet with King Hassan—at Hassan's suggestion. I considered the trip to be of the greatest importance for Israel-Arab relations. Other reactions from both the left and the right were not so positive. The attitude of the right was best expressed by Shamir, who stated that Peres did not have a mandate from the government to make any substantive agreements with Hassan. This was most unfair, but rather typical of Shamir. He had known about this trip well in advance and had said nothing. His statement was an attempt to maintain a "hands-off" relationship with Peres, while still being kept fully in the picture by Peres on all secret missions. The left wing maintained that the prime minister was ignoring and bypassing the more pressing Palestinian problem. As soon as I observed the hesitation on the part of the national leadership to endorse the trip, I made a public statement saying what an important development it was for an Israeli prime minister to fly to an Arab country in an Israel air force plane and be received with all due honors. In my view, this was part of an historic process which had been going on since the visit of President Sadat to Jerusalem. That occasion had brought us across an historic watershed, and had created a new situation for us in the Middle East whereby Arab negotiations with Israel were by now an accepted fact of life.

Peres returned two days later. King Hassan had wanted the basis for the negotiations to be the 1981 Fez Declaration by the Arab states, which demanded the return of all territories, including Jerusalem, to the Arabs. Peres rejected this out of hand, but the king, in a television broadcast, still did not specifically rule out further negotiations. Peres's trip was most important symbolically. Syria immediately broke off relations with Morocco but no such action was taken by any other Arab country. That visit became part of the historic evolution of Israel's acceptance in the Middle East. As usual, Peres showed imagination and intelligent initiative, creating a pattern, the importance of which could not be overemphasized.

Peres told me when he returned that in his private meeting with Hassan the king had spoken very openly about the difficulty of working with the Arab world, but that he had asked Peres how long we felt we could continue to rule over two million Arabs. He wanted to know how we could continue to maintain a society which was constantly involved in this conflict, and how we could go on year after year in a state of war without moving toward some form of compromise. The straightforward-ness of Hassan's language obviously struck a deep chord with Peres.

As PRESIDENT, one has many problems but also curious small pleasures. I was visited by a young American named Little Sun, who was reputedly the head of the Sioux tribe. He hailed from Spokane, Washington. His maternal grandmother was Jewish, thus his mother was Jewish, hence he was Jewish. He had come to Israel to celebrate his bar mitzvah at the Wailing Wall. According to his mother, who looked much more Indian than Jewish, he was a fifth-generation descendant of the famous Crazy Horse, who had led the Sioux in their final battles against the Americans at the end of the nineteenth century. The last real chief in the tribe was his grandfather, and according to his mother, Little Sun was the only successor, although he would have to be appointed by the council of elders of the tribe. He was the first Jewish American Indian I had ever met and, I expect, he'll also be the last.

On 10 October 1986, it was time to implement the rotation agreement. After two years in office, with an almost unbelievable popularity rating of 79 percent, Prime Minister Shimon Peres was to resign so that Likud Party leader Yitzhak Shamir could assume the office for two years, retaining the same bipartisan cabinet that Peres had led.

By law, I had to go through the motions of creating a new government, and each party made recommendations in accordance with its political inclinations. The result was a foregone conclusion, since Labor, the largest party in the Knesset, would opt for the nomination of Shamir for the second two-year term. I refused to invite Kahane to consultations, so he demonstrated outside the gates and tried to force his way in. His people distributed very unpleasant flyers about me, which I suppose was to my credit.

Naturally, another political crisis blew up. Peres, who would become vice premier and foreign minister in the new Shamir government, was not prepared to agree that Yitzhak Modai, after his acrimonious dismissal, should return to the cabinet. The Likud insisted on bringing him back as a matter of principle, although privately a number of its leaders made it quite clear they would be only too happy if he did not return to the cabinet. Both Peres and Shamir wanted their own man as ambassador to Washington, and neither would back down. If ever I had seen an exercise in political futility, this was it.

The public was disgusted by this kind of horse-trading, but no one had a solution. Frustrated with Shamir, who would not agree to anything he proposed, Peres regarded the role of ambassador in Washington as a crucial political weapon to be filled by a politician. He was not prepared to hand it over to a career diplomat; he wanted his own man there to maintain contact with the leaders with whom he had cultivated such good relations.

The next day, Shamir called on me and held forth about Peres's obduracy, maintaining that Peres was a prisoner of the extremists in his party. I looked at him, smiled, and said, "What about you?" He stopped for a moment, smiled, and said, "In all probability, me too."

The current ambassador, Ephraim Evron, would continue until the end of his appointment, May 1987. Some months before that, the foreign minister would need to appoint a replacement with the prime minister's approval. As prime minister, Shamir would agree to a candidate put forth by the foreign minister, Peres, and would not rule out any candidate peremptorily. Peres agreed to Shamir's proposal but wanted the number of candidates for the ambassadorship to be limited to four, so that Shamir could not turn down an unlimited number of candidates. That was agreed to, and we could now move forward.

It was indeed a historic moment when, for the first time in Israel's history, the secretary-general of the Labor Party, Uzi Baram, proposed the leader of the party that had been Labor's enemy since 1920, to be prime minister.

Formally invited to compose the government, Shamir presented it three days later. For a change, it finally included a woman, Shoshana Arbeli-Almoslino, the new minister of health.

ON 2 NOVEMBER 1986, I set off with Aura on a state visit to Australia, Oceania, and Southeast Asia. One of the more impressive individuals that I met in Canberra was Robert Hawke, the Labor prime minister, whose tough, outspoken ways reflected the behavior of a no-nonsense political animal from a labor background. He was a down-to-earth leader who made no secret of the fact that he appreciated the joys of life. He was also a staunch friend of Israel and through him I solicited Australian support in respect of our attempts to improve relations with China and with India.

As a special gesture, both Australian houses of Parliament unanimously adopted a resolution calling on the United Nations to revoke the Zionism-Racism resolution of 1975. A year later, both houses of Congress in Washington adopted this resolution word for word.

On the Sabbath morning, I presented a gift of a Sefer Torah from Israel with suitable adornment to the Tourak Synagogue in Melbourne. Since then, each year the Sefer Torah has been transferred from one synagogue to another in Australia for a period of one year.

Australia was a revelation. It was a giant in the midst of awakening, culturally and socially exciting, and quite beautiful. Australia's connections with China and its membership in the Pacific Forum, based in Fiji, added considerably to its importance for Israel. The Jewish community there is a very resilient and warm one, with 80 percent of the children attending Jewish day schools and receiving Jewish education. I could address the children freely in Hebrew in all the schools.

As we left Melbourne to board our air force plane at the airport, information was received that some Libyan-trained citizens of the island of Vanautu, with which Qaddafi's Libya had maintained a close association, were allegedly planning to attack our plane. We were therefore directed along a very devious route which was changed by radio as we proceeded in our cars, until we finally reached our plane, which had been moved to a remote part of the field.

Shortly thereafter, a group of Vanautans was arrested in Australia.

AMONG ALL the countries I visited on this trip, I experienced the greatest degree of left-wing propaganda in New Zealand. They had a population of three million then in an area ten times the size of Israel. The Jewish population numbered approximately 5,000.

New Zealand was gradually becoming a leading voice against nuclear tests by the French and Americans, against the presence of nuclear submarines, and in favor of the Third World approach, emphasizing the importance of the developing countries with at times a distinct bias in their favor in the various international forums. It was becoming less and less a representative of the Anglo-Saxon world, and more and more a left-wing-oriented society (politically, not economically), which was trying to establish a leading position in the Pacific Forum at the head of the new Island States. The New Zealanders were obviously trying to become an important force in the Third World. Prime Minister David Longe, who was one of the more impressive heads of state I met on my trips, told me that he had given the left-wing parties a free hand politically, from an international point of view, while retaining a free hand for himself in the economic field. His pragmatic approach had achieved economic miracles.

From there we flew to Fiji, where we were met by Governor-General Ratu Sir Penaia Kantabaru and Lady Ganilau, Prime Minister Kamisese Mara and his wife, and the chief of staff and other dignitaries. Standing in the bright sun in such an exotic setting, hearing "Hatikvah" being played, was something new even for the oldest and most cynical of travelers.

Fiji is, in effect, the capital of the Pacific. It is the home of the Pacific Forum, the central political body of sixteen Pacific nations, including Australia and New Zealand. Here too is the central economic organization of the islands, the headquarters of the United Nations Development Project in the Pacific, as well as the University of the Pacific. It supplies a battalion of troops to the Multinational Force in Sinai, and a battalion to Unifil in Lebanon. It has close links to China, and at the time of my visit was interested in developing closer links with Israel. Prime Minister Mara was a most impressive and dignified individual. A graduate of Oxford, he was a poet of some renown and a composer of classical music, and had been studying medicine when he went into politics. Like all the traditional leaders we met, he wore the native skirt and sandals.

On the grounds of the governor-general's residence, we went to a very special reception at which I was given a whale's tooth, making me an honorary citizen.

There followed, to the sound of ritual singing, an incredible war dance. Warriors bounded around with spears, each of which featured blue-and-white ribbons and bobbins.

Afterward, I had talks with the prime minister and his advisors. He raised many issues on which he wanted cooperation with Israel. They wanted the troops in the Fijian battalions to stay in kibbutzim and moshavim and train before they returned to Fiji. He promised to authorize the establishment of an Israeli embassy, based in Fiji, to cover most of the Pacific Forum, but only after the forthcoming elections, as he did not want to antagonize the small Moslem vote. He expressed grave reservations and concern about Libyan and PLO penetrations into the area.

I laid a wreath on behalf of Israel at the military cemetery, where there were nineteen graves of Fijians who died in Lebanon or in Sinai. After we left, several more graves were added.

TONGA WAS AN hour's flight away from Fiji. The king had repeatedly invited me, and I was happy for the opportunity to accept. We were visiting a country very friendly to Israel, and what is more, we were visiting a Polynesian government. In Fiji we had visited the Melanesians; in receiving the representatives of the Marshall Islands I had met with the Micronesians. It seemed only fair to meet the Polynesians.

Tonga is a small, independent kingdom in the Pacific, with probably the oldest royal dynasty in the world, dating back 1,000 years. It comprises three groups of islands, separated one from the other by stretches of ocean, and with a total length of approximately 300 miles. The population is somewhere in the region of 150,000. The country has had a constitution for hundreds of years. Its parliament is composed of twenty-eight people—one-third of them are ministers of the Crown who are appointed directly by the king, one-third of them are nobles who are elected by the nobility, and one-third of them are commoners who are elected by the people of the country. It is an extraordinarily civilized country.

We arrived at Fua'amotu airport and were met by the acting prime minister, Baron Vaea, and Baroness Tuputupu. After the usual state ceremony, we departed from the airport to the capital, Tufumahina. On the morning of Friday, 14 November, we went to the royal palace, where Aura and I were ushered into the presence of the king, Taufa'ahau Tupou IV. With him was Queen Halaevalu Mata'aho. The king is a man of very considerable proportions, as was his late mother, the renowned Queen Salote, who captivated the British people in the Coronation Day parade in London in 1953. He was seated in a thronelike chair, sufficiently wide to accommodate his girth. He wore the skirt customary in Fiji and Tonga, with sandals on his feet, and of course the broad cummerbund of straw matting around his waist, which indicated that he was a member of the nobility. The queen was a tall, attractive, stately figure wearing the richly colored clothes in which the local women dressed. The king revealed an intimate knowledge of the Bible, and a great affection for Israel, displaying a particular expertise in Phoenician history and art.

During the course of my visit, I met with the various ministers and palace officials, and received their requests for aid in the field of agricultural planning, pest control, water-control systems, and solar energy. The king was concerned about Arab attempts to invest in his country. Tonga had maintained its independence for hundreds of years and he did not want to lose it now to Arab businessmen.

As we traveled around the country, we noticed that whenever a royal car drove along the road, the population stood and bowed. When we took off, I felt as if we were leaving behind a delightful little touch of paradise.

IN HONG KONG I went to see the governor, Sir Edward Youde, a British sinologist who had been ambassador in Beijing and was fluent in Mandarin. In the tradition left by the British, Government House was a delight of quiet luxury and character. We had tea, and the governor discussed in great detail and with considerable optimism the future between Hong Kong and China. Unfortunately, this very pleasant and exceedingly intelligent man passed away on a visit to Beijing just three weeks later.

Lord Lawrence Kadoorie called on me. He was then eighty-seven years old, and one of the two legendary Kadoorie brothers. The family came to Hong Kong from Shanghai. They had originated, like most Jews in China, in Baghdad. Their father had established the Kadoorie school in Palestine, in which both Yigal Allon and Yitzhak Rabin studied. Lord Lawrence told me that he had just concluded a deal for the construction of nuclear power plants to provide electricity in China. This agreement had been negotiated in conjunction with President Mitterrand of France and Prime Minister Thatcher of England, for a total of $3 billion.

We sailed around Hong Kong harbor, and then met the Jewish community, numbering about 350, in the Jewish community center. Here we visited the magnificent synagogue, well over one hundred years old, with an Ark of the Law containing the most exquisite Sifrei Torah, a testimony to the history and origins of the community. In talking to the community, I emphasized the importance of *aliyah*—immigration—to Israel as they looked to the future.

From Hong Kong we flew to Singapore. The Malaysians bitterly attacked my visit to Singapore, and Malaysia, Indonesia, and Brunei withdrew their ambassadors in Tel Aviv for consultations for a few days. There were threats in Malaysia to cut off Singapore's water supplies, which originate in Malaysia. Fortunately, thanks to Israel and its military mission in Singapore, the country was well equipped to defend itself and to deter Malaysia.

I was most impressed by Prime Minister Lee Kuan Yew. He was really a father figure in the nation, and I felt that I was sitting in the presence of another Ben-Gurion. We had a long argument about Israel's various policies. He told me at one stage he had been a success because he had observed our mistakes and avoided making them.

My main impression of Singapore was that it was an outstanding example of a well-run country: the extremely efficient civil service, the cleanliness, the traffic solution (a car may not enter the center of Singapore unless it is carrying four people), the effective arrangements for investments, and of course the very successful economy. Some years earlier, Deng Xiou Ping had asked when he visited Singapore, why, when a few Chinese can do what he had seen there, could not the millions in China do the same? That visit had a direct effect on his thinking and on the later formulation of Chinese economic policy.

From Singapore we traveled to Sri Lanka, where, despite the fact that no diplomatic relations existed between the two countries, Israel was quite popular.

A special helicopter flew us from the airport to Colombo, where I was received with full military honors at the residence of President Jayawardene. We drove through the streets of Colombo in the president's Rolls-Royce, suitably adorned with the flag of Israel. The president was eighty years old when I met him, very alert and obviously a clever man. The magnificent Presidential Palace, a veritable museum, displayed portraits of the governors of Ceylon from Portugal, Holland, and Britain respectively, not to mention the various kings and queens of these countries.

Sri Lankans were experiencing an armed uprising organized by the Tamil population in the north of the country. Not only did Israeli-constructed patrol boats guard the Pak Straits against infiltration from South India, but wounded Sri Lankan soldiers were accepted for rehabilitation in our hospitals, and Israeli experts were at the head of an ambitious agricultural rehabilitation program there.

All in all, we were on the road eighteen days. Sometime later, Ariel Sharon, who had become minister of trade and industry, told me that as a result of this trip to the Pacific, Israel's annual trade with this part of the world had increased by over half a billion dollars.

CHAPTER 25

The Presidency—1987

WHEN NEW YORK's Cardinal John J. O'Connor came to Jerusalem in early 1987, Israel's complicated relationship with the Vatican was still one of old-fashioned, inbred religious prejudice. The Vatican had been run by the most conservative elements in the church, and it had never officially recognized Israel. Cardinal O'Connor eventually helped overcome that obstacle, aware as he was of the importance of Jews in American life. However, his superiors were making the church's adaptation to the modern world quite difficult.

Apostolic delegates had been calling on me in my office for quite some time. But now it was proposed that Cardinal O'Connor would visit me only in my home and would see Peres, the foreign minister, only in his apartment. The message was clear: this was a personal visit and the Vatican was allowing no official recognition. I phoned Prime Minister Shamir to tell him that I intended to receive the cardinal in my office, as I received everyone else. (In Beit Hanassi, the presidential residence, as in the White House, the offices were downstairs and Aura and I lived above them. We lived above the shop, so to speak.)

The Vatican had long had diplomatic relations, for instance, with Kuwait, and despite stronger historical links with Judaism than with Islam, the Church seemed intimidated by the Arabs. A Vatican emissary once told me that Pope Paul VI had surrounded himself with conservative and dogmatic advisors. He had great difficulty making up his mind and was very indecisive even on matters of great importance. When dealing with the pope, the emissary always recommended the opposite of what he really wanted because the pope always responded, "That's true, but on the other hand . . ." That way he could then say, "Yes, you're right as always, Your Holiness."

In this particular confrontation, the Vatican backed down. The cardinal arrived at my office, although he was wearing a clerical suit rather than his official robes. I suppose it was an acceptable symbolic compromise for him. No mention was made about our minor conflict. An attractive and wise individual, he wanted to know why I did not treat the Vatican representative to Israel with more respect. Because I got none in return, I replied. When a state dinner was given for Lech Walesa, the Catholic president of Poland, the Vatican representative did not even deign to come. Cardinal O'Connor, clearly aggravated at such behavior, said, "He'll now come to everything you invite him to"—and indeed he did, on direct orders from the Holy See.

This meeting with Cardinal O'Connor and my various sessions with him in New York were stepping-stones on the road to the establishment of formal relations between the Vatican and Israel, which took place in 1994.

THE DESTRUCTIVE CAPABILITIES of our potential enemies were brought home to me in horrific films that showed the effects of chemical warfare in the Iran–Iraq War; Syria, too, now had large quantities of nerve gas at its disposal.

In a strange way, people are resilient and able to cope with the most terrifying possibilities. In Israel, we never really dwell on the dangers of our day-to-day situation. We are constantly reminded, of course, with daily warnings on television to "never ignore an abandoned suitcase." But our awareness is subconscious, like that of a tightrope walker who never allows his fear to become paralyzing.

The man in the street does not spend his day obsessed with nerve gas or Arab threats or even landmark peace talks. He thinks about his paycheck and his kids' education and the quality of his health care. Politicians can become so obsessed with their own importance and their role in world affairs that they forget about the real and pressing needs of ordinary people. But those ordinary people don't forget. Margaret Thatcher told me, "Tell Mr. Peres that elections are not won on foreign policy." Look no further than George Bush's campaign in 1992 to affirm the truth of her insight.

Ordinary people were being affected by the strained relations between Peres and Shamir, and the tension was growing. Shamir had rejected the idea of an international conference that might lead to direct peace talks, even though it had been approved by the cabinet in Begin's day and four times in the Knesset. This was not only a slam at Peres but an attempt to bolster Shamir's standing within the Herut Party. He was definitely looking over his shoulder at the oncoming Sharon and Levy.

Peres favored bringing down the government and going to elections, but I warned him against this; the public would never forgive the party responsible for causing such havoc. Nor was an international peace conference a good electoral issue. Calling for elections at that stage made no political sense, but it emphasized Peres's difficulty in accepting a secondary situation. If he kept it up, he would ruin his outstanding image as prime minister.

A few hours before Shamir returned from a visit to America, Peres left for a meeting with Egyptian president Mubarak. It was very bad behavior on Peres's part. Shamir was prime minister. He was returning from discussions with the president and the secretary of state of the United States. Peres, as second in command, should have been there, and running away to Cairo was a blatant attempt to ignore the fact that Shamir was prime minister. Totally subverting the concept of a unity government, his gesture created the impression of two governments at odds with each other. Peres had had his two years under the agreement and it was Shamir's turn now.

THE DEVELOPING DRUG PROBLEM in Israel was another new threat. Some 30,000 people were addicted to hard drugs; another 200,000 used "recreational" drugs. In other words, 5 percent of our population was taking drugs. I convened a special meeting of representatives of government departments to discuss the problem.

Much of the world's supply of hashish and heroin comes from Lebanon, and we are right in the middle of the Lebanese drug-smuggling route. Drug peddling is a several-billion-dollar-a-year business, with some 40 million "fixes" of heroin alone imported into Israel each year. At the conclusion of this discussion in Beit Hanassi, we decided to appoint an interorganizational steering committee to organize drug-fighting activities throughout the country. As a result of our efforts, the prime minister's office decided to set up a fairly powerful government agency, with an appropriate staff, to coordinate all the efforts in the country to combat this danger.

This was an example of the Israeli system at its best. We had a problem and we came up with a logical solution to try to fix it. There was none of the hysteria that rises in the United States when a problem like drugs is brought up. Israeli society is not puritanical, and we deal with drugs and sexual issues practically and unemotionally. There is no hue and cry about our excellent sex education. Ads for condoms appear on television, and we have a visible and rational AIDS-prevention program. We are quite open and simply use good common sense in dealing with such subjects.

BUT ONE ELEMENT in Israeli life could never be dealt with rationally and logically: terrorism.

In October 1986, an Israeli air force navigator, Ron Arad, was shot down over Sidon, in Lebanon, and taken prisoner by the Amal Shi'ite organization. There was talk of an exchange of prisoners: they would release Arad, we would release terrorists from the Amal group and an additional 400 jailed Palestinians. Arad's family begged me to pardon any terrorists demanded by the Arabs in return for their son. But relatives of the victims of terrorists had recently demanded and received a Superior Court order forbidding such an exchange.

Smadar Haran had lost her husband and her two children in a terrorist attack in Nahariya. To prevent the child she was hiding with from crying out and revealing their location, she covered its mouth and unwittingly suffocated it. The terrorists did not find her, but they shot her husband and drowned him, and smashed her other child's head on a rock. Sentenced to life imprisonment, one of the terrorists was released in a prisoner exchange in 1986; there were now rumors that the other would be included in this new exchange. Haran begged me *not* to grant any new pardons. Shaken by the dilemma and by the moral complexity of the issue, I asked her how she would behave were she in the position of Ron Arad's mother. She refused to buckle, adamant in her opposition to releasing terrorists under any circumstances.

There is no proper answer. Decisions have to be based on principles, without pandering to basic human instincts, however justified they might be in an individual case. Fortunately, the issue never came to me for a decision. Ron Arad, who has been held in prison with no communication with the outside world for over ten years, was handed over to an extremist group and is believed to be either in Iranian custody or held by an Iranian-controlled organization in Lebanon.

—

THE CONTROVERSY SURROUNDING my state visit to Germany did not have quite the same impact as my Shin Bet decision, but nonetheless emotions ran high. Some of those who opposed my trip were quite hypocritical, happy to take money from the Germans for war reparations and happy to do business with them. But they would not accept the president of Israel going there as a symbol. Ben-Gurion said that while we dared not forget, the last testament of those who died in the Holocaust was that the Jewish people be strong; our first priority, therefore, was to keep the Jewish state strong. Since 1965, when Israel and Germany established diplomatic relations, Germany had done more to strengthen Israel than any country other than the United States. I respected any Holocaust survivor who opposed my visit with integrity. But I believed that the moment a German guard of honor presented arms to a president of Israel, as our flag was hoisted to "Hatikvah," would be a moment of victory over the criminals who had perpetrated the Holocaust. Its six million victims would be with me when it happened.

WE STOPPED FIRST in Basel, where at the Casino Hall the first World Zionist Congress had convened ninety years earlier. Theodor Herzl, the founder of the congress, wrote in his diary, "In Basel I founded the Jewish State." Aura and I entered the hall ceremoniously, to the sound of organ music, and as I looked at the familiar and historic stage, I conjured up the photograph of that first congress which is so familiar to all Zionists. I could see them all sitting in their white-tie formality, dressed for what they believed in their hearts was a great occasion. The commanding figure of Herzl was in the middle, others such as Max Nordau and David Wolfsohn were seated. They seemed quite alive to me as I stood in the hall. In a sense they *were* alive. Certainly their ideals had lived on—perhaps the greatest way one can achieve immortality. Herzl's room in the Drei Koenig Hotel was small and modest—apparently he did not have the per diem that today's president of the Zionist organization has. Herzl had posed on the balcony overlooking the Rhine, and I was photographed on it in the same position. The two photographs were published together as "A Dream and Its Realization."

On 6 April 1987, at the Koeln-Bonn airport, the president of the State of Israel stood on German soil for the first time in history. At the official residence of President Richard von Weizsaecker in Bonn, I took the salute of the presidential guard of honor, and "Hatikvah" was played. My decision had been correct. If there could be an hour of triumph for the victims of the Holocaust, it was this.

Over forty years before, German soldiers in a different uniform had stood at attention before me as we interrogated them in the midst of battle. At the frontier barrier in Geilenkirchen, the Nazi emblem lay crushed in the snow near the little customhouse, in the destroyed German towns with white handkerchiefs and sheets hung from every building.

Our first act in my state visit was a trip to Bergen-Belsen, with its mass graves marked by stones inscribed HERE LIE 2,500 VICTIMS. We approached the obelisk memorial, and I slowly mounted the steps and placed a wreath in the form of a blue-and-white Star of David on the Hebrew-inscribed monument. I stood in silence as a *hazan* intoned the memorial for the dead, *El Malei Rahamim,* and then I said kaddish, the prayer for the dead. Immediately after that, I addressed the victims in the graves:

> . . . In this awesome place, the "Vale of Slaughter," and at the outset of my journey on this soil, I leave as a memorial, my brethren and sisters, victims of the Shoah, a stone hewn from the rocks of Jerusalem. On it are carved the words of the Psalmist, as testimony to the decimation of my people: "My pain is with me forever."
>
> I was here for the first time forty-two years ago. Then I was a Jewish soldier from the Land of Israel, participating in the destruction of the Nazi regime, "plucking the brands snatched from the fire." The memory of those shocking sights will never, ever leave me. Now, accompanied by some survivors, I return as president of the State of Israel, the independent Jewish State, by decision of its sovereign government—to bear witness before you that the ultimate destiny of the Jewish people will never be betrayed, and that the Jewish people lives on!
>
> I do not bring forgiveness with me, or forgetfulness. The only ones who can forgive are the dead; the living have no right to forget. Thus "I will surely remember, with a heavy heart."
>
> You bequeathed to our people the precept of life, the imperative of existence; to ensure that never again would the Jew be a helpless victim, and that never again would Holocaust and destruction be the fate of Israel. You bequeathed a testament to build the future of the Jewish people in its homeland, proud and free. A people strong in its moral right and in its moral force no less than in its ability to defend itself; a people that arose from the ashes of the Holocaust to a constructive, creative new life . . .
>
> The grief of your death will eternally be with us. Not as a perpetual

hatred; not as a barren, paralyzing hostility; but as a call to strength and steadfastness. A call to understand the depths to which the human soul can sink, and a call to rise above them. To fulfill with all our very being the antithesis of evil, of wickedness: "Turn away from evil; and do good. Seek peace—and pursue it."

In the name of the Jewish people, and in the name of the State of Israel, I repeat our oath never to forget you, and to be forever faithful to your bequest—the imperative of life.

At the conclusion of my speech, I walked over to a rock that we had brought from the hills of Jerusalem and unveiled it.

Ten survivors of Bergen-Belsen had come from America; I remembered some of them from the months after the liberation. Advancing with linked arms, together they laid a wreath. We walked in total silence to the international memorial. Behind it is a wall with inscriptions in the languages of every country whose citizens were massacred here. Under the Yiddish inscription, I laid a wreath. The ceremony was over.

The state dinner took place at Schloss Augustusburg, one of the ancient, magnificent residences that had survived the war. President of the Federal Republic Richard von Weizsaecker made a speech, again talking about how the German people were responsible for the Holocaust and would continue to bear that responsibility throughout the generations.

The main square in Bonn was packed with cheering crowds waving Israeli flags. I had fought the Nazis not far from there. The mayor talked about Bonn's twin-city arrangement with Tel Aviv and presented me with a set of Beethoven's complete works. For a moment, great art overcame images of brutality.

Chancellor Helmut Kohl is the son of Catholic parents, fearlessly outspoken, very knowledgeable, and exuding common sense. He was not very keen on Shamir but had taken a liking to Peres and proposed that Peres visit him to discuss Peres's idea for a Marshall Plan for the Middle East. Kohl accepted full German responsibility for the crimes committed against the Jewish people, maintaining that the blame would attach to the German people throughout history. Germany owed a debt in light of the past, he said. It could be paid by ensuring Israel's security.

WE FLEW TO WORMS with President Von Weiszacher. Worms had once been an important Jewish center; there was only one Jew left. The community in nearby Mainz looked after the synagogue and cemetery. The synagogue, destroyed by the Nazis, had been restored to its original condition, but the basement *mikve* (ritual bath) was the original, built a thousand years earlier.

Next to the synagogue is the Rashi House, the small chapel where Rashi—Rabbi Shlomo Yitzhaki, possibly the greatest Biblical and Talmudic commentator—lived in the eleventh century. In the so-called Miracle Wall is a dent reputedly made by Rashi's mother. While bearing him, she stepped back to avoid being crushed by soldiers. The wall saved her child, according to tradition.

The Jewish cemetery in Worms is the oldest in Europe, with the earliest identifiable grave dating from 1060. The Maharam, the renowned eleventh-century Rabbi Meir of Rutenberg, who because of his beliefs was tortured to death by the local duke, is also buried there. The Nazis had ordered the destruction of the cemetery. Sometime before that, the head of the SS, Heinrich Himmler, had been taken around Worms by the city's archivist, Dr. Ilter. Himmler showed great interest in the cemetery, so when the order came to destroy it, Ilter went to the local Nazi authorities. Since Himmler had been so taken with it, he said, they should not touch it until they received orders directly from him. They decided not to make an issue, and the cemetery survived intact.

On Kristallnacht in November 1938, when Germany's synagogues were burned by the Nazis, Ilter smuggled the famous illustrated Worms *machzor* (prayer book) out of the synagogue. Kept safe under the flagstones of the cathedral, it is now in the National Library in Jerusalem.

THE PLOETZENSEE PRISON in Berlin houses a bare room with five meat hooks suspended from the ceiling; on a table is a portable guillotine. Those accused of attempting to assassinate Hitler in July 1944 were done to death here, their agony lasting hours as they hung suspended by piano wire. The documentation relating to the executions offers grisly evidence of the Nazis' systematic and orderly cruelty. Incongruous instructions were given to lawyers, ordering them to wear dark suits when attending the executions; detailed bills down to the last pfennig were submitted to the families to cover the cost of the executions.

Our moving and truly historic state visit concluded with a speech broadcast from the Press Club in Berlin, beamed to an audience estimated to be over seventy million.

—

PERES WAS STILL obsessed with the idea of an international conference meant to open up direct negotiations with Jordan, even though most people were less than enthusiastic about the idea. An election, even with no guarantee that he and Labor would win, was a greater priority for him than concentrating on the nation's economic and social situation. He did not look well and was apparently suffering from a strong dose of self-delusion. He was our best prime minister after Ben-Gurion, and it was painful to see him reduced to this internecine struggle.

A government crisis was looming. Peres had reached an understanding with King Hussein in London in the so-called London Document, and U.S. Secretary of State George Shultz passed on to Shamir the details, which in fact had been worked out by Peres with the Jordanians. Peres believed that these developments were a major breakthrough toward peace and that, on this basis, he could run for election. (In effect, this was the last attempt to negotiate a peace without directly involving the Palestinians. I was never convinced that the London Document would enable Israel to bypass negotiations with the PLO, but Peres obviously felt differently. He believed that Shamir sabotaged his dealings with King Hussein and said publicly on many occasions, "You did not want King Hussein; now you will have to deal with Arafat.") I believed that this issue would bring about no change in the balance of power in the Knesset; the problem here was the complete mistrust that characterized relations between Shamir and Peres.

By May, Peres had rushed into a crisis without guaranteeing a majority of the Knesset in favor of elections. He had failed to get support for the international conference and for the dissolution of the Knesset; the government was split and talking in two voices.

Shamir and his supporters were up in arms because Peres had allegedly developed the negotiations with Jordan behind Shamir's back, although Shamir knew all about Peres's meetings. Most Israelis did not want the international conference that Peres was pushing for and were disenchanted with the national unity government.

IN SEPTEMBER, a song called "The Little Journalist" was introduced by one of our leading folk singers, Arik Einstein. To my delight, it tore Israeli journalists to pieces for the cruel manner in which they pry into people's business and destroy their reputations. It was a damning condemnation, and long overdue, of the level to which Israeli journalism had sunk. The reaction was most interesting. Believing in freedom of speech for themselves but not for others, the journalists demanded that the electronic media stop broadcasting the song. To their credit, a few important journalists like Matty Golan in *Ha'aretz* and Tommy Lapid in *Ma'ariv* supported Einstein's song and decried attempts to stifle criticism of the press. It was high time the press began to look at itself. What it would see would not be pretty. The press performs one of the most important functions in a democracy, but like the people and the institutions it criticizes and judges, it must be open to fair criticism, praise, or condemnation.

EARLY IN OCTOBER, Aura and I left on a state visit to Denmark, and on arrival were greeted by Queen Margarethe II and the prince consort, Prince Hendrick. The main theme at the state dinner was the rescue of the whole of Danish Jewry from the Germans by the people of Denmark in 1943. (Some years after that trip, the Danish wife of the PLO representative in Denmark, who had been involved in smuggling arms and explosives to Israel, revealed in court that there had been a plan to assassinate me on the occasion of my visit to the Copenhagen city hall, but according to her, Yasser Arafat vetoed the plan.)

Our state visit included the fishing village of Gilleleje, from which some 20 percent of Denmark's Jews had been clandestinely transferred to Sweden in 1943. In the church, in the attic of which the Jews had been hidden before being smuggled and shipped out of the country, the pastor delivered a moving address about the Holocaust, reading the first three sentences of Genesis in Hebrew. The queen and I went on board one of the small ships which had smuggled the Jews across the sound. They had lain in the storage place for the fish like sardines, and been covered by fish. Gilleleje was a most moving experience, recalling the courage of a nation under tyrannical German occupation.

IN NOVEMBER it was time for my state visit to the United States to mark the fortieth anniversary of Israel, the first by an Israeli president. Peres briefed me before I left. He was very annoyed with Secretary of State George Shultz. Israel and the United States had worked out a plan whereby Reagan and Gorbachev were to invite King Hussein, President Assad, and Shamir to meet with them during their summit conference in Russia. It was presumed that the Arabs could view this meeting as an international conference (which they favored), whereas the Israelis (who did not favor such a conference) could take the opposite view. It was all semantics and politics, of course, but it was valid and probably would have worked. These five leaders would meet and then decide on future bilateral meetings. Shamir had accepted all this in principle, trusting Shultz implicitly not to betray Israel's interests and turn the proposed meeting into an international conference. The Americans would try to add foreign ministers in this initial session, so that Peres could attend, too.

As it turned out, King Hussein rejected the proposal out of hand. As a result, Peres wanted me to urge Reagan and Shultz to keep up the pressure for a wider-ranging international conference. My position, which Peres rejected out of hand, was that Hussein would always find an excuse not to attend any conference, while pretending to be all in favor of one. Peres was unwilling to listen to any other point of view. I suspected that neither the prime minister nor the foreign minister really wanted me to go to the United States. Each had his own international agenda and was obsessed with advancing it. However, my visit was the result of the U.S. government and the U.S. Jewish community's initiative, and our government would have looked petty and unfriendly had it been canceled.

So on 9 November 1987, Aura and I arrived in New York. From Kennedy airport, we were flown on Air Force One, the president's plane, to Andrews Air Force Base near Washington. There we were met by Secretary of State George Shultz, helicoptered to Washington, and driven to the Willard Hotel on Pennsylvania Avenue, near the White House (Blair House was under repair). It was the same hotel Lincoln stayed in the night before he was shot. I decided not to take that as any kind of omen.

In our first talk in Washington, Shultz told me that he was convinced that time was running out for Israel. The demographic clock was ticking, and the situation in the West Bank and Gaza was becoming much more serious. He did not know how long it could go on that way without exploding, and it was essential to proceed as rapidly as possible with the peace process. We were well aware of the danger, which would doubtless be a major factor in the next Israeli election. The issue would have to be dealt with in Israel in a democratic manner—no one person could decide—but we had to do everything possible to move forward.

In discussing the war between Iran and Iraq, Shultz said quite pointedly, "We are not happy with your attitude. Please do not cross us." Israel allegedly was still supplying arms to Iran, flouting U.S. policy to cut off all their sources of weapons.

Israel had been a major supplier of arms to Iran under the shah, but the authorities had clamped down and stopped individual channels of supply. By now, all the holes had been plugged. Shamir and Peres both confirmed to me that Shultz's allegations were baseless.

Shultz and, by implication, Reagan very much resented Israel's attitude. The president was unhappy with remarks attributed to Rabin, in which he favored Iran over Iraq. Rabin denied making this statement, but it was clear that Reagan meant business.

To avoid leaks, I cabled a report by a special route directly to Shamir, Peres, and Rabin. Two days later, details of my talk with Shultz were headlined in *Ha'aretz* and *Davar*. The newspapers had obviously been given the information by one of the recipients. It certainly was not Rabin; it would not have been to his advantage, since he was responsible for the policy Shultz was condemning. An ordinary citizen in Israel can be sent to jail for up to seven years for divulging secret information, but at times apparently government leaders allow themselves to breach security with impunity.

On Tuesday, 10 November, the state visit began officially. The beautiful weather which had greeted us had turned into a continuous downpour, which meant that the full White House ceremony—the honor guard, the pipes and drums, etc.—would have to take place indoors. President and Mrs. Reagan greeted us at 10 A.M. to the sound of a 21-gun salute. We walked through a guard of honor to the largest room in the White House, the East Room, entering to the tune of "Hail to the Chief" and preceded by Marines carrying the American and Israeli flags.

After the two national anthems, President Reagan spoke. To my surprise, though there had been no coordination, we both opened our speeches on the same theme. Reagan noted that the date was the forty-ninth anniversary of the Kristallnacht, the night the Jewish synagogues in Germany were burned down, and also the twelfth anniversary of the Zionism-Racism resolution in the United Nations. He discussed my part in the debate, my role as a kind of conscience for the rest of the world. When it was my turn to speak, I too referred to the historic background of the date on which we were meeting.

In the Oval Room, where we posed for "photo opportunities" for the media, Reagan asked me if some of the TV people were ours. I replied that ours were on strike, and his reaction was "How did you do that?"

One of the reporters asked the president how much further the dollar would drop. His reply was that the dollar had dropped enough (which, incidentally, was not in accord with the U.S. administration's policy). This was headline news throughout the world, served to highlight my visit, and incidentally raised the value of the dollar.

At our meeting in the Cabinet Room, Reagan opened by reading from cards. He talked about the peace process and the current Arab summit conference in Amman. Never deviating from these prepared remarks, he gave the impression that he was not overly aware of what was going on— which was absolutely incorrect. Reagan knew exactly what was going on. He had a reasonable overview of things and was most moved by small events that he had experienced. It was vital to prevent Iran and Khomeini from succeeding, he said; that was the only way to bring stability to the area. The United States did not want to see a victorious or a vanquished state, merely an end to the war.

I felt that there was no appreciation in the world of the danger from Islamic fundamentalism. In the 700-page transcript of the trial of Sadat's assassins, not once was the Egypt–Israel peace treaty mentioned as a reason for his murder, though it was widely believed that the cause of the assassination lay in Islamic fundamentalist beliefs. I wonder if my words were taken to heart. The dangers of religious fundamentalism were a little too remote for Americans at that time. I quoted a Palestinian leader who said to me, "You, sir, have never gone to bed fearing that you would wake up in the morning with a bullet in your head."

After Secretary of Defense Caspar Weinberger reemphasized U.S. policy about stanching the flow of arms to Iran, Shultz talked about the demographic clock ticking in the West Bank and Gaza; in his view it was dangerous and we had no right to sit with folded arms.

After a luncheon at the State Department with top newspaper editors, publishers, columnists, politicians, and leading members of the American Jewish community, I moved on to the U.S. Congress, to address both houses, the first president of the State of Israel ever to do so. I must say, it was one of the most moving moments of my life. I was introduced by the speaker of the house, Jim Wright, then delivered my speech. I talked of the special relationship between our two countries, and what America meant to the ordinary people around the world, whether living in bondage or in freedom. In the course of my remarks, I said:

> . . . I stand here representing a democracy aged forty years, in the heart of the greatest democracy in the world, celebrating the two hundredth anniversary of its Constitution. I represent an ancient people and a young state, but what binds us is not our age but our values. Israel rep-

resents the belief in man and in his right to the basic freedoms and to peace. We believe that the democratic system of government is the only one valid for mankind. In the great trials of our times between totalitarianism and democracy, democracy has invariably emerged triumphant. We believe that man must help his fellow man. We believe that prosperity comes only to those who share it with other fellow men. We . . . see ourselves as a bridge between the developed world and the developing world. Our great ally, the United States, unselfishly supports other nations in the world. So do we, as a matter of national policy, aid, support and share our experience and our progress with developing countries who require it.

. . . We live in a world in which hundreds of millions of people wake up every morning hungry. We live in a world in which the scope of ignorance exceeds that of education, in which helplessness exceeds ability . . . We live in a world of Holy Wars, racism and prejudice, a world which experienced two world wars and has been incapable of putting an end to war . . . It is a world which is in dire need of hope and of aid and which instinctively turns to this country, the powerful keeper of the seal of democracy in the world, a fortress that no upheaval, political or economic, can move from the basis which was created by its Constitution two hundred years ago.

. . . Like you, we have never known one minute without democracy.

. . . Today in the Near East the longest war in this century is being waged—a brutal bloody war motivated by fanatic religious fundamentalism on the one hand, and the ambitions of a megalomaniac dictatorship on the other hand. Tens of thousands of prisoners have been shot out of hand. An unconventional weapon, poison gas, has been introduced, and the world has stood by in mute helplessness. The figure of those killed has gone well beyond the million mark.

. . . How blind were the so-called experts in analyzing the developments in our area . . . Thus again and again the Western world was taken by surprise when the real focus of danger erupted.

. . . Today you know as well as I do that if the Israel–Arab conflict were to be resolved and to disappear, as I certainly hope and pray that it will, all the centers of bloodshed, war, instability and fundamentalistic religious fanaticism from the Atlantic Ocean to the Persian Gulf, would persist. It is against this background that we must view the sole bastion of democracy in our region—Israel.

. . . We have never achieved any advance without negotiations. We have never negotiated with our Arab neighbors without achieving an advance. This is our message . . . we are moving inexorably towards peace . . . That peace will be achieved because we want it and because the people of the Middle East want it . . .

Never in history has a nation given to mankind in so unselfish a manner what the American people have made available to the world. Mindful of the unique role that Providence has bestowed upon you, I stand before this great assembly today, in the year of our fortieth anniversary, and extend to you the greetings of a grateful nation and a staunch ally. God bless America.

I was very moved by the frequent applause and the warmth of the reception accorded me. It was overwhelming.

─────〜∞∞〜─────

The Presidency—1988

ALL IN ALL, 1987 proved to be an eventful year. I would not have minded if 1988 had been a little less eventful.

For the first time, Peres voiced his belief that Israel had to get out of Gaza; the Jordanian police would be far more effective there, he said, than the Israeli forces in maintaining order. His obviously explosive theory sparked immediate and passionate debate. Everyone understood the danger facing our society, but there was absolutely no indication of any consensus as to a solution. One thing was clear—and Peres was more aware of this than anyone: if we did not move forward, the Arabs would soon realize our weakness, our inability ultimately to govern the territories, and would realize their own strength. Israel would then be in serious trouble. Again, in politics perception is crucial—and we could never risk the perception that we were weak, particularly since we were now facing a popular Arab resistance known as the *intifada*, which had broken out in November 1987.

The political clock was also ticking; our presidential elections were approaching. Whether to run for a second term was not an easy decision. Although I found the job fascinating and satisfying, and there seemed to be a reasonable chance I would be reelected, life in a glass cage, continually exposed and bereft of any real private life, gave me pause. I made my decision early, after much consultation in the family circle: I would run again. I felt that I had more to contribute, and in a country whose leaders too often shied away from taking a position on difficult issues, I believed that I could provide a voice for those very issues.

—

PERES WAS ANNOYED by some of my recent remarks. I had said in a speech that both he and Shamir wanted peace, and that their debate was only on the approach, specifically on the issue of the international conference. Peres insisted that Shamir did not want peace, and that I had no right to say otherwise. (I had taken my statement verbatim from Peres's speech to the last UN General Assembly.) Launching into an almost hysterical tirade, Peres ran Shamir down in the most derogatory terms, incensed that I had once said that Peres was not behaving properly toward him. I didn't back down in our meeting. I told him that I was of the opinion that if a person held the position of a prime minister, whatever his views and my opinion of them, he must be treated as prime minister. When Peres was prime minister, he expected to be treated as such by everyone, whether they agreed with him or not. He could not believe differently in regard to Shamir.

That did not end our disagreements, however. Peres was disturbed by a speech I'd made in response to a British minister, David Mellor, who had slammed our policy in Gaza. Israel had been condemned in the United Nations for building housing and taking some 60,000 Palestinians out of refugee camps. I thought this the height of cynicism. On the one hand, Mellor was characterizing the camps in Gaza as "an affront to human dignity"; on the other hand, his ambassador had voted two months earlier to remove the Arabs from the decent housing that Israel had built for them and send them back to those camps.

Peres saw the new situation—the *intifada*—as a national tragedy brought upon us by Shamir and his government. Unfortunately, he forgot that he was part of Shamir's government. The policy in the territories was being carried out by two Labor Party ministers, Rabin as minister of defense, and Bar-Lev as minister of police. Peres was disavowing everyone and everything, even if they were on his side.

I could understand Peres's frustration, but felt that leadership requires a far greater degree of self-control. Peres was too brilliant and too important to the government to appear to be out of control.

As far as the West Bank was concerned, we had to deal with the realities of the day. The Arabs had to be represented in the Jordanian Parliament as Jordanian citizens; the Israelis in the settlements had to be represented in the Knesset. Hussein, we were led to understand, was willing to take over Gaza, provided we cut it off territorially from Sinai, surrounded it, and demilitarized it. The problem was how to open negotiations. I doubted that it would work. As far as involving Jordan in Gaza was concerned, we had missed the boat. It was too late.

YITZHAK RABIN ADDED to the controversy and aggravated the tension by issuing a statement that was totally uncalled for. In response to the violence in the territories, he announced a "no shooting, no killing" policy. Had he stopped there, all would have been fine, but unfortunately he kept going to reveal that we would have a "breaking bones" policy.

Suddenly world attention was focused on Israel's official "beating-up policy." Why couldn't politicians keep quiet? Was it any real surprise to learn that Israeli soldiers would beat up rioters? We were no better or no worse than other countries faced with the same problems. If people were hurt by officials during a riot, attention might be paid—but it would hardly become a media event. And yet, thanks to Rabin's statement, that is exactly what was happening. Rabin's intentions were good, to avoid any more killing, but his presentation was unfortunate.

The Americans concluded that something had to be done in light of developments in the territories. They could not use the word "autonomy," because it was anathema to King Hussein. However, they wanted to turn the process from a procedural one (international conferences, direct negotiations) into a substantive one, by introducing an expanding process of autonomy without actually calling it that. They would talk about "accelerated interim arrangements" and would considerably advance the time frame arranged at Camp David; the discussions on a solution for the territories would be moved up from three years ahead to the current year. Suddenly, negotiations were set for December 1988. George Shultz, a committed friend of Israel, foresaw us facing a much more difficult situation with the new Bush administration; it would be in our interest, he said, to open negotiations with the Arabs on the basis of guidelines agreed upon under the Reagan administration.

Shamir had gone along with the general idea, although he was later attacked in the cabinet by—who else?—Sharon and Levy, who said they would agree to autonomy only as it had been laid down in the Camp David agreements. Labor agreed to back the Shultz proposal, although Peres was still arguing for the inclusion of an international conference. (Shultz, incidentally, admitted that he was totally against an international conference.) The next stage would be to sound out King Hussein. If his reply was positive, Shultz would follow up with a visit to the Middle East in March 1988.

Shamir and Peres were evidently incapable of getting their act together; their differences were irreconcilable. The issue was no longer substantive but, rather, a complete collapse of personal trust. There was no
need to antagonize Secretary of State Shultz; as usual, the Arabs would
get Shamir off the hook. The PLO had already issued instructions
forbidding the Palestinians to meet with Shultz. King Hussein suddenly
remembered that he had an urgent appointment with a dentist in
London—exactly coinciding with Shultz's visit, which was on the direct instruction of President Reagan and with the complete support of
Congress.

ON 23 FEBRUARY 1988, the Knesset officially voted me in for a second
term. I was endorsed by the entire coalition, indeed, by 116 members out
of 120, a historic first in Israel.

The "Who is a Jew" amendment would have given a total monopoly
on Jewish life to the Orthodox in Israel and created a worldwide schism,
particularly in the United States, where they are outnumbered by Reform
and Conservative Jews. In January 1988 it was defeated in the Knesset,
along with a bill granting pardon to all members of the Jewish underground. Designed to bypass the sole discretion of the president, the latter
bill was a threat to our democracy, and the danger inherent in it influenced my policy in respect of the underground.

IN FEBRUARY 1988 the Palestinian Arabs were living under a reign of terror. They wanted to meet with Shultz, but the PLO would not allow it
for fear they would lose their leadership to a younger, homegrown group
that was emerging in the territories. While Shultz had made good
progress on the road to autonomy, he was engaged in a war of semantics.
I did not see him making any major advance unless he could sit down
with some of the Palestinians, and to do that he had to walk a linguistic
tightrope. He could not appear weak with the Arabs, yet he could not offend them. He could not seem too devoted to Israel, yet he had to make it
clear that Israel had total U.S. backing. There seemed to be a growing gap
between Arab leadership in the territories and the Arab governments.
Arab leaders did not want a solution; they wanted victory. There was no
chance of a solution then because there was nobody rational to talk to.
While that had generally been true in the past, there had always been one

exception—President Sadat. Unfortunately, there were no Sadats around at that time.

Shultz met with King Hussein in London and then rendezvoused with President Reagan in Brussels. He then returned to Israel to meet with Shamir and Peres, before going to Egypt and Damascus. His amended proposal was now that the key ministers of Israel and Jordan would meet with U.S. representatives in an initial conference in April. Also attending that conference would be delegations from Egypt, Syria, Jordan (including Palestinian representatives), Lebanon, Israel, the United States, and the Soviet Union. This conference would be followed by negotiations for an "interim settlement"—autonomy. The goal for a final settlement was December 1988.

The international opening conference posed a major political problem for Shamir because of opposition within his own party. He had little time to solve that problem because he was due to visit the United States ten days after Shultz's visit, and Shultz expected him to give an answer to President Reagan. Shamir's staff had put him on the spot by arranging such a meeting in Washington. They had not, of course, expected these latest developments, but there was no way to back out now.

The nation was confused and torn, as was the government. This was an emotional issue, and there were many voices—most of them passionately convinced their point of view was the only correct one.

I saw nothing wrong in accepting the Shultz proposal; it was a question, once again, of perception over reality. The Palestinians would reject the Shultz initiative if Israel accepted it. But if that happened, Israel would not appear as the stumbling block on the way to peace. I recommended that Shamir behave as Begin did at the time of Camp David: he wrote a letter to President Carter setting out his views, in effect rejecting any ideas that had been put forward, for instance, on Jerusalem, and reserving his right to present his own approach in future negotiations. In this case, I suggested to Shamir that he write a letter to Shultz referring to each of the proposals and setting out his understanding of them—for instance, that the international conference would have no executive powers and that each successive phase in the negotiations would not begin until the previous phase had been agreed to and completed. Shamir said he would consider this possibility at the meeting in Washington, but he was not prepared to accept it at this stage.

It was suggested that I try to get Shamir and Peres on the same track, but I saw no point to such an effort. The depth of their animosity would preclude any positive results. Nevertheless, personal likes or dislikes had no place in this situation. The leaders of Israel's two biggest parties had to come and could come to some agreement on such major issues as the geographical alignment of Jerusalem, the rejection of a withdrawal to the 1967 lines, the idea of a Palestinian state, and the River Jordan as Israel's defense border. Peres, however, was too bitter about the Likud's campaign against him to meet with Shamir. There were as many as fourteen vicious attacks on him per day, and they were clearly orchestrated. Peres maintained that we lost ground in negotiations because the Likud and Shamir had sabotaged his agreement with King Hussein in the London Document. Unfortunately, the manner in which the London Document had been organized—Shamir said that Peres had done it behind his back—created great antagonism on Shamir's part. Peres was right, but that didn't make his stubbornness any less frustrating.

Shamir left for Washington, where Shultz apparently failed to move him on the issue of the international conference. President Reagan issued a veiled threat, noting that anyone who turned down Shultz's proposal—he added quickly that Shamir had not done so—would have to answer to his people and to the future for having missed an opportunity for peace. This was about as tough a threat as Israel had received for some time, and it did not go unnoticed. Nonetheless, Shamir remained adamant and spoke out against the conference. Clearly, he was paying less attention to what he heard in America and was already running his election campaign in Israel.

Shamir comported himself very well in Washington and was popular with the American public. He managed to convince Reagan about the futility of holding a nonbinding international conference, but of course Reagan would not say anything to that effect, since he was being totally directed by the State Department on this issue.

Contrary to his expectations, Shamir did not feel pressured by the Americans. He put his case over fairly effectively in the media and before American Jewry, whose support at rallies in his honor impressed and encouraged him. Finding a much more pro-Israel atmosphere in Congress than he had expected, he had no intention of committing himself and risking an antagonistic response. He preferred to pass the ball to the Arabs, particularly to King Hussein.

Passover arrived. Every year we had maintained an empty chair at the seder dinner for Ida Nudel, a prominent Jewish "refusenik" who was denied permission to leave Russia for many years. This year, Passover 1988, Ida Nudel occupied her chair at our seder. What a triumph for hope, faith, and courage! This time we left an empty chair for Yuli Kosharovsky, another refusenik who had waited over twenty years for an exit visa. I called him in Moscow and told him that next year he would occupy the chair. He did. In 1996 his name was put forward as Israel's ambassador to Russia.

METULLA, AT THE TIP of the panhandle of northern Galilee, was founded by Baron Edmond de Rothschild and some fifty intrepid settlers in 1894. Surrounded on three sides by Lebanese territory, it was a prosperous village with some 3,000 inhabitants and was popular with summer tourists. After World War I, it was administered by the French in Lebanon and in 1924 it was returned to the British in Palestine. Much of the land of the early settlers was in what is today Lebanon. The village was the main target for Katyusha rockets when the PLO took over in south Lebanon, until the Israeli incursion drove them back in 1982. Metulla's kindergartens and schools stand only a few yards from the Lebanese border; new housing was built with backyards abutting the border fence. Well run and successful, Metulla was as inspiring a lesson for Israel as one could envision.

The border is known as "the good fence." Thousands of Lebanese citizens come into Israel every morning and leave every afternoon. Most of them come to work, some to receive medical treatment. General Antoine Lahad, a Christian formerly of the Lebanese army, is commander of the South Lebanese army, created by Israel in the "security zone" north of the border. His troops were becoming an effective fighting force, their officers and men trained by the Israel Defense Forces. The security zone has Christian, Moslem, and Druze populations, each of which is represented in the South Lebanese army. Strangely enough, Lebanon's civil administration in Beirut was operating even in south Lebanon, and Lahad had apparently unofficial contact with Beirut. There is a small port on the Israeli border at Nakoura, the headquarters of the United Nations forces in Lebanon, with direct contact by sea to Beirut. It was a typical Middle Eastern situation: governments at war as deadly enemies, with daily contact between citizens who dealt with each other as neighbors.

ON MONDAY, 9 MAY, I was sworn in for my second term at 7:27 P.M., the exact moment of the setting of the sun. Again, the mounted escort of police led Aura and myself to the Knesset. Again I entered into the hall with two Yemenite shofars being sounded. As the whole House stood, I raised my right hand, put my left hand on the family Bible, and took the oath of president. In the course of my remarks, I said:

> . . . As I view the state of Israel today, I cannot but be moved by and proud of everything we have accomplished in the forty years of the existence of the state. In every corner of the country, I find vitality and progress. The cultural revolution taking place in our midst comes to uplifting expression in the community centers, in music, in dance, in the theater, in literature and art, in science and medicine, in all aspects of the academic world, in the study of Torah and of Judaism.
>
> . . . However, with all the magnificence of the achievements and the brilliant success of the Zionist movement, it is impossible to ignore the clouds and the dark shadows which threaten us. . . . This malaise has many faces, beginning with irresponsible interparty incitement, a poisoned atmosphere and a tendency to demonize one's political opponent. This, in addition to outbreaks of racism, and the encouragement of hatred between Jew and Jew, and Jew and Arab. We are witness to violence in industrial relations and the conduct of industrial struggle on the back of the ordinary citizen, and even of the sick, wounded, disabled and old. We are witness to an unfair approach as far as the dignity of the individual is concerned, and a lack of sensitivity in regard to the sanctity of a citizen's good name.
>
> . . . Above all, we must protect the democratic nature of our country, for without a democratic society based on the will of the people, the State of Israel will have no future.
>
> . . . Israel has always proposed dialogue, free negotiations, peace talks. The Arabs of Israel are an element which could exercise a positive influence. This, on condition that they assume an active and moderating role as loyal citizens of the State of Israel and a determination to advance the cause of understanding and peace between nations, and not the reverse.
>
> . . . On the other hand, I fear that at times we do not have the inherent feeling of the basic national justice of our cause, a cause which represents the realization of the Zionist dream and the establishment of the State. Of course, we have made mistakes, and self-criticism is healthy and justified. But such criticism must strengthen the basis of our cause and not weaken it. The self-flagellation and a tendency to a guilt complex on the part of parts of Israeli society must of necessity create divisions in the basic feeling of the justice of our cause in the people. Regretfully, there seem to be no such doubts in the camp of our enemies. Everything on their side is black-and-white, simple and clear.

. . . We must appreciate the nature of the world in which we live, and particularly of our region. We dare not despair of peace. We dare not change our character, but we must appreciate that a very long road to peace faces us. There are no magic formulae to resolve the conflict, and a full acceptance of Israel in our region is as yet far away. Peace is our aim and our dream, but it is not necessarily waiting for us around the corner.

. . . Our desire for negotiations and peace with our neighbors is not because justice is with them more than with us. On the contrary, the rise of the State of Israel represented a rectification of an historic wrong lasting thousands of years. Our desire for peace is because we have always been a people of peace, and because of our awareness of the fact that the problems between us and between our neighbors can only be resolved by peaceful means.

Several weeks afterward came the first great news of my new term: in the midst of a luncheon in honor of the president of the German Bundestag and his wife, Aura and I were notified that our first grandson, Noam, had been born to Michal and Bouji, our youngest son. We cut the lunch short and rushed down to the hospital in Tel Aviv, making our first acquaintance with the new arrival, whom we unanimously decided was both handsome and brilliant.

IN THE OPENING shot of the upcoming election campaign, Ariel Sharon, the minister of industry and trade, publicly attacked Yitzhak Rabin, the minister of defense, for failing to bring about law and order in the territories. Politically, it was a very smart move. Rabin had become a major asset for Labor. He had emerged as a rational and capable leader. Peres was threatened by Rabin's rise; he knew there was a real threat that Rabin could replace him as party leader—and thus become prime minister-to-be. In his attack, Sharon was, in fact, killing two birds with one stone. He was not only focusing attention on Rabin, he was also undermining Shamir, who had given his unequivocal support to Rabin's policies in the territories.

Sharon had his own very specific idea on how to handle the territories. His policy was to divide and rule, and it was possible to do that within the Arab population. He told me that many Arabs were giving support to his idea of Palestinizing Jordan.

Around this time, the parties had their internal elections to nominate their lists for the Knesset. There were no real surprises for Labor, other

than the fact that Abba Eban did not make the list. It was Labor's loss
—they needed my brilliant brother-in-law far more than he needed
them—but it made me quite sad. I didn't like the fact that there was no
room in the political system for men like Abba Eban.

On the Herut List, David Levy emerged in first place, Sharon in second, and Moshe Arens in third. The leader of the party remained Shamir,
and while there was no indication who would take over after he left the
post, the results did give Levy a clear lead.

Levy was a good, articulate, smart politician. He tended toward pom-
posity and self-importance. He'd come from Morocco as a boy; when he
was a little older he worked as a bricklayer. He has always wanted to be
the head of the Likud. It doesn't appear he'll ever succeed, but he will become a respected elder statesman.

Other Likud members also made a name for themselves. Binyamin
"Bibi" Netanyahu achieved fifth place, and Benny Begin, Menachem
Begin's son, came in seventh. Labor had a more attractive list, mostly because Herut had no Druze or Arab representatives, few women, and no
new faces from the development towns. I was never certain exactly how
to evaluate such results. I had never been sure that women vote for
women, Moroccans for Moroccans, or Ashkenazis for Ashkenazis. Shamir's team had a clear majority in the Knesset Likud caucus, but it looked
as though that party caucus would be split by the three contenders for
leadership succession—Levy, Sharon, and Arens.

In July 1988, King Hussein of Jordan dramatically announced the severing of all administrative and legal links with the West Bank. He was thus
handing the baby back to the PLO and Israel. The Jordanian parliament
was dissolved, all West Bank representatives were removed, and many of
the citizens of the West Bank were no longer full Jordanian citizens. The
king was rightly convinced that the *intifada* would spill over into his
country and endanger his regime. Indeed, he went out of his way in a press
conference to deny that Jordan is Palestine, and that Palestinians constituted the majority in Jordan, a fact which, incidentally, was inaccurate.

There was considerable speculation about what steps would now be
taken by the PLO. In the background, for the first time voices were being
heard from the PLO calling for some sort of compromise. Necessity and
an all-too-human weariness of violence was causing reason to creep in to
a heretofore unreasonable organization. This development became the
subject of much debate in Israel's pre-election campaign.

Our minister of health, Shoshana Arbeli-Almoslino, called on me as leader of a delegation of the heads of the various hospitals in the country. They described the impossible situation that had been reached in the health services, whereby they were plagued by constant strikes in the hospitals and throughout the system.

Accordingly, at a dinner given by the Weizmann Institute of Science, I called for the establishment of a government commission of inquiry into the health services. The situation, I warned, was impossible. It had gone too far and had lasted too long. That night, the prime minister announced that he accepted my proposal, as did the minister of health. The chief justice appointed an outstanding commission headed by Supreme Court Justice Shoshana Netanyahu, which included the leading authorities on the subject in the country. This was to be the beginning of a process which could revolutionize our health services.

ON 17 OCTOBER Aura and I left on an official visit to France. We crossed the Champs-Elysées in the cavalry-led procession to the Marigny Palace, where we were accommodated. We looked up this magnificent boulevard, possibly one of the most beautiful in the world, lined by hundreds of French and Israeli flags stretching right up to the Arc de Triomphe. I was very moved. President Mitterrand noticed this, and he asked me, "What are you thinking about?" I answered, "I am thinking of the Nazi flags that adorned the Champs-Elysées forty-eight years ago, when the German army marched down the boulevard." He nodded and said, "I understand you." As we passed the crowds lining the route I saw many in the crowd, obviously Jews, weeping openly. The Marigny Palace was grand and impressive, although Napoleon's bed, in which I slept, was somewhat short. Aura was more comfortable in Marie Antoinette's bed.

In his spacious and elegant private office at the Elysée Palace, Mitterrand told me of a long discussion he had had with Gorbachev about the Middle East. Gorbachev's first priority in Mitterrand's view was to get out of Afghanistan. He also wished to change his country's approach to Israel, and had decided that from now on he would coordinate with Europe and with the United States. Mitterrand was very impressed with Gorbachev. He expressed his deep concern about the demographic problem we were facing with our Arab neighbors. Our state dinner at the Elysée Palace in Paris was entirely kosher. For a week the chief rabbinate had koshered the plates, and special Jewish waiters wearing yarmulkes accompanied us everywhere, pouring wine in accordance with Jewish tradition.

In the Hôtel de Ville, Aura and I were greeted by Jacques Chirac, the mayor of Paris, and his wife. Over one thousand people were seated in the magnificent Salle des Fêtes, a medieval-style hall with banners and coats of arms hanging from the ceiling, very like the banners hanging in Gothic cathedrals. In my speech I relived my childhood and talked about the attachment of my family to Paris. I recalled my late grandfather, who had officiated as a rabbi in his synagogue on the rue Pavée, and the sounds and smells and memories of the city.

Our trip to Normandy included Asnelles, where a Nazi artillery bunker was preserved as a monument to the last position on the coast to be reduced on D Day. On the beach and in the sea could be seen the remains of the famous Mulberry Port, which was towed from Britain to Normandy. I laid a wreath, the Last Post was sounded, and we stood for a minute of silence. Three British generals who had crossed the Channel for this occasion attended the ceremony. One of them had commanded the unit of the 147th Regiment of the Essex Yeomanry that had taken this position on June 6, 1944.

At Arromanches, where I landed in the Allied invasion in 1944, we visited the museum of the invasion. We also visited the Museum for Peace in Caen, where I planted a cypress tree which we had brought with us from Jerusalem. Back in Paris, we visited my grandfather's synagogue and his home at 29 rue des Francs-Bourgeois, where we stayed when I was a boy. After nearly sixty years, it had not changed. There was the balcony from which Yaacov and I used to drop pebbles, taking turns trying to hit a table in the outdoor café below. On one occasion a pebble hit the bald pate of a gentleman who happened to be a *policier*, and there was hell to pay. Giving full vent to his colorful vocabulary, he was ready to arrest us, and it cost my grandfather several hundred francs to placate him. But instead of punishing us, my father and my grandfather realized what a scare we had had. In an act of real understanding, they took us to the Bois de Boulogne to ride ponies.

I have a mixed recollection of Paris. My indelible images are of an eight-year-old boy riding a pony in the park and of a young soldier standing on the Champs-Elysées watching Churchill, De Gaulle, and Eden drive past in a victory parade on Armistice Day, 1944. To these memories are now added the moving friendship of the president of the Senate, Alain Poher, a visit to the expanded Louvre Museum accompanied by the world-famous architect I. M. Pei, who designed the addition, and a trip to the Holocaust Memorial.

—

Rabbi Gamliel was well into his eighties in the autumn of 1988. An advisor to the imam of Yemen, he had come to Israel forty years earlier, having spirited out of Yemen the archives relating to the Jewish community. His mother-in-law was now 118 years old and still going strong. It is a Jewish custom to tell people that you wish they'll live to be as old as Moses was when he passed away. This presented a slight problem of protocol when I paid Gamliel a visit. How could I avoid being rude by wishing the elderly woman a long life—"till 120"? Instead of that blessing, the rabbi suggested, I should substitute "until the arrival of the Messiah."

In Israel, election day is a national holiday, which is economically wasteful and a complete anomaly. In general, our election laws are almost as absurd as our electoral system. Candidates for the Knesset, including the heads of government, cannot appear on television for a month before the elections; sailors may vote abroad, but consuls general who provide them with ballot boxes cannot; prisoners in jail, even convicted murderers, have a vote; but in 1988 neither Israeli ambassadors nor members of the foreign service could vote (this piece of useless bureaucracy was later changed).

The results of the 1988 election were a disappointment because they were so inconclusive. The Likud received forty seats in the Knesset, Labor received thirty-nine, and Shas emerged as the third-largest party, with six seats. The right wing—the Likud together with the religious parties—had gained sixty-five seats; the left wing, including the Arabs, took fifty-five. Recrimination in the Labor camp over the defeat was directed against Peres, as this was his third defeat at the polls, and he was attacked for letting a personality cult dominate the campaign. The main domestic issues had been largely ignored, and Peres's advocacy of an international conference was not popular. Despite numerous calls for his head, no alternative leadership was available; no one had yet emerged with the proper stature. The Israeli Arabs had been their own greatest enemies. Because of an internecine struggle, they refused to sign a single surplus-votes agreement, thereby losing over 30,000 Arab votes and a historic opportunity to wield real political power.

The ramifications of this election were disturbing. In the Knesset, one member in five was either opposed to Zionism or was a non-Zionist (strictly Orthodox and Arabs). And the Moledet Party, under Rehavam Zeevi, advocated the "transfer" of the Arabs out of Israel.

ONCE AGAIN, a member of the Knesset had the task of forming a government. Naturally, the Likud proposed Shamir as prime minister. I had been inundated with letters, cables, and phone calls, demanding a national unity government; if Likud and Labor joined, they would neutralize the increasingly powerful non-Zionist elements. The Labor group proposed Peres, as was to be expected. My consultations were serving only to expose the utter inadequacy of the Israeli electoral system.

One of the most sensible presentations was given by the Shinui Party, led by Amnon Rubinstein. After opting for a government led by Peres, he recommended that the two major parties form a national government without any of the small parties—including his own. This would avoid the blackmail of the religious parties, but unfortunately the two major parties would not accept this coalition. Each was busily trying to win over the religious parties with one inducement or another. Labor's agreement to give the Aguda Party the "Who is a Jew" legislation could cause an irreparable split in world Jewry—and this, after the party had consistently voted against this legislation. The Likud, trying to keep up, would offer the Aguda the same.

Rabin, anxious that a broad government be formed, was prepared to serve as minister of defense under Shamir. In his view, the Likud would give Labor the treasury for Peres, while they retained the Foreign Ministry and the premiership for themselves.

The Orthodox Aguda representatives, considering themselves the guardians of the Torah and Jewish ethics, demanded the release of the Jewish underground prisoners. My education, based on the Ten Commandments, taught me that "Thou shalt not kill." As deplorable as many of our prison conditions were, not once since I had become president had a rabbi come forth to plead for prisoners. Why, I asked, was the Aguda distinguishing between people of the same blood? I had eased up on those prisoners who honestly repented and would continue to. But without sincere repentance there would be no clemency. I turned down their requests.

On 14 November, I entrusted the formation of a government to Shamir. Peres was understandably very down but understood that I had no choice.

Ours was not the only government in flux. Secretary of State George

Shultz, one of Israel's dearest friends, was about to be replaced by James Baker. There was some concern about this in Israel. We had a wonderful relationship with Reagan and Shultz; Baker was somewhat of a cold fish and a WASP. We had many questions about the newly elected president, too. Bush was on record as saying that Jewish settlements must stop. His chief of staff, John Sununu, was of Lebanese descent and not at all well disposed toward Israel. It looked as if we might have problems on an international plane, too: Bush and Margaret Thatcher were talking about a move forward with the PLO.

Not only were we having problems with the American government, we were having serious problems with American Jews. The General Assembly of the Jewish Federations in the United States and Canada was in total revolt against the "Who is a Jew" legislation, and an American delegation was coming to Israel to protest. We could hardly afford a major split with American Jewry. Meanwhile, a large delegation representing British Jews arrived in Israel. World Jewry was up in arms about this new legislation.

Israelis were disgusted with the political wheeling and dealing, the open blackmail, and the ugly image they created. Our leaders, far from helping us out of the morass, were pushing us straight in. I was constitutionally powerless to avert the rift with American Jewry, to change the political system, and to stem the loss of confidence in politics. But my public influence and backroom expertise made me far from helpless.

Unsuccessful in forming a government, Shamir received a final twenty-one-day extension.

I hoped to create an atmosphere leading to a resolution of the national crisis. The Israeli people felt disgraced by what was going on in the government. Major problems were being ignored because of unseemly political negotiations. Other countries set up a stable government immediately after elections, and France achieved stability after changing its system. The will of the people called for a broad government; Shamir and both major parties had to renew peace negotiations. There had to be a better way to do things.

A week after a speech by me on the subject, the Labor Party agreed to negotiate for a broad government and, toward the end of December, agreement was reached. Labor got most of what it wanted. Labor and the Likud would have the same number of ministers. Peres was not only minister of finance, but Labor would appoint the chairman of the finance committee of the Knesset. The two parties would advance the peace process, and if the government fell, no alternative government would be formed; the Knesset would be dissolved and the country would go to elections. This was to remove the Likud's fear that Peres would negotiate with the extreme Orthodox parties behind the party's back.

The religious parties cried foul and called Shamir a traitor and a liar—the first time I heard them say "traitor" in conjunction with our prime minister. Unfortunately, it was not the last.

Shamir was frightened by the ultimatums of the right-wing parties and by the extreme demands of the religious parties. There had been no alternative, he said, and no chance to form a satisfactory narrow government. Skipping over several ministers, he added three young faces, Dan Meridor as minister of justice, Ronni Milo as minister of police, and ultimately mayor of Tel Aviv, and Ehud Olmert as minister of health, and ultimately mayor of Jerusalem, in a courageous move to shake up the cabinet and advance a new and promising generation.

I hoped such courage would translate into the real world—or as real as Israeli politics ever gets.

The Presidency—1989

ISRAEL IS BASICALLY a very civilized society; as a people and a government we tend to be both forgiving and rational. We live in a welfare society. Criminals are given every opportunity for rehabilitation. We absorb immigrants at a rate surpassed by few other countries, and they become Israelis, regardless of color or social status.

Israel tends to be a military society more from need than desire, but it is certainly not a militaristic society. All Israeli men enter the army at the age of eighteen. Women are required to serve too, although for religious reasons they can opt for national service such as teaching, police work, or social work. Men serve for three years and women for two, with changes in the period of service in the offing. Women are not required to serve if they have children. Soldiers and officers can join our academic reserve and complete their education while receiving professional training and fulfilling their service requirements. We try to be rational, yet we must be realistic. Above all, we must survive.

The *intifada* pushed our society to the brink of cruelty. Fear does that, and the *intifada* made many fearful.

The word means "shaking up" in Arabic. It was first used, in reference to the territories, in December 1987. The Palestinians wanted to shake things up, to move out of the lethargy that came with passive acceptance of their occupation. The *intifada* began in the streets, not as something stirred up and created by the PLO. Young Palestinians formed gangs and started throwing rocks at Israeli soldiers, believing that they would not be countered with a barrage of bullets. The rock throwing quickly got out of hand, and our soldiers began retaliating with rubber bullets and tear gas.

When an Israeli truck careened out of control in the Gaza Strip and crashed into a car, killing four Palestinians, wild rumors spread that it was a plot to kill Arabs. Rioting began, even as Israel denied any intent to harm. Great cruelty developed and Palestinians killed Palestinians as an excuse to settle any and all accounts. If you called *anyone* an Israeli sympathizer, you could literally get away with murder. During the *intifada*, 40 percent of the Palestinians murdered in the territories were killed by Israeli soldiers; the others were killed by their fellow Palestinians.

We tried to curtail the violence and did cut down on the casualties, but the situation had become intolerable. Without a solution to the problem, the Middle East was going to explode.

Amid all this tumult, something happened that indicates what Israel is all about. Even when surrounded by cruelty, our people will not succumb and lose their humanitarian instincts. At the end of 1988, Soviet Armenia was hit by a fearful earthquake that caused the deaths of an estimated 50,000 people and injured hundreds of thousands of others. Cities were completely destroyed and razed. Israel immediately sent two rescue teams, led by the chief of Haga (civil defense), that saved many people buried for days under the ruins. A field hospital and operating room were set up in subzero temperatures and brutal weather. The Russians would never have been able to mobilize such an efficient operation on their own. Yet there was controversy over this mission. Why should we be so humane to a country that had acted so inhumanely toward Israel? Because we felt that we owed it to other people not to behave toward them as they had behaved toward us. The two rescue teams, despite their different ethnic backgrounds and approaches to religion, created something important and wonderful. Why could this not rub off on our leaders and politicians?

TOWARD THE END of 1988, Emperor Hirohito of Japan was in very poor health and not expected to live much longer. A state funeral seemed imminent.

Within the Israeli government, there were those who felt that we should not honor the memory of an emperor who had been an ally of Germany in World War II. But the Japanese did not adopt an anti-Jewish position in the war. Indeed, they were effective in saving the lives of thousands of European Jews as a matter of policy. To escape the Nazis, Jews crossed into Japan through Russia; my father had negotiated with the Russians to allow them passage.

The funeral was attended by 164 delegations, and the pomp and circumstance was overwhelming. Politics is often encumbered by a powerful veneer of display, but make no mistake, that's not all there is to it. In this case, a political agenda drove everything forward. The new emperor, Akihito, responded favorably to our desire to become involved with Japan on a technological basis. In perfect English, the empress expressed their gratitude for my decision to attend the funeral.

Among the national leaders in Tokyo was King Juan Carlos of Spain. Tall, pleasant, and very well spoken, he puts one immediately at ease and is both intelligent and sophisticated, as well as a superb conversationalist. His close friend King Hussein really wanted peace, he said—I was certainly glad to hear that. But the main reason for our meeting was the upcoming 500th anniversary in 1992 of the expulsion of the Jews from Spain. One of the king's titles was king of Jerusalem, making it even more important that he come to Jerusalem. It would be unpardonable to allow this period to go by without ensuring a historic reconciliation.

President Mubarak of Egypt, who was attended by an entourage of 180 people, is a hail-fellow-well-met, a sort of diamond in the rough. He was very favorably impressed by Moshe Arens, our foreign minister, and was willing to guarantee that an international conference would be only a formality—one or two meetings—with no powers of decision, and would lead to direct talks and serious negotiations.

We had a long heart-to-heart exchange of views. How would the Arabs in the territories react to Rabin's proposal, he wondered. Those living in the territories were hesitant to speak their mind, I explained, for fear of Arab terrorist action against them; Arafat and his people were preventing any sort of local leadership from emerging. Mubarak's insight was that if local leaders were to emerge, we should not kill them with kindness. By embracing them publicly and running after them, as we were doing with Faisal Husseini, the Palestinian leader from Jerusalem, it only made them appear soft and too pro-Israel. Mubarak definitely understood the political and psychological games one had to play.

I replied that terrorist outbreaks, carried out with Arafat's approval, made it impossible for us to deal with him. Conversely, if these attacks were being carried out against his wishes, what point was there in talking to somebody who did not control his own organization?

Mubarak felt that Arafat was the boss and still had maximum control in the organization. We had to deal with him; he was the most reasonable man of power in the PLO. Many other factions were led by what President Mubarak characterized as "murderers and sons of whores," who were sabotaging him. One could still talk to Arafat, and if anything were to happen to him, there would be chaos. "All of us, including you, will regret his departure," Mubarak added. The Palestinians' claim to "the right of return" was a nonexistent problem: the bulk of the Palestinian diaspora would *not* wish to return.

Both Mubarak and Hussein had problems with the Islamic fundamentalists and the restraints that they put on the development of our bilateral relations. Mubarak explained in reply to a question of mine that he did not invite Shamir for a meeting because of Arab public opinion. He was awaiting a good opportunity or a specific reason. Moreover, after a good exchange of views, our prime minister tended to issue statements that caused Egypt embarrassment—I couldn't disagree with that—even though Mubarak's statements occasionally embarrassed *us*. He agreed with me and declared that he had decided not to issue any more. Like Sadat, who understood the importance of talking to the people of Israel directly, Mubarak was happy to be interviewed on Israeli television.

Mubarak had a point about Arafat. The great irony is that Israel has come to rely on his importance and centrality in the peace process. Though the uneasiest of bedfellows for Israel, bedfellow he is. He led the Fatah, a major terrorist organization. He proved himself to the Palestinians during their most difficult period, after they were driven out of the state-within-a-state they had established in Lebanon. Arafat led them to Tunis, where he established a government-in-exile.

I had said all along that the Arabs would recognize Israel only when it became apparent that they had to. For Arafat, that time came when all other options were removed. He needed money; he needed a new way to keep the PLO viable. To his absolute credit, he recognized that the time had come and had the strength to act.

At the American embassy in Tokyo, I met with President Bush, who greeted me as an old acquaintance. Secretary of State James Baker, General Scowcroft, the head of the National Security Council, and White House Chief of Staff John Sununu were also present at this session.

Bush supported my approach to curtailing the Islamic fundamentalists' activities by boycotting any country that showed support for them—I believed in unequivocal war with no mercy. A peace plan *had* to be a long-drawn-out process, and there was no way to do it quickly. It was all so intricately political, psychological, and emotional. There was much to commend in Rabin's peace plan. The Palestinians were weary of the continuing struggle, and terrorism occupied the overwhelming position in the Palestinian consciousness.

I was not overly happy with the atmosphere. Baker and Bush both seemed knowledgeable and committed, and I felt an unexpected surge of optimism—perhaps we were moving in the right direction, after all. But they seemed to lean toward the PLO on certain points and too pro-Arab for my liking.

EMPEROR HIROHITO'S FUNERAL ceremonies lasted for thirteen hours, but the visiting heads of state were obliged to attend for only four. A light, freezing rain fell over the solemn procession, led by the imperial family and composed of Shinto priests carrying flags and ceremonial objects. The Sikaren, a huge carriage containing the imperial coffin, appeared, borne by fifty-two priests in black robes. Music heard only at a royal funeral was played.

Boxes accompanying the emperor to his burial place were laid around the coffin. They included his favorite dishes, prepared by his favorite chef; his microscope; a particular melon that he loved to eat; and other objects identified with him and designed to facilitate his passage to the next world. After a moment of silence, observed throughout the country, a 21-gun salute was fired.

Addresses of condolence were delivered by the speaker of the House of Representatives, by the president of the House of Councillors, and by the chief justice of the Supreme Court. Then each head of state was called, and we walked slowly to the coffin, bowed, then turned and moved a number of steps toward the emperor and the imperial family. Again, we each bowed to the emperor, who bowed in return, and then we went back to the hall and to the exit, where our respective convoys arrived—to the second—to whisk us away.

Since I could not travel because of the Sabbath, I moved to the Akasaka Palace Hotel, which was but fifteen minutes' walk from the Akasaka Palace, the site of that evening's formal state reception. King Hussein was staying at this hotel and there was much conjecture as to my purpose in moving. The purpose was simple—I didn't want to walk for an hour each way to and from the reception.

It is impossible to describe the interest the media had in my going on foot. I was accompanied by a large crowd of TV cameras and photographers, whose spotlights and flashlights blinded us and made it almost impossible to get to the palace. I'm sure that my stroll was the most widely covered event concerning a head of state attending the funeral. As delegations all rolled up to the palace in their luxurious limousines, one head of state walked through the light rain and arrived on foot. It became a major story.

The palace itself is the official government guest house, and is, together with the grounds, modeled after the palace at Versailles. At the head of the magnificent staircase, the prime minister and his wife greeted the guests, and I found myself in one of the great receptions of the century, attended, I was told, by the largest gathering in history of heads of state and national leaders.

I had interesting discussions with numerous kings, queens, presidents, and their foreign ministers. President Mubarak took me aside, and with his arm over my shoulder, whispered to me something he would like me to pass on to Arens—it was his reaction to Shamir's negative approach to the idea of an international conference. The duke of Edinburgh, who noticed this brief meeting, came over to me and said that regretfully he did not know the president of Egypt, would I do him the honor of introducing him? I thought to myself, who in the long history of the Zionist Movement would have dreamed that the prince consort of Great Britain would have to ask the president of Israel to introduce him to the head of an Arab state?

President Mitterrand took me aside and gave me his mostly positive impressions of his meetings that week with Shamir in Paris. The only frustrating moment was when, from a distance, I saw the prime minister of Pakistan, Benazir Bhutto, eyeing me. I was keen to talk to her—and it was clear that the desire was mutual—but it was not to be. Because she is an extreme Moslem, I could not approach her. She and other Pakistani and Indian leaders have to kowtow to their Moslem population. If I'd gone over to her, she would have had to turn her back on me. It was a great pity because not only is she one of the more interesting world leaders, she is extraordinarily attractive.

We left Tokyo on Monday, 27 February. Many of the hotel staff lined the red carpet leading from the elevator to the lobby, and then to the car. I shook hands with each one of them, and many bade me farewell with the Hebrew words *"shalom"* or *"lehitraot"* (au revoir).

Overall, the visit had been important. The Japanese prime minister publicly affirmed Japan's policy of developing and improving relations and increasing economic ties with Israel. Note the changing times: Japanese reluctance to do business with us was based on their main supply of oil, the Arab world. But now the Arabs—mostly Egypt—were selling oil to Israel, there was one less restriction to worry about. As always, our relationships developed through diplomacy but were based on economic realities.

Prime Minister Shamir was very concerned by Mubarak's statement that Israel would ultimately have to talk to the PLO. He would be on the spot during his forthcoming visit to Washington and wanted to avoid a clash with the U.S. leaders. I had a vague suspicion that the Americans were to some degree coordinated with the Soviets and I advised Shamir against going to Washington if he had nothing concrete to offer. Bush seemed interested in the Rabin plan and it was Shamir's best bet. The PLO would probably reject its approach, thus maneuver themselves into a situation whereby they did not support elections in the Arab population. Shamir could not hope for a better situation when facing the American public.

MOHAMMED ABU ZULLUF, owner, publisher, and editor of *El Kuds*, the leading Arab daily in the territories, told me why King Hussein had dramatically severed Jordan's link with the West Bank in 1988: his popularity there had dropped to less than 10 percent. Abu Zulluf had encouraged him to appreciate the political realities that would ultimately affect him. He convinced Hussein that he was being misled by sycophants who reported only what he wanted to hear: that the Arabs in the territories loved him. The king sent four trusted envoys to the West Bank to meet with its leaders and the ordinary public. When they reported that Hussein had no support, he cut official ties.

The *intifada* could have been stopped within months of its beginning, Abu Zulluf said, but now, tired and weary as they were, the Palestinians realized that it could give them leverage. However frustrated they were, they would continue to suffer in order to sustain the impetus.

On 23 March, I gave the keynote address to formally open Prime Minister Shamir's Conference on Jewish Solidarity at the Convention Center. Some 1,700 delegates, a most impressive gathering of world Jewish leadership, had arrived. In the course of my remarks, I said:

> . . . *whatever* the conditions, whatever the circumstances, there is a universal first requirement of leadership. That requirement is ideological conviction. The great Hebrew poet Nathan Alterman, who accompanied and interpreted the revival of Israel in his majestic verse, once wrote on what I believe is a dominant issue today facing the Jews of Israel and, indeed, World Jewry, an issue which we all must face up to. I believe that in his immortal poem he encapsulated the main problem facing this conference and indeed, our people today. I quoted it in the

Knesset on the occasion of the inauguration ceremony of my second term as president last May. These are his words in loose translation:

... Then Satan said: How can I subdue him?
    For he has the courage and the ability,
    The weapons, the resourcefulness and the wisdom.
    And he said: I will not weaken him,
    Nor curb nor bridle him,
    Nor inspire fear in him,
    Nor soften him as in days of yore.
    I will do only this: I will dull his mind
    And he will forget that his is the just cause.

This is the main issue facing us today. Our belief in ourselves and in the justice of our cause.

SOON AFTER THE CONFERENCE Shamir went to Washington to meet with Bush and Baker. The plan he was presenting included elections in the West Bank and Gaza and an interim arrangement of autonomy. He would also indicate his willingness, after the period of autonomy, to enter into a discussion on the final arrangements. This, as far as the Americans were concerned, was seen as a breakthrough, because Shamir had been unwilling to make any commitment on a final arrangement. He would reiterate his acceptance of Security Council Resolution 242 and would propose an international effort to solve the problem of the Arabs in the refugee camps without prejudice to the political solution. In effect, he was adopting Rabin's plan, as I had advised him to do.

The trip went very well. By opting for elections in the territories, Shamir had given the administration an opening that it would use to advance further. The Americans had pressured President Mubarak of Egypt to use his influence on King Hussein and the PLO, so there would be no out-of-hand rejection of Shamir's proposal. They had obviously indicated to Mubarak that if he was successful with Hussein and Arafat, the United States could bring pressure on Israel for further compromises at a later stage. In all, Shamir had acquitted himself well.

Moreover, the visit had been easier than Shamir had initially imagined. His proposal had been reasonably well received, and he found Bush and Baker pragmatic and willing to listen. On all bilateral problems, the meetings were positive. When he met alone with Bush, the president raised the question of settlements and, in a very polite way, said that they would much appreciate it if the Israeli government would not "rock the

boat" by establishing new settlements. Shamir clearly did not fully understand that such a request by the president of the United States, however
polite the terminology might be, still had to be addressed seriously—in
fact, it was a demand. I sensed that we might have trouble over this.
Shamir was most impressed by how much weight American Jewry carried
with Bush.

Peres, as minister of finance, resented Shamir's basking in the warmth
of public approval following his visit to the United States. Peres and
Rabin had first proposed the idea of elections in the territories—exactly
what Shamir used as his innovative proposal in Washington—at a press
conference before the last elections to the Knesset. Peres was even more
bitter when he recalled how he had achieved the London Document with
King Hussein, which would have made Jordan the center of negotiations,
only to have it rejected by Shamir and the Likud. He had warned that if
Israel would not talk to King Hussein, we would have to talk to Arafat,
and that was happening now, with the Americans acting as go-between.
According to Peres, Arens went to Washington, on Shamir's instructions,
to sabotage Peres's negotiations with Hussein, and Arens was now proposing publicly that Jordan be brought back into the negotiations. Peres
maintained that had Shamir given him full support when Peres reached
the agreement with Hussein, there might have been a positive result. It
was clear to Peres that Levy, Modai, and Sharon were taking a strong
stand against Shamir's policy.

In many of the great ventures that he had launched, Peres considered
himself maligned and slandered. He had battled with Isser Harel when
Harel was head of the Mossad, and with Golda Meir. Golda had leveled
accusations against him in connection with Israel's special relations with
France, which Peres was responsible for. He had been attacked by Sapir,
then minister of finance, for his initiative to develop the nuclear research
reactor in Dimona. He was bitter over his letdown by Dayan in the Rafi
Party period and his difficulties with Ben-Gurion during the Six-Day
War. A lack of mutual confidence had existed between Rabin and himself, he said.

Peres seemed depressed to the point of wanting to give up public life,
although he knew he could never do it. Despite his unique drive, imagination, and ability, he had apparently made many political mistakes and
enemies.

—

THE ARAB REACTION to Shamir's proposal for elections came quite soon. Some eighty Palestinian leaders in the West Bank and Gaza rejected his proposal out-of-hand, despite indications from Arafat that Shamir's plan was acceptable under certain conditions.

The government voted by a slim majority to adopt the Shamir-Rabin proposal to hold elections in the territories as a first step in a peace process. The elections were to lead to five years of autonomy and, ultimately, to negotiations on a final political solution for the West Bank and Gaza. Two ministers voted against the plan, maintaining that it was better to talk directly with the PLO than to hold elections that could bring forth even more extreme elements with whom Israel would have to negotiate. Sharon, Levy, and Modai from the Likud and Shaki of the National Religious Party vehemently opposed the plan, fearing it would lead to a Palestinian state.

A few days after the vote, with emotions running high, Modai called on Shamir to resign, demanding that elections be held, with the plan of action a major issue. It was typical of the inherent weakness in our system of government that a minister could publicly call on his prime minister to resign and emerge unscathed. In any well-run democracy the minister would have tendered his resignation, or the prime minister would have fired him on the spot. Shamir did nothing, adopting his usual noncommittal approach.

IN MAY, the *intifada's* hostile activity peaked, as the Israeli army imposed a curfew on the entire Gaza Strip and ordered all of the residents to return to Gaza from Israel. Overnight some 100,000 workers were removed from the Israeli labor market and after a few days the situation began to take its toll on the economy. Building construction slowed down and the sanitation departments in most towns curtailed services or even closed. The policy was meant to make it clear to the population in Gaza that Israel was under no obligation to give them jobs; they could not benefit from our economy and take back some $700 million a year while fomenting unrest and violence. The new plan was to regulate entry into Israel by means of colored identity cards; those convicted of security or criminal offenses would be excluded. Unfortunately, by also restricting people who were not terrorists and taking away their livelihood, we were turning them into potential terrorists.

Our actions exacerbated our problems with the United States. Secretary of State Baker was annoyed with our hard-line foreign minister, Arens, who took a very tough stance on his visit to Washington. Calling on Israel to forgo the dream of a "greater Israel," to recognize the Palestinians, and to reduce the level of violence in the territories, Baker was obviously enunciating the policy of the new administration. Baker was tough and determined, and Shamir did not quite appreciate the seriousness of these developments.

Trying to smooth Israel's ruffled feathers, Bush invited Arens to the United States. The administration apparently used a system in which Baker played bad cop and Bush played good cop. Shamir, who was then in London, seemed to be the bad cop wherever he went, and since his was the only voice that really counted as far as Israel was concerned, this was not good news. After very unwisely dismissing Baker's remarks as "unimportant," Shamir was received for the first time by Margaret Thatcher, who clearly did not think Shamir's plan for the territories was adequate. He fared better in Spain, where, despite reservations, the government appeared to accept and support the proposal. Shamir was now under heavy attack from his own party. Only Levy could save him, and it was reasonable to assume that he would extract a heavy price for it.

Peres, meanwhile, saw no solution to the impasse with the *intifada*. He was obviously moving toward the necessity for a meeting with the PLO, because he did not see any other interlocutor emerging in the territories. He was also moving in the direction of creating a Palestinian state. He did not know of anybody in Israel who wanted to retain Gaza, with its 650,000 Arabs (in 1995 there were 800,000). Had a poll been taken, 90 percent of Israelis would have voted to give up Gaza. Peres has talked of Gaza's becoming a new Singapore. There's certainly plenty of cheap labor —and given Peres's imagination, if he ever gets the chance, I wouldn't put it past him.

ISRAEL HAS BEEN THROUGH a number of wars and many battles. By 1989 it had 34,000 wounded veterans. I attended many memorial ceremonies, but one remains indelibly impressed in my mind. It was at Latrun, where I had served in the War of Independence with the 7th Brigade. Many of the wounded veterans participated in a very moving reunion. Most stirring of all was the father who had been blinded, holding hands with his fifteen-year-old daughter whom he had never seen, praying to God in front of the vast assembly, in a beautiful poem, for one more moment of vision so he'd be able to see her. His daughter broke down and cried; most of the audience were near tears themselves. It was an important reminder that under the politics of war lie all-too-human tragedies.

THE JEWISH UNDERGROUND members who were still in jail were becoming heroes to the right wing, and Dan Meridor, the minister of justice, warned me that there could well be a bill passed in the Knesset freeing all members of the underground. I had to preempt developments by taking the initiative.

My policy was to split the organization and bring about its demise; the members initially sentenced in 1984 had to remain in prison long enough that the example of their punishment would deter others. When the Stern Group murdered Count Folke Bernadotte in 1948, Ben-Gurion, realizing that this issue could split the nation, allowed a law to be passed in the Knesset that resulted in a mere two-month jail term for the perpetrators. In October 1956 forty-seven Arab villagers were murdered in Kafr Kassem by the Israeli Border Police. The two officers in charge were sentenced to fifteen and seventeen years in jail, respectively, but were freed after less than three years.

I resolved that such leniency would not be allowed in this case. For five years I had withstood public pressure for clemency. The prime minister had voted for an unsuccessful bill designed to release the underground members. I decided they should continue to languish in jail for several additional years.

Yielding to police advice that these prisoners were a greater danger to society in jail than out of it, I decided to review a sentence only if the prisoner wrote to me in his own handwriting, asking for a reduction, expressing sincere regret, and decrying the policy the group had adopted. As in previous cases, this led to a split and internal confrontation in the underground. Of the twenty-nine people arraigned in court, twelve wrote such letters. The organization broke up and eventually disappeared.

None of this group had any connection with the current unrest in the territories. In fact, everyone who had gone free proved to be a power in the struggle against the extremists. Despite the *intifada*, there had been no Jewish underground activity for eighteen months thanks, I believe, to my policy. Some prisoners were in their sixth year in jail—they never believed they would be there that long. If I reduced their sentences so that the end was in sight, their effectiveness as a focus for protest would be greatly reduced. The situation was becoming more dangerous with them in jail, once they had rejected their own philosophy and expressed regret.

Not one was pardoned, but I reduced their sentences so that they would be released in 1991 or 1994, depending on the prisoner and the crime. As usual, there was an uproar, especially from the left-wing press. But I had stood up to very heavy pressure over the years, and believed that I had acted in the best interests of law and order, and of justice.

Both the minister of police, Haim Bar-Lev, and the head of the Shin Bet informed me that they fully supported the move I had made. They reiterated their view that this had been the right move, and that my policy on this issue had led to the breakup of the underground.

BOUTROS BOUTROS-GHALI, the Egyptian minister of state for foreign affairs, came to Israel to create a situation in which Egypt would be an intermediary between Israel and the PLO. Shamir had turned down his proposal; our prime minister was not ready to deal with Arafat in any way, shape, or form. But Boutros-Ghali was convinced that Arafat wanted to move forward. Arafat did not control his entire organization, and acts of terror were still being carried out by constituents of that organization, but the PLO could still play a central part in any plan for peace, and it was important for Israel to talk to its leader. Our fear was of autonomy among the Palestinians—that extreme fundamentalists would take over. The fundamentalists were responsible for frequent terrorist outbreaks in Egypt and also constituted a danger to the Jordanians, who were as opposed to them as Israel was.

Egypt's prospects were disturbing. They had to suspend construction of the irrigation canal in Sudan because of civil war and bombing by Egypt's "Libyan brothers." Egypt inhabited only 3 percent of the Sudan and had no additional water to grow food, feed a rapidly growing population, or develop tourist sites on the Mediterranean and the Red Sea.

Egypt was importing $3 billion worth of food annually; pessimists said it would use up its oil reserves in ten years; optimists, twenty years. The revenue from oil paid for imported food. Two million Egyptians working in Iraq and perhaps another million elsewhere constituted a brain drain, while those who contributed little to the domestic economy were consuming food. Furthermore, all the countries around the headwaters of the Nile were at war or involved in disputes. They all wanted to develop and increase irrigation, and the only source of water for irrigation was the Nile, which meant further problems for Egypt.

When Boutros-Ghali had completed his sorrowful tale, I said to him, "Why do you come to us to deal with a problem which pales into insignificance beside the problems facing you in Egypt?" His only answer was to reply with a bitter laugh.

ON 26 JUNE 1989, Aura and I arrived in Ottawa, Canada, for a state visit. At the entrance to the grounds of Government House, we transferred to an open, horse-drawn carriage. A cavalry escort of the Royal Canadian Mounted Police preceded us through the gardens to the dais at the entrance to Rideau Hall, where we were received by the governor-general, Madame Jeanne Sauvé, and her husband, Maurice Sauvé.

On Tuesday, 27 June 1989, I addressed both Houses of Parliament in the Commons, an unusual honor. My predecessors on such occasions included Winston Churchill, President Reagan, President Bush, Prime Minister Thatcher, President Mitterrand, Chancellor Kohl, and the Queen of Holland. The chamber was packed, and the public gallery was filled to capacity with representatives of the Jewish community. I described in detail the problems facing Israel in the Middle East, and sang the praises of Canada as reflected in the famous poem by John Service in "The Song of the Sour Dough."

An event occurred that was very special to me: a visit by my former commanding officer in the British army, Colonel Robert (Tex) Noble. He was an outgoing character who had not changed since he had been my boss in Germany in intelligence. As he walked in, he said in his loud, brash voice, recalling the years we faced the Russian occupation forces in Germany and the Communist movement, "Well, we finally beat the bastards."

IN JULY 1989, the Likud's central committee met. Shamir had, to a degree, capitulated to Sharon, Modai, and Levy by including in his keynote speech their reservations regarding the plan for autonomy in the territories. As a result, he gained a unanimous vote in favor of his plan. Those reservations—no vote for the East Jerusalem Arabs, no negotiations until the conclusion of the *intifada*, no Palestinian state, and no foreign activity in the area of the territories—would guarantee an Arab rejection of the plan. By bending, Shamir had surrendered his exclusive control of the party and gave the recalcitrant three a standing that they previously had not had. At the meeting he did not shake hands with Sharon, but that did not detract from his initial weakness. He had made a mistake, and it looked as if Labor might be obliged to leave the unity government as a result. They could not agree to such conditions based on what was essentially Rabin's plan. This did not bode well for Shamir; the struggle would now begin in earnest within the Likud for the leadership position.

The Labor Party Bureau did indeed decide to recommend to the central committee that it withdraw from the unity government. This was a mistake. Were a narrow government to be formed by Shamir, it would be right-wing and clerical, bound to be unpopular, and, in fact, unformable in the Knesset. Labor could then, by default, hope to put together its own government. But Peres was fed up. It was difficult for him to be not only number two to Shamir but also engaged in a developing interparty struggle with Rabin for leadership of the Labor Party. After a remarkable political comeback from his first term as prime minister, Rabin was now perceived as both tough and honest—an unbeatable combination for a leader. He was clearly the new favorite within Labor and with the man on the street. Peres's time seemed to be over—at least as leader of the party—although he was far from ready to admit it.

In the meantime, the reverberations of the events of the Likud Central Committee could still be felt. Minister of Justice Dan Meridor and his colleagues, who were Shamir's closest confidants and backers, were completely surprised by Shamir's about-face. Shamir had a clear majority guaranteed, and his colleagues understood that he would force the issue and put it to a vote. Shamir's supporters were utterly flabbergasted by his surrender to Sharon's dictates. I was told by many that one of Shamir's former colleagues in the Stern Group had influenced him to change his attitude. According to the story, the person caught Shamir just before the meeting and intimidated him by saying that the prime minister did not have a guaranteed majority in the central committee. (A leading Israeli political columnist confirmed this account.) In yet another political crisis, with the central committee of the Labor Party to be convened in a month, Peres was urging his party to leave the government; Rabin and many of the ministers were against such an action, each for his own reason. There was much talk in the Labor Party of exchanging Rabin for Peres as leader.

Shamir was desperately trying to hold on to a national unity government, but he had only himself to blame for the situation that he had created. When Minister of the Interior Aryeh Deri asked a question in the Knesset of Shamir about the peace plan, Shamir replied that no change whatsoever had occurred. In other words, he was completely ignoring the additional conditions set out by the Likud Central Committee, which he himself had agreed to. That caused a major blowup between Shamir and Sharon. Soon afterward, Shamir refused to divulge certain confidential information to Sharon for fear it would be leaked. Sharon apparently told Shamir that he despised him, and there was now an open split between the two. Normally, a prime minister would have fired a minister who spoke like that, but the ever passive and indecisive Shamir did nothing of the sort. He considered Sharon to be very dangerous but chose to ignore his very existence.

AT THE OFFICIAL welcoming ceremonies in Jerusalem for President André Kolingba of the Central African Republic and his wife, I faced a problem peculiar to Israel. As they moved along, shaking hands with the welcoming delegation, there was a slight incident. Some of the religious ministers, including Rabbi Peretz of Shas, did not take Mrs. Kolingba's outstretched hand, because they do not shake hands with women. I whispered to her not to give her hand to rabbis, whom she would easily recognize by their beards. She was therefore surprised and flustered when the bearded Armenian patriarch extended his hand. I whispered that if the bearded gentleman was wearing a cross, it was all right to shake hands. Then when we reached the chairman of the Foreign Affairs and Defense Committee of the Knesset, Eliahu Ben-Elissar, who is bearded but not Orthodox, and he offered his hand, she was completely perplexed. At this point I gave up. From then on I whispered instructions to her for each individual.

FOLLOWING HIS MEETING with Secretary of State Baker, Rabin paid a surprise visit to Cairo. President Mubarak had recently proposed a ten-point program to the Palestinians, which included giving a vote in the proposed elections in the territories to residents of Jerusalem; inclusion in the delegation for negotiations of two Palestinians from outside the territories, as part of the ten proposed to be members of the delegation (these could be people who had been expelled from the territories); and the principle of the return of territory for peace as the basis for negotiations. These and other points were totally unacceptable to Shamir, in the inner cabinet of Shamir, Peres, and Arens. Labor had no objection to the program as a starting point for negotiations. Thus, Israel could and should go to a meeting without committing itself in favor of Mubarak's points, and it could reject them if necessary during any session. Mubarak's ten points had a plus side: no mention was made of a Palestinian state or of the Palestinians' claim to a "right of return."

Basically, what emerged was openness on Labor's part, a pragmatic approach to try out the Palestinians' readiness for peace, as opposed to a total rejection by the Likud of any approach except on their own terms.

Shamir was very disturbed by Rabin's visit to Egypt; Rabin, on the other hand, vehemently denied that he had done anything behind Shamir's back. The meeting had come about at Baker's urging, and after receiving an invitation from Mubarak, Rabin went only after reporting to Shamir, Peres, and Arens. Once again we were being done in by big egos and petty jealousies, even as peace seemed to be within view, if not in our grasp.

ON WEDNESDAY, 4 October, a court in Ramle sentenced Abie Nathan— a flamboyant Israeli pilot, originally from India, and a man who had devoted much time, energy, and money to helping his fellow man in many parts of the world—to six months in jail and one year on probation for meeting Yasser Arafat. This was in accordance with the law passed by the Knesset a year previously, at the instigation of the Likud, forbidding contacts with proscribed terrorist organizations. The law was in my view a disgrace, as was the sentence pronounced on Abie Nathan. In a democracy, it cannot be against the law to talk to anyone about anything. But it was the law, and it had to be observed, although Nathan could have been sentenced without actually having to serve jail time. The only positive aspect was that it would undoubtedly turn Abie into a martyr and might bring about a move in the Knesset to change the law. I met with every group who asked to see me in order to protest the sentence, but Abie Nathan, as a matter of principle, refused to ask for a pardon—which I would have granted.

SOON THEREAFTER, I was able to welcome, once again, a close friend. It was the seventieth birthday of Lord George Weidenfeld, the well-known and quite brilliant English publisher. George, a bon vivant and patron of the arts who regularly holds court in his salon in London, had been going around the world celebrating this birthday with his friends and admirers and partners in New York, London, Vienna, and now in Jerusalem. Aura and I gave a luncheon in his honor. George has been a great and true friend of Israel over the years and, among others, Shamir, Rabin, and Meridor were happy to toast this charismatic man before whom all doors seem to open automatically. George's publishing company, Weidenfeld & Nicolson, has showcased many of Israel's best writers, and his stable of authors also came to pay him homage. At our luncheon, he reminisced about his long ties to Israel as well as his colorful past. He began as a member of Betar in Vienna, escaped as a refugee to England, where he established himself as a publisher, and worked his way up to become an advisor to Dr. Chaim Weizmann, Israel's first president.

George is a unique individual who, despite his enormous success in life and his peerage, has remained a good and proud Jew and a very loyal Zionist.

Sometimes, in the midst of political struggles, when one is participating in decisions and events that have international and historical ramifications, it is easy to lose sight of the everyday pleasures and problems of a normal family life. This was brought home to me when our dog, Charlie, fell ill. For eleven and a half years Charlie, an extremely handsome cross between a German shepherd and a Great Dane, had been part and parcel of the family. When the vet called to advise me that Charlie's illness was terminal, and that he recommended putting him to sleep, I have to say that, for the moment, all I cared about was the fact that I was losing someone I had come to love, even if he was a four-legged someone. I went with my daughter Ronit to say farewell to Charlie and I put him through his paces, going through all the exercises that I had ever taught him. Then I bade him a sad goodbye. For those moments, everything else was irrelevant, and in a way, I was glad to have a reminder of what was important and personal.

SOON AFTER MY LUNCH with Lord Weidenfeld, I had another happy reunion. After the formation of the State of Israel in 1948, a small group of volunteers organized the emigration of Iraqi Jews to Israel via Iran. One of those volunteers was a young man named Yehuda Tajjer. In 1950, Tajjer was arrested by the Iraqis and sentenced to death. They suspected him of spying for his new country. He was placed on the scaffold, hooded, and, with the rope around his neck, waited for fifteen minutes to be executed. He said all his prayers several times and in those fifteen minutes his hair turned totally white. Then, for no reason, he was suddenly taken down from the scaffold and sent to a prison in the Iraqi desert that was reserved for Communists and the worst criminals in the country. He was never given any reason for the executioners' change of heart, but he spent ten years in that prison. In 1960, the leader of Iraq, Brigadier Abd-ul Karim Qassem, an eccentric and very strange individual, to say the least, heard about Tajjer, invited him for a talk, and at the end of their conversation set him free.

When Tajjer returned to Israel, I was one of those who received him. On the way back from a ceremony at which I awarded him, in my capacity as director of military intelligence, the War of Independence medal, he told me that he was officially inviting me to the wedding of his future son—although he himself was not yet married. Tajjer was ultimately sent to the Israeli embassy in London as a Middle East expert, took his doctorate in Middle Eastern affairs, and became a lecturer at Tel Aviv University. In November 1989, I received a letter from him, reminding me of our agreement in the car on the way back from that ceremony nearly thirty years earlier. He had married and had one son, who was now about to be married. Of course, I attended the wedding, which was most joyous, and certainly proved once again that where there is life, there is hope.

THE YEAR ENDED with a new bombshell in Israel: on 31 December Shamir announced that he was dismissing Ezer Weizman as a minister. Weizman had allegedly had contact with representatives of the PLO in Switzerland. He did not deny the allegations, but he had no advance warning and learned of his dismissal at a governmental meeting. Shamir had told Rabin and Peres about his intention, but neither of them saw fit to inform Weizman. Shamir was flabbergasted, having assumed that they would deal properly with a leading member of their party. Peres and Rabin may have considered it not their job to pass on messages from Shamir. It was an unpleasant situation, and Weizman certainly did not deserve such treatment. He was convinced that he was the one man who could communicate with Arafat and the PLO. As a result, he was accused by Shamir of working against his own government. Stunned by Shamir's stance, many Labor ministers threatened to resign and bring down the government should Weizman's dismissal remain in effect. So, as the 1990s dawned, Israel was in *yet another* political crisis. If things could not be worked out, I would try to form *yet another* government.

The Presidency—1990

EARLY IN 1990, Shamir came to see me about his dismissal of Weizman. Shamir had obviously known about Weizman's meetings with the PLO in July 1989. He had been hoping that such meetings would not recur but had been moved to act because Weizman was scheduled to leave on a visit to Moscow. Shamir felt that Weizman could truly damage the government's position, and to remain passive would make him a party to Weizman's actions.

But Shamir had given Weizman no chance to defend himself. It seemed to me that the fairest thing to do would be to place the accusations and proof in the hands of an independent legal personality or body before whom Weizman could appear to deny any allegations or defend himself against them. If Shamir wished to dismiss Weizman for being a bad minister, that was his prerogative under the law. But as he was accusing him of a very serious offense, I said, it should have been done in a proper legal manner. Shamir felt I was right, although he decided that he could and would suspend Weizman during the period of the inquiry.

That evening, in a special broadcast before the news, Shamir spoke to the nation and made the accusations against Weizman. He offered the beleaguered minister every opportunity to reply. Weizman did reply, but it was not the most successful response. He was unprepared and spoke haltingly and stumblingly. The gist of his defense was that all he'd done was have a chance meeting with the PLO in Geneva. That answer didn't have much credibility in the eyes of the public, as critics maintained that one didn't just stroll into a session with the PLO by accident.

Peres, of course, wanted to bring down the unity government immediately. Rabin did not agree. He was convinced that a government with only a narrow majority would be incapable of running the country at that time, with the *intifada* still going strong, with the economic situation still shaky, and the peace process still moving forward. That night Rabin began to negotiate with Shamir through Dan Meridor to try to salvage something out of this situation.

The next morning, Rabin called in Weizman and presented him with the proposed compromise: Weizman would resign from the inner cabinet for a period of eighteen months, would remain minister for science and infrastructure, and would have no more meetings or be involved in any more talks with the PLO. At first Weizman turned down the proposal. However, when he realized that he would be abandoned by his colleagues in the Labor Party if he refused, he accepted. Shamir took back his original letter of dismissal and gave Weizman a letter setting out the new arrangements. Shamir furthermore approved Weizman's trip to Russia. In the ensuing public debate, Shamir was discredited for caving in and Peres was attacked for remaining on the sidelines and for sandbagging Weizman by not even warning him of his dismissal. Rabin was the only one to emerge from the situation with added strength and authority.

DR. LOUIS WADE SULLIVAN, the U.S. secretary of health, education and welfare, called on me during his visit to Israel. In the course of our discussion I learned that he controlled the fourth-largest budget in the world —between $400 and 500 billion a year. The largest was that of the United States government as a whole, the second largest was that of the Soviet Union, in third place came Japan, and then came the budget of the U.S. secretary of HEW. Despite that incredible figure, I was amazed to learn that 28 percent of the American population (over 30 million people) did not have health insurance. By contrast, 97 percent of Israelis have workable health insurance.

Our doctors will even treat foreign citizens. One of the saddest groups that came to visit me was sixty children, survivors of the Chernobyl nuclear disaster, who were invited to Israel by the Histadrut for medical treatment. They arrived with several grownups from the town, including a few firemen who had fought the blaze in the reactor. It was the quietest group of children I had ever seen in my life. They did not utter a sound except when told to. Their silence was understandable. Although we were doing what we could to help them, I was told that they were all doomed and could not live very long, and I'm sure they realized that.

The firemen, who were all doomed too, told me about their experiences. It had been a classic bureaucratic mix-up. The fire was not reported to Moscow. Only after thirteen days, days when the whole village was exposed to the deadly radiation, did Moscow find out what had happened—and that was only because the Swedes filed a protest when they discovered high levels of radioactivity in their air. The area around Chernobyl was then evacuated, and the reactor was being buried under tons of earth. But that all came too late to save the children or the brave men who tried to rescue them.

OUR SUDDENLY SHAKY RELATIONSHIP with the United States got a lot shakier when Shamir spoke about the need for a "greater" Israel to absorb a great number of immigrants. "Greater" was immediately taken to mean "bigger," as in "more and more settlements." The PLO and Arab countries attacked his statement ferociously, the European parliament condemned it, and Secretary of State Baker was livid over what he saw as a genuine betrayal. Shamir tried to amend matters—he meant a "stronger" Israel, he explained, not a "greater" one. As Chaim Weizmann said, "It was a fine speech, but it was not as good as keeping quiet."

That week, the *intifada* was stepped up. The internal struggle among the Palestinians was becoming more marked: all seven Palestinians killed in the territories that week were slain by other Palestinians. Almost simultaneously, an attack on a busload of Israeli tourists in Egypt, apparently mounted by Islamic fundamentalists answering to Teheran, killed ten and wounded seventeen. Iran was still instigating and supporting international terrorism, and we were basically helpless to stop them.

Rabin was emerging as a real leader. By blocking Peres's move to bring down the government, he had become the central figure in the Labor Party—paradoxically, because of his close relationship with Shamir. Shamir was happy with Rabin as minister of defense, and Rabin appeared happy with Shamir as prime minister; he did not interfere with Rabin's work and had blocked most of the criticism from within the Likud about Rabin's policies.

ON 25 FEBRUARY, Aura and I gave an official dinner to mark the seventy-fifth birthday of our brother-in-law, Abba Eban. Every president would have wanted to honor this brilliant man, and I was thrilled that I had the opportunity. Abba was the first Israeli ambassador to the UN and our second ambassador to the United States. For almost a decade, he was both simultaneously. He had been a member of the Knesset since 1959, until Labor, in the most recent elections, had unwisely not seen fit to include him on their list. He had also been deputy prime minister, minister of education, and minister of foreign affairs. He is a brilliant speaker and writer and is fluent in Hebrew, English, French, Spanish, Arabic, and Iranian. His only flaw as a politician is that he was too honest for Labor to deal with. My own feeling is that *all* politicians should have that flaw.

SHAMIR NOW SEEMED bitter and depressed. A man under siege, he was being attacked from within his own party, while Labor was still threatening to bring down his government. Even as he became more bitter, he became tougher and more determined to face the fact that the curtain was closing on his political career.

On 15 March, for the first time in the history of Israel, the government fell on a no-confidence vote in the Knesset. It was now my task to invite a member to form a government.

Shamir was very much to blame for this debacle. Despite sensible advice to go easy with the United States and particularly with Secretary of State Baker, he had made every possible mistake. He had opened every front at once—with the United States, with Labor, within his own party, with Sharon, with Levy, and with the Aguda, which voted against him because he had not honored signed agreements. Instead of proving himself, he and his government had elicited only malaise.

I had to move quickly. Immigration from the Soviet Union was becoming an overwhelming problem, and unemployment was rising to almost 9 percent. Ten ministers had resigned in the wake of the no-confidence vote, and by law only the prime minister could act in their place—a ridiculous and unworkable situation. We were now functioning with no defense minister and no foreign minister.

For the fifth time, I began the search for a candidate with the necessary majority in the Knesset to form a government. Labor, of course, proposed Peres, and the Likud recommended Shamir.

The Shas group, the religious party, backed the Likud, which was a complete surprise: they had been the single most important voting bloc in bringing down Shamir's government. They did not specifically mention Shamir, just the Likud, which complicated matters somewhat, since the parties are required to propose a specific member of the Knesset. Things got more complicated when, a few hours after my inconclusive meeting with Shas, Chief Rabbi Ovadia Yosef, the Shas mentor, called me and begged me to ignore everything that the Shas delegation had said, imploring me "in the name of God" to nominate Peres. Late that night, Rabbi Aryeh Deri, the Shas leader and minister of the interior, came and told me that they now favored Shamir. Brushing aside my questions about Rabbi Yosef, he explained that Shas now opted for Shamir. It was difficult to fathom what kind of political negotiations and promises were being brokered behind the scenes. I'm not sure I even *wanted* to fathom them.

It was the power and influence of Rabbi Yeheskel Schach, the nonagenarian leader of the *haredi* extreme Orthodox movement, that had forced Rabbi Yosef's hand. In a rambling speech at a *haredi* convention, Rabbi Schach attacked the kibbutzim, emphasizing how removed they were from traditional Judaism. The kibbutz movement was deeply and rightfully insulted. At a memorial service by the graveside of Yigal Allon, I described my feelings as I surveyed the graves of the soldiers who had fought with Allon and looked at the audience gathered there, including many officers and commanders from the kibbutzim who had fought the length and breadth of the country. I said I felt that the nation as a whole should go to the gravesides of the boys who had fallen and ask their forgiveness. I characterized the public debate going on as a disgrace. Men who had led our forces to victory were being labeled as traitors by those who had never heard the sound of war; underground leaders were being maligned by those who never knew what they did; and people who had served the nation were being vilified by those who had never done anything in their lives.

THE RACE BETWEEN the supporters and opponents of Peres was neck and neck. I had to decide rapidly and concluded that the first choice must be Peres. Because the Likud government had been defeated in a no-confidence vote, giving the successful opposition its chance made constitutional sense.

Shamir took my decision well. I had recommended him for prime minister three times, but things were different now: the government had fallen on a no-confidence vote. There were problems in the territories, a military threat on our northern border, and increasing unemployment. The Knesset faced a recess with vital economic decisions held in abeyance for lack of a full-time minister of finance; with the new fiscal year only ten days away, there was no national budget; and thousands of Jews were

arriving daily from the Soviet Union. No nation could operate this way—
we had to change our system of government.

With twenty-one days to form a government, Peres began maneuvering, even as a growing movement was protesting our system of government. Many of the movement's leaders were on a hunger strike, seeking
the appointment of a presidential commission to examine the system and
submit alternatives to a referendum. Sick and tired of politicians, Israelis
were becoming disenchanted with politics—and, unfortunately, with democracy.

Wednesday, 11 April, was one of the more dramatic days in the story
of Israel's governments. A week earlier, Peres had advised me that he had
the necessary majority. Accordingly, the Knesset had been called into session so that he could present his government. The evening before the
Knesset meeting, he had addressed the central committee of the Labor
Party to announce what was happening. He did not seem to be at ease,
and it was not the best of his speeches. He refused to present a full government to the committee at that time, limiting himself to naming the
same Labor Party ministers who had served in the national unity government, then promising to add some five new ones, including at least one
or two women. In his speech, he criticized the mass demonstrations
against the electoral system. I later told him that this had been a serious
mistake, and advised him for his own good to meet the hunger strikers
because they really represented the majority of the public. He made a further mistake by giving a newspaper interview to Dan Shilon in *Yedioth
Ahronoth,* the headline of which was "I Will Be Prime Minister the Day
After Tomorrow."

At a certain point in the Knesset session of 11 April, Labor asked for
an adjournment, maintaining that circumstances had changed, and thus
Peres was prevented from presenting his government. What had occurred
was that two members of the Aguda, Rabbi Avraham Verdiger and Rabbi
Eliezer Mizrachi, had suddenly announced that they had been in touch
with advisors of the Lubavitcher Rebbe in New York. They indicated that
the Rebbe did not wish them to vote for Peres because the Rebbe was
against any territorial compromise or any party that would support territorial compromise. The move by these two Aguda members took away
Peres's majority.

Peres had heard of the Aguda shift during the night. At six in the
morning, he had gone to Rabbi Ovadia Yosef to tell him that he was two
votes short of forming a government. (It should be recalled that Rabbi
Yosef's Shas party had been instrumental in bringing down Shamir's gov-

ernment.) According to what Peres told me later, Rabbi Yosef promised him two votes from Shas, which had previously decided to abstain. Assured once again of the majority, he went ahead with his plans, and even invited his wife, Sonia, to come to the Knesset for his swearing-in as prime minister. But at ten that morning, Aryeh Deri had called him and told him that despite Rabbi Yosef's promise, the two votes from Shas were not available to him. He was therefore left without a majority. He had also been publicly humiliated. He asked to meet with me, since his mandate of twenty-one days would expire that night.

Peres arrived, looking the worse for wear. He was very bitter that a rabbi in New York could dictate to members of the Knesset—*in Israel*— on how to vote. He asked me for an extension according to the law. He had been told of Rabbi Yosef's telephone call to me during the consultations, and said that he believed the rabbi had not changed, but had been forced into this new situation because of the danger of a split with Rabbi Schach, a leader in the *haredi* world. He needed time, and he begged me to give it to him. I gave him an additional fifteen days to accomplish what he needed.

All the political commentators had a field day trying to explain why our meeting had gone on for over an hour. The reason was that Peres was on the verge of collapse when he arrived at my home. Because it was the Passover, no food or drink was served in the Knesset and he had not eaten anything all day long. The secretaries in my office noted that he looked faint and was in a very weakened state. We went up to my apartment and Aura quickly fixed a meal for him. Peres was physically, and perhaps mentally, at the end of his tether.

Some days later, when I learned that the two recalcitrants in the Aguda refused to resign or to change their position, I called Peres and told him I did not see why he was waiting till the end of the period I had given him. He now had no chance for a majority, should call it a day and cut his losses, and return his mandate to me in a dignified manner. I was aware of the fact, as he was, that people in the party were mobilizing behind his back to unseat him in favor of Rabin.

Stubborn to the end, Peres advised me that Rabbi Yosef would come to see me and would confirm his support for him. He would do this under the guise of visiting me to wish me a speedy recovery from a minor illness. At midday on 13 April, Rabbi Yosef telephoned. He went into a long monologue of blessings for my recovery, wishing me the best, and promptly hung up, with not one word about coming to see me. I called

Peres and told him what had transpired. Peres insisted that this was impossible, since the rabbi had made a promise to him.

A bit harshly, I told Peres it was about time that he woke up and realized that people were misleading him. It was time for him to draw the necessary conclusions. I recommended that he return the mandate I gave to him. But even now, he still believed he could form a government. He talked of hints from the extreme right-wing group Moledet, led by Rehavam Zeevi. He was going to make any deal he could to regain the position of prime minister.

To add to the insanity, Aryeh Deri came to call on me. According to him, the pressures on Rabbi Yosef were enormous, and the rabbi was sick and tired. I had no sympathy; he, Deri, was, after all, to blame for all this. He was the one who had talked Rabin into supporting Peres to bring down the government. Why, I asked, had Yosef started it in the first place, if he had no intention of going through with it? Deri replied that they had made a mistake, they had underestimated the opposition of Rabbi Schach and the tremendous power he wielded. Rabbi Yosef was, according to Deri, incapable of standing up to Rabbi Schach, who controlled the entire yeshiva (Talmudic seminary) world. I said that the conclusion I drew was that he, Deri, lacked courage. He replied that he did not lack courage, but that the distance between courage and a willingness to commit suicide was at times not very considerable. He felt his life was in danger in Bnei Brak, the *haredi* center. He was brokenhearted, because while Rabbi Yosef wanted Labor to form the government, he would not go against Rabbi Schach and they would therefore vote for Shamir—even though they had no confidence in him and indeed felt that it could be a tragedy for the country. I was amazed at the sad state of political life in Israel.

In the midst of all this, President Vaclav Havel of Czechoslovakia, the first head of state from Eastern Europe to visit Israel, arrived, bringing with him some thirty advisors, who obviously had very little experience. Havel clearly was unsure how to behave as a president, but I had no doubt that he could learn. With no formal education, he had taught himself English during his five-year stay in jail. Anyone who could do that could certainly teach himself how to be president.

Havel said that on his visit to Prague a few weeks earlier, Yasser Arafat had seemed to be preoccupied with issues of protocol; the PLO leader wanted to be treated like a head of state. Arafat told him that he wanted to meet with Israelis and work out an agreement, feeling that time was of the essence. He spoke in a conciliatory and moderate tone in private but changed his attitude completely in the presence of others. Havel felt that he was not honest.

Havel continued, having Austria as a friend was important for Czechoslovakia, but he did not know how to go there without seeing President Waldheim, whom he did not want to meet officially because of his Nazi connections. President von Weizsaecker of Germany, who also avoided official dealings with Waldheim, suggested that he take Havel to the Salzburg festival, where they would meet Waldheim and shake hands, obviating the necessity to hold discussions in Vienna in accordance with the requirements of protocol.

We had a successful and eventful state dinner that night. I advised Havel that since there was worldwide media coverage of the event, he should prepare a speech in English, which he did; it was greeted with great enthusiasm.

The dinner, however, was marked by tension, because Yitzhak Modai, the leader of a breakaway faction in the Likud Party—the New Liberal Party—had declared that he would announce his support for either Peres or Shamir on the nightly television news broadcast at 9 P.M. His decision would determine which man would be able to form the new government. We sat down to dinner soon after 8 P.M., and Shamir, who was sitting next to me, was handed an envelope. He showed it to me as soon as he opened it. It was a note from Modai advising Shamir that he had Modai's vote. Peres received a note that night also. It was not the message he'd wanted to receive.

After the dinner, a devastated Peres told me he would, the next day, hand back his mandate to form the government. And indeed, when he arrived the following evening, he did so. He said that he felt betrayed, and was particularly bitter at having been let down by Shas and by Rabbi Yosef. I had warned him that would happen.

Shamir now began *his* endeavors to form a government, the same Shamir whose government had been given a no-confidence vote. If ever there was proof of the ludicrousness of our system, this was it.

Rabin, ever the pragmatist, insisted that a new leader of the Labor Party be appointed going into the next elections. Naturally, Peres resisted, maintaining that he had been elected for four years and would remain leader until the party's convention in 1991.

There was a very real possibility that Shamir might fail to obtain a majority, and absolutely no possibility that Rabin (according to Rabin himself, in a private conversation with me in my home) could mobilize sixty-one votes. My only options if Shamir failed were to create a broad national unity government or call for new and full elections. Enmity between leaders of the main parties made a unity government almost impossible to achieve; as for elections, I had no power under the law to call for them. The most likely scenario was governmental paralysis. Peres would accept a unity government on the conditions of parity between the two parties and the continuation of the peace process. Rabin declared himself to me to be in favor of a national unity government provided Levy was named foreign minister. Shamir, however, could not forget that Peres had caused his downfall and refused to name him as part of any new government. It was a stalemate.

Meanwhile, the world moved on. President Bush held talks with Mubarak and Hussein, but because of our internal turmoil and instability, no Israeli leader was included. Shamir was livid, and I couldn't blame him. On the other hand, who could blame Bush? There was no guarantee that any political leader would be part of our government from one day to the next.

Finally, on 8 June, Shamir called to tell me that he had formed a government. He had Ephraim Gur's vote—Gur crossed over from Labor—in return for his, Gur's, appointment as a deputy minister and the guarantee of a seat in the next Knesset. It was political bribery, pure and simple. Aryeh Deri of Shas had also changed his vote. After fighting to bring down Shamir's government, he was now its devotee. A series of articles alleging that he was corrupt and using his position to direct financial resources to institutions and yeshivot of Shas led to a police action that may have influenced his political stand.

After all this horse trading, Shamir's proposed government was voted in with a majority of sixty-two to fifty-seven, with one abstention. For better or worse, Israel was back in business.

IN THE WAKE of this political turmoil, I made a state visit to Sweden. The sentiments of the Swedish government were strongly in favor of the PLO. I suggested to the foreign minister, Sven Andersson, who was on his way to a meeting of the Socialist International in Cairo, that he ask Arafat why he did not convene the Palestine National Council to rescind the covenant calling for the destruction of Israel.

Some days later the Swedish prime minister, Ingebor Karlsen, told me that their delegation had indeed introduced such an amendment at the conference. To their surprise, the concept was not rejected by the PLO.

This was an enormous turnabout, a clear indication of a change in attitude which ultimately led to the Oslo talks.

TED TURNER, who revolutionized TV news with CNN, allowed national TV stations to broadcast for three minutes every week. Apparently, Israeli TV did not bother to take advantage of his offer. Although he controlled one of the world's greatest communications complexes, he had a prejudiced idea about Israel on his brief visit and expected to find a bunch of Arab-bashers spitting fire. He was struck by the difference between the image of Israel presented abroad—by, among others, his own CNN—and the reality in Israel itself.

He was somewhat taken aback by that reality when he met Rabbi Raphael Pinhasi, our new minister of communications from the Shas religious party. For religious reasons, the rabbi had no TV at home and there was no basis whatsoever for discussions between them.

THERE WERE OMINOUS rumblings coming from Iraq. Moving away from his threats to Israel, which he was determined to destroy, Saddam Hussein began moving against Kuwait and the United Arab Emirates. Hussein insisted they were flooding the market with oil, causing a reduction in price with heavy financial losses to Iraq. His threats were not to be ignored, and Kuwait appealed to all the Arab countries for help. The United States had confirmed its support, hinting that it would defend Kuwait in case of attack. It was obvious that Saddam Hussein was going to be the source of considerable trouble in the Middle East.

Iraq was in a very recalcitrant mood because of reduced oil prices, and, under pressure from Saddam Hussein, OPEC agreed to raise the price to $21 from $17 a barrel; Hussein wanted $25. The world still looked on this conference as just another inter-Arab struggle that would disappear after a compromise was reached.

On 2 August, Iraq invaded Kuwait with an army of over sixty divisions and took control of the entire country, in an action condemned not only by the free world but also by the Arab world except for King Hussein of Jordan, the Yemenites, and the PLO. The megalomaniac from Baghdad had turned Arab against Arab.

As Saddam Hussein threatened to "burn half of Israel" by firing missiles with chemical warheads at us, Israel showed great restraint—following the advice of the Americans—and did nothing to retaliate. By dealing with this as an Arab-versus-Arab issue, we kept anti-Israel emotions out of the fray. It was not easy but it was effective, and we gained new respect from much of the Arab world. Arens put heavy pressure on Shamir to move against Iraq and violate Jordanian airspace, but Shamir held fast, saving us from a debacle and enhancing his standing with the Americans. It was, however, a terrifying time in Israel: we were under attack, with our hands bound.

The Israeli public, informed that a Scud missile onslaught was imminent and preparing for chemical warfare, was very nervous. In my monthly radio broadcast, I tried to quash the media-fed hysteria by analyzing the Iraqi army as undistinguished in eight years of fighting with Iran, despite its size. We were not facing a monster; the Iraqis could—and were—easily handled by a Western army with air superiority. I did not believe that Saddam Hussein would widen the war by initiating a full-scale attack on Israel. The conflict was one thousand miles away, and the only party possessing the option of a major military attack was the president of the United States.

On 8 October, the Gulf War was overshadowed in Israel by an internal tragedy. While the Temple Mount was teeming with thousands of Jews praying at the Wailing (or Western) Wall and thousands of Moslems praying over the wall on the Temple Mount, a group of Arabs apparently organized themselves surreptitiously and closed off the Temple Mount, burned the Israeli police post, and showered the Western Wall plaza with rocks. It was a clear move mounted by the PLO to divert attention from the Gulf War crisis, revive the *intifada,* and create an alternative issue to stir up the Arabs, who were for the most part more anti-Saddam Hussein than anti-Israel. Taken by surprise and outnumbered, the Israeli police opened fire, killing nineteen Arabs and wounding approximately one hundred; some twenty Jews were wounded by the barrage of rocks.

It was obviously a tragic overreaction. The new team leading the police was inexperienced in such matters. Under its previous leaders, not one Arab had been killed in Jerusalem during the entire *intifada.* The loss of lives created a worldwide uproar, and Saddam Hussein achieved his goal: the UN Security Council was dealing with this problem and not with the Gulf crisis.

The next day, an official independent inquiry commission was created to head off a team appointed by the Security Council to investigate the situation. But the Temple Mount affair would not go away. The Security Council passed a resolution, with United States backing, condemning Israel for the incident and for not agreeing to receive the secretary-general's delegation. This refusal was a personal decision on the part of Shamir against the better instincts of his government. President Bush pleaded with Shamir to give them a way out, but Shamir rejected the request without consulting anyone. The whole situation was aggravated by Shamir and Bush's mutual lack of trust.

From the commission's report, which was attacked by the left wing, there emerged a picture of serious omissions on the part of our police. Despite several unanswered questions, the report would have been well received at the UN if the Israeli government had had the good sense to receive a UN delegation. But Shamir had dug in his heels and would not budge.

IN THE MIDST of the tension in the Middle East, Japan enthroned its new emperor. Aura and I attended the coronation of Emperor Akihito. The detailed instructions given to us for the enthronement ceremony required men to wear uniform or white tie; suspenders were to be white and no other color. For Aura, no skin could be uncovered; she was to wear a long dress closed to the neck, with long sleeves and gloves, and a small hat with a veil.

The imperial procession was led by the emperor, dressed in the traditional brown robes with a long train carried by aides. The empress, wearing fourteen layers of clothing, shuffled along very slowly, followed by ladies-in-waiting and the princesses. She sat motionless, like a doll, throughout the ceremony. The emperor's proclamation of his own enthronement was followed by three calls of "Banzai!" by the prime minister, and the crowd cheered.

Vice President Dan Quayle, with whom I met while in Tokyo, was at a loss to explain why, even though Saddam Hussein had specifically declared Israel destined for destruction, we were the only country against which members of the UN had ganged up. He was as unhappy as I was about the UN's position. Contrary to media reports about him, I found him highly intelligent and articulate, accompanied by a first-class staff. Israel was being attacked in the UN while in Beirut one thousand people had been killed, and heavy casualties were being inflicted when Hindus attempted to destroy a mosque in Ayodhya, India. The UN ignored these massacres and all it had time for was Israel. We had to bring our relationship back to a reasonable level.

I planned to invite UN Secretary-General De Cuellar to Israel, with a view toward stopping the Security Council's ongoing attacks on Israel's handling of the rioting on the Temple Mount. Since Shamir felt the UN could not be objective on this subject and would not meet with him, we would use Jerusalem mayor Teddy Kollek as our representative. Quayle promised to help me, and he kept his word. Our meeting in Japan was of great help in the top-level relationship between the United States and Israel.

Some good also came of my meeting with Prime Minister Kaifu of Japan, who accepted my invitation to visit Israel and announced the immediate reactivation of the joint consultative committee between Israel and Japan. The embassy in Israel would now receive a commercial attaché—an important step forward: Japan was by now our number-three trading partner.

President Bush called me when I was in Los Angeles on my way home to Israel. He had heard of my objections to the UN attacks on Israel. He realized it had been a mistake to seize upon the Temple Mount incident and move the center of interest from Saddam Hussein and the Gulf; Bush said he would do everything to take the matter out of the Security Council, although there was opposition to this. He also said he would welcome a face-to-face session to "cry on your shoulder" over the strained relations between our countries.

He thanked me profusely for the complimentary remarks I'd made in San Francisco about his leadership. As he put it, "I need it." I told him I was not impressed by the line the United States was taking, and explained the danger of Saddam Hussein to the American people. He told me he agreed with me, and added that if I would read his interview in *Newsweek* the following week, I would see that he had changed his approach. Shamir was very encouraged by this talk.

The deadline for the withdrawal of the Iraqis from Kuwait was 15 January 1991. There was no intention of negotiating with the Iraqis, President Bush said, merely of putting them on notice as to American intentions. Israel could only hope that the Americans and their allies would attack and destroy the Iraqi potential for destruction, particularly their nonconventional weapons. And we could only pray that they would bring an end to Saddam Hussein's reign.

CHAPTER 29

The Presidency—1991

ON 16 JANUARY 1991, the Americans led the coalition in attacking Iraq with high-level bombing. They claimed that they had destroyed much of the Iraqi military infrastructure, but we saw just how inaccurate that boast turned out to be that night, when Iraqi Scud rockets landed in Ramat Gan and Azur, near Tel-Aviv.

The next night, a large area in Ramat Gan was destroyed. Thousands of apartments were damaged during one week of bombing, with four thousand people rendered homeless; loss of life was, fortunately, minimal. Of the forty Scuds fired at Israel, many missed their targets and caused no damage.

The government came under heavy pressure, especially from the right wing, to take action against the Iraqis, but the Americans and the coalition members begged us to do nothing, so as not to embarrass them with their Arab allies. Shamir held fast and acquiesced in the American requests; if anything went wrong, Israel would have been blamed for sabotaging the war effort. Suddenly, we were popular again. Shamir's stand was courageous and wise, and we were inundated with goodwill and offers of support.

In the afternoon of 18 January, President Mitterrand called me. In my radio talk to the nation a few days before, I had referred to the groveling attitude of some of the European countries, which had clearly not learned from the era of appeasement years ago. This hurt Mitterrand very much. He was also offended by the chairman of the Foreign Affairs and Defense Committee of the Knesset, who had attributed French technology to the Scuds, when in fact they were Russian. I did not back down. I told Mitterrand that what hurt *us* was what happened at the UN Security Council. The UN was trying to negotiate with Saddam Hussein to withdraw from Kuwait. As part of a compromise, the French suggested the UN agree to open up the Palestine question once again. How could they possibly link the two issues, I asked. There was no justification for it; it was a grave mistake. Mitterrand did not back down, either. He emphasized that he was very much against Saddam Hussein, which was why he had sent 12,000 French troops into the Saudi desert.

I clearly had struck a nerve. After another Scud attack two days later, Mitterrand sent me a cable, and then a few days after that he sent his deputy foreign minister to Israel. He also delivered a broadcast to France, which was picked up around the world. We talked several more times, and in one of our conversations he reminded me that while he had indeed supplied arms to Iraq, he was no better and no worse than others who had done so, and he himself had fought very hard against Iraqi attempts to rebuild the nuclear facility which Israel had destroyed in 1981. I accepted his political sincerity, although I still did not agree with him and it must be said that the record of the French in international relations was not always exemplary.

Scuds kept falling sporadically, primarily in Tel Aviv and its suburbs. As a battle-tried nation, Israel had faced great dangers with courage and determination. But this was a new type of war, with an enemy attacking from over 600 miles away with less than a few minutes' warning. Anyone who says it was not unnerving is lying.

Damage in the Hatikva Quarter of Tel Aviv, where some of the first Scud missiles landed, and which Mayor "Chich" Lahat and I inspected, was considerable, and many houses were leveled. Luckily, quite a few people had gone to public shelters and were saved; many others tried to reach the main shelter near the football stadium. Fortunately, no one reached it in time: a missile landed twelve feet from the entrance and completely demolished it.

In nearby Ramat Gan, the situation was much worse; one district was almost completely destroyed. Aura and I visited it with the mayor, Zvi Bar. Miraculously, only one person was killed. Despite the great sense of unity, of pulling together, there was no sense of heroism. This was a passive war, and all we could do was stay strong and wait.

One controversy emerging from the war concerned the effectiveness —or otherwise—of the Patriot antiaircraft missiles, which we were sent generously by the Americans, the Dutch, and the Germans. The Israeli experience did not confirm the missiles' effectiveness. The Scud missile disintegrated when coming down, its component parts providing targets for the Patriot. Unfortunately, the warhead frequently continued to the target unaffected.

While the public showed enormous inner strength, some of the authorities did not always. They were dictated to by civil defense authorities and, against the prime minister's wish, closed the schools. People could not get to work because they had to stay home to look after their children. Entire businesses were collapsing, which affected industrial plants throughout the country and sent the economy plunging again. Any other country in a war doubles its efforts to produce and to advance economically, yet we were doing just the reverse. Shamir was against this policy, but the ministers had decided otherwise.

THE ARAB REACTION to the war was very complicated. Among Arabs, the wealthy Gulf states, like Kuwait, were unpopular; but Saddam Hussein was fairly popular, regarded by the man in the street as a fighter against the imperialist West—even when the West was represented by their own Arab nations. There were violent pro-Hussein protests in Syria, Tunisia, Libya, and Algeria; grassroots support in Jordan; and a student riot in Egypt in a show of solidarity. My own opinion is that Bush stopped the military push too soon, two days before his forces would have reached Hussein, because President Mubarak of Egypt needed an end to the internal pro-Saddam Hussein rioting. There was an overwhelming feeling of frustration and loss of honor in the Arab world, and Bush's early end to the war was a political acknowledgment of that—as well as an enormous error that he has since conceded. As long as Saddam Hussein remained on the scene, the war was not concluded but only postponed.

Despite his ignominious defeat, Hussein managed, by concentrating the remaining military forces loyal to him and by the effective use of an extensive security apparatus, to retain power. He appeared on TV, promising reforms and calling for national unity. He had the nerve to use his propaganda machine to declare victory. As the truth came out, the Shiites, backed by the Iranians across the border, revolted. But they were ruthlessly and brutally suppressed by the revolutionary guard units of Saddam's army. In Kurdistan, the same thing happened. The revolt of the Kurds, which had the support of the Turkish government, was a little more successful; areas of Kurdistan in northern Iraq remained in the hands of the Kurds.

Israel was not happy with the war's resolution. President Bush sent a tremor through part of Israel's society by emphasizing that the American policy, as far as our conflict was concerned, would be that of "territory for peace," and he emphasized the urgency of a satisfactory resolution of the Palestinian issue. All this came while Secretary of State Baker was in the Middle East gathering information, and Bush was riding high with the American people. We would have to play our cards very carefully to succeed with this administration.

Baker arrived in Israel to listen and learn, not to talk. He asked the right questions and absorbed the answers. Both he and Bush disliked Shamir and did not want to see him continue as prime minister, but Baker was very impressed by Rabin. I realized that the Americans had a strong preference for an Israeli prime minister—and it was clearly for Rabin.

Fulminating against Sharon, Baker insisted at one of our meetings that he was sabotaging U.S. peace efforts by establishing and enlarging settlements. The Americans had a tendency to exaggerate as far as settlements were concerned; at least 50,000 so-called settlers lived in the suburbs of Jerusalem, which Baker could see from his hotel window. This was a natural process of urban expansion, no different from the spread of suburbia anywhere. I explained to him that it would be wrong to suspect Mayor Teddy Kollek of duplicitous behavior.

Baker seemed particularly impressed by President Hafiz al-Assad of Syria—much more than by Mubarak of Egypt—although he recognized how cruel Assad could be. Baker saw things in strictly political terms; cruelty—at the presidential level, at least—probably did not register on Baker's moral compass. Despite his intelligence and ability, Baker was mishandling his shuttle diplomacy, both with us and with the Arabs. He had not achieved a single concession from the Arabs; all compromise was coming from Israel. Shamir and Arens were becoming resentful, and the Arabs were beginning to think they had total control of the situation. It was not the way to handle either side.

THE DETERIORATING RELATIONS between Israel and the United States were reflected in an incident involving Ariel Sharon, who was in America. He was about to make a courtesy call on his opposite number, Jack Kemp, the U.S. secretary of housing and development, but Baker, with Bush's backing, forbade Kemp to receive him. Accordingly, Kemp came to see Sharon at the embassy. This was a deliberate slap in the face. Such an event had never occurred before. Word reached us that Bush was furious about Sharon's setting up two settlements at the time Baker was negotiating. Sharon made a public statement, while still in the States, that he was carrying out the policy of the government of Israel. Sharon was in the wrong. There had been no point in broadcasting the movement of a few prefabricated buildings as a major expansion of the settlements. He was trying to show his strength and fearlessness—in contrast to what he indicated was Shamir's indecisiveness and weakness. It was his way of trying to take over the Likud leadership.

In April 1991, Baker returned to Israel. Tom Friedman of *The New York Times* arrived with him. He told me that Baker was a very cold and aloof man; the peace negotiation was just another job at which he wanted to succeed. Friedman also said that the subject of Israel, the territories, and the Palestinian problem had become an obsession with Bush. The feeling among the other newspapermen in Baker's party was that Jordan deeply appreciated Israel's understanding of Jordan's behavior in the recent Gulf crisis. The fact is that we understood, far more than the United States did, King Hussein's dilemma and his decision to support Saddam Hussein, although we did not agree with him. Bush and Baker were not at all happy with Jordan's stance during the war.

Baker met together—for the first time—with Shamir, Arens, and David Levy, the three politicians most involved with the peace process. Baker had insisted on this one meeting, fed up with concluding an agreement with one minister only to be told by the others that it was not valid. This time, they all managed to come to a broad agreement for a regional conference. However, Baker had not made any advance with Syria, so the conference would now be limited to Israel, Egypt, Jordan, and the Palestinians—in addition, of course, to the United States and the Soviet Union.

President Lech Walesa, who arrived with his wife on the first state visit by the head of the Polish state, proved to be tough, honest, outspoken, and fearless. The presidency did not change his way of life; he remained a worker and an electrician, returning home every weekend from the presidential palace to his apartment in Gdansk. He was quite aware of the tension and controversy surrounding his visit, having allegedly made anti-Semitic remarks in his campaign, for which he was now being held accountable. Walesa addressed the Knesset, despite criticism over the invitation, but there was no need to worry. His plea for forgiveness for what had happened to Jews on Polish soil did not seem to be an empty gesture.

Born in 1943, Walesa told me he had never even seen a Jew while growing up and was overwhelmed by what he saw in Israel. Convinced that he would arrive to strife and bloodshed in the streets, he found the atmosphere pastoral and the people relaxed, with life continuing normally. Despite our problems, there was great pride in our achievements, and Walesa decided that Polish industry was a hundred years behind ours. "Leave the pope to me," he said about Israel's relations with the Vatican. "I will talk to him as a Pole talks to a Pole."

FOUR MEMBERS OF the Knesset, Uriel Lynn, Amnon Rubinstein, David Libai, and Yoash Tsiddon, visited me to mobilize my support for a bill calling for the direct election of the prime minister. They promised that the next step would be an attempt to legislate in favor of a constituency election system, which is what I had been rooting for all along. I saw virtue in their bill provided it would lead to a system such as the one used in France to elect their president, or to a mixed system—50 percent constituency, 50 percent national list—such as in Germany. But I suspected that under the system proposed, Israel's small parties would grow at the expense of the large parties. I felt that the only way to bring the small parties down to their natural size was to move to constituency elections and to increase the threshold from the current 1.5 percent to 4 percent, the European average. (My fears proved valid. When the elections took place in May 1996 under the new system, the horse trading that took place showed that the smaller parties had been strengthened and the larger parties weakened. Without a major overhaul in our electoral system, we will never achieve internal political stability.)

YITZHAK RABIN WAS NOW determined to go head-to-head with Peres to gain leadership of the Labor Party. He decided to throw his full support behind, and demostrated total identification with, the proposed modification of the electoral system that would turn the vote for prime minister into a direct, popular election. Peres opposed this stubbornly, while Rabin realized that this change could give him a distinct edge. For the first time, Rabin was making a concerted effort to ingratiate himself with Labor members as well as others in the Knesset. Though hardly his normal style, this showed a certain enlightened self-interest. Peres went to every wedding and bar mitzvah of every Labor member. Rabin had never done that sort of thing—until now. This "new" Rabin was clearly on his way to becoming our next prime minister.

JAMES BAKER CAME on his fifth shuttle visit to Israel. Assad had now concluded that the United States was the only superpower, and he could no longer rely on the Soviet Union's backing. Therefore, his only option was to enter the U.S. orbit and adapt to the new situation. As always, unless one is dealing with the most fanatical of fanatics, reality and pragmatism won out in the political arena. Without Soviet support, Assad had to negotiate with Israel because the United States was insisting on it. Assad accordingly toned down his extreme position and indicated a new approach to President Bush. Without going into details of the Palestinian question or making specific demands about the Golan Heights, he was finally prepared for his negotiators to meet face-to-face with Israeli negotiators after the formal opening of a regional conference, and to bargain without preconditions. From a public relations standpoint, Assad had clearly outmaneuvered Israel. The world suddenly saw this cruel dictator and manipulator of terrorist organizations as a great paragon of peace. Now Israel was seen as the only reluctant player in the game.

Baker met with Palestinians in Jerusalem under the leadership of Faisal Husseini. Baker had problems because of Israel's insistence that there be no representatives of the PLO or of East Jerusalem in the conference delegation. The Palestinians maintained that to yield on this issue, to forgo a voice, would be impossible.

As the debate intensified within Israel, there was a threat that some right-wing parties might bolt from the government. Peres announced in the Knesset that Labor, without asking for any consideration or political reward, would give Shamir the necessary parliamentary support to advance the peace process. It was a statesmanlike move—and the right thing to do.

Polls indicated that some 70 percent of Israel's population favored going to the conference; 59 percent opposed the return of any part of the Golan to the Syrians. Shamir again announced that he would not go along with any territorial concessions whatsoever. We would now face essential issues, and Shamir would now be exposed to considerable international pressure.

Baker returned again at the end of July. He had received quite a few concessions and position clarifications from Shamir, who still saw the principal problem as the composition of the Palestinian delegation that would be part of a Jordanian-Palestinian delegation; he insisted that only Palestinian residents of the West Bank and Gaza be eligible and excluded residents of Jerusalem and representatives of the Palestinian diaspora. Shamir agreed to recommend that Israel attend a regional peace conference in October. Arafat declared that there would be no delegation without the PLO's approval. President Assad responded by highlighting the folly of the PLO, which had taken the side of the aggressor in the invasion of Kuwait instead of representing the Palestinians.

The agreement to attend the conference was welcomed in Israel by a sound majority, although Sharon came out openly against it—of course —along with the extreme right-wing parties. Our real troubles were just beginning. After interminable procedural negotiations as part of the Baker shuttle diplomacy, we were facing substantive issues, and it was not in Shamir's nature to agree to anything substantive.

A new situation was now being created in the Middle East. The Likud Party in Israel had been strengthened. President Assad of Syria had become more realistic or was smartly outwitting everybody—which amounted to the same thing. President Mubarak of Egypt was obviously a "favorite son" as far as President Bush was concerned. King Hussein was following developments closely in the hope that Jordan could return to the political mainstream. There were many indications of a distinct improvement in Jordan's attitude toward Israel; Hussein's appreciation of Shamir was growing. Peace was now needed as much by the Arabs as by the Israelis. For this reason alone, it was actually possible.

ISRAEL'S LEADERS HEADED consciously toward a collision course with the United States. Israel submitted an application for a $10 billion loan guarantee to absorb immigration, which was running at about 100,000 a year—ignoring Secretary Baker's request to Shamir for a four-month postponement of the application. President Bush asked Congress to reject the proposal, at least temporarily, in the interests of the peace negotiations. Israel replied, quite correctly, that there could be no linkage; a purely humanitarian move could not be related to political issues.

If the loan guarantee was not approved, Israel would find itself unable to absorb its influx of immigrants. Sharon was guilty of exceeding his budget by some 400 million shekels. Yet no action was being taken against him, and Shamir refused to acknowledge any existence of the problem.

Bush was clearly losing his temper. His obsession with Israeli settlements could do us great harm unless dealt with, yet Shamir refused to go along with him on something as simple as a loan postponement. To add insult to injury, every time Baker came to Israel on a shuttle visit, Sharon saw to it that prefabricated buildings were very publicly moved into a village in the territories, adding to an existing settlement or even creating a new one. When attacked, Sharon replied obstinately that his every move had been approved by Shamir. At the very least, Shamir certainly did nothing to stop Sharon's self-destructive moves. Bush was furious and had obviously decided to teach Israel a lesson that could prove to be very costly.

In the stupidest move of all, Israeli television broadcast a program depicting the scope of new and existing settlements. The film was sent to President Bush, who hit the ceiling and called an unscheduled press conference. Without mentioning the settlements, he said he did not want this issue of loan guarantees to prejudice the peace process. He banged the podium as he spoke, obviously under great pressure. If Congress voted to approve the loan guarantees, he would veto the resolution.

Bush did not like us—plain and simple—not from any anti-Semitism but because of our policies. And he obviously disliked Shamir, who had sailed too close to the wind and had maneuvered himself into a corner that he had been trying desperately to avoid.

Bush summoned the leaders of AIPAC, the Israeli lobby in Washington. He had only just begun to fight; if necessary he would explain his policy to the entire nation and mobilize the American people to force Congress to postpone the guarantee. Our government's Micawberish assumption that "everything will turn out all right," combined with our leaders' total failure to understand Bush's motivation, had created a dire situation. Without U.S. support, we would be considerably weakened. An editorial in *The New York Times* was headed "We Are Fed Up with Shamir."

Shamir's situation was now lose-lose. If he did not suspend settlement activities in the territories, he would have a major confrontation with the president of the United States. If he did suspend them, he would lose the support of the Israeli right wing, which would probably bring down his government.

Meanwhile, President Bush won in Washington. Congress agreed to postpone dealing with the loan guarantees by four months. It was portrayed by the U.S. media as the first resounding defeat of the Jewish lobby.

OUR SECOND VISIT behind the Iron Curtain was as guests of President Vaclav Havel of Czechoslovakia. President Havel had by now become an experienced and very popular president. Prague is a beautiful city full of Jewish memories, tradition, and heritage. In my meetings in Prague, I raised the issue of the Jewish religious property which had been gathered by Adolf Eichmann in Prague for the purpose of creating a museum recalling what the Germans believed would be an extinct nation, the Jewish nation. I had many meetings on this subject with the officials of the Czech Republic and the parliament of the Czech Republic. At the state dinner held in the magnificent hall of the famous Hardcany Castle, my neighbor was Alexander Dubcek, the speaker of the parliament and the man who stood up against the invasion of the Russians in 1968. He told me that contrary to what was generally believed, he was not flown lying on the floor of a plane to Moscow, but instead was spirited to a place outside Prague, where he lay bound on the floor of an army tank for over two days.

Dubcek presided when I addressed the national assembly. When in my speech I raised the question of confiscated Jewish property, and the anomaly whereby the Czechs were continuing to honor Eichmann's testament instead of restoring this property to a living Jewish people, I was greeted with loud applause.

Everywhere we were reminded of the great history of the Jewish people—in the synagogues, which had been converted into museums, and in the ancient Altneuschul Synagogue, dating back to 1270, in which the legendary Maharal, Rabbi Loew of Prague, had prayed.

The official ceremony marking the fiftieth anniversary of the creation of the Nazi concentration camp in Theresienstadt took place in the Smetana Theatre in Prague in front of 2,000 people and was broadcast live on TV. President Havel delivered a most moving speech on anti-Semitism, which he told me he had sat up all night to write. After I spoke, we joined the Havels in the royal box and heard the Czech Philharmonic Orchestra and the Prague Choir give a most magnificent rendition of Verdi's *Requiem*. At the time of the Nazis, this great work had been performed fifteen times by an obsessed conductor who had repeatedly gathered together an orchestra and a choir in Theresienstadt, only to lose them after each concert when the musicians and singers were shipped off to Auschwitz. The last concert, the fifteenth, was given in the presence of Adolf Eichmann and guests from the International Red Cross, to whom Germans were trying to prove that Theresienstadt was a normal town. After performing in front of Eichmann, the conductor committed suicide. His sister was present in the audience and a number of those attending fainted from emotion. It was probably the most moving concert I have ever attended, full of human significance and tragedy, making the evening and the trip truly unforgettable.

ON 30 OCTOBER the Madrid Peace Conference opened. It was an American show, and the Russians appeared as poor relations. Israel was in turmoil until the very last moment, because this time Shamir had humiliated his foreign minister, David Levy, who was due to head our delegation until Shamir decided that he himself would lead it. The United States, Russia, Egypt, and the European Community also sent delegations to this meeting, the first ever of its kind.

The Israeli and Palestinian delegations both spoke in terms of accommodation if not of compromise; Israel offered a transitional phase of autonomy, and the Palestinians indicated a willingness to accept it. Israel insisted that the bilateral talks that would emerge from this conference take place in the Middle East, alternately in Israel and an Arab country. Syria insisted they be held in Madrid; the Americans wanted Washington. In any case, the process had begun and, in the long run, would be irreversible.

HERE IS HOW ludicrous politics can get. Many of the gains made in Madrid were lost because the politicians could not agree on where the follow-up bilateral talks should take place. Shamir tried to influence Bush and Baker to have the meetings in the Middle East—if not in Israel or an Arab country, then Cyprus or somewhere nearby. Without saying a word to him, the Americans issued invitations to participating countries for a meeting in Washington the first week of December. It was a real slap in the face and part of the bullying process by the United States—especially after Shamir had gone out of his way to praise Bush for getting the whole process moving. Shamir told Bush that he would recommend to the government of Israel that it not accept the invitation.

Israeli and American delegations arranged to discuss some of the substantive issues certain to come up at the bilateral talks. Beforehand, Shamir and Bush met privately, for what was supposed to be five minutes, but the conference lasted forty-five minutes—the entire time originally allotted to the meeting of the delegations. Vice President Quayle, waiting outside, was beside himself with anger, while Shamir wasted forty valuable minutes with the president of the United States discussing a mere administrative point: where the meeting was going to take place! But the issue of venue was not unimportant. The Arabs were trying to push the whole process back to an international conference, which Israel had always opposed. They were basically trying to ignore Israel and concentrate on talking with the United States. Israel wanted to set up face-to-face sessions with the Arabs by mutual agreement and without U.S. supervision. At that time, the Arabs were unwilling to have them.

The Washington meeting was called for 4 December. The inner cabinet announced that Israel would come five days later, in order to emphasize that it could not be dictated to on any issue—administrative or substantive. A State Department spokeswoman characterized the move as childish. She was being charitable. This was hardly the level of diplomatic dialogue we should have reached.

Sharon was bitter and frustrated about the lack of leadership in the government, sensing not only hostility all around him but also complete indifference to the great problems facing the state; Modai, our minister of finance, had the same feeling about his colleagues. Despite the apparent absence of leadership the public did not seem excessively bothered by it. It was a strange and anomalous situation.

ON 16 DECEMBER 1991, the UN resolution equating Zionism with racism was revoked by the General Assembly by a surprisingly large majority. Without the Americans, who took the lead and pushed to have the resolution adopted, this outstanding victory could never have been achieved. The countries revoking the resolution—all the former Communist countries, many Third World and nonaligned countries, even the Soviet Union and India—were a revelation. Sixteen years earlier we had been subjected to attack, diatribe, condemnation, and calumny. The world had changed considerably.

—

As THE SOVIET UNION approached its end, many constituent republics, such as Georgia and Armenia, asked Israel to recognize them and establish diplomatic relations. In December, the U.S.S.R. was replaced by a Commonwealth of Independent States, with the Russian state, led by Boris Yeltsin, predominant. If ever there was poetic justice, it was in the ceremony at which the Soviet ambassador presented his credentials. For twenty-four years, since the Six-Day War, there had been no diplomatic relations between our two countries. The Soviet Union had now decided to establish relations, but a few days left before it would disintegrate; this was to be its last official public function in the world in which the red flag with the hammer and sickle would be raised and the Soviet Russian national anthem would be played. It took place at the president's residence in Jerusalem. On 31 December all ambassadors of the Soviet Union became ambassadors of the Russian Republic.

Ambassador Alexander Bovin, a professor and writer in *Izvestia,* arrived in the dress uniform of the Soviet Foreign Service, but he had forgotten his sword and hat. He had come to Israel via Cairo and across the Sinai Desert, he explained to the press, because it was much cheaper. How the mighty had fallen.

———— ⊶✹⊷ ————

The Presidency—1992

WHEN CARDINAL O'CONNOR of New York called on me in 1992, he was dressed in full canonicals and arrived with a complete delegation. He had come on an official visit; the Vatican wanted to improve relations with us.

The time had come—the Vatican had to recognize us officially for political reasons. China, India, and Russia were building ties to Israel, and the Vatican was now in the minority on this issue. If it held out much longer, it faced the risk of becoming irrelevant and isolated.

We would be happy for the pope to visit Israel, but only as one head of state visiting another. There would be no crossing the border at some unofficial point, as Pope Paul VI had done in 1964. Islamic fundamentalism constituted a danger for Jews and Christians alike, and prejudice was clouding the Vatican's vision on this issue. The pope was now in full agreement with Israel on this point.

The Vatican had also made a major change of policy on Jerusalem. It no longer had political reservations about Israeli control of the city; it only wanted to ensure the safety and freedom of Christian residents and institutions as well as freedom of religion and access. Such conditions had always been and would continue to be acceptable to Israel.

Another distinguished ecclesiastic who called on me was the Archbishop of Canterbury, George Carey, who came with a number of aides, including the Anglican bishop. It's safe to say we were not on the same wavelength. The archbishop was quite critical about certain aspects of our relations with our Arab neighbors. I pointed out to him that the actions he was objecting to, such as expulsion orders, were all based on laws which the British had promulgated in Palestine. Indeed, our prime minister, Yitzhak Shamir, had been exiled by the British under the same law. When the archbishop persisted about our restrictive policies, I compared England's behavior toward the IRA with Israel's behavior toward the PLO. I pointed out that, at that time, no spokesperson of the IRA was allowed to be heard on the British media. In contrast, Yasser Arafat appeared regularly on Israeli TV. We would listen to anyone and allow anyone to speak. What we wouldn't allow was any action that directly threatened the existence of the state. All in all, quite a reasonable policy.

SHIMON PERES AND YITZHAK RABIN were struggling to win leadership of the Labor Party, and it was no longer a friendly contest. The polls indicated that Shamir would beat Peres if he were elected Labor leader but would be beaten by Rabin if he were elected. Peres thought all pollsters were dishonest and refused to be influenced by them. Rabin, ever the pragmatist, did not understand why Peres would not just get out of the way and clear the path for a Labor victory. Their political relationship was singular: they did not like each other yet complemented each other like no team in Israel's history. Their success with the Peace Plan was a perfect example. Peres had spent years looking for a link to the Arabs and ultimately decided on Arafat when many thought the choice was lunacy. But Peres could never have carried the plan out without Rabin's strength, cautiousness, and the trust he inspired in the Israeli people. It had been agonizing to watch them vie for power, but such is the nature of politics.

Following the Madrid Conference, direct talks began between an Israeli delegation on the one hand and Jordanian-Palestinian, Lebanese, and Syrian delegations on the other. The multilateral talks in Moscow that opened in January were attended by Israel as well as by representatives of all the Gulf States, led by Saudi Arabia.

Subcommittees were created to handle disarmament, ecology, water, economics, and refugees. Canada, the United States, Belgium, and Turkey were to host their meetings, scheduled for May and June; the process would involve Egypt, China, the Gulf States, Saudi Arabia, Tunisia, and Jordan. This development indicated a major advance; full diplomatic relations between India and Israel were announced.

IN THE RACE for Labor Party leadership, Rabin won 40.6 percent of the votes; Peres finished with 35 percent. This comeback was an extraordinary personal triumph for Rabin, who had been forced to resign as prime minister in 1977. Perceived as tough and strong, Rabin was allowed to show a flexibility that would have been called weakness in another leader. This is why Nixon could open the door to China, when a "weaker" Democrat would never have been given the opportunity by the American public.

Peres accepted his defeat with dignity but took first spot on the list in the Knesset primaries. The rank and file voted him in in a big way. He felt that this gave him the basis for a continued central leadership role in the Labor Party. In addition to vitriolic remarks about Shamir, he was critical of Rabin, though he obviously did not want him to lose. He took to heart the words of Felipe Gonzales, the prime minister of Spain, who said that Rabin could win an election, but only Peres would know what to do with the victory.

In the Likud Central Committee elections Shamir emerged with a vote of 46 percent, somewhat of a disappointment, considering he was the incumbent prime minister. The results promised an interesting race in the national elections. Rabin had the distinct advantage of being attractive to those Likud members who were disappointed with the actions of the Likud leadership.

AURA LED A DELEGATION to a conference in Geneva of the wives of heads of state. The purpose was to discuss the position and role of women in the village and on the farm, and it was linked to the Food and Agriculture Organization of the United Nations. It was presided over by Fabiola, queen of the Belgians, and was attended by sixty-three wives and daughters, including Queen Noor of Jordan, Queen Sofia of Spain, Mrs. Suzy Mubarak of Egypt, Qadaffi's daughter from Libya, a princess of Morocco, and the wife of the president of Tunis. Aura spoke about the role of women in Israel and developed a friendly relationship with Mrs. Mubarak, who chaired her committee. She returned very satisfied that some good came out of the conference. The women seemed more able than their husbands to rise above political maneuverings.

In general, I would say women are fairly equal to men in Israel's society. There is still a push for better treatment and a furthering of women's rights, but all in all it is not the major issue that it is in America or England. It is not an obsession (of course, *every* cause in America becomes an obsession). In Israel, laws have been passed to assure certain rights. There must be a certain percentage of women on the boards of public companies. We have had several women ministers and Supreme Court justices, although not enough. The Labor Party and the Likud guarantee a minimum number of women on their national list for the Knesset. The courts have confirmed the rights of women to serve on the religious councils which run municipal religious affairs.

MEANWHILE, OUR RELATIONSHIP WITH the Americans was becoming increasingly strained. In March, President Bush had obviously decided to teach Congress and the Jewish lobby a lesson; the confrontation that had developed over loan guarantees for immigration to Israel was a major miscalculation in relations with the United States. Unable to move out of the corner into which he had maneuvered himself, Shamir assigned responsibility for his miscalculation to leaders of the American Jewish establishment and friends in Congress. President Bush's reaction came as a complete surprise to him.

Israel was soon facing allegations of giving away technology received from the Americans. On Israel's insistence, an American defense mission was sent to examine published complaints, and nothing was found. The atmosphere was such that the mission did not have the good grace to apologize publicly.

MY STATE VISIT to Spain marked the 500th anniversary of the expulsion of the Jews by King Ferdinand and Queen Isabella and the historic reconciliation of the Spanish and Jewish people. Somewhere, somehow, the Jews who had been burned at the stake, tortured, and exiled five centuries before because of their faith were witness to the developments in Madrid.

The great Jewish statesman, philosopher, and biblical exegete Isaac Abrabanel, who was in the service of King Ferdinand and Queen Isabella, appealed in vain to revoke the edict of expulsion of Spanish Jewry signed on 31 March 1492. On our way to Spain, Aura and I read the most moving appeal, and realized that we were now becoming part of a great national experience. Little did Abrabanel realize that it would be five hundred years to the very day before the edict was revoked, and Spain, represented by King Juan Carlos and Queen Sofia, achieved a reconciliation with the Jewish people represented by the president of a Jewish state reestablished in its ancient homeland.

Aura and I went with King Juan Carlos and Queen Sofia to the synagogue where the ceremony of reconciliation took place. It was a small house of worship located on the third floor of the Jewish community center building. We were received by the heads of the Jewish community. It was the first time a Spanish king had ever visited a synagogue. Queen Sofia had, however, been introduced to Judaism by a theologian who regularly taught her about our religion.

After our formal arrival, the four of us entered the synagogue to the singing of a choir and orchestral music. When we approached the Ark of the Law (*Aron Kodesh*), the king and queen sat to the left of the *Aron Kodesh*. Aura and I took the two seats to its right.

Several members of the community spoke. Edmond Safra, representing the world's Sephardi Jewish community, talked about his grandparents' great-grandparents, who had been exiled from Spain, and he gave voice to great emotions. A most moving memorial prayer was intoned by the cantor in memory of those who had died at the hands of the Inquisition. The blessings for the royal family and the president of Israel were given by a local rabbi. At the end, I spoke in Spanish, and was followed by the king. We both were conciliatory about the past and hopeful about the future.

It was incredible, to me, to be a part of this repudiation of such a vile part of history. Whereas I was usually the symbol who caused others to cry with emotion, this time it was the symbol who shed the tears.

WITHIN A FEW MONTHS we moved from one sad and tragic chapter in the history of the Jewish people to another. Our state visit to Poland began in Warsaw, most of whose Jewish inhabitants had been annihilated; it is in effect the capital of the world's largest Jewish graveyard. As I stood there and listened to Israel's anthem, there flashed across my inward eye that haunting picture of a little Jewish boy in Warsaw with his hands held up in surrender as mocking German soldiers direct their weapons at him. In the Umschlagplatz adjoining the ghetto, Jews were assembled before being shipped in crowded trains to the annihilation camps; on Sienna Street a remnant of the ghetto wall had been uncovered and become a place of pilgrimage.

Auschwitz was shattering. Each of the various blocks had its specific function of death and torture. The dreadful remnants of the Holocaust were preserved in showcases—hair cut off before victims were gassed, thousands of spectacles, shoes, and children's clothes. Perhaps the most poignant exhibition was of suitcases and valises, each bearing the owner's name and date of birth with an occasional observation that the owner was an orphan or a small child on his or her own. This exhibition of cold-blooded efficiency applied to the murder of children was heartrending. Birkenau, adjacent to Auschwitz, housed the death machines—gas chambers and incinerators that worked overtime; the remnants of human bones and ashes still protrude from the soil.

We drove in total silence to Cracow, whose old Jewish quarter, Kazimierz, had produced great leaders and geniuses. Seven synagogues survived the Nazis because they were used as stables; the Rama synagogue was very badly maintained. The Jewish community today comprises about 200 people, most of them intermarried but clinging desperately to Jewish traditions and origins. They gave me a volume of the Tractate of the Talmud, Pesachim, published in Vilna by the renowned widow Roehm at the end of the last century. I happened to own a copy of exactly the same Tractate, from the same printer, found in Hitler's bunker, having been brought there from Katowicz. It belonged to my father, who recorded its story in the volume in his own handwriting.

Two hundred kilometers northeast of Warsaw, we came to the township of Tikocin. The Jewish community had been led by a series of important rabbis, and in the Jewish world it was known as Tiktin. The entire Jewish community, some 3,000 people, was taken one morning during World War II to a nearby forest, where they were murdered and buried in three adjacent mass graves.

Because it, too, was used as a German military stable, the ancient synagogue in Tikocin survived the Holocaust and the war. It is a beautiful building dating back to 1640. The synagogue itself is large and impressive, with prayers written all over the walls in large, artistic letters. Upstairs is the rabbi's study, with many of the old prayer and Talmudic books on display. The *bima* was of exquisitely carved wood. A non-Jewish lady came especially from Warsaw to explain everything to us in perfect Hebrew.

The entire population of Tikocin gathered outside the synagogue as we left for the drive to the town's old cemetery. On one 200-year-old tombstone, on the grave of a woman, my colleagues found the name Herzog. As Tikocin is near Lomza, where my grandfather had officiated as a rabbi and my father was born, there likely was some family connection.

The mayor of the town, in which not a single Jew survived, delivered a very nostalgic speech. He said that all those who were old enough still recalled the Sabbath eves, when various melodies emerged from the Jewish homes in which prayers were being sung. It was a beautiful memory, which none of the old-timers could forget, he declared.

We drove to the forest, to the site of the mass graves, where the delegation and I intoned the Kaddish and where I laid a wreath. A Polish farmer who had been a young boy tending cattle in the forest when the massacre took place described it all to us. He saw everything. With tears in his eyes, he gave us a vivid picture of the terrifying scene. We stood in choked silence and again contemplated the results of the evil of man.

Lomza, some ninety miles northeast of Warsaw, is where my grandfather had served as a rabbi in the last century and headed the local Hovevei Zion movement, forerunner of the Zionist movement. As we entered the town, we passed the river, which I recalled from my grandfather's stories of his youth. On one occasion he dived into the river and rescued a drowning Polish boy. The Jewish community of some 10,000 had been wiped out during the Holocaust, the synagogue and ghetto totally destroyed. All that remained was a plaque and a fading photograph of the synagogue.

On 28 May, I addressed a joint session of both houses of the Polish parliament, the Sejm and the Senate. I opened by saying how moved I was to stand there, the grandson of the rabbi of a small town in Poland, who had participated in the struggle against the Nazis and who had fought for the independence of his country and who was now president of Israel. I recalled the names of the Jewish members of the Sejm and the Senate who had served in the period between the wars, including two who were to become ministers in the government of Israel and two who were later members of the Executive of the World Zionist Organization. I talked about the 1,000-year-long history of the Jews in Poland, the terrible tragedy of the Holocaust which had befallen us, and when I dealt with political developments in the Middle East, I warned about the great danger of Islamic fundamentalism. I raised the question of the growth of anti-Semitism in a country such as Poland, where so few Jews remained. It was a delicate subject to broach, but the response was positive. Once again an expression of the dramatic change in Jewish history: the head of an independent Jewish state speaking to the parliament of the country in which Auschwitz existed, with its terrifying memories.

—

ON 14 JUNE 1992, Mikhail Sergeyevich Gorbachev, the former Soviet leader who gave rise to glasnost, and his wife, Raisa, came to Israel. They attended a state dinner, along with some one hundred other guests, which we organized in their honor. The guests included Natan and Avital Sharansky. Gorbachev, meeting Sharansky for the first time, was visibly moved. Raisa said that she remembered Avital: she had seen her demonstrating against them on their first visit to New York. The friendly meeting between Gorbachev and Sharansky perhaps more than anything else signified the amazing revolution that had occurred.

At the dinner, I emphasized the unique place that Gorbachev now held in history, the gratitude of the Jewish people to him for opening the gates for the Jews of Russia, and also for the major part that he had played in reducing the tension between the major powers in the Middle East. In his remarks, Gorbachev admitted that he was not enthusiastic about the emigration of Russian Jews to Israel and did not want to lose their skills or brains. But he certainly believed in their right to leave if they wished. He spoke very highly of Ronald Reagan, wondering if Israelis really appreciated the value of the Reagan-Shultz team. We most certainly did—they were our greatest friends. Far from expert in complicated Israel–Arab relations, Reagan saw things in black and white. Because we were the good guys, he rode with us all the way. Although I didn't say this to Gorbachev, it was this black-and-white attitude of Reagan's that led to his firm anti-Communist policies, which ultimately had much to do with the demise of the Soviet Communist Party.

The evening with Gorbachev was a great thrill. He will undoubtedly be remembered as one of the truly important figures of the twentieth century. It was exciting to see him on a personal level, not as a remote historical figure. He struck me as unusually intelligent and alert, surprisingly free of dogma. We had expected Raisa to be difficult and abrasive, but she was very subdued and pleasant.

What impressed me most was the way the Gorbachevs toured the country. They wanted to meet real people and get to know the land. And this they did. They fell in love with the kibbutz at Ein Gedi, and indeed, because of their infatuation, arrived over two hours late at a ceremony held in their honor at Ben-Gurion University in Bersheba.

They conducted themselves with dignity, and I sensed no regret on Gorbachev's part at the way his political life seemed to be concluding. The regret came from the Israelis. We knew what he had meant to Jews the world over and we would never forget it.

ELECTION DAY ARRIVED on 23 June. Rabin had a clear majority and enough votes to block any possibility of the Likud's forming a government. Labor gained forty-four seats, and the Likud dropped from forty to thirty-two seats. The left-wing Meretz Party gained twelve seats, and the Arab Democratic Party gained two. The outstanding success was the right-wing Ometz Party, led by "Raful" Eitan, which rose from two seats to eight. Tehiya, the extreme right-wing party that had entered the elections with three seats, failed to get even one and was in effect eliminated as a party.

In the midst of the celebrations, Peres made political and programmatic remarks that annoyed Rabin, who stated quite pugnaciously that he was boss, and the power of decision making was his alone. He would guide the negotiations, he would appoint ministers on the basis of ability rather than loyalty to any faction. He alone would run the Labor Party.

Rabin's speech was hardly gracious or tactful, but someone was finally showing strong, firm leadership. There was nothing timid about Rabin, but as gruff as he could be, the people of Israel were ready to give him their goodwill. The reaction from Washington was positive: President Bush, who disliked Shamir, invited Rabin to America and made available the elusive loan guarantees, the issue among others that had helped bring down the Likud. Rabin was also invited to Egypt by President Mubarak. He could not have gotten off to a better start internationally.

The Likud knives came out—and they were sharp. Shamir announced his withdrawal from public life. Arens announced his withdrawal from politics, fed up with his colleagues and the internecine battles. The candidates for Likud leadership were David Levy, Ariel Sharon, Binyamin "Bibi" Netanyahu, and Benny Begin. My feeling was that one of the two younger candidates would win, not Sharon or Levy. A new era had dawned for Israeli politics.

A prime minister must maintain authority over his ministers, and Shamir had not always displayed the necessary leadership. He had obviously caved in to Sharon. He brushed off much as unimportant—even our conflict with the United States over loan guarantees. He said confidently that he would bring them, but everybody knew this was untrue. The Likud had obviously distanced itself from the people, as Labor had done in 1977, and it lost much of the major constituency that had brought it to power: the Oriental community, particularly the North

Africans. Internecine conflict had also had an effect; the Likud had proved to be its own worst enemy. The Israeli people wanted a strong government and a strong leader.

On 13 July, with the traditional three knocks of the gavel on the desk, I announced the opening of the thirteenth Knesset and called on the oldest member to come forward to be sworn in. He was Yitzhak Shamir.

In his speech Rabin called on the Arab heads of state to meet him in Jerusalem or receive him in their capitals, and he invited the Jordanian-Palestinian committee to meet with him. The Arabs were obviously unsure about how to react to a speech like this.

Rabin was not a politician in the traditional sense. Although he had smoothed out some of his rough edges and had learned how to play politics with the Labor rank and file, he was still a blunt, honest, no-nonsense man—and that's the kind of prime minister he became. When he decided he was right, no one could dissuade him.

The next day, Rabin presented his government to me. No one realized it at the time, but his ascension signaled the most thrilling, important, turbulent, and emotional era of Israeli politics since the formation of the state.

To MARK THE 500th anniversary of the arrival in the Ottoman Empire of the Jews who had been expelled from Spain, the government of Turkey, together with the Turkish Jewish community, decided to hold special celebrations. We were invited to come to Istanbul as guests of the celebration committee and of the Turkish government. This was an encouraging development—to be invited by a Moslem state. We were accommodated in the magnificent Ciragan Hotel, which was located on the shores of the Bosporus and was an old Turkish palace. The Turkish government was not sure how I would be received by the population, and therefore initially gave a low profile to the visit. Gradually, as they discovered that the reaction was not hostile, and frequently very friendly, they raised its status until it began to approximate a state visit.

The celebration was like a new edition of the Thousand and One Nights from Baghdad. Aura sat between President Turgut Ozal and Prime Minister Demirel, who did not speak (their relations had been very strained for some time and the word was that we had succeeded in bringing them together). The evening opened with a ballet and opera depicting the exile of the Jews from Spain and their arrival in the Ottoman Empire. After speeches by Jak Kamhi, a leading industrialist and the chairman of the celebrations, and President Ozal, I addressed the audience, mentioning our relationship with the Arab world and the peace process which was ongoing at the time. I was followed by Prime Minister Demirel. Several orchestras played, and the entire event had to be seen to be believed. Dr. Theodor Herzl, the founder of modern Zionism, had cooled his heels for hours, waiting to be received by the Ottoman sultan, possibly in this very palace. The sultan must surely have turned in his grave at the sound of the "Hora" and other Israeli songs being sung at this event. Prime Minister Demirel told me that Turkey had not seen such a magnificent event for fifty years. He remarked that it had taken five hundred years for this event to take place and it would probably be another five hundred before there would be another such celebration.

This was the beginning of a substantial and productive relationship between the two countries. We now even have a military air training and cooperation agreement.

When I returned to Israel, Rabin briefed me at length about the latest political developments. Baker now appeared to be losing enthusiasm for the Palestinians—they talked a lot and were starting to wear thin with the Americans. There might be a chance of progress in Syria with Assad; Mubarak and the Americans were pressing in that direction. Shortly after taking office, Rabin had called on Mubarak, who was disenchanted with the Palestinians, was unhappy about King Hussein, and was very concerned about Saddam Hussein in Iraq.

Rabin's visit to President Bush's summer home in Kennebunkport, Maine, opened a new page in U.S.-Israeli relations. Israel would now benefit not only from "drawing down" weapons and equipment on a grant basis but also from the broadened prepositioning of U.S. equipment in Israel and cooperation in weapons development.

During the election campaign, Rabin declared that he would never countenance Israel's withdrawal from the Golan Heights as part of any arrangement with the Syrians. But only four months later, he refused to commit himself to a delegation of Golan settlers who called on him for support. Over 80 percent of the settlers had voted for Rabin, and his policy shift caused much bitterness and controversy. For months thereafter, the Likud broadcast his campaign promise to show how he had allegedly broken it.

It was generally anticipated that all or part of the Golan would have to be sacrificed for peace, and, in the grand scheme, many citizens did not argue with the prospect. But on a personal level, it was heartbreaking; lives could be irrevocably altered. Children presented appeals against being forced to go, and choirs sang a specially composed song about not leaving their homes. During a visit to the Golan Heights, as I stood at Haruv, looking down on much of Israel, I, too, was filled with anxiety. Placing the Syrian army in these strategic positions had already given cause for regret. Surrendering Mount Hermon, "the eyes of the country," and giving Syria access to our main water reservoir, the Sea of Galilee, were difficult to accept emotionally. Founded in 1967, Merom Golan was the first kibbutz—indeed, the first Jewish settlement—on the Golan Heights. What about its future? Israel was ready to do a great deal for peace, but so much effort and life had been invested to preserve our position on the Golan, especially in the Yom Kippur War. I did not envy Rabin's hard decisions.

To achieve peace we would have to compromise—but certainly not with total withdrawal, as in Sinai. I favored a Hong Kong–type solution: combining an acknowledgment of Syrian sovereignty in most, if not all, of the Heights with a fifty-year lease to Israel. Syria was as interested, in the long run, in reaching a peace agreement as we were, especially as Assad no longer had the backing of the Soviet Union. If they could negotiate in a tough and intractable manner, we could too.

RABIN'S GOVERNMENT WAS COMING under heavy criticism, much of it deserved, for both its domestic and foreign policies. Many of the ministers he appointed were ineffectual, and he was disturbed about internal politics in the Knesset. At this point, Rabin seemed slightly overwhelmed by the premiership and its responsibilities. Minister of the Interior Aryeh Deri compared the Shamir and Rabin governments he had served in. The Likud was a pack of wolves without leadership; Labor was a bunch of amateurs and sheep with leadership.

MY TERM as president would end in less than a year. I'd had feelers about running for a third term, and many people felt the two-term law should be changed to encourage me. Several political groups asked whether I would run if the law was adjusted. The job was exhausting, the existing law reasonable, and in public life one should know when to get up and leave, I said; nobody was irreplaceable. The paradoxical result of my statement was a growing public demand that I reconsider and run for a third term if the law was amended. But my decision was firm. I was now officially a lame-duck president.

That didn't mean I didn't have work to do. On 23 December, I left for the first state visit of a president of Israel to China. En route in the plane, we lit the fourth Hanukkah candle.

At the international airport of Beijing, we were received by the minister of railways, Han Zhubin, and his wife, Gao Xiuquin. As we drove the thirty kilometers through the countryside to the city, a soldier or policeman was stationed every few hundred yards, facing outward. It was easy to see the central role that the bicycle played in Chinese transportation. My escort told me that there were 200 million bicycles in China. In Beijing alone, with a population of 8 million, there were 6 million bikes and only 350,000 motor vehicles.

Aura and I were each given a huge apartment in the guest compound in Beijing, exquisitely decorated with Chinese furniture and intricate wood carvings on every door. After a lunch of vegetables and rice, Minister Han escorted me to the official ceremony of welcome. En route, the minister told me he controlled some 57,000 kilometers of railways. I related to him the story of the late Menachem Savidor, the speaker of the Knesset, who, when he headed Israel's railways, visited the United States and was asked about the length of our railway system. Too ashamed to admit the truth, he averred that he had forgotten the length, but he did know that the width was the same. I said to my escort that this reply was apt for me as well.

In Tiananmen Square, Chairman Mao's giant portrait was prominently displayed, flanked by the flags of China and Israel. That was a sight I never thought I'd see. I joined President Yang Shangkun, eighty-six years old but still quite commanding, on a raised platform. The band then struck up "Hatikvah." That was another event I had never conjured up in my wildest dreams.

Our first meeting was in the Hebai Room of the Great Hall of the People. President Yang spoke of his respect for Israel's achievements. He wished us well in our endeavors to advance the peace process.

In my reply I pointed out that we were the only two ancient people who over thousands of years had not changed their language, their folklore, their beliefs, their religion, or their country. This definitely linked our two peoples. I talked about the Chinese Jewish community in history, dating back to the immigrants from Iraq and Iran in the Middle Ages, and the Jews of Kaifeng, Tientsin, Shanghai, and Harbin. It emerged that as far as the modern Chinese were concerned, there was no distinction whatsoever between Israel and the Jewish people.

I dwelt at length on the dangers of Islamic fundamentalism. The president admitted that his countrymen were beginning to feel its effects among their Moslems, too. The party secretary-general, Jiang Zemin, came to see me. He was the number-one strongman in the country, and was taking over from Deng Xiou Ping. He was to be appointed president a few months later when Yang's term concluded. Jiang was effusive in his praise for Israel—he said he admired the Jewish mind, our international trading success, our technological advances. He made it very clear that China was looking forward to working with us in many areas and that there was an enormous potential for cooperation and growth. The conversation was both encouraging and frustrating. As with most of the Chinese officials I met, they were sincere in their desire for a full rapprochement with Israel. But they wanted everything on their own terms. They acknowledged no wrongdoing, no errors in policy. Still, it was an important breakthrough, one that can only strengthen Israel's economy and, in fact, world standing.

In Shanghai, I was escorted by a deputy mayor, who on occasion stood in for Mayor Huang Ju. In the course of our visit and our talks he related to me all that happened to him, and indeed to all the intellectuals, during the Cultural Revolution. He described that period as one of sheer madness and utter chaos. It set the country back many, many years. A professor, he had been taken from his home to a "re-educational" institution. It was actually a form of concentration camp in which 300 to 400 academics were forced to work the land with the local farmers. The farmers lived under the most backward, primitive conditions. He was cut off from his family and was not allowed any visits or correspondence. The only "education" they received was the mandatory study of Mao's Little Red Book. Huang decided that he was going to excel, even in those conditions. He did, and was therefore released after only eighteen months. He told me that he now lived with his family, along with one other family, in a four-room apartment. He paid a monthly rent of $10 and earned the equivalent of $50 a month.

Shanghai is a mixture of ancient Chinese history and new glass skyscrapers. It is a modern metropolis of 13 million people, one that can vie with the other great cities of the world. Huang talked to me about plans to turn Shanghai into the main industrial center in China that would even outstrip Hong Kong. He pointed to Shaul Eisenberg, a leading Israeli industrialist, who was in my party. Eisenberg was involved in joint ventures with twenty plants in the city, and 250 plants and projects throughout the rest of China. Huang talked about the history of the Jewish community in the city, and the fact that it had received and accommodated thousands of Jews who had fled from the Nazis during World War II (including my Uncle Reuben).

One evening we went with our party of Israelis and Chinese escorts to a nightclub in the Peace Hotel in what was originally the Sassoon Building on the famous Bund waterfront, to celebrate Nissan Limor's birthday. The hotel was reminiscent in every way of the 1920s. An orchestra comprising Chinese and European musicians played nonstop jazz all evening. We danced not only with members of our own delegation, but with all the Chinese interpreters and bodyguards, men and women, who were with us.

The next day the deputy mayor told me that our little celebration the night before was the talk of the town. The people were tremendously impressed by a society in which the head of state could feel free to go to a nightclub and dance with members of his staff and the Chinese escorts and security.

We visited the sites of the Ashkenazi and Sephardi synagogues. The Sephardi synagogue, Ohel Rachel, had been founded in 1900 by the Kadoorie family. It is used now as a public meeting hall. In my honor they removed the covering of the Ark of the Law to reveal the traditional Hebrew words "Know before whom you stand." The Ashkenazi Ohel Moshe synagogue had served also as the headquarters of Betar, the Revisionist Zionist organization. It was adjacent in the Japanese-occupied area of the city to a poor ghetto where the Jews had lived.

Air China flew us to Xian, the capital of the Shaanxi Province. There we were taken to the Xian satellite monitoring and control center. The purpose of the visit, our hosts explained, was to encourage growing cooperation with Israel in the field of space satellites. They had already launched thirty-four satellites into space. We promised to send a qualified delegation.

It was when I returned to Israel that the impact of this trip really hit me. Who would have dreamed of the Israeli flag gracing Tiananmen Square, adorning Mao Zedong's giant image? This vast country is due to become, in the not-too-distant future, one of the great economic powers in the world, if not *the* greatest. It already had, when I visited, a $50 billion trade surplus with the United States. The population was 1.2 billion. China has huge problems but enormous potential. It has pursued a policy of moving toward a Western capitalist-style economy while maintaining the political restrictions of a Communist society. That is indeed an incredible achievement, one which the Western powers do not approve of, but which seems to be solving the problems in China. Many of the Chinese leaders believe that under a democracy such as exists now in the Soviet Union, the situation in China would be uncontrollable chaos. There is no doubt that the Chinese *do* function better than the Russians. And they *will* become a democracy. I really believe that it's inevitable. Perhaps the gradual process will be better for their people than the sudden shock of the Russian democracy. It's a difficult moral call as to whether they're right or wrong.

CHAPTER 31

The Presidency—1993

A CLOUD HUNG OVER Israel's government. Four hundred Palestinians had been expelled to Lebanon from the territories, creating a worldwide uproar. The expulsion had been initiated by the army after a wave of terrorism and destruction. The Palestinians were leading members or supporters of Hamas, an Islamic fundamentalist organization dedicated to the destruction of Israel. It is based in the area controlled by the Palestine Authority as well as Palestinian areas held by Israel, with an outside headquarters in Damascus. Hamas does not believe in any political solution or compromise for the Arab–Israeli problems; its only solution is an end to the Jewish State. For that reason, it is an outlaw organization in Israel.

Because the Lebanese government refused to admit them, the 400 Palestinians were basically homeless, living outdoors in makeshift tents in no-man's-land in Lebanon. Their situation had become a cause célèbre; and international pressure was brought to bear to allow them to return home. But Rabin was adamantly opposed to backtracking on this issue: if the Supreme Court found in favor of the expellees, the government would honor its decision. Otherwise they were not coming back. The Supreme Court's decision found the mass expulsion illegal but the individual expulsions legal; individual expellees had the right of appeal.

This issue constituted Rabin's first real experience as prime minister at dealing with the new U.S. administration, and he found President Clinton and Secretary of State Warren Christopher to be straightforward and understanding but not pushovers. The United States was involved because the UN had decided to intervene, and Israel could not succeed in a UN vote without a U.S. veto. Rabin and Christopher reached an agreement on a negotiated compromise that Israel and world opinion could live with. One hundred Hamas expellees would be returned to the territories immediately and the rest by the end of the year. All of them would have the right of appeal to special committees set up for this purpose. The United States would move to prevent the convening of a Security Council meeting that would impose sanctions on Israel. Rabin was attacked publicly in Israel for this arrangement; it did not satisfy the left or the right, but the government approved it.

Rabin told me that he was very happy with the compromise. When all was said and done, only one hundred expellees returned to Israel.

I CONTINUED TO BE concerned about the developments in the Supreme Court and the direction in which it seemed to be moving. At a meeting with the chief justice, Meir Shamgar, I expressed my concern about the tendency of the court to insinuate its way into various areas which should belong to the legislative or administrative authorities. I could not accept the contention made by some judges that everything was subject to judicial review, including, for example, declaring war or signing a peace treaty, public appointments, whether or not to issue gas masks, and at what time TV programs should be broadcast. There was a tendency to impinge on the independence of the Knesset; the borders between the three authorities—legislative, judicial, and administrative—were gradually being erased. In my view, the government was supposed to govern, the judges were supposed to judge, and only in exceptional cases were those judgments to come at the expense of the government. I feared that there would eventually be a sharp reaction from the political sector, and this could affect the long-term standing of the Supreme Court.

AFTER ALL THIS TIME, Ariel Sharon and I actually had a good relationship. Our politics or approach to the world could not be more different, but we were among the founders of the Defense Forces and had a lot of history in common. Sharon was not putting forward his candidacy in the Likud leadership race because he knew he did not stand a chance within his own party. He believed that Binyamin "Bibi" Netanyahu would be the new party leader, a prospect that did not arouse his enthusiasm. At the time, Sharon indicated publicly that he considered Netanyahu a lightweight who owed his popularity to style rather than substance— something no one could accuse Sharon of—and a Johnny-come-lately.

Frequently sad and depressed, Sharon desperately wanted to lead the country and was now forced to come to grips with the fact that he probably never would, despite his being a bulldozer with unquestioned ability, climb to the top of the political heap.

Following the Likud victory in the elections in May 1996, Sharon indicated that he desired one of three appointments, namely, minister of finance, minister of defense, or minister of foreign affairs. Much pressure was exerted by the right-wing elements in the Likud party in favor of Sharon's demands. Finally, an ultimatum delivered to Netanyahu by David Levy, the deputy prime minister and minister of foreign affairs, forced Netanyahu to appoint Sharon as the minister in charge of a newly established ministry of national infrastructure. This gave Sharon authority over power, water, the lands administration, the airports, the railways and public works, to name but a few subjects. A very formidable ministry indeed with much political clout.

I ENTERED WHAT can only be called a lame-duck period in the presidency. I worked as hard as ever, but some of my time began to be taken up with a kind of farewell tour. I spent much time going to plants and factories and speaking to youth groups, urging them to go into Israeli industry as a career. I visited quite a few towns and villages, Arab and Jewish, including settlements in the territories, and tried to calm the fears of change and displacement. And I did my best to ease the transition on an international level. I knew that what I had achieved as an international communicator had frequently proved to be most useful.

On my official visit to Great Britain in March, Aura and I were received at Buckingham Palace by the queen, who greeted us as old friends. The commander of the guard invited me in flawless Hebrew to inspect the guard.

Standing at the side of the queen as I listened to the strains of "Hatikvah," with the Brigade of Guards guard of honor presenting arms, I thought of the stalwarts at 77 Great Russell Street in London, home of the Zionist Organization, and the leaders of Anglo Jewry, who had struggled to create the Jewish homeland. Lord Rothschild represented that group at the luncheon tendered by the queen.

At a luncheon, Prime Minister John Major told me that by not giving meaningful concessions to the Palestinians, we were not enabling them to save face and move forward. The Palestinians have always experienced great internal strife; at best, the PLO was always an uneasy coalition of a number of organizations whose individual leaders were afraid to show weakness or moderation for fear of being pounced upon by the others. Many PLO members are intelligent and realistic and, like other rational human beings, unwilling to endure perpetual violence. Their meetings and talks with Israelis have shown that there is room for legitimate compromise. Events are making clear just how much the Palestinians and mainstream Israel have in common. After the tragic assassination of Rabin, whoever would have imagined that one of his first mourners would be Yasser Arafat? The horrible irony of Rabin's murder is that it may ultimately bring together many of the Middle East's disparate groups.

IN HOLLAND, we were guests at the palace in The Hague of Queen Beatrix, one of the most charming women one could ever hope to meet, and certainly one of the outstanding monarchs in the world today. We reciprocated the magnificent state dinner with an impressive Israeli-organized and -conducted concert attended by the queen and the leadership of the Netherlands.

Holland has historically been a great and true ally of Israel, and my trip there reiterated our friendship. The Westerbork camp, which we visited with the queen, was the site from which some 102,000 Jews of a community numbering 120,000 were sent to their deaths. In Amsterdam, I laid a wreath at the memorial to the dock workers who had struck at the time of the Nazi occupation in protest against the oppression of Jews and were summarily executed by the Germans.

IN THE PRESIDENTIAL elections of 24 March 1993, Ezer Weizman won by a handsome majority over Dov Shilansky, the former speaker of the Knesset.

Binyamin "Bibi" Netanyahu won the leadership of the Likud with 52 percent of the vote, his election signifying a radical break with the past and a virtual revolution in Israeli politics. He was, after all, only forty-three, just a baby in Israeli political terms. His election was healthy from the point of view of Israeli politics; we needed an injection of youth. But, despite being personable, an excellent speaker, and more than handsome enough for the TV cameras, Netanyahu was not considered by many substantial enough to justify such a position. What Netanyahu did bring to politics was a new dimension, an Americanization of the process: effective use of the media, dependence on sound bites, and awareness that easy answers were often more popular than much-needed depth.

At the outset of Netanyahu's political rise, he adopted the line of all Israeli hawks: "Don't give in to the Palestinians." He and others on the right spoke out against the peace process, but they offered no alternative solution.

As the election campaign for prime minister moved forward, Netanyahu changed his approach and came out in favor of the continuation of the peace process, adopting the slogan that he would ensure "peace with security." By dint of a very effective campaign, as opposed to an ineffective campaign by Labor, the majority proved to be convinced by Netanyahu's approach.

Following his election, Netanyahu declared his intention to honor all of Israel's obligations under the Oslo Agreements. Despite his previous protestations to the contrary, he and his colleagues agreed to meet with Arafat and the leadership of the PLO. In July 1996 Deputy Prime Minister David Levy first met with Arafat.

While the process may now be slowed down, there is no doubt that Netanyahu will have to adapt to and honor the agreements made by the Labor government. If he fails to do so, he will face enormous problems not just in the Arab world but internationally, particularly in Washington.

Netanyahu will now have to move from slogans to a clear policy. Decisions will have to be made. It will be interesting to see how he reconciles his earlier rhetoric with the need to move toward peace.

THE FANATICISM AND HATRED that ultimately led to Rabin's assassination were already evident by March 1993, which saw fifteen deaths in the territories. The opposition, led by Netanyahu, and settlers from the West Bank, engaging in demonstrations, laid the blame on Rabin. Netanyahu's first move as Likud leader had been to blame the government. Each time blood was shed, the Likud tried to make political gains. Rabin accused Netanyahu of "thriving on political blood."

After the Oklahoma City bombing occurred, Rabin praised the American people for coping with the tragedy and not turning it into a partisan issue. When the IRA broke the cease-fire amid negotiations with Britain and exploded a bomb in East London, the Labour opposition rallied behind the government. As opposed to this approach in the spring of 1993, Rabin, seen as the symbol of government, was brutalized because of it. Whenever a Jew was killed by an Arab, angry demonstrators appeared at his house. At times they seemed to hate Rabin more than the Arab killer. This hatred ultimately brought tragedy.

The media escalated the charged atmosphere with screaming headlines five times the size of those used at the outbreak of the Six-Day War. If at the time of the War of Independence we had the media we have today, I shudder to think what might have happened.

ONE OF THE MORE MOVING farewell ceremonies to honor us was given by the General Security Service (Shin Bet) and attended by all the senior members of the organization. The head of the Shin Bet made a very emotional speech about Aura and myself, commending me "for having saved the Shin Bet." I thanked them for having looked after us so well over the years, and for the quality of the young men who had been with us everywhere, some of whom had become close to us. I would always be proud of the fact that I had saved the Shin Bet in its hour of trial.

ON MONDAY, 5 APRIL, we held what was to be our last seder in Beit Hanassi. This time we limited the guests to our family. All our children and grandchildren came, as did Yaacov's family, Abba and Suzy Eban, and our in-laws, the Afeks. It was a memorable occasion, full of love and tenderness. For the first time Bouji's son Noam and Joel's daughter Renée asked the traditional questions.

EGYPT'S AMBIVALENT ATTITUDE toward Israel was emphasized by President Mubarak's announcement that he would meet with Rabin. Mubarak proposed that the meeting take place at Taba, inside Sinai, on the Egyptian side of the border; Rabin agreed to Taba but proposed that Mubarak join him for lunch at the Princess Hotel in Eilat on the Israeli side of the border. The Egyptians would not agree. They had enough trouble with the Islamic fundamentalists without giving them a reason for additional eruptions. Mubarak was hesitating as he faced the fundamentalists: this attitude has been the basic flaw in our relations with Egypt.

Tension was growing between Rabin and Peres. Frustrated with Peres's approach, Rabin felt that he was ready to give in too rapidly to the Arabs on many issues. In this instance, I felt Rabin's caution was an advantage.

Some vaguely noncommittal remarks of Peres made it clear that some contact existed with the PLO and some form of secret negotiations were afoot. Peres later said that I was the only one to whom he even dropped hints about what was happening. I did not know the full story, but something was brewing and it would later be revealed when the Oslo Agreement was announced. This would have explained the tension between the two Labor leaders.

ON 14 APRIL, I officiated for the last time at the ceremony of receiving credentials from foreign ambassadors. One of the diplomats was from the African country of Gambia. When I asked him if his country, which lies on both banks of the Gambia River and is entirely surrounded by Senegal, would ever unite with Senegal, the Gambian ambassador laughed and exclaimed, "How can we? They don't know how to play cricket."

EVEN SOMETHING AS important and moving as the opening of the Holocaust Memorial Museum in Washington was politicized. Before I accepted the invitation to attend, it was made clear that Israel would be given no special consideration in the dedication ceremonies. The chairman, who had donated millions of dollars to the museum, insisted that the dedication was an American event, and so the president of Israel would not speak. Rightly incensed by this insult to our national dignity and the historic injustice that it demonstrated, Rabin responded that if I did not speak, no representative of Israel would participate. President Clinton thereupon ruled that I was to be invited to address the opening ceremony.

Secretary of State Christopher entertained some 250 guests at a luncheon. In the anteroom I met some of the presidents who had also come for the ceremonies—from Poland, Hungary, the Czech Republic, Slovakia, Slovenia, Croatia, Romania, Bulgaria, and Portugal, in addition to the prime ministers of Albania and Moldavia. I studiously avoided President Franjo Tudjman of Croatia, whose invitation to participate had been widely criticized. And rightly so. He had written anti-Semitic comments and had tried to play down the seriousness of the Holocaust. It was common knowledge that the Croatians were among the most loyal allies of the Nazis in World War II, and they were active participants in the massacre of Jews and Serbs.

In the afternoon, I was invited to a meeting with President Clinton at the White House. Anthony Lake, head of the National Security Council, was there, as was Martin Indyk, also of the NSC (who would later be appointed U.S. ambassador to Israel). I was accompanied by Itamar Rabinovich, our ambassador, and Nissan Limor, my director-general. The president and I discussed the peace process, of course, and I reiterated the great danger facing the world from Islamic fundamentalism.

I was very impressed with Clinton on an intellectual level. He was quite frank and open—he said he had no idea how complicated the Palestinian problem was before assuming office. He agreed with my warning that Iran was at the forefront of terrorist action, but said that Iraq was also dangerous as long as Saddam Hussein still ruled. While favoring strong action against Iran, Clinton had one big problem: every time the Americans decided to boycott Iran and close off certain economic avenues, he woke up the next morning to find that one of his European allies had come to a secret deal with the Iranians that rendered the U.S. actions meaningless.

Jonathan Pollard, who had been convicted for spying for Israel in the U.S., had been in solitary confinement for eight years and was becoming deranged. Clinton promised to look into the issue and had asked for a recommendation from the Department of Justice. I told him that my authority was the same as his: I got a recommendation from the minister of justice but did not have to accept it.

I left the White House believing Clinton was going to act on the Pollard matter not from a legal but from a humane point of view. Unfortunately, he did not.

Thereafter, the scheduled reception took place in the White House for heads of state. At the same time, Aura was entertained by Hillary Clinton. Vice President Gore and Secretary of Defense Les Aspen were there but the president did not join us, as we had expected. He had originally planned to meet only myself, Lech Walesa, and Vaclav Havel in private, but with the problem of Bosnia weighing heavily on him, and the fact that most of the visiting heads of state were from areas neighboring on Yugoslavia, he decided to ask each one of them privately their views on the subject. Thus we were left as a group standing at the reception for three hours. There was not one chair in the room. The heads of state were infuriated, but we all kept quiet. In the end, we had a group photograph taken with President Clinton—and everyone was smiling.

During the long wait, the president of Bulgaria, Zhelu Zhelev, said to me that in protest against the fact that his country had not been mentioned in any ceremony for saving its Jewish population (there had been observances at the Capitol Rotunda and at Arlington Cemetery in connection with the Holocaust Museum dedication), he was sending an official protest and was considering not attending the main ceremony. I told him that he must attend, and that I was certain the matter would be resolved.

As we prepared to go on stage the next morning, Vice President Gore asked me if it was true that the Bulgarians had in fact saved the Bulgarian Jewish community. I answered yes, the people had risen as one man and had not allowed the Nazis to take the Bulgarian Jews to Auschwitz. I also said that in my view the president of Bulgaria was justified in his complaint. On the spot, Gore wrote out an addendum to his introduction to President Clinton and showed it to me. He said that everyone knew about Denmark's courage, but fewer people knew about Bulgaria, and then he went into the details.

AFTER THE CEREMONY inaugurating the Holocaust Memorial Museum, a superb and moving memorial to the holocaust, we joined the Clintons for coffee, welcome after being wet and cold from a heavy downpour. President Clinton asked for clarification on the peace talks. President Assad of Syria was negotiating, I said, while allowing terrorists to operate against Israel and permitting a Palestinian extremist radio station to broadcast diatribes from Damascus against the peace talks. After my lecture, Clinton knew what he was dealing with: an unprincipled, two-faced character.

WE TOOK LEAVE OF all the workers in Beit Hanassi and their spouses in an emotionally charged ceremony, testimony to the very special relationship that existed between the staff and ourselves. I had reached my last day in office, which was covered in its entirety by television cameras. My sculptured head was placed in the row of busts of former presidents.

Throughout my decade as president, I endeavored to represent Israel with dignity and to bring our message to Jewish communities throughout the world. But as I look back and sum up the years of the presidency, I draw particular satisfaction and pride from the social aspects of my work within the State of Israel. I was not always successful in my endeavors, and did not always achieve what I set out to achieve. I am aware of the fact that some of my decisions were not always well received, but I tried at every stage to be a servant of the public in good faith, against the background of a deep concern for the fate of the nation and a deep belief in Israel's destiny.

The farewell ceremony in the Knesset on 13 May 1993 began just before sundown. We drove through Jerusalem past waving and cheering crowds. The presidential flag was raised for the last time in my honor; the Knesset was packed to overflowing.

I had worked hard on my last speech as president of Israel. It was my swan song. Recalling the opening prayer of my speech ten years before when I was sworn in, I spoke a prayer of gratitude for having been allowed to serve as president. I described the dramatic changes which our country had experienced during my time in office. Ten years earlier, Israeli soldiers were fighting in Lebanon in defense of the country's northern border. Today we were engaged in peace talks with our Arab neighbors. The evil Soviet empire, whose falsehoods and weaknesses had been exposed before the world, had collapsed, and blessed sources of immigration (*aliyah*) had welled up. In this same period, hostile activity against our population had begun in the form of the *intifada*. The acute problem of our relationships with our neighbors was being tested daily at the peace talks, at the negotiating table, and by the harsh realities in the streets. My years in the presidency had seen the Gulf War, where long-range missiles had been used against our civilian centers for the first time, but also the beginning of the peace process in Madrid.

I remarked that in the diversity and changeability of Israel's fate at this time, we saw the familiar pattern of intermingled joy and sorrow, peaks of hope and depths of despair, striving for peace and involvement in strife past and future. I described the centrality of the presidency in the very heart of Israel's life. I recalled the four prime ministers with whom I had worked, half of all those who had officiated as prime minister in Israel since its establishment: Begin, Shamir, Peres, and Rabin. I praised the degree of cooperation I had enjoyed from them, and also expressed appreciation to the cabinet secretaries who had served during my period of office: Dan Meridor, Yossi Beilin, and Elyakim Rubinstein. I emphasized the fact that I had been involved six times in the process of deciding on and recommending a member of the Knesset to lead the government. I took one last opportunity to use that as an example of the inherent weakness in our system.

Discussing the change in the law that was now imminent, the direct election of the prime minister, I said that it did not guarantee success, as it had never been tried before. However, I emphasized that unless we had true democracy, unless the members of the Knesset were directly responsible to the public in their constituencies, we would not succeed in eradicating many of the evils evident now in our system.

I talked about the acute problem of the division of powers, and the recent developments which indicated that the Knesset was losing its independence. It had been called upon by the courts to answer for its behavior, while in my view it should be answerable only to the electorate. I made a very strong plea for a strict division of powers.

I said that having served as president, I was even more convinced than in the past of the importance of the office of president. The Israeli people need such an institution, which symbolizes statehood and the fundamental unity that goes beyond divisive political disputes—an institution that serves as a unifying focus for the people of the country and for the Jews of the Diaspora and gives expression to our national pride. I believed that the presidency was significant too as a bridge between the various entities—the religious and secular, Jews and Arabs, Israel and the Diaspora, Israel and other nations. I described my effort to build bridges in all these areas, and was proud that I had led the fight against the ugly phenomenon of racism and had shut the doors of the presidency to its representatives. I expressed pride at the trust and respect that characterized the relationship of the Arab and Druze communities to the presidency, its nature and spirit.

I called for the protection of the dignity of every man and woman, his or her right to a good name and personal freedom, and the right to be judged in a court of law and not in the media, to equality before the law without distinction of race, faith, sex, or economic and social status. We had to be a society supportive of the poor and weak among us. I expressed the fear that we had a long way to go before we reached these goals.

I evoked the memories that the name Weizmann recalls in the early history of Zionism, and described my first meeting with the new president on the battlefield along the road to Jerusalem during the War of Independence. I talked about Weizmann and his wife, Reuma—they had been married by my late father—and thanked the entire staff and team of the presidential residence, led by Nissan Limor, the director-general. I talked about the team that Aura and I had constituted and her contribution to creating the character and image of the presidency. I expressed my appreciation of the Knesset for its cooperation.

I mentioned that I belonged to a generation that had seen both the Holocaust and our national redemption, and I could never take anything about our national identity and independence for granted.

I concluded by thanking the Almighty for having vouchsafed me this great privilege of heading such a wonderful people. I quoted from the

Bible about the importance of peace and unity, and concluded with the words of the prophet Isaiah: "How beautiful upon the mountains are the feet of the messenger that brings good tidings, that announces peace. . . ." At the conclusion of my speech, Ezer Weizman was sworn in as my successor. The speaker of the Knesset called out "Long live the president!" and the Knesset replied "Long may he live!" three times. Two shofaroth were blown, and we concluded with "Hatikvah."

After a reception in the Chagall Hall in the Knesset, Aura and I took our personal belongings and went home to Herzliya, to a house bursting with flowers and full of friends and neighbors. The next day, I went out to play golf.

CHAPTER 32

The Present . . . and the Future

FOR TEN YEARS, I had not stepped into or out of a car without having every move orchestrated. I had not walked down a street or gone into a café without security precautions being taken. I had had protection by my side every minute of every day and had not been able to enter a bookshop and browse because my arrival was seen as a major event. Protection was at my side every minute of every day. Suddenly I was a free man and the feeling was exhilarating.

I am no longer subject to daily media scrutiny. I can openly discuss and express myself on any subject, no matter how public. Surprisingly, my dialogue with the public seems more open and honest now that I am out of office. Some people who fawned over me when I was president moved on to greener pastures. It is only human. In any case I never took the flattery seriously. In the final analysis, one's true friends remain. Solid relationships stay solid and continue to enrich one's life.

As I have stated often, one cannot forget the past, but one must live for the future. I am proud of what I have accomplished, and prouder still of what I've seen achieved around me. But now I live for the present and the future. My children—and now my grandchildren—are my pride and joy. Joel, my eldest son, is in business as an international trader, as is his wife, Marguerite. He has four children, ranging from twenty years of age down to five. Michael is a colonel in Israel's armed forces, an Arab scholar, and was a member of the teams negotiating peace with the Palestinians, Jordanians, and Syrians. His wife, Shirin, an up-and-coming lawyer, recently gave birth to a son, Erel. Isaac, aka "Bouji," is a successful lawyer, prominent in the Labor Party, and he showed considerable ability and skill as chairman of the recent primary elections in the party. He and his wife, Michal, also a lawyer, have two children, Noam and Matan. Ronit, our daughter, the good-natured baby of the family, is a psychologist, married to a fellow psychologist, Ami Bronsky. She recently published her first paper in an American scientific journal and has a baby daughter, Noga.

We're friends, all of us. I could have given them more time when they were growing up, certainly, but they have always been an important part of our lives and will continue to be so. I believe they understand and even approve of the fact that the State of Israel was also a part of our family.

I would never admit it to her, but Aura is a brilliant, wonderful, and extraordinary woman. On Israel's tenth anniversary she initiated the annual International Bible Quiz. She set up the Arts Council of Israel, working with the minister of education and culture. In that capacity, she instituted and organized government aid to the arts—theater, dance, and museums. At the request of the Knesset Interior Committee, she set up the Council for a Beautiful Israel, and has devoted more than twenty-five years of her life as its volunteer chairperson. Its purpose is to educate the country—children as well as adults—about the environment. This is her passion now. Her center in Tel Aviv is one of the truly progressive organizations in the world in the areas of ecology, urban planning, and landscape design. As if this weren't enough to keep her busy, she is also chairperson of the Public Council of the Schneider Children's Hospital in Tel Aviv. And in her spare time, she manages to be a loving, attentive wife and mother.

For my part, I have gone back to writing for the press in Israel and abroad. I serve on the boards of several prestigious corporations in Israel and overseas. On occasion I have represented Israel, as at President Nixon's funeral, and at the fiftieth-anniversary celebrations of the liberation of Brussels. I am involved in the formation of the Center for Middle East Studies and Diplomacy at Ben-Gurion University in Beersheba.

I only wish that Israel's present were as comfortable and pleasant as mine. In so many ways, be it by choice, coincidence, or a twist of fate or timing, my life has paralleled that of my country. When I was young and angry, growing into manhood, exploring my limits, so was Israel. As I matured into middle age, learning what my limits were, Israel did, as well. When I became a politician and statesman, craving peace and reason, so did my country. Now, however, as I settle into a period dominated by the pleasures of family and intellectual pursuits, I can only hope that the country I cherish will rise above turmoil, violence, and hatred and be allowed to live in peace as the beacon it can and should be.

Yitzhak Rabin's assassination was a devastating loss from which the country is still trying to recover. Something new and horrible had come to our society: a Jew was killed by a Jew—an obsessed, fanatical Jew. The nation awoke the next morning to a sense of chaos. We were used to war from without; we were not used to this kind of violence from within.

The full impact of Rabin's death—or, more accurately, his life—was not felt until his funeral. Leaders and ministers from over eighty countries came on a day's notice. Much of the Middle East was represented: Egypt by President Mubarak, who spoke; Jordan by King Hussein, who eulogized Rabin very movingly; Oman, Qatar, Tunis, Turkey, and Morocco by their foreign ministers. The funeral showed the world that we were no longer standing alone; we were finally part of the Middle East. All this would have been incredible some twenty years ago. It took Rabin's death to demonstrate what he had managed to accomplish: the humanization of the peace process and, in fact, of Israel. His coffin was placed before the Knesset, and approximately a million people filed past, nearly one-fifth of our population. Rabin was buried on Mount Herzl, our national and military cemetery. In a painful and tragically unnecessary way, his death was the ultimate price for the peace plan.

I was with Rabin during his last trip abroad, at the end of October 1995. He went to the UN for its fiftieth-anniversary celebration, and I went with him to New York. During the flight, he told me how hard it was to fight the forces within the government bureaucracy that were trying to hold up his programs and plans. When we landed, I had a strange feeling. As we left the plane I said, "For God's sake, look after yourself." Those were the last words I ever spoke to him.

There was, for a while, a change in political behavior in Israel as a result of Rabin's murder. The extreme right wing had been calling him a traitor and even showed doctored pictures of him wearing an SS uniform. Many believed this had a hand in creating the atmosphere that led to his assassination. Speeches are not uttered in a void. Words stir up passion; passion results in action. And when action is taken, responsibility for the repercussions must also be taken. For a time after the assassination, those passions cooled and then, of course, as terrorism again reared its ugly head and the election drew near, mud was slung and emotions were once again stirred.

Peres lost the May 1996 elections by a very small margin. But one vote can decide the majority in a democracy. For one who has been associated in one way or another with Peres for close to fifty years and who admires him as a statesman, it was a blow. Israel lost a leader who was guiding the

Middle East toward peace. Time alone will tell whether or not he can be replaced by a leader of stature.

When the results were announced giving Binyamin Netanyahu a majority, the question facing all of us was whether or not the peace process would continue. I trust that it will. Menachem Begin, a hard-line leader of the Likud, orchestrated negotiations that led to peace between Egypt and Israel, much as Nixon, the great anti-Communist, opened the door between the U.S. and China. They are the role models Netanyahu must pattern himself after, using his power and position to mediate peace.

On assuming office, Netanyahu committed himself publicly to continue the peace process, and indeed sent an envoy to the Palestinian Authority to emphasize this point. But while promises are fine, our new prime minister must deal pragmatically with the issues, and to do that he must forge relationships with the Arab leaders, particularly Arafat, Hussein, and Mubarak. Much will depend on the negotiations, opened in May 1996, to resolve the Palestinian issue. Those negotiations will also directly influence vital strategic relationships between the United States and Israel, particularly on the successful technological and military levels which the Labor government achieved with the U.S. This will, in turn, have a direct effect on Israel's economic welfare and progress and on its ability to absorb immigration.

Netanyahu will be judged by his performance on two critical fronts. The first will be his approach to Israel's relations with the Palestinians. Should he fail to advance the solution for the Palestinians, the country could easily find itself receding into a renewed cycle of terror and a revival of the *intifada*. If he succeeds, however cautiously and slowly, we will eventually have peace. On a domestic level, Netanyahu must close the gap between the various divisive components comprising the Israeli population, especially between the secular elements and the various religious elements, who gained much strength in the elections. Netanyahu had considerable support from the religious population. The trick will be for him to keep that support without giving in to their extremist elements.

The situation is so volatile, so much changes on a daily basis, it is almost impossible to predict what will happen. However, I know what I would like to see happen, and I have what I think are reasonable expectations. I am not a utopian. I am a realist. And, realistically, what I see in Israel's future is peace. I've always felt that to look ahead, one must first look back. And so, to put things in context, to see what can and will happen politically and socially in the next few years, we need a bit of history.

In 1979, the Egyptian peace treaty was a huge breakthrough. That came about through Sadat's and Begin's vision. When we survived the Yom Kippur War, Sadat realized that he could never defeat Israel militarily, so he was forced to attempt a political reconciliation. His crusade for peace led him to Jerusalem and the Knesset through diplomatic means. Our peace with Egypt is a cool peace, but that is better than no peace. The border is open, 70,00 Israelis have been to Egypt, and many thousands of Egyptians have returned the visit. Trade has developed and flourished.

When Egypt made peace with Israel, it was expelled from the Arab League; now it heads the league. That is probably the biggest symbol of the changing times. A serious "sin" is now acceptable. In essence, this reembracing of Egypt made it kosher to make peace with Israel. The rhetoric about destroying Israel has disappeared, at least officially.

The Madrid talks came in 1991, led by Bush, Baker, and Gorbachev. Israel, headed by Yitzhak Shamir, sat at a table with Arab representatives from Egypt, Syria, Jordan, Lebanon, and the Palestinians. The barriers had broken down.

Following the Gulf War, the Arabs realized the danger emanating from Iraq and Iran, from within the Arab world. The actions of those two countries were threatening the peace of the entire Middle East. This greatly accelerated the Israel–Arab relationship, which in turn led to much thinking about finally dealing with the Palestinians. We did have a running dialogue with the Palestinians for quite some time, but not with the PLO. The Arab communities and countries urged us to talk to the PLO—even though they themselves were not enamored of the organization—because the crux of the problem between Arabs and Israelis has always been the Palestinian problem.

Following its 1992 election victory, the Labor Party, led by Rabin and Peres, began to look seriously for peace. The Madrid talks, while wonderful symbolically, had become a barren dialogue, more flash than substance. Arafat was unofficially calling all the shots and pulling all the strings behind the scenes, so Peres and his closest advisors secretly began conversations with a surprisingly willing PLO. With Rabin's support, those conversations soon turned into a negotiation. The Oslo Agreement, which had majority support in Israel, was followed by the Gaza-Jericho agreement and the interim agreement that set up the Palestinian Authority in the West Bank and the Gaza Strip. The basic aim behind these accords was to create a partner that would fight with us to end terrorism and violence and build a new relationship based on Palestinian self-rule.

The violence has not yet ended, so it remains to be seen how that partnership will work out. Do I think it will? Yes, for two very simple reasons. The Palestinian entity is very dependent economically on Israel; they cannot survive without us. If terror ceases, they can revitalize their economy. Without peace, they cannot. Furthermore, they know that terrorist activity will militate against their political aspirations. They need peace even more than we do. That is why it will ultimately happen.

FOR MANY YEARS, we had had unofficial talks with King Hussein (Yaacov started conversations as far back as 1963). The Jordanians felt betrayed by the PLO because they were kept in the dark about our negotiations, which affected vital Jordanian positions and needs. Because events were passing them by, Jordan, led by the great realist King Hussein, suddenly agreed to negotiate with us, and we quickly reached a peace agreement with them. We now had official peace with Egypt and Jordan, and arrangements for autonomy with the Palestinians.

The two major problems now facing us, on a practical political level, have to do with negotiating a lasting and abiding peace with Syria and reaching a permanent solution with the Palestinian Authority that will guarantee peaceful relations at all levels. First and foremost is the need to decide what the map of the territories will look like. Ultimately, it all comes down to the issue of control of land and thus, in turn, people. We could have a quilt pattern to the settlements, but if there is Arab terrorism—and there certainly could be—that would make many aspects of daily life untenable. Transportation, among other things, would be extremely difficult. After so many years of hatred, no law or peace treaty can make Arabs like Jews or Jews like Arabs—not, at least, overnight. So the solution to the settlement problem is to set out specific borders. One proposal is to annex part of the West Bank for Israel. I would favor going along the lines of Israel's Institute for Strategic Studies, which showed that we could annex only 17 percent of the land and absorb 70 percent of the Jewish population there. We could then concentrate the Jewish settlers in blocs of settlements along the so-called Green Line. Combine that with a system of cantonization: linking the remaining Jewish cantons to Israel and the Arab villages to the Palestinian Authority. The Palestinians now have complete civil authority (but not over Israeli citizens) in Gaza and the West Bank's major cities. Israel has overall control of security. That works and it should stay that way, at least for the immediate future.

Negotiations for the final arrangement began early in May 1996; they should be completed within three years. As long as terrorism is kept under control, the Palestinian problem can be solved by the end of the century.

It is clear that in the course of negotiations, concessions will have to be made, and the problem facing the government will be to make those concessions as painless and viable as possible.

The other side must and will make concessions, too. The bulk of the Middle East has realized that if the peace talks fail, the Palestinians will suffer most. Their extremism will cost them again because they will have renewed strife and another war. The difference is that Arafat is now aware that his future, too, depends on peace. Everything is dependent on Arafat's controlling Hamas's fundamentalist terrorist contingent. That is Arafat's responsibility. It can be done, but the means might not be pleasant. Arafat has to act firmly and with determination.

The United States is the only power that can stop fundamentalism in a nonviolent manner. Together with other Western powers, it must impose economic sanctions on all countries that allow Islamic fundamentalists to flourish. Trade between much of the West and Middle East is irreconcilable with terrorism, and if fundamentalism is not economically viable, it will disappear. One of the greatest threats is the marriage of Islamic fundamentalism to weapons of mass destruction. That threat will be contained only if a strong stand is taken economically and militarily.

There are rational political solutions to the Middle East antagonisms. Facts must be faced: in all probability, there will ultimately be a Palestinian state linked in a federation or confederation with Jordan. The question is whether that state will be another Libya and Syria, or whether it will prove to be rational and forward-thinking. The Palestinians are insisting that Jerusalem be their capital. This cannot and will not happen. It is part of Jewish history, prayer, and belief. No Israeli government prepared to compromise on Jerusalem will ever have the backing of the people. But accommodation for the city's Moslem holy places (not to mention Christian sites) will have to be agreed upon. That will not be so easy, not because of Israeli resistance but because the Arabs are arguing about who will have authority—Saudis, Jordanians, or Palestinians—in these holy places. Once that is settled, a rational and likely solution is to set up a Palestinian capital in either Gaza or in Ramallah, just north of Jerusalem.

The next big problem is Syria, which constitutes a serious military danger to Israel. If we can achieve peace with Syria, the other Arab countries—Saudi Arabia, Algeria, almost all but Libya, Sudan, and Iraq—

would fall in line. President Assad has made Israel's return of the entire Golan Heights a prerequisite to peace. Rabin encountered considerable political opposition to this. He might have been able to push it through in a national referendum, but even he always spoke of withdrawal *in* the Golan and not *from* the Golan. Total withdrawal is not realistic; partial withdrawal is a necessity. This bitter pill could be sweetened Hong Kong– style: Israel remains in the Golan for a number of years while acknowl- edging Syrian sovereignty over parts of it. Israel, as part of our negotia- tions, has demanded a full peace—exchanging embassies, unhindered trade, and free travel. We have also demanded a military early-warning system, a mutual reduction of military forces, and an end to the terrorist activities of the Hizballah against Israel's northern border and of the Palestinian terrorist organizations based in Damascus. So far, Syria has not been forthcoming.

We are obviously going to have to compromise with Syria—all negoti- ations are about compromise. But we do not have to accept every Syrian demand. In fact, we must not accept many of them. There are tremen- dous benefits to a mutual peace, but we dare not ignore our vital defense interests.

Withdrawal from the Golan Heights can be contemplated only if mil- itary and strategic conditions are agreed upon. Such arrangements must be reliable and guaranteed for a long period, ensuring a reliable defense against surprise attack.

In this context, we must maintain our strategic control of Mount Her- mon. Our presence there gives us a dominant military position that will deter Syria from contemplating any renewed attack on Israel. It is the only way to ensure the continuation of peace and quiet on our mutual border. Any early-warning equipment located on Mount Hermon must also remain in place until peace with Syria has become an established fact. We cannot give up total control of the Sea of Galilee, as the Syrians are demanding. That reservoir contains one-third of Israel's water supply. Be- fore the Six-Day War in 1967, the Syrians implemented a plan to divert water away from Israel. We cannot risk allowing that to happen again by agreeing to their becoming a riparian state. Because Syria does not need water from the Sea of Galilee, Israel must continue to control the water supply (keeping our agreement in place with Jordan to supply them with water), turn back some of the Golan to Syria, and control the line of the high ground on the Golan Heights. That is a compromise that might ul- timately be reached. It will require patience and time; Assad must eventu- ally realize that accommodation with Israel is in Syria's interest.

Assad is an absolute dictator and, although ruthless, he is clever. He knows that peace is to his benefit, particularly with pressure from the United States. But one reason we cannot make concessions that would greatly weaken us is that we do not know who will replace Assad. Syria's next ruler might be just as ruthless, but less clever and even more stubborn. We cannot negotiate ourselves into a position that leaves us wide open for future disaster.

As the peace process ripens and leads to peace with Syria and a permanent arrangement with the Palestinians, our country will have to accommodate the two peoples—the Jews and the Palestinians. We must be prepared for the fact that it will take many years before the wounds are healed and the area achieves any kind of pattern of normal relations. The only truly democratic society in the region is Israel, and it will take a long, long time for democracy to be totally accepted in the Arab world. Israel faces the dilemma of being a Western-oriented entity in the midst of a different culture. This situation will create many dilemmas, which is why it is so vital to retain the comparative strength of the Israel Defense Forces during this transition period.

If Israel is able to bring about a comprehensive peace, the question becomes "What next?" The answers are exciting, the potential almost limitless. And it is this potential that will ultimately bring the region together. If a warm peace occurs and we are able to combine our talents, the Middle East will become a major economic, technical, and agricultural force. Israel certainly has a lot to offer in such a scenario. Right now, 5.5 million Israelis have a higher gross domestic product than 85 million Arabs in the neighboring countries. The average annual Egyptian income per capita is $600; in Syria and Jordan it is between $1,200 and $2,000. In Israel it is $16,000. With a warm peace, the Arab income will most certainly rise. The Arabs could gain know-how and use us to improve their industry. They would become less dependent on their sole resource, oil, and Israel would have peace—a very fair trade, in my opinion. As it is, our defense expenditure has dropped considerably since the peace with Egypt (we don't have to maintain a large army on the Egyptian border). The more we lower our defense costs, the more we can improve our living standards.

Israel will have to continue the struggle, together with all moderate governments, against Islamic fundamentalism. But fundamentalism is nurtured in misery, hunger, unemployment, and frustration. Therefore, it is essential that Israel help advance the societies in the Middle East, raising their standards of living. As one of the leading countries in medical science and treatment, we could contribute significantly to efforts to raise health standards throughout the Middle East.

The Middle East is 95 percent desert, arid and semiarid. At the birth of the State, David Ben-Gurion emphasized that Israel must turn that desert into a source of life. The main requirement is water, which is in short supply throughout the region. Even with brackish water, Israel has demonstrated that the desert can be transformed into a fruitful and food-producing area. Additional freshwater sources are being created by an expanded program of waste-water purification for agricultural purposes and desalinization of seawater for urban use. If we have peace, the entire region can flourish and grow.

Israel can contribute greatly in areas such as solar energy. And what better field for the Middle East to dominate? One thing we have is sunshine. Think of the possibilities for joint infrastructure of railways, roads, health centers, ports, and airfields. A project has been proposed to create electricity by means of a joint canal between Israel and Jordan dug from the Red Sea. If peace comes and Israel and the Arabs join forces, we can reduce poverty and starvation throughout the region.

It is not just outside its borders that Israel must turn to solve its problems; we must also turn inward. Israel was created to become "a light unto the nations." To become such a light, we must remain true to the principles of Judaism. That requires maintaining the highest possible civilized standards in our relationship with our minority population. Chaim Weizmann, Israel's first president, said that we would ultimately be judged by our relationship to our Arab minority. I believe that, and I believe that Israeli soul-searching in this area will mean that we are ultimately judged in a very positive light.

Many crucial internal problems have not been adequately handled because of external pressures. As the peace process advances, we will have to address those internal problems. Israeli society must deal with the question of its collective identity. We could be heading for a very bitter cultural struggle on this issue. At the center will be the questions of Jewish identity in Israel and the significance of having a Jewish State.

To ensure its strength and stability, the Jewish people in the Jewish State must remain true to the Jewish cultural and religious heritage that has sustained our people for thousands of years. A synthesis must be achieved between Judaism and democracy, as was undertaken in our Declaration of Independence. This may indeed be the greatest challenge facing the Jewish people. The state must be a center and home for world

Jewry, living in the Diaspora. It must be a base for Jewish thought and creativity, one that will give stimulus to Jews wherever they may be.

Fundamentalism is the main problem confronting the world of Islam and its neighboring countries; Israel, too, must deal with fundamentalism and extremism. The confrontation between an extreme philosophy and those not committed to it has already led to the assassination of a prime minister. Such a rift between Jews is unforgivable and an extraordinary danger. There is also a rift between our extreme religious segment and the rest of the country. Today's religious leadership must follow the lead given by my father and Rabbi Kook if that rift is to close. If we cannot bring about peace within our borders, how can we expect to achieve it outside them? Again, rational thought must prevail. New realities must be faced. If we learned anything at all from Rabin's assassination, it is that reason and understanding must prevail over irrationality and fear.

I HAVE ALWAYS believed with unquestioning faith that the State of Israel must base its existence on strong foundations if it wishes to live and thrive as a unique, ethical society. I see those foundations as the rich Jewish legacy that has preserved us through the generations, the values that underlay the Zionist undertaking here, the sound security and economy that enabled us to withstand the attacks of those rising up against us, and, above all, moral strength creating individual and universal justice.

I cannot take Israel's independence for granted, for I have seen the Jewish people emerge from the terrifying depths of the Holocaust to ascend the heights of the State of Israel. During all my years in the military, in security, in politics, in the law, in journalism, in economics, in diplomacy, and in government, I was inspired by my belief in the eternity of Israel and the compulsion to work toward it. Beyond every setback I see the saga of remarkable achievements in every field of life. The tragedies that befell the Jewish people in my lifetime have no equal. But our victories and achievements have surpassed the dreams of generations. That is why one can dream, one should dream. One must dream.

INDEX